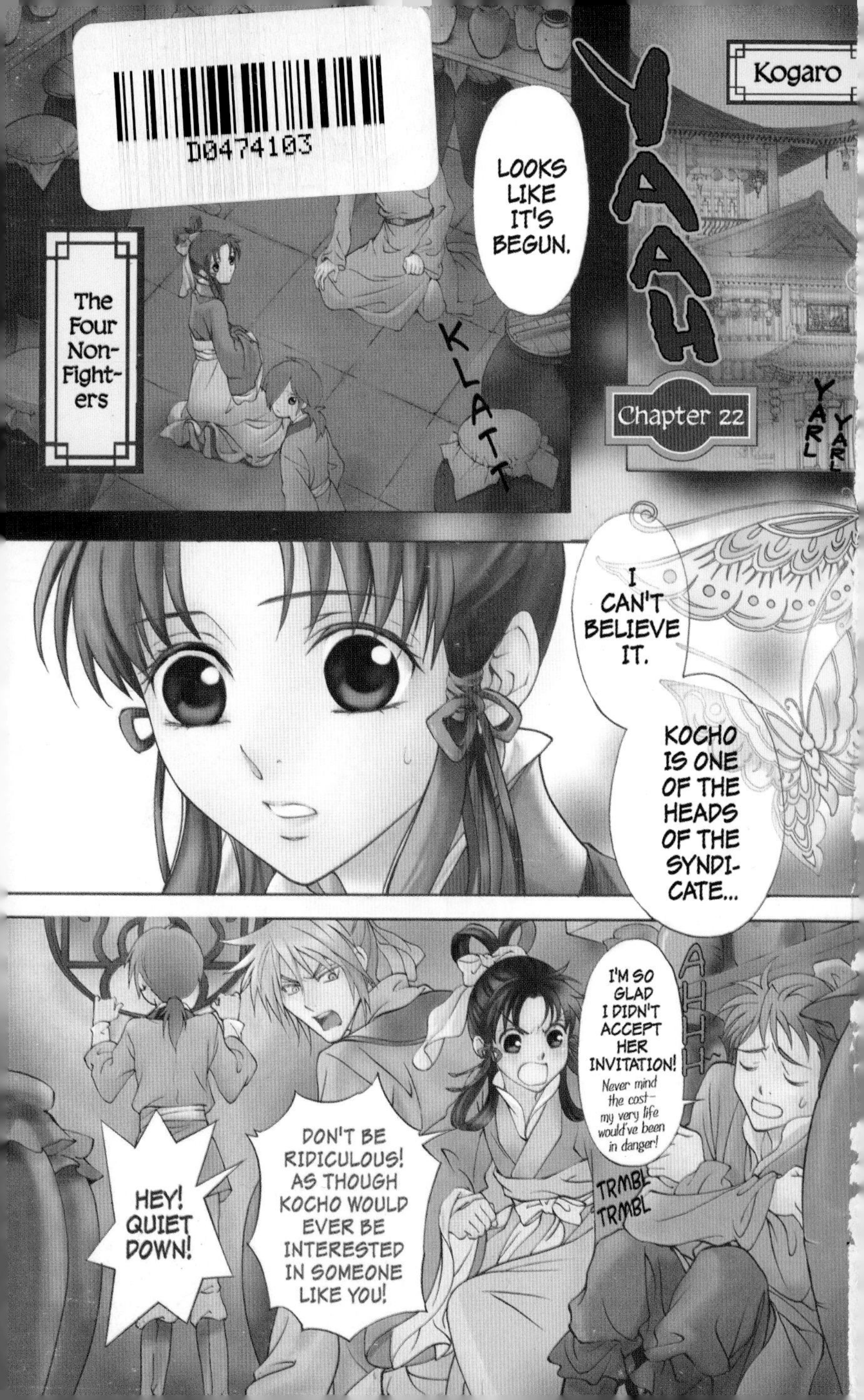
Kogaro
YAAH
Chapter 22
YARL YARL
LOOKS LIKE IT'S BEGUN.
KLATT
The Four Non-Fighters
I CAN'T BELIEVE IT.
KOCHO IS ONE OF THE HEADS OF THE SYNDICATE...
I'M SO GLAD I DIDN'T ACCEPT HER INVITATION!
Never mind the cost—my very life would've been in danger!
AHHH
TRMBL TRMBL
DON'T BE RIDICULOUS! AS THOUGH KOCHO WOULD EVER BE INTERESTED IN SOMEONE LIKE YOU!
HEY! QUIET DOWN!

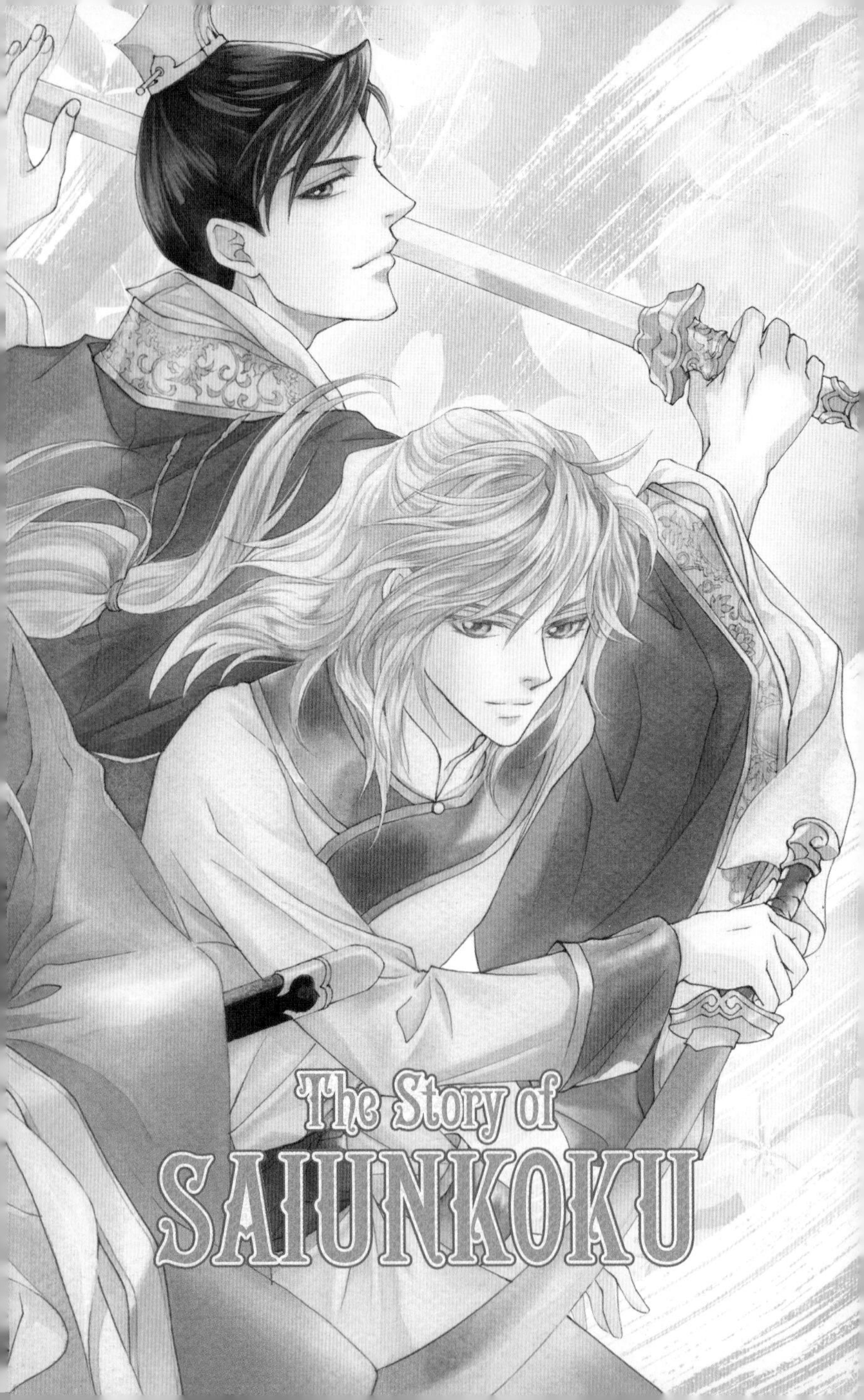
The Story of
SAIUNKOKU

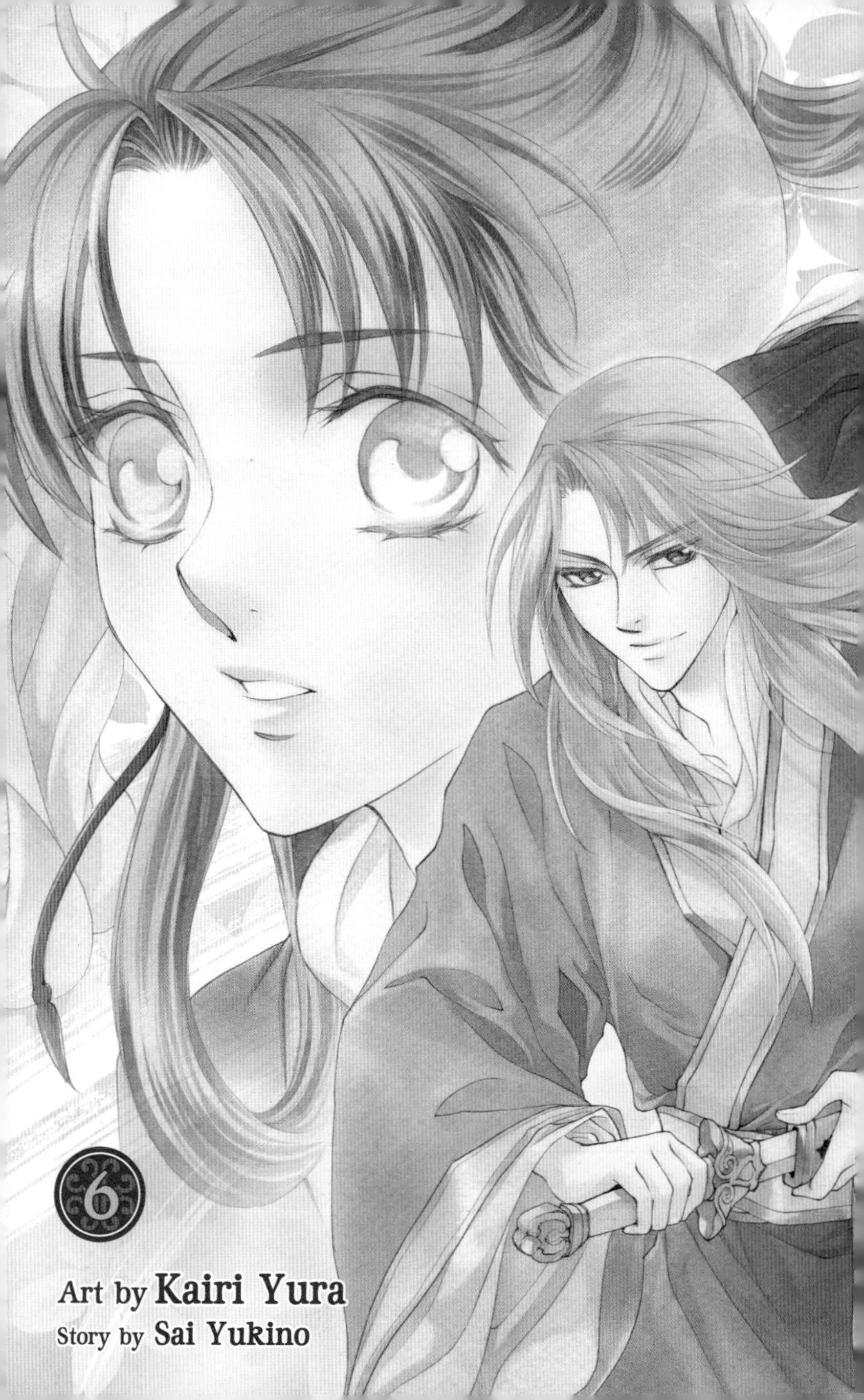
6
Art by Kairi Yura
Story by Sai Yukino

Volume 6
Contents

Story Thus Far

When Ryuki, the young emperor of Saiunkoku, proclaimed that women shall be permitted to take the Imperial Civil Exam, the way was opened for Shurei to fulfill her long-cherished wish to become a civil servant. She prepares for the exam, believing it to be the final hurdle between her and her dream, until the mysterious youth Eigetsu comes bursting onto the scene with the "Blue Scarf Gang" (a new gang of thugs terrorizing the streets of Kiyo) hot on his trail. A fierce battle for the red-light district breaks out between the Blue Scarf Gang and the combined forces of Kocho's syndicate and the emperor's retinue (Ryuki, Shuei, Koyu and Seiran)—with Shurei caught in the middle!

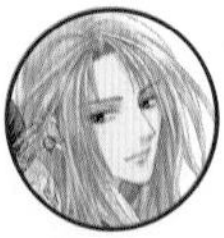

Ryuki Shi
The young emperor of Saiunkoku. He has been pining ceaselessly for Shurei since her departure from the Inner Court.

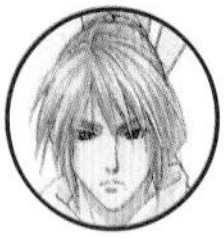

Koyu Ri
A civil servant renowned throughout the court as a genius, currently stuck in a frivolous position (perhaps?) serving Ryuki. He has a hopelessly bad sense of direction.

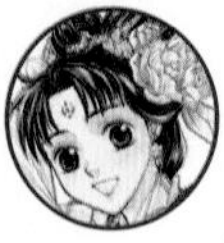

Shurei Hong
A young noblewoman of the prestigious but impoverished Hong Clan. She dreams of becoming Saiunkoku's first female civil servant.

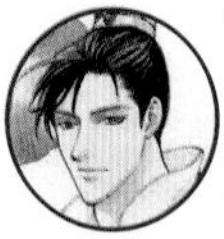

Shuei Ran
A military officer. He is a general of the Yulin Guard, a squad of soldiers charged with protecting the emperor. He is inseparable from Koyu (much to his friend's ire).

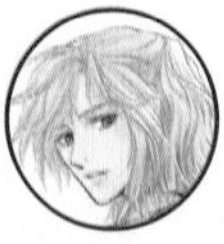

Seiran Shi
After being taken in by Shurei's father, Shoka, Seiran has served the Hong household as its faithful retainer ever since. He is actually Ryuki's older brother.

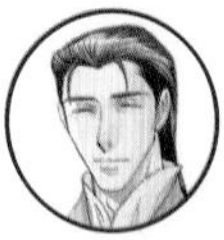

Shoka Hong
The eldest son of the Hong clan and Shurei's father. He holds a leisurely post as the Imperial Archivist, but there is a darker side to this ex-assassin as well.

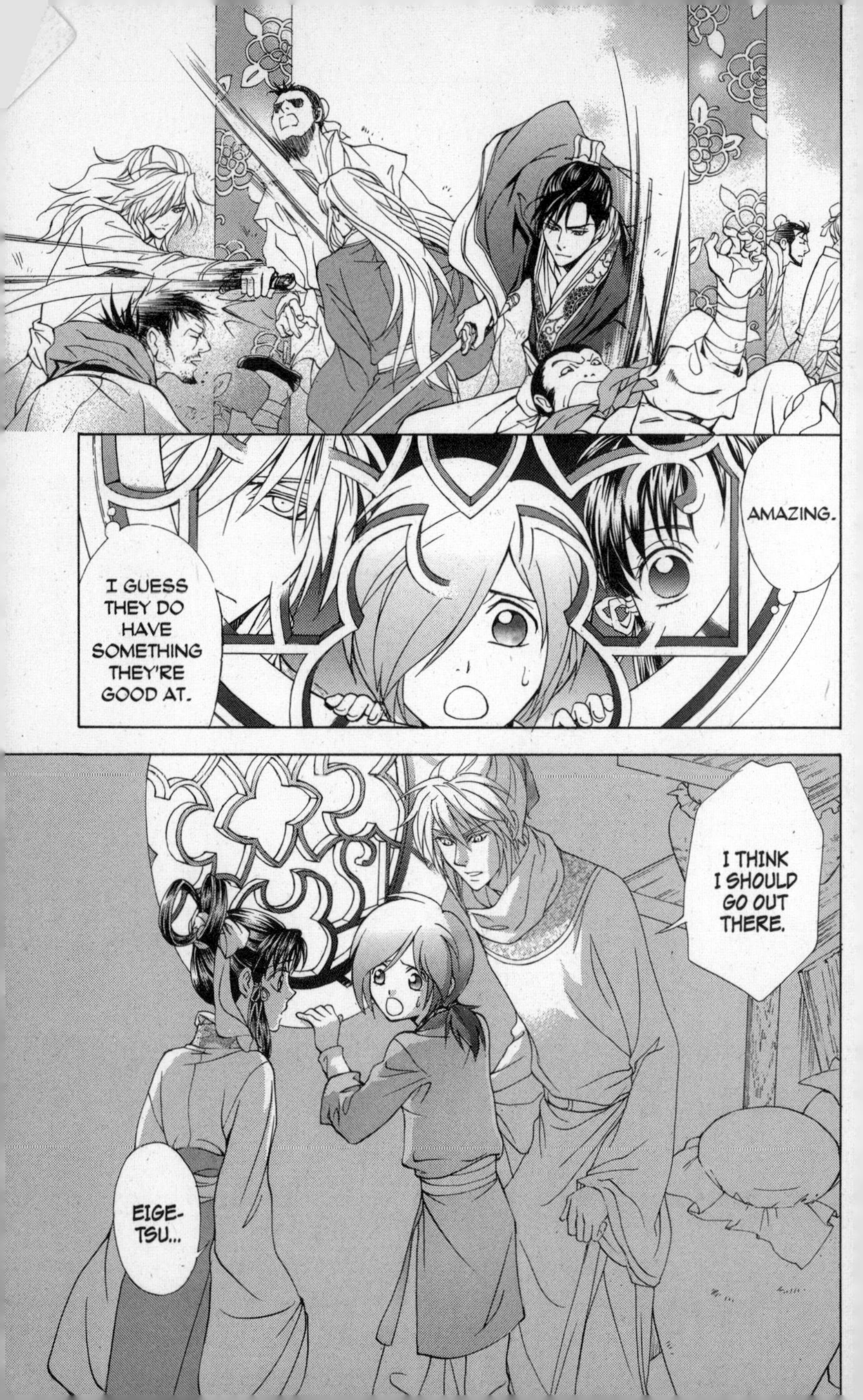
AMAZING.
I GUESS THEY DO HAVE SOMETHING THEY'RE GOOD AT.
I THINK I SHOULD GO OUT THERE.
EIGE-TSU...

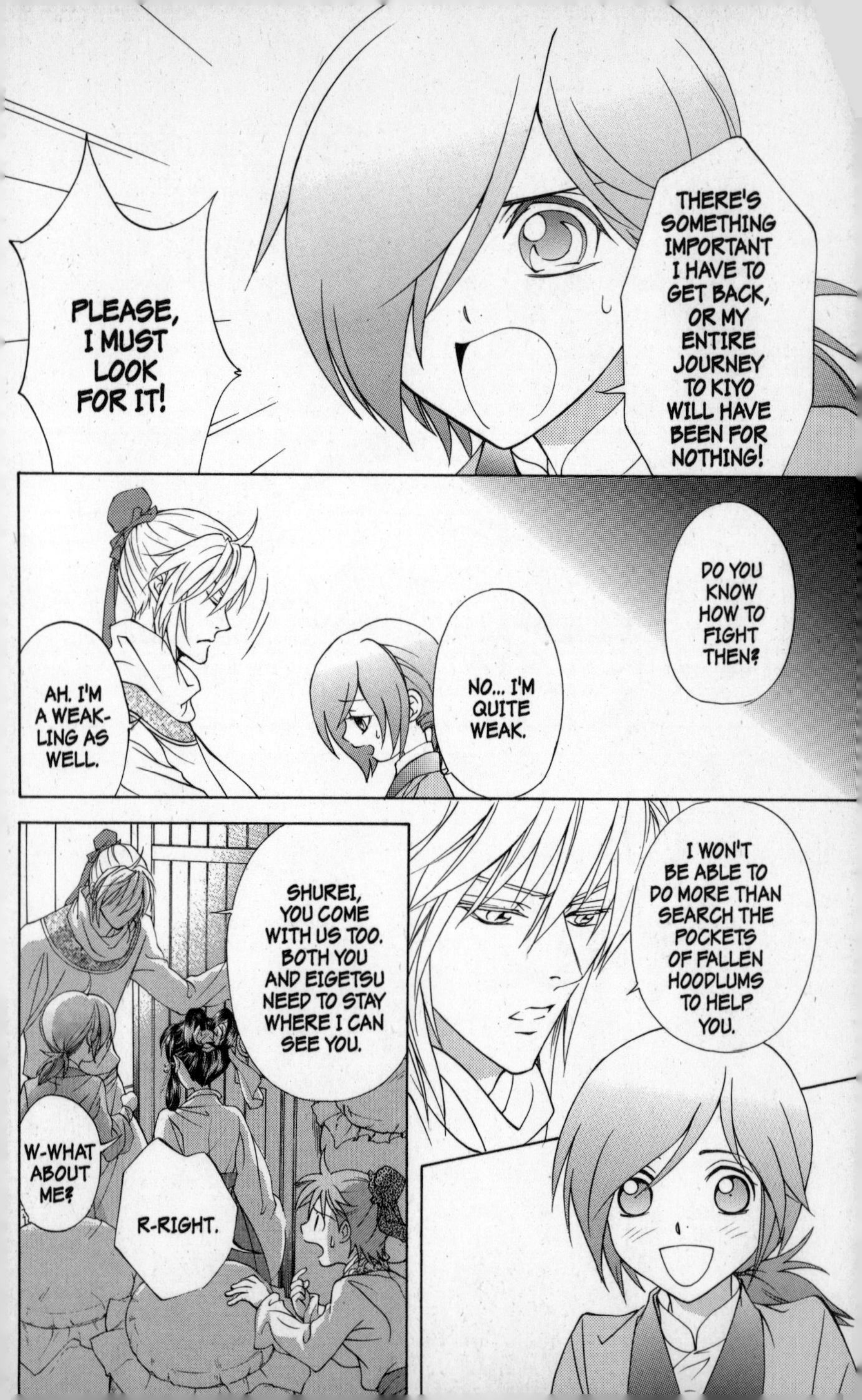
THERE'S SOMETHING IMPORTANT I HAVE TO GET BACK, OR MY ENTIRE JOURNEY TO KIYO WILL HAVE BEEN FOR NOTHING!
PLEASE, I MUST LOOK FOR IT!
DO YOU KNOW HOW TO FIGHT THEN?
NO... I'M QUITE WEAK.
AH. I'M A WEAK-LING AS WELL.
I WON'T BE ABLE TO DO MORE THAN SEARCH THE POCKETS OF FALLEN HOODLUMS TO HELP YOU.
SHUREI, YOU COME WITH US TOO. BOTH YOU AND EIGETSU NEED TO STAY WHERE I CAN SEE YOU.
R-RIGHT.
W-WHAT ABOUT ME?

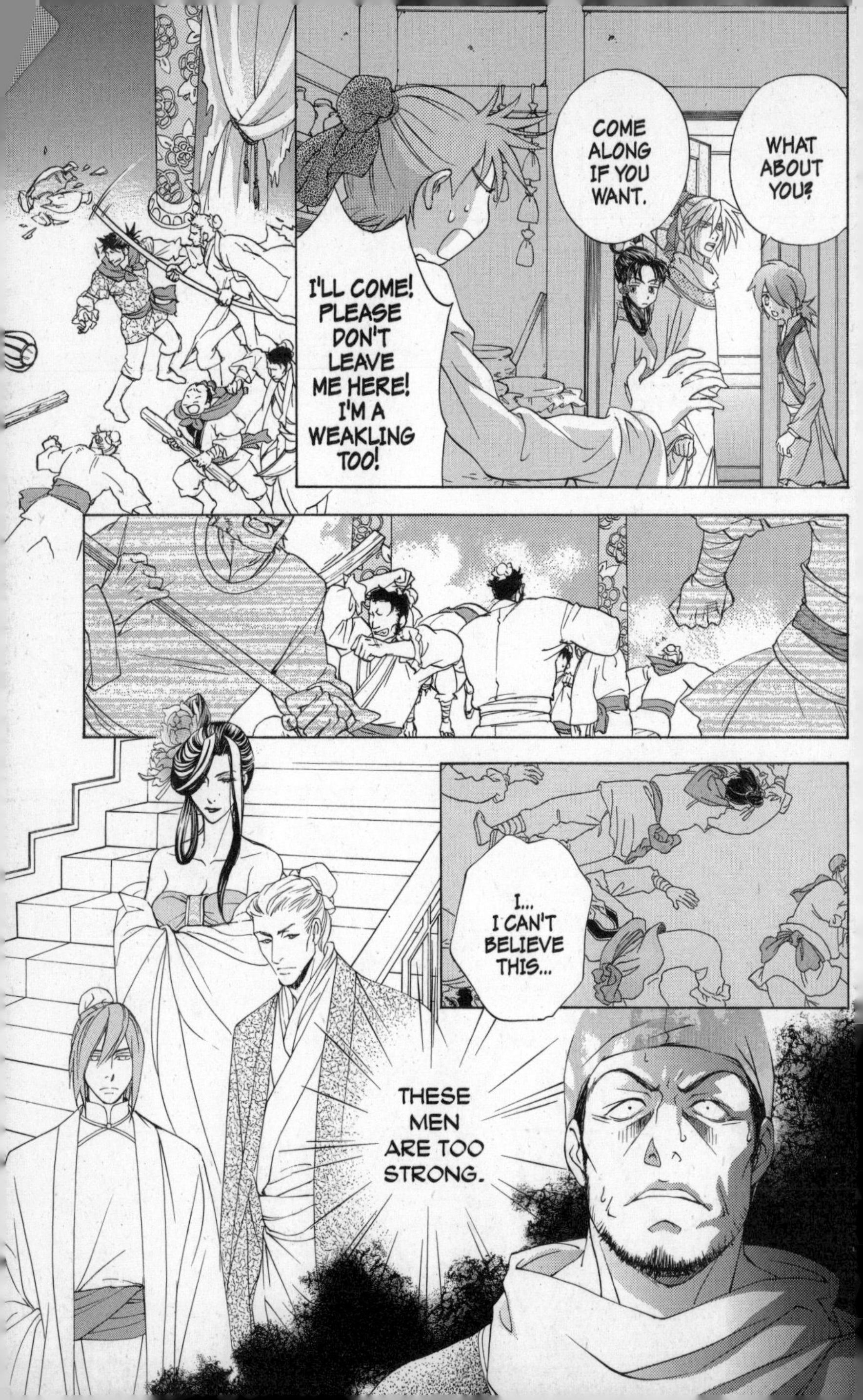
WHAT ABOUT YOU?
COME ALONG IF YOU WANT.
I'LL COME! PLEASE DON'T LEAVE ME HERE! I'M A WEAKLING TOO!
I... I CAN'T BELIEVE THIS...
THESE MEN ARE TOO STRONG.

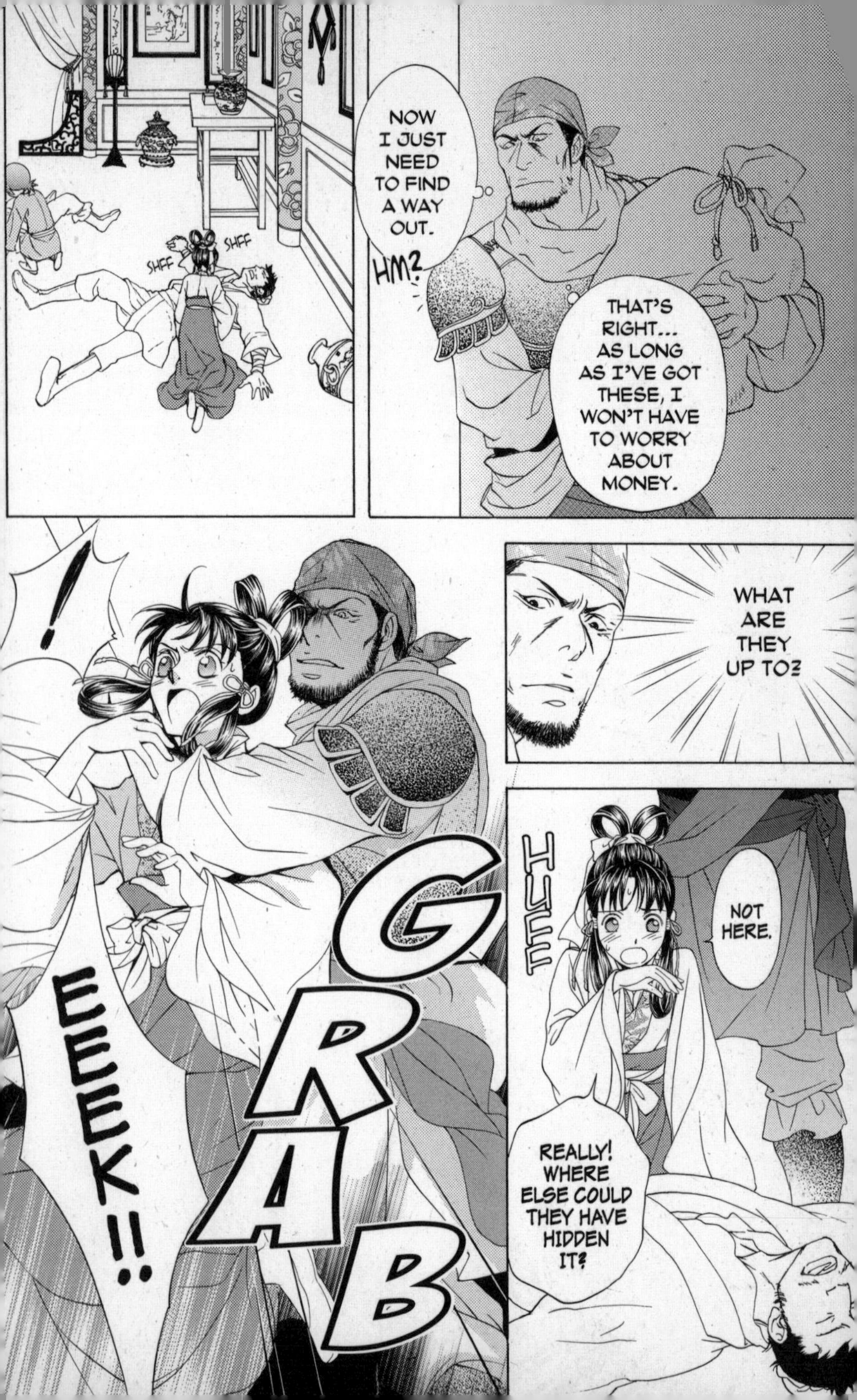
THAT'S RIGHT... AS LONG AS I'VE GOT THESE, I WON'T HAVE TO WORRY ABOUT MONEY.
NOW I JUST NEED TO FIND A WAY OUT.
HM?
SHFF
SHFF
WHAT ARE THEY UP TO?
NOT HERE.
HUFF
REALLY! WHERE ELSE COULD THEY HAVE HIDDEN IT?
!
GRAB
EEEEK!!

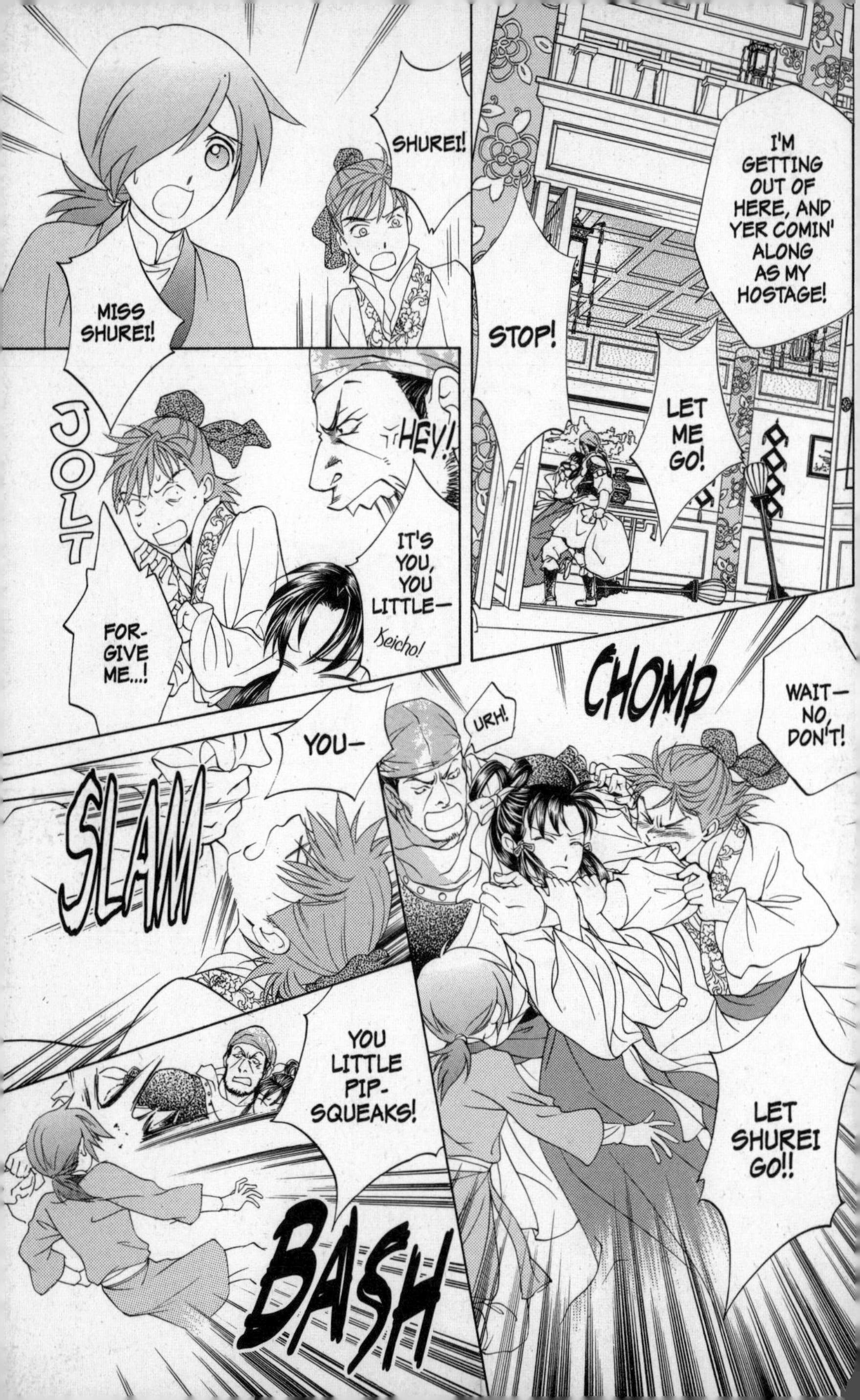
I'M GETTING OUT OF HERE, AND YER COMIN' ALONG AS MY HOSTAGE!
STOP!
LET ME GO!
SHUREI!
MISS SHUREI!
HEY!
IT'S YOU, YOU LITTLE—
Keicho!
JOLT
FOR-GIVE ME...!
WAIT— NO, DON'T!
CHOMP
URH!
LET SHUREI GO!!
YOU—
SLAM
YOU LITTLE PIP-SQUEAKS!
BASH

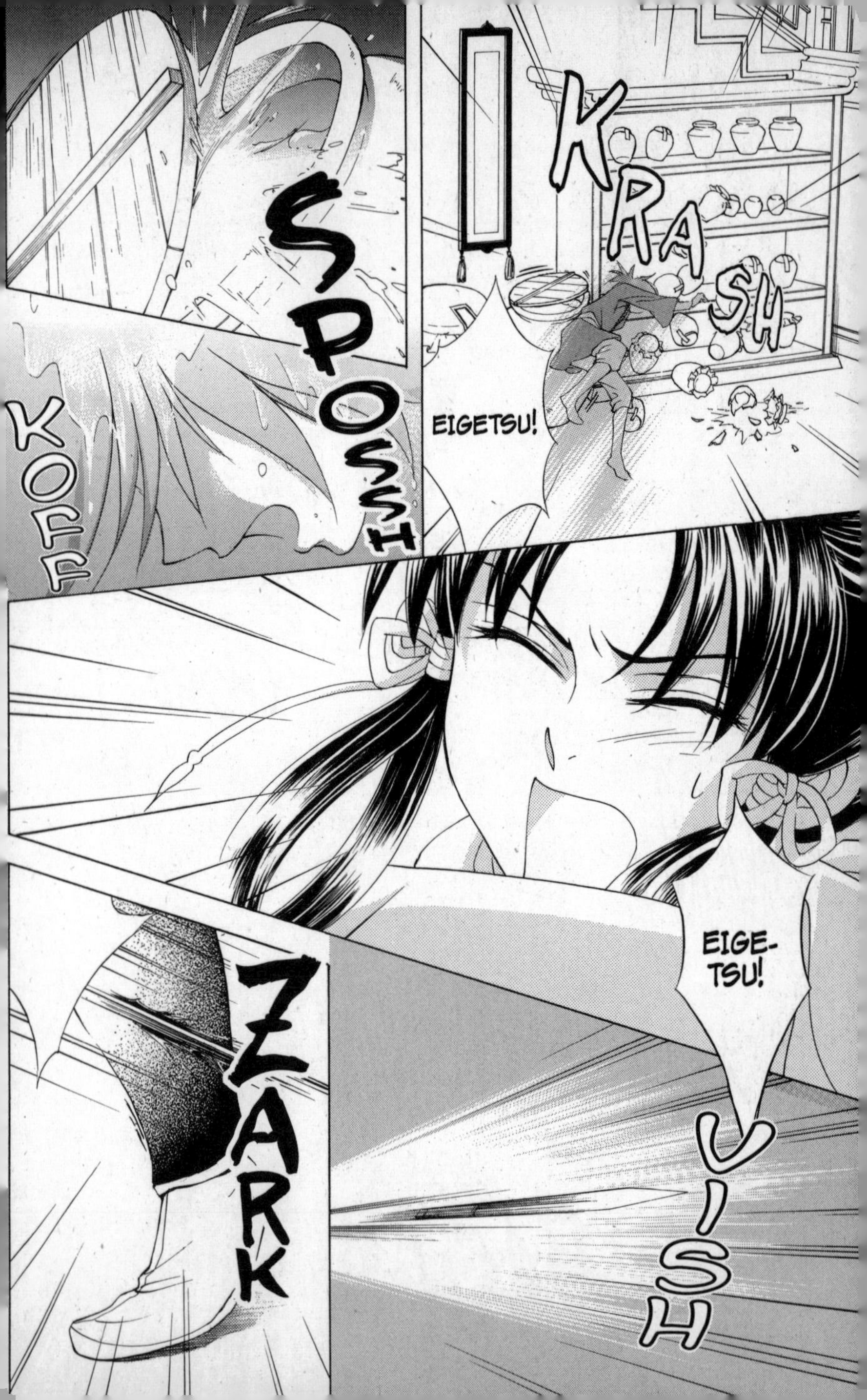
KRASH
EIGETSU!
SPOSSH
KOFF
EIGE-
TSU!
VISH
ZZARK

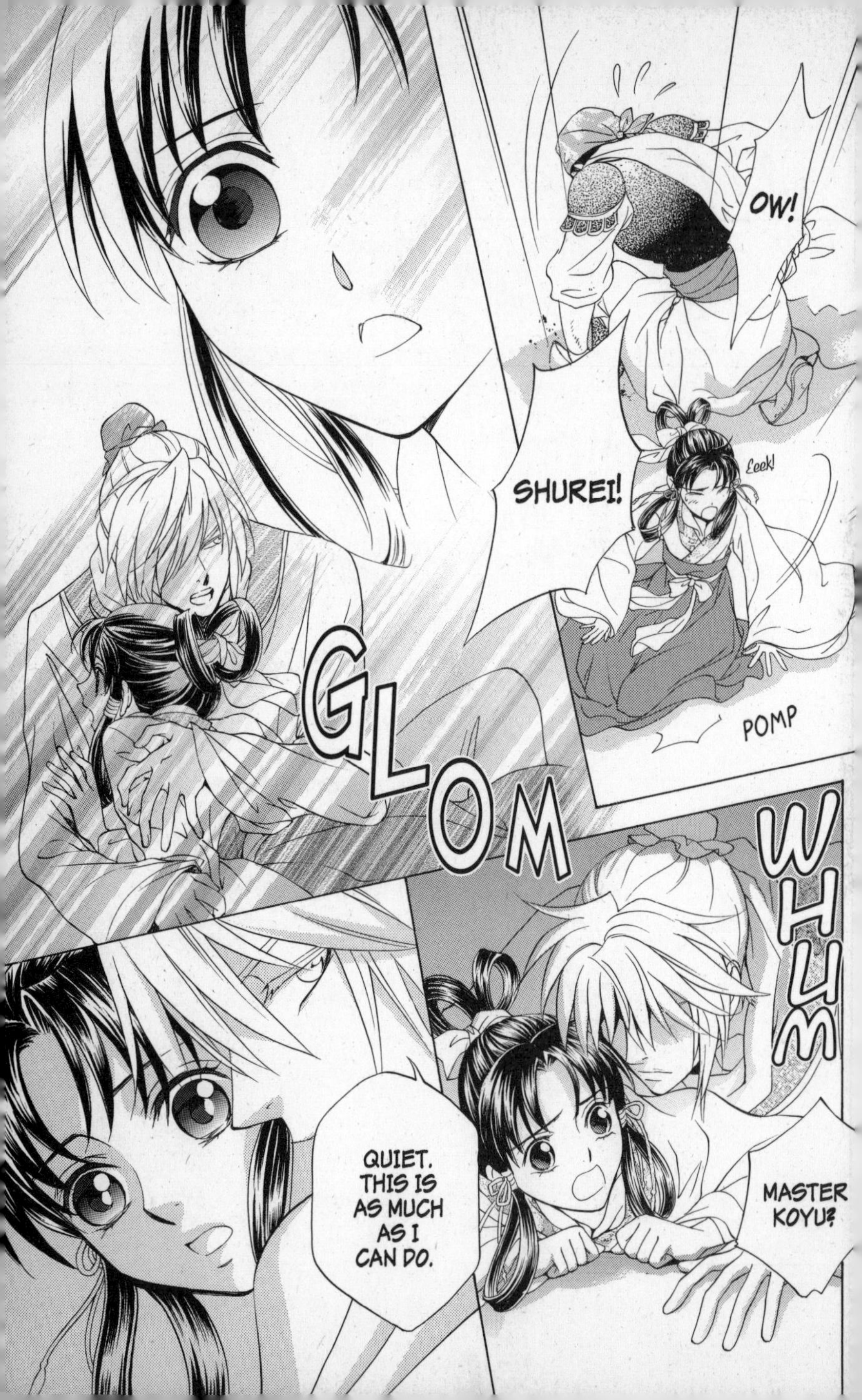
OW!
SHUREI!
Eeek!
POMP
GLOM
WHUMP
MASTER KOYU?
QUIET. THIS IS AS MUCH AS I CAN DO.

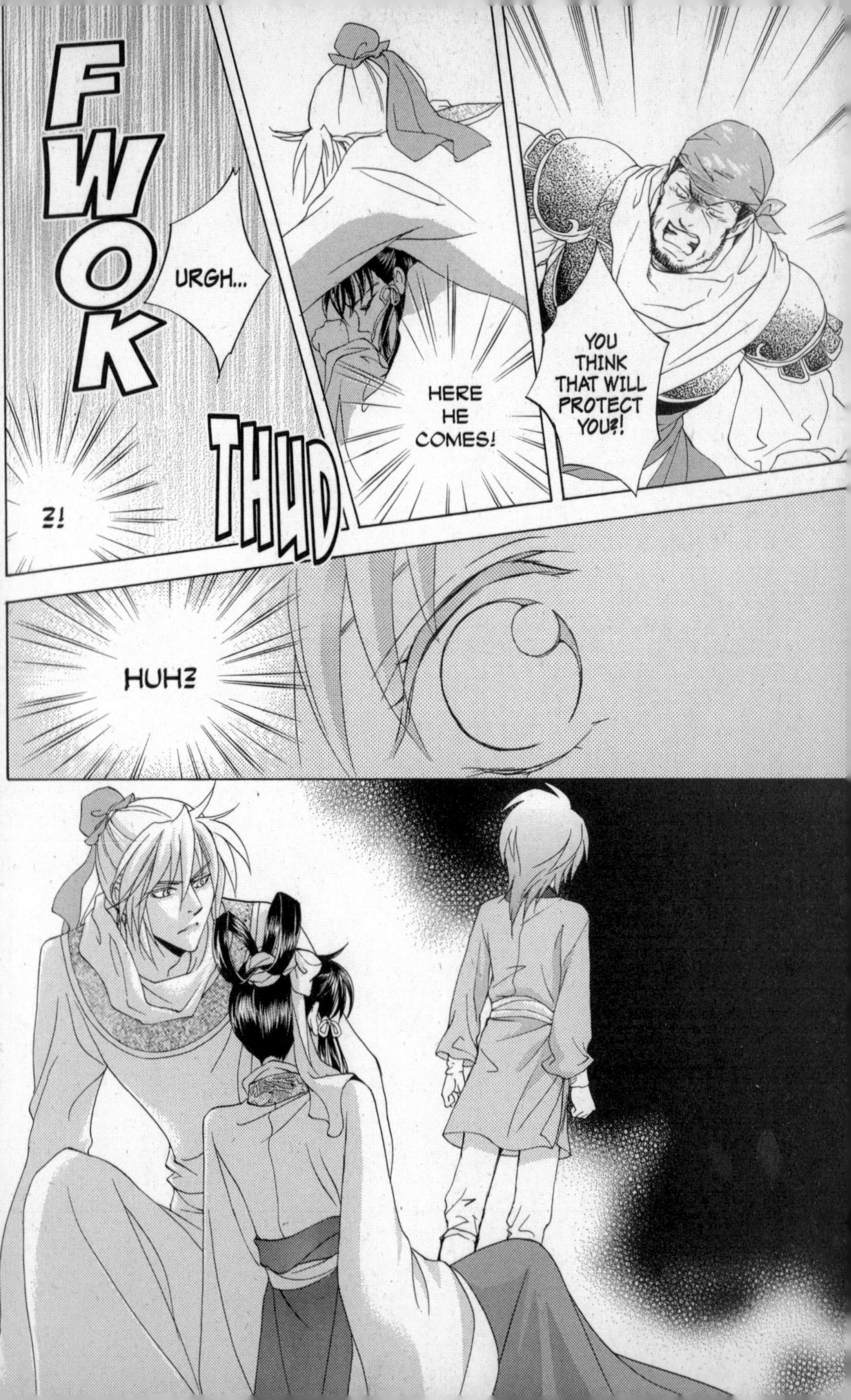
YOU THINK THAT WILL PROTECT YOU?!
HERE HE COMES!
FWOK
URGH...
THUD
?!
HUH?

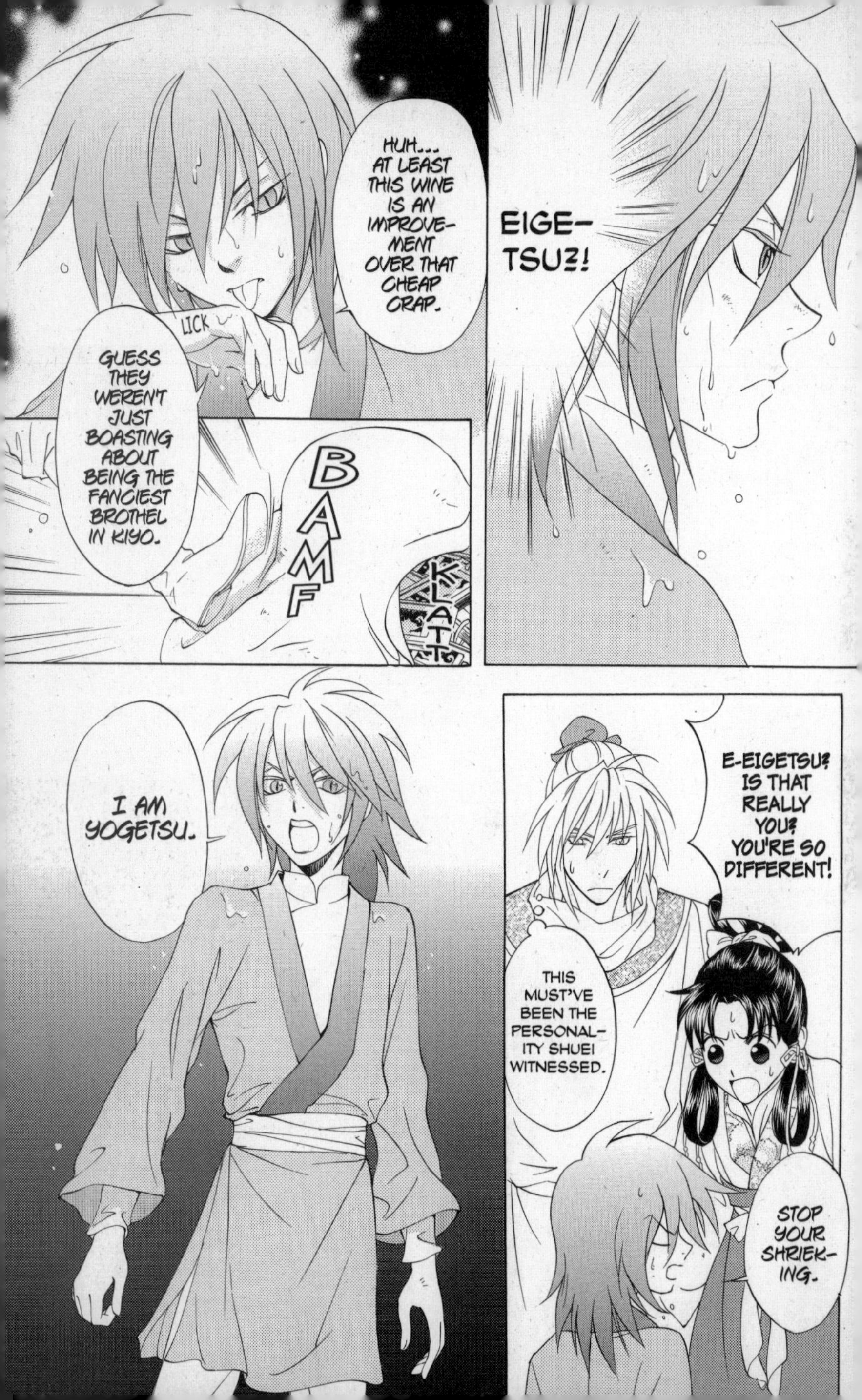
EIGE-TSU?!
HUH... AT LEAST THIS WINE IS AN IMPROVE-MENT OVER THAT CHEAP CRAP.
LICK
GUESS THEY WEREN'T JUST BOASTING ABOUT BEING THE FANCIEST BROTHEL IN KIYO.
BAMF
KLATT
E-EIGETSU? IS THAT REALLY YOU? YOU'RE SO DIFFERENT!
THIS MUST'VE BEEN THE PERSONAL-ITY SHUEI WITNESSED.
STOP YOUR SHRIEK-ING.
I AM YOGETSU.

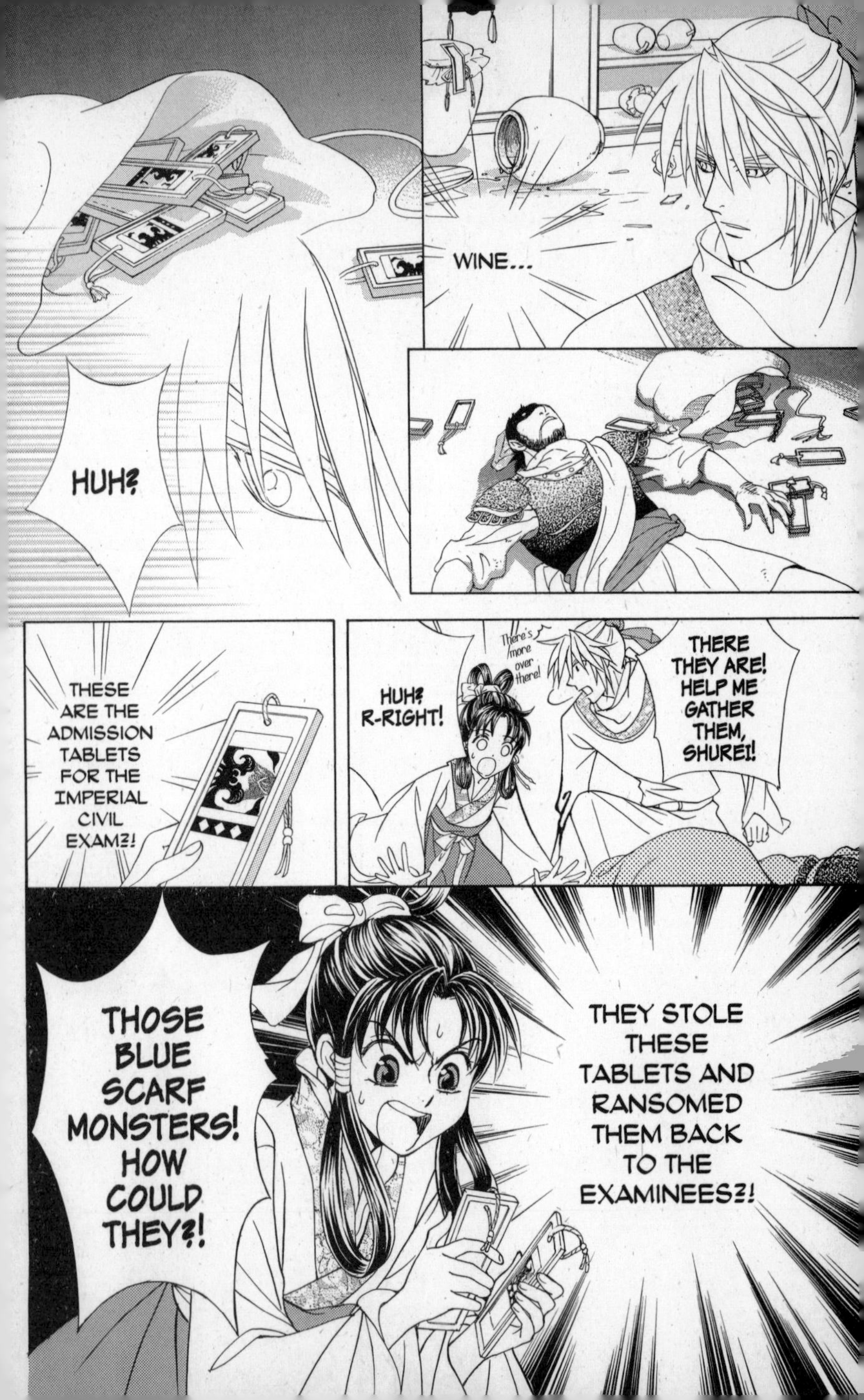
WINE...
HUH?
THERE THEY ARE! HELP ME GATHER THEM, SHUREI!
There's more over there!
HUH? R-RIGHT!
THESE ARE THE ADMISSION TABLETS FOR THE IMPERIAL CIVIL EXAM?!
THEY STOLE THESE TABLETS AND RANSOMED THEM BACK TO THE EXAMINEES?!
THOSE BLUE SCARF MONSTERS! HOW COULD THEY?!

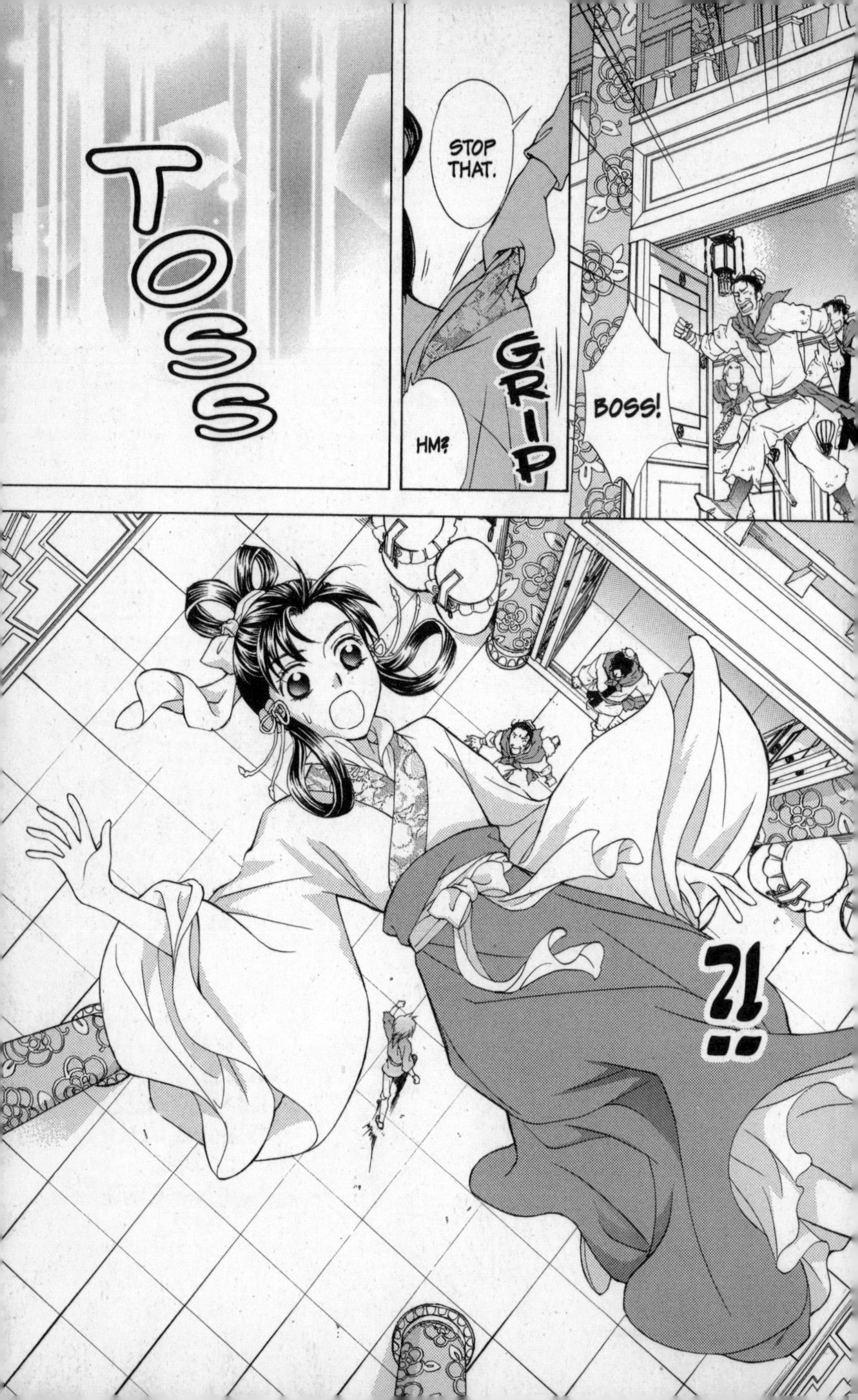
BOSS!
STOP THAT.
GRIP
HM?
TOSS
?!

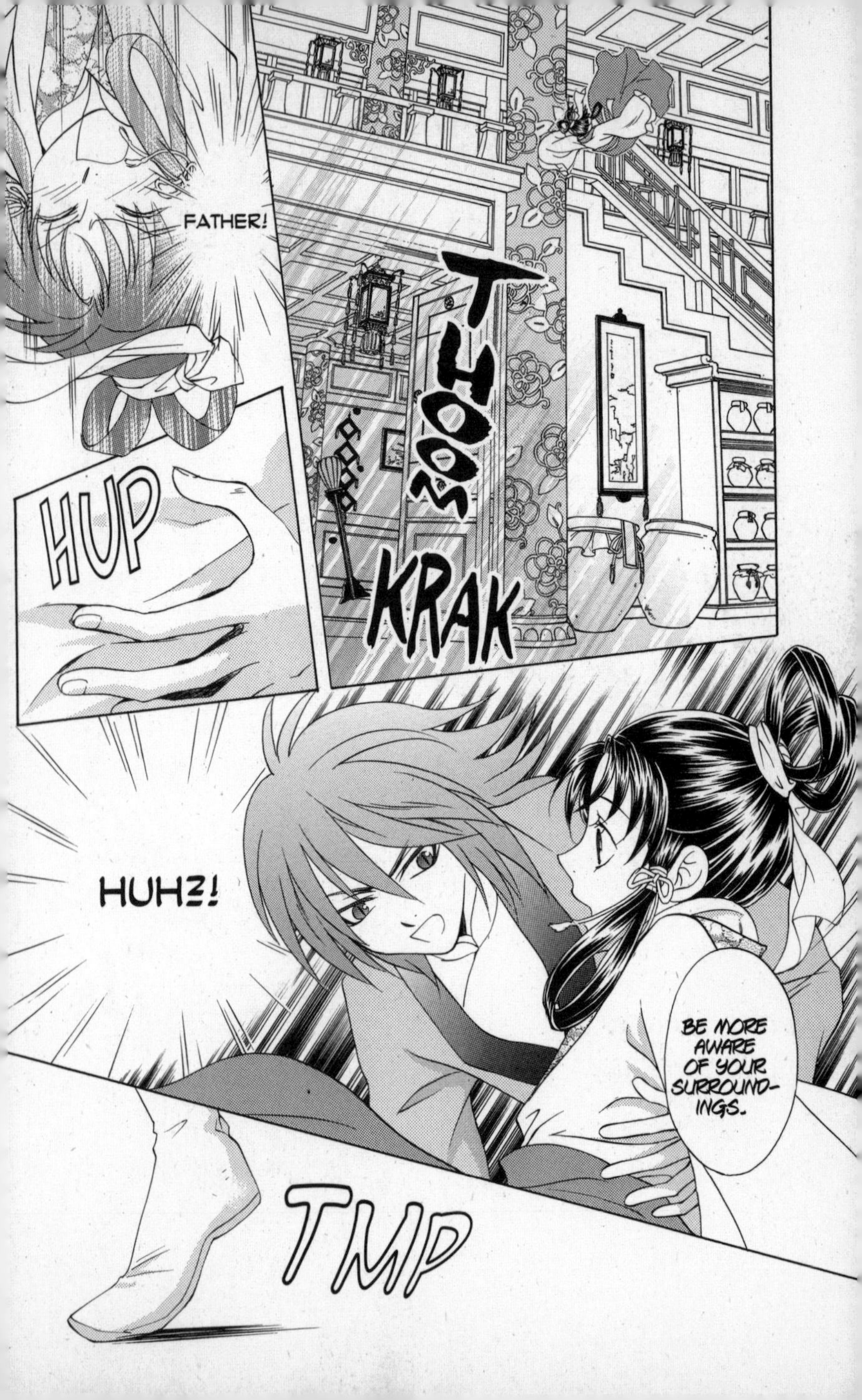
THOOM
KRAK
FATHER!
HUP
BE MORE AWARE OF YOUR SURROUNDINGS.
HUH?!
TMP

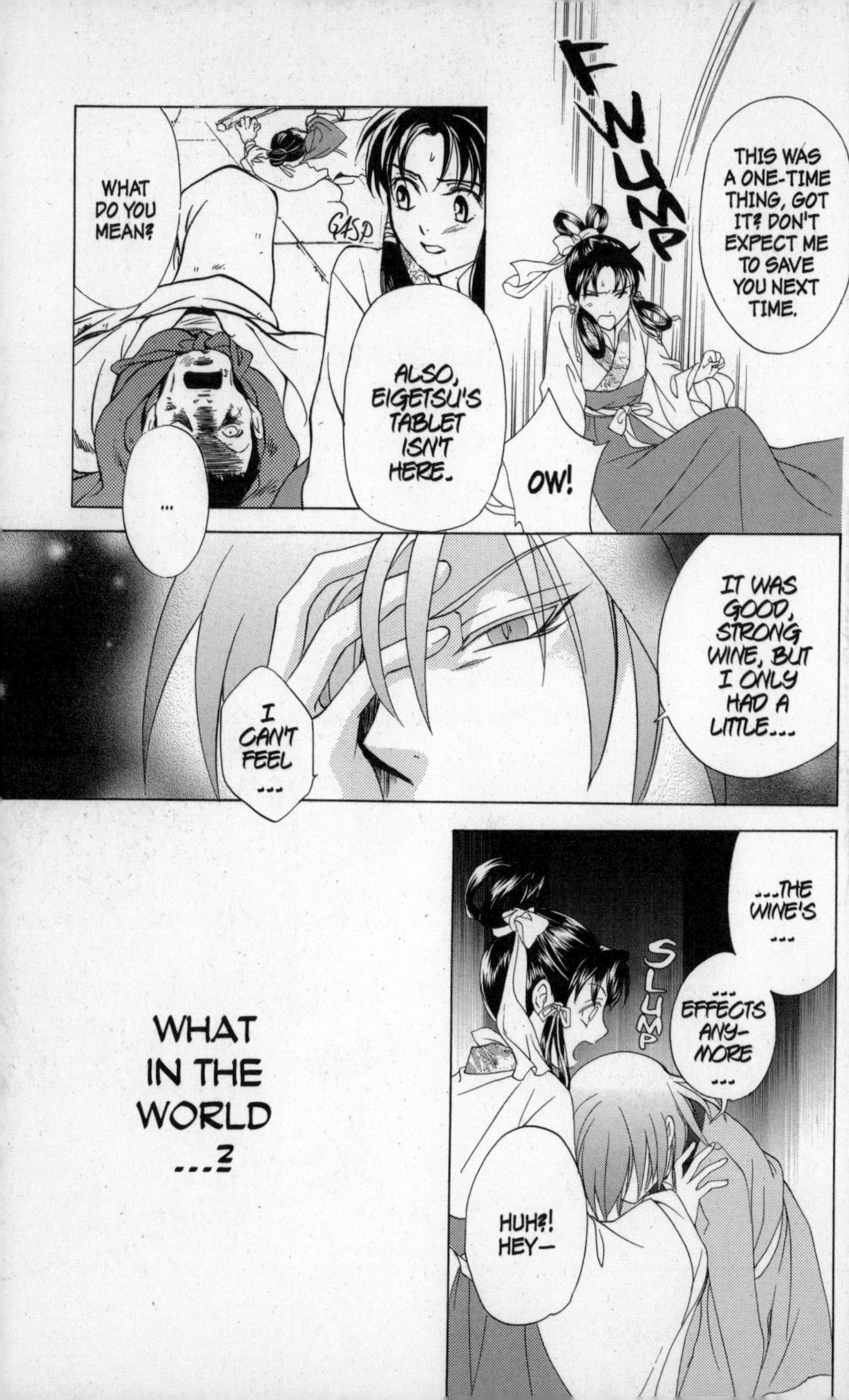
FWUMP
THIS WAS A ONE-TIME THING, GOT IT? DON'T EXPECT ME TO SAVE YOU NEXT TIME.
OW!
GASP
ALSO, EIGETSU'S TABLET ISN'T HERE.
WHAT DO YOU MEAN?
...
IT WAS GOOD, STRONG WINE, BUT I ONLY HAD A LITTLE...
I CAN'T FEEL ...
...THE WINE'S ...
... EFFECTS ANYMORE ...
SLUMP
HUH?! HEY—
WHAT IN THE WORLD ...?

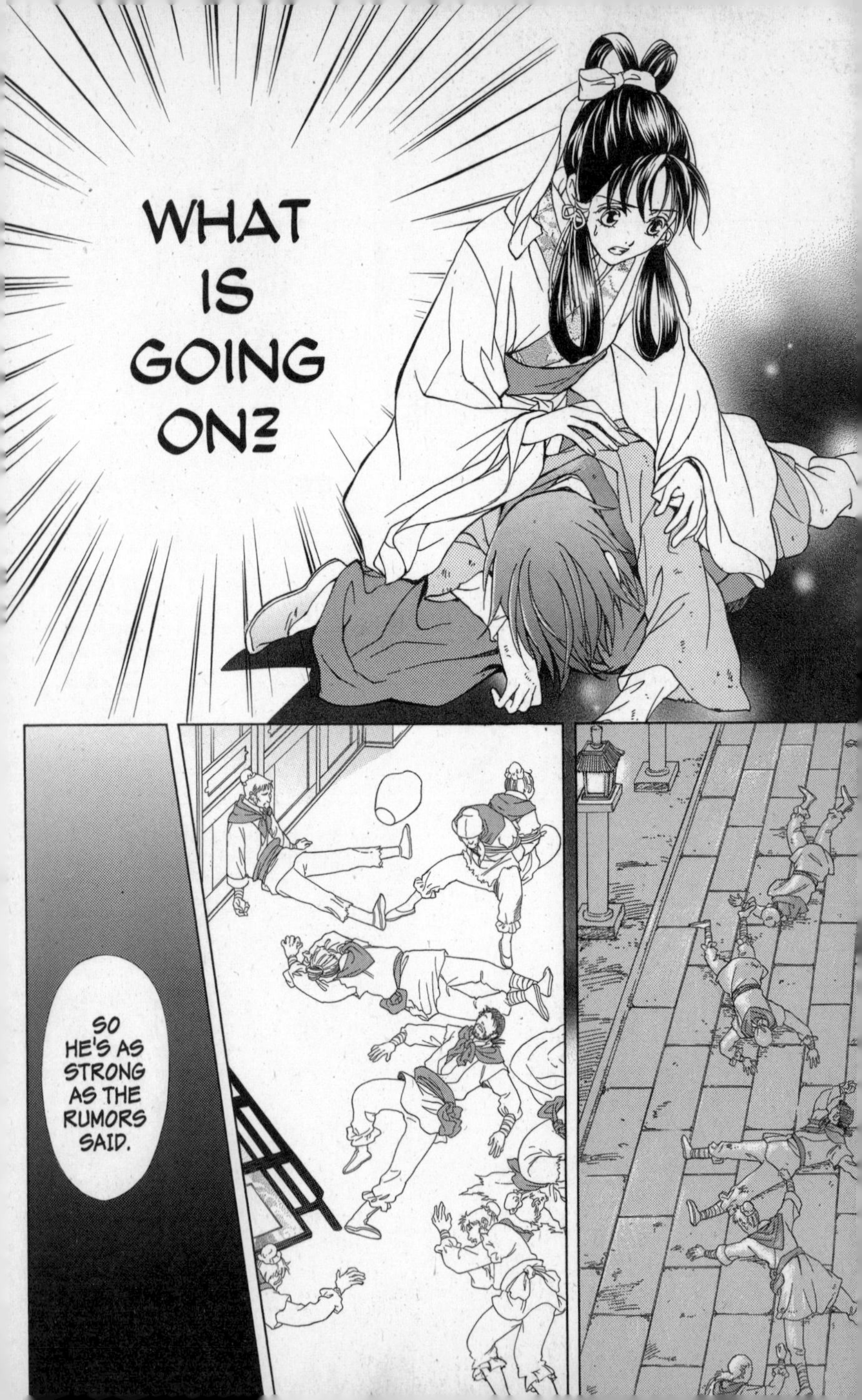
WHAT IS GOING ON?
SO HE'S AS STRONG AS THE RUMORS SAID.

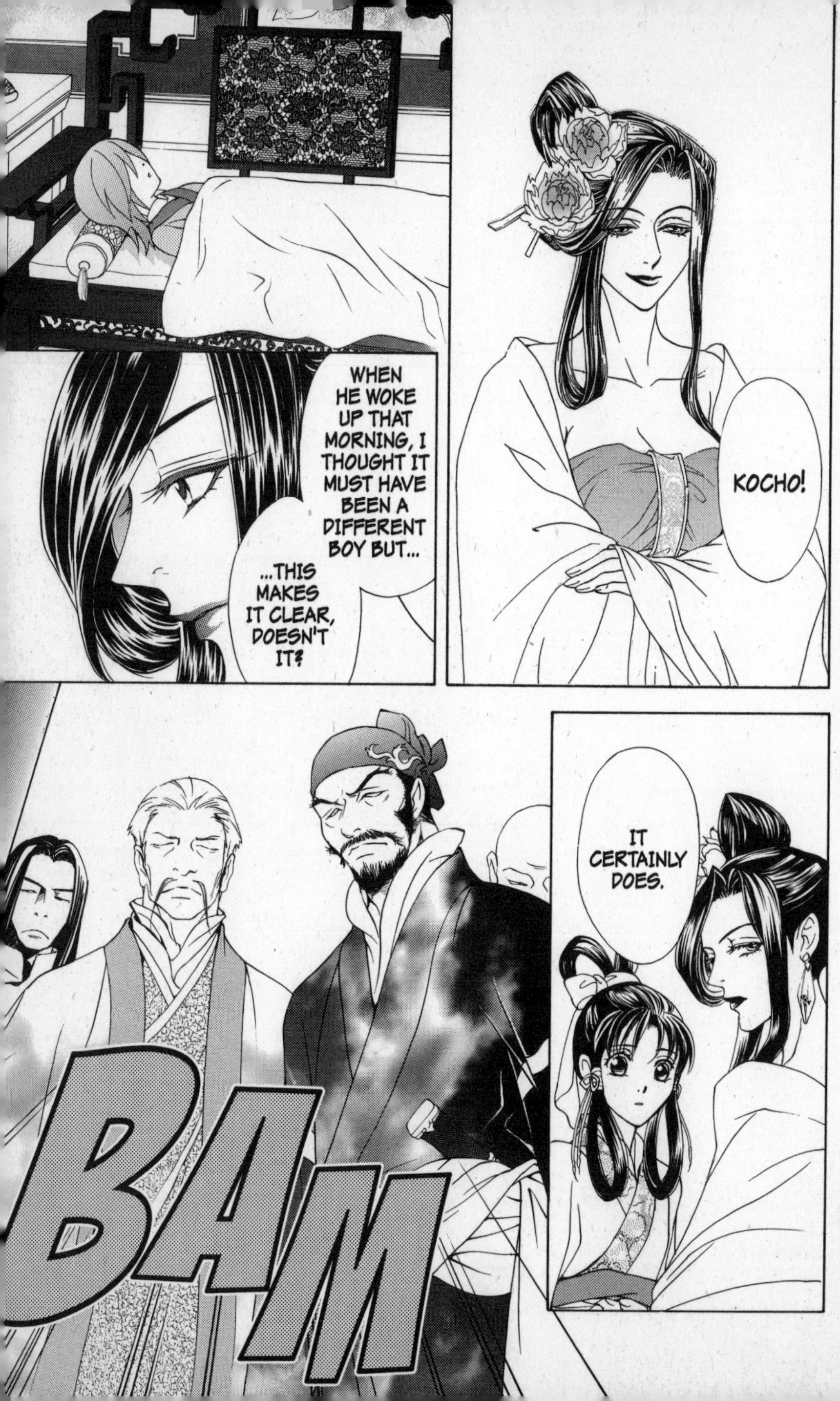
KOCHO!
WHEN HE WOKE UP THAT MORNING, I THOUGHT IT MUST HAVE BEEN A DIFFERENT BOY BUT...
...THIS MAKES IT CLEAR, DOESN'T IT?
IT CERTAINLY DOES.
BAM

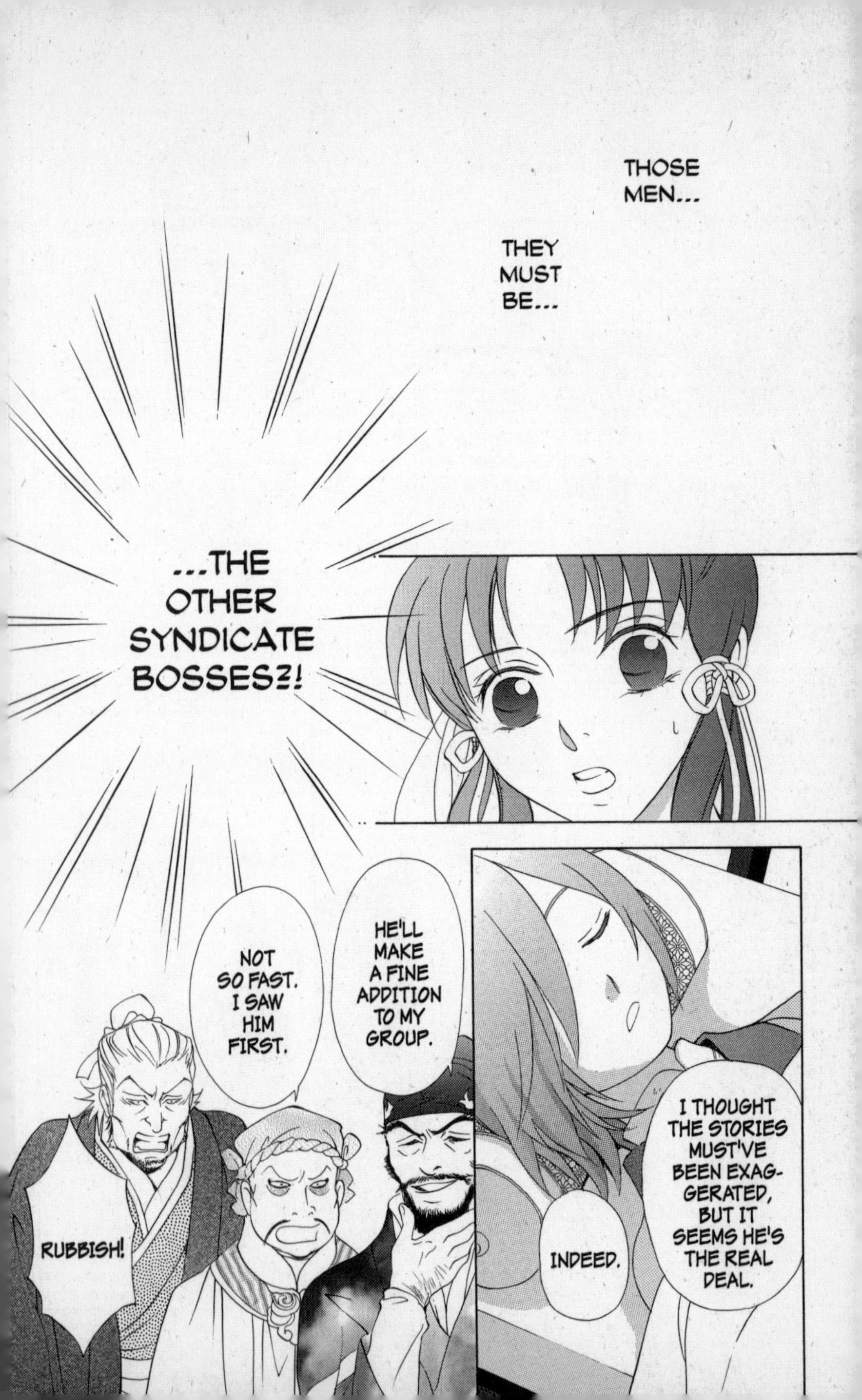
THOSE MEN...
THEY MUST BE...
...THE OTHER SYNDICATE BOSSES?!
I THOUGHT THE STORIES MUST'VE BEEN EXAG-GERATED, BUT IT SEEMS HE'S THE REAL DEAL.
INDEED.
HE'LL MAKE A FINE ADDITION TO MY GROUP.
NOT SO FAST. I SAW HIM FIRST.
RUBBISH!

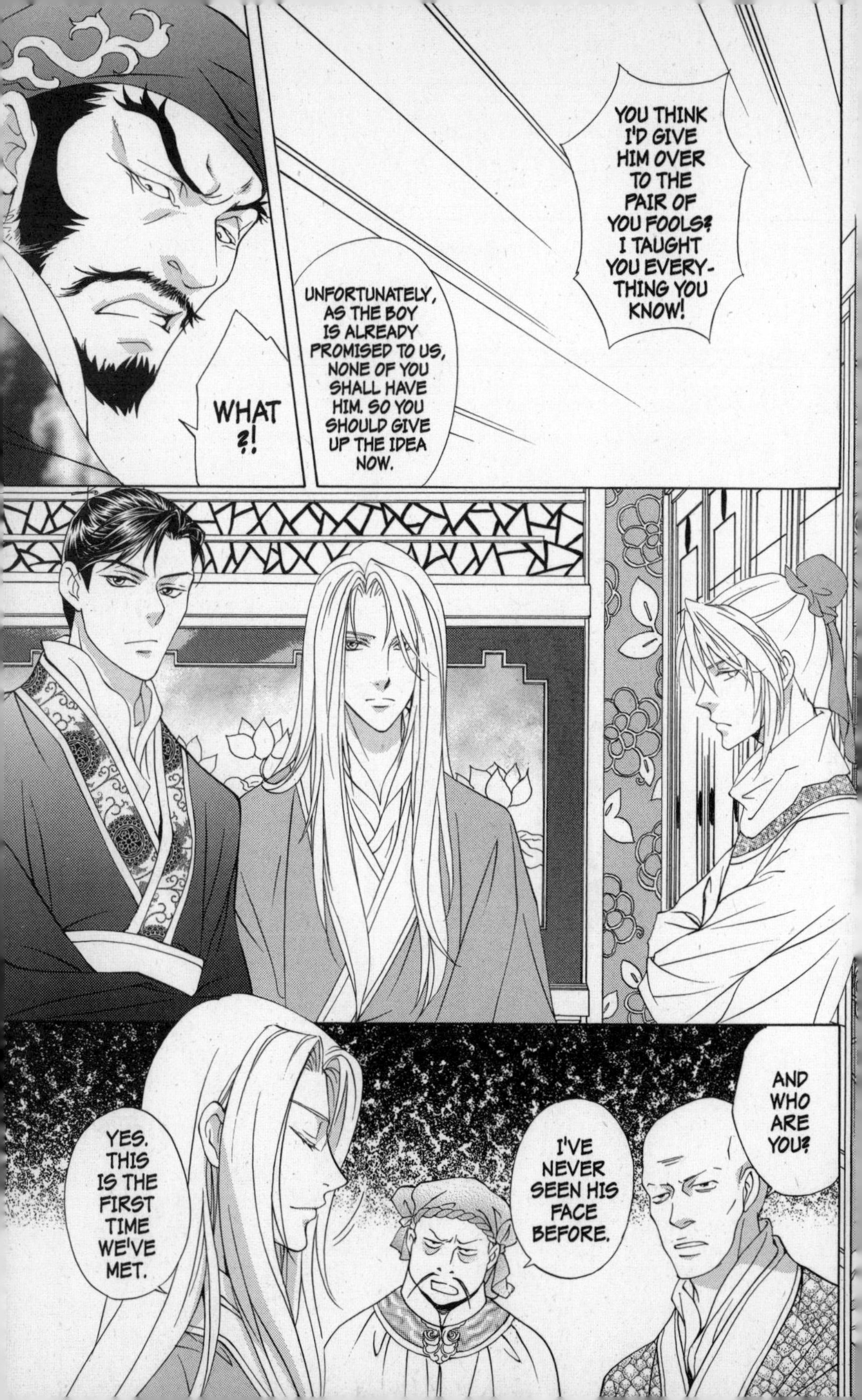
YOU THINK I'D GIVE HIM OVER TO THE PAIR OF YOU FOOLS? I TAUGHT YOU EVERY-THING YOU KNOW!
UNFORTUNATELY, AS THE BOY IS ALREADY PROMISED TO US, NONE OF YOU SHALL HAVE HIM. SO YOU SHOULD GIVE UP THE IDEA NOW.
WHAT?!
AND WHO ARE YOU?
I'VE NEVER SEEN HIS FACE BEFORE.
YES. THIS IS THE FIRST TIME WE'VE MET.

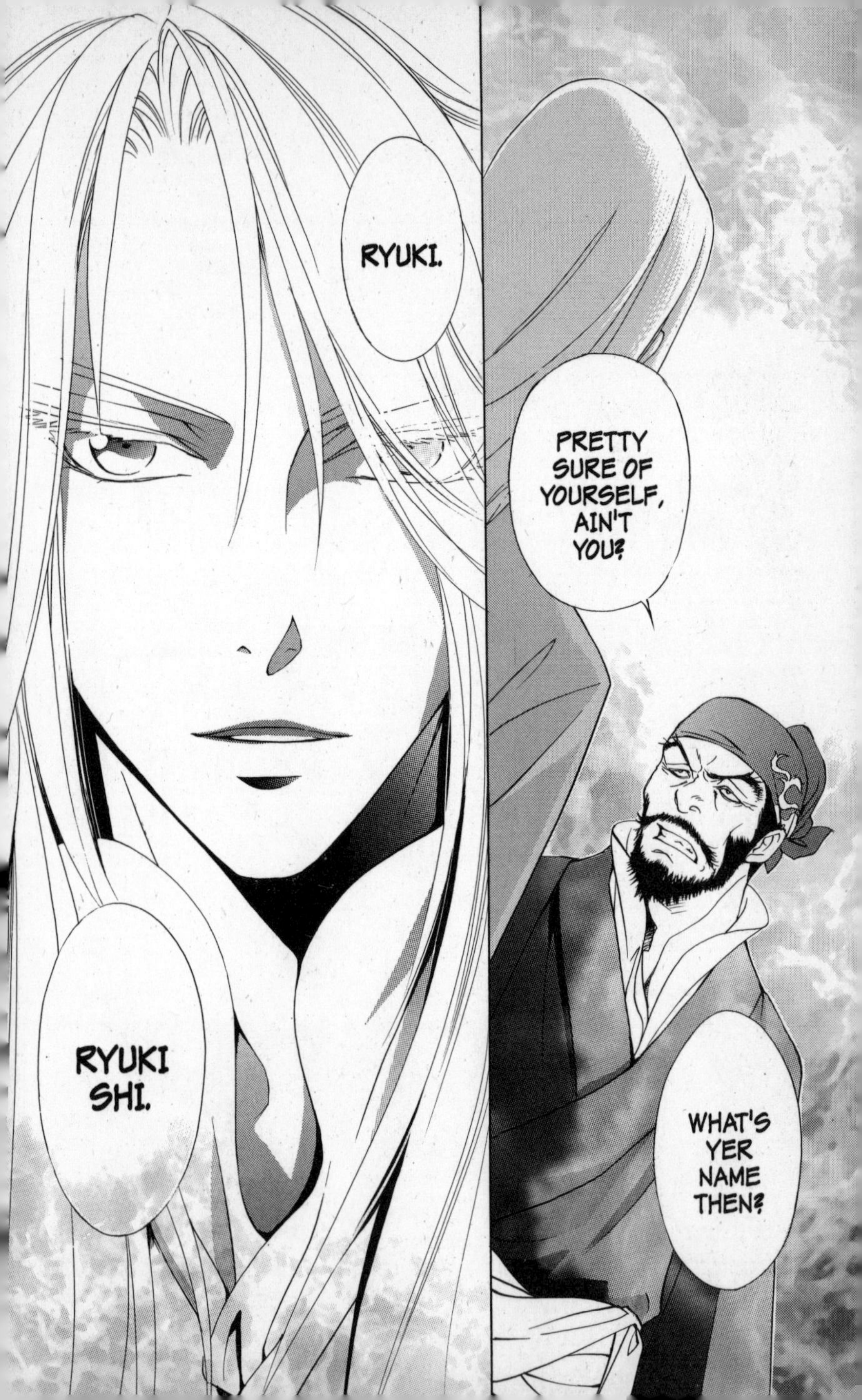
PRETTY SURE OF YOURSELF, AIN'T YOU?
WHAT'S YER NAME THEN?
RYUKI.
RYUKI SHI.

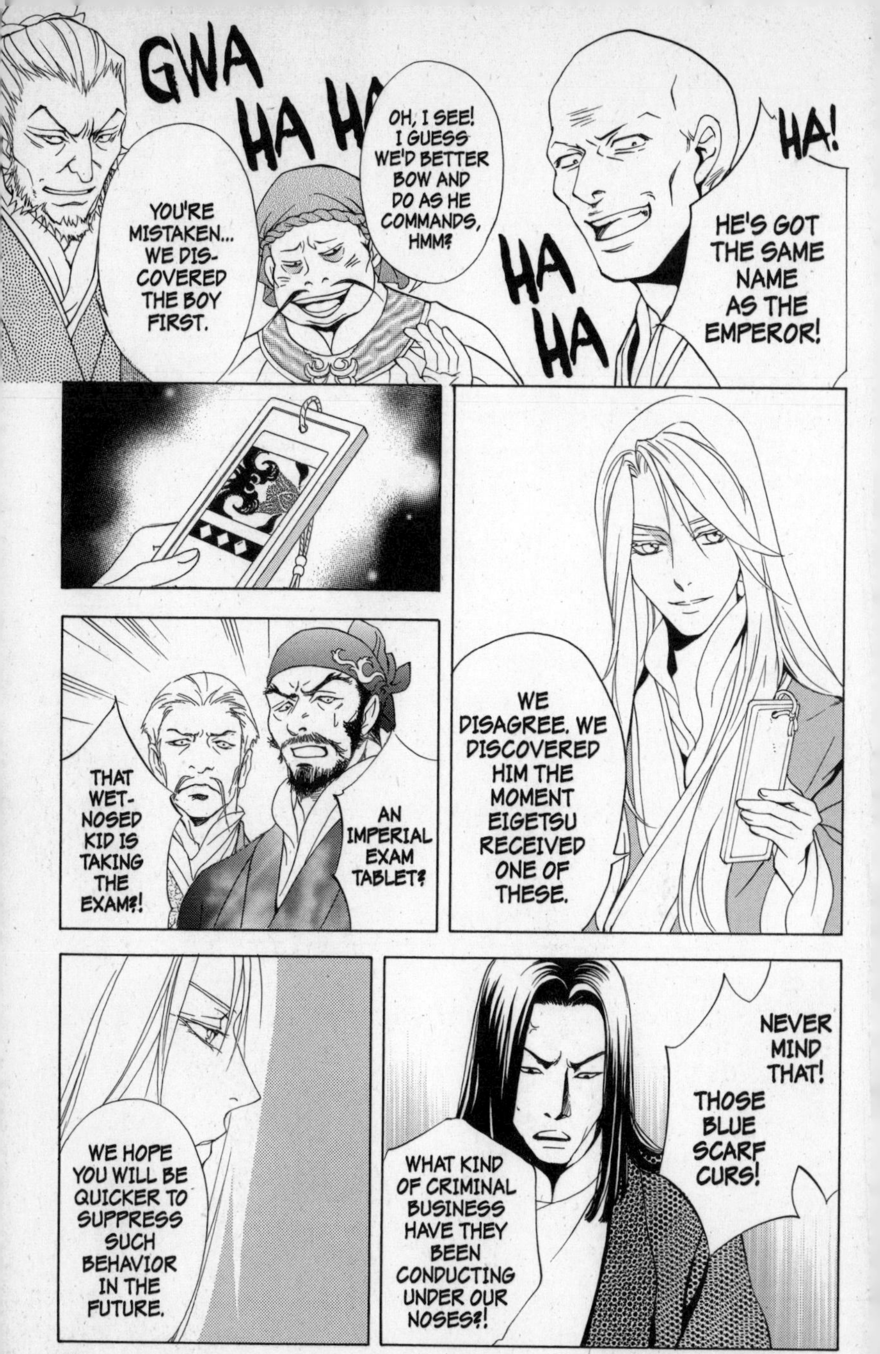
HA!
HE'S GOT THE SAME NAME AS THE EMPEROR!
OH, I SEE! I GUESS WE'D BETTER BOW AND DO AS HE COMMANDS, HMM?
GWA HA HA
HA HA
YOU'RE MISTAKEN... WE DISCOVERED THE BOY FIRST.
WE DISAGREE. WE DISCOVERED HIM THE MOMENT EIGETSU RECEIVED ONE OF THESE.
AN IMPERIAL EXAM TABLET?
THAT WET-NOSED KID IS TAKING THE EXAM?!
NEVER MIND THAT!
THOSE BLUE SCARF CURS!
WHAT KIND OF CRIMINAL BUSINESS HAVE THEY BEEN CONDUCTING UNDER OUR NOSES?!
WE HOPE YOU WILL BE QUICKER TO SUPPRESS SUCH BEHAVIOR IN THE FUTURE.

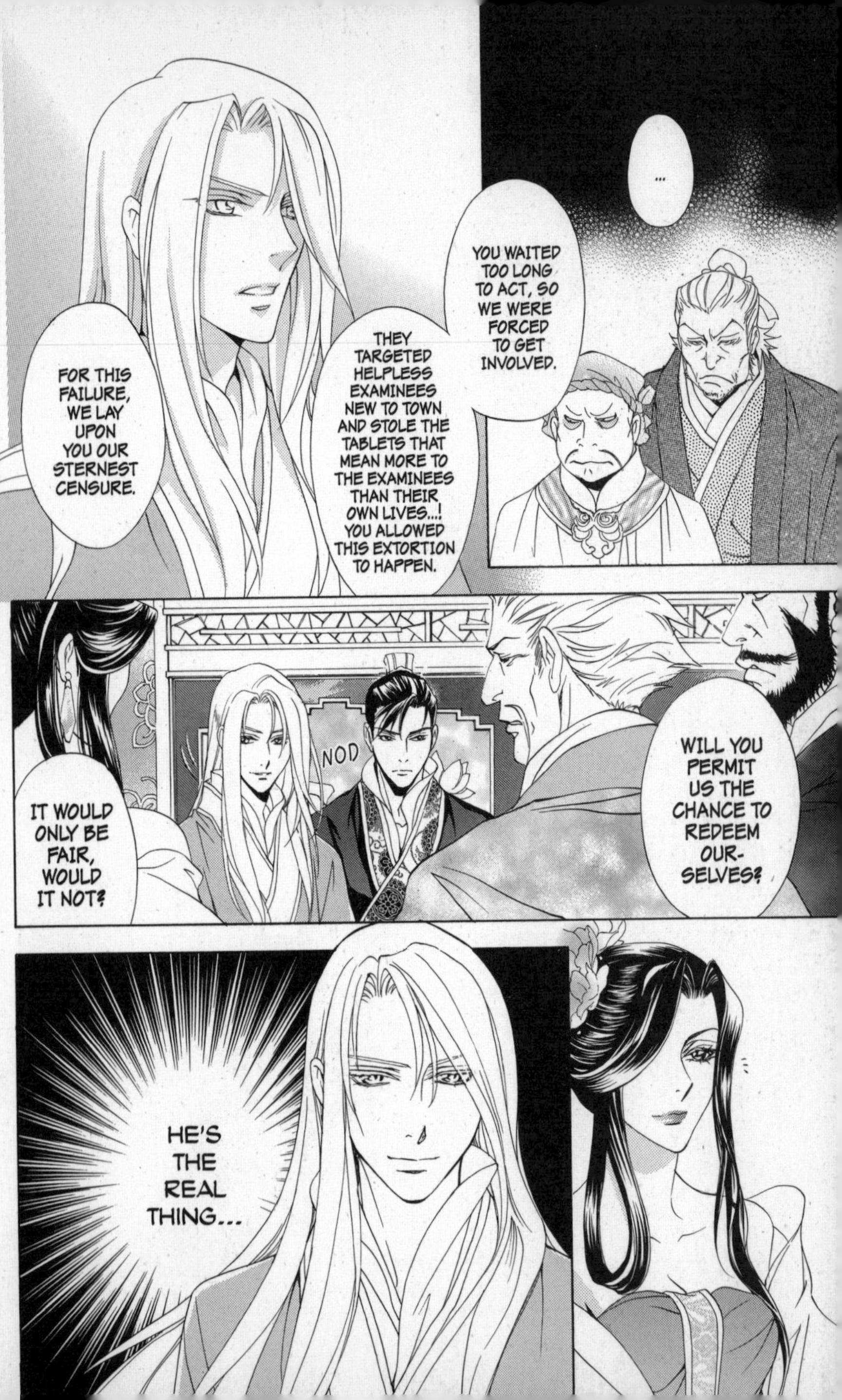
...
YOU WAITED TOO LONG TO ACT, SO WE WERE FORCED TO GET INVOLVED.
THEY TARGETED HELPLESS EXAMINEES NEW TO TOWN AND STOLE THE TABLETS THAT MEAN MORE TO THE EXAMINEES THAN THEIR OWN LIVES...! YOU ALLOWED THIS EXTORTION TO HAPPEN.
FOR THIS FAILURE, WE LAY UPON YOU OUR STERNEST CENSURE.
WILL YOU PERMIT US THE CHANCE TO REDEEM OUR-SELVES?
NOD
IT WOULD ONLY BE FAIR, WOULD IT NOT?
HE'S THE REAL THING...

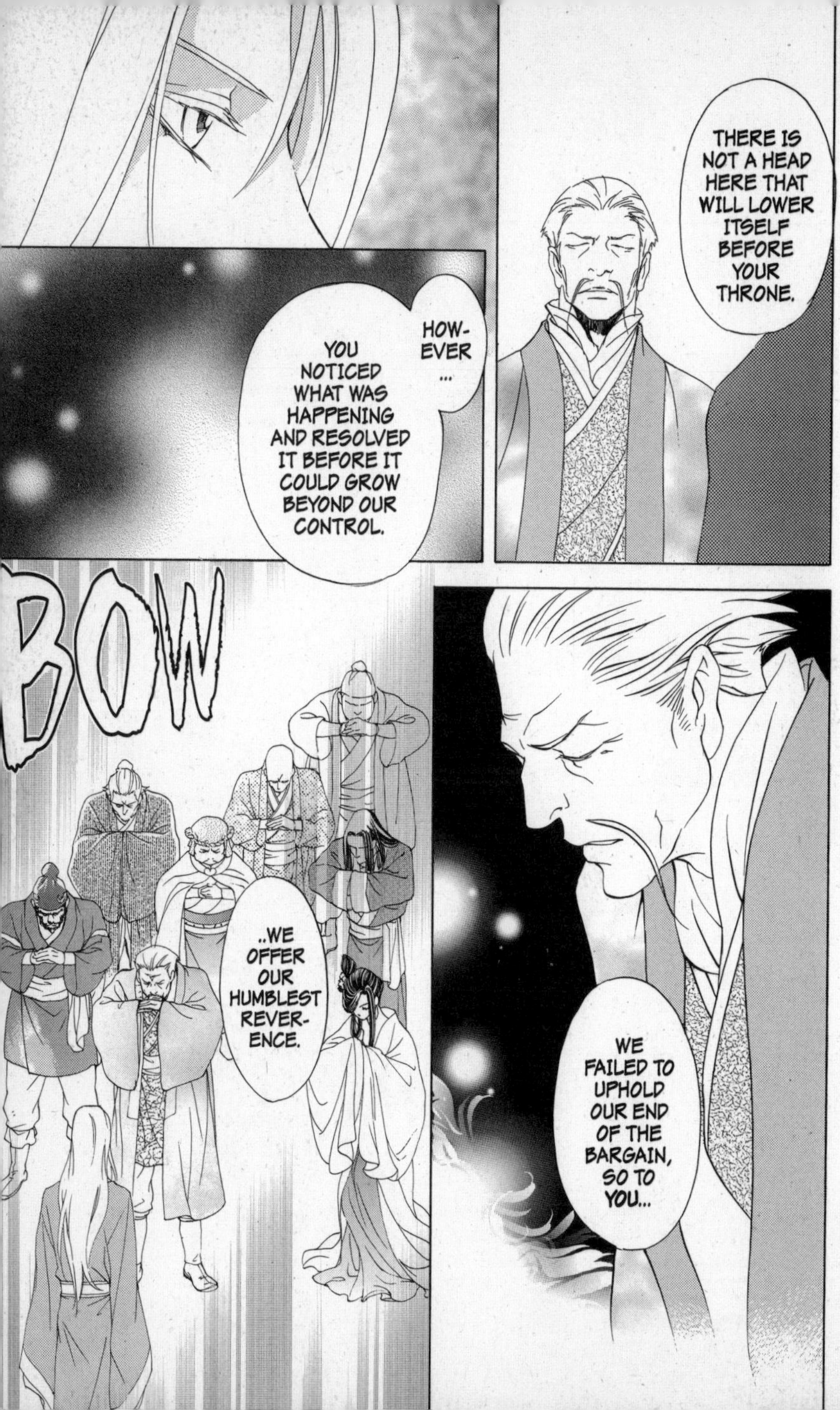
THERE IS NOT A HEAD HERE THAT WILL LOWER ITSELF BEFORE YOUR THRONE.
HOW-EVER...
YOU NOTICED WHAT WAS HAPPENING AND RESOLVED IT BEFORE IT COULD GROW BEYOND OUR CONTROL.
WE FAILED TO UPHOLD OUR END OF THE BARGAIN, SO TO YOU...
BOW
..WE OFFER OUR HUMBLEST REVER-ENCE.

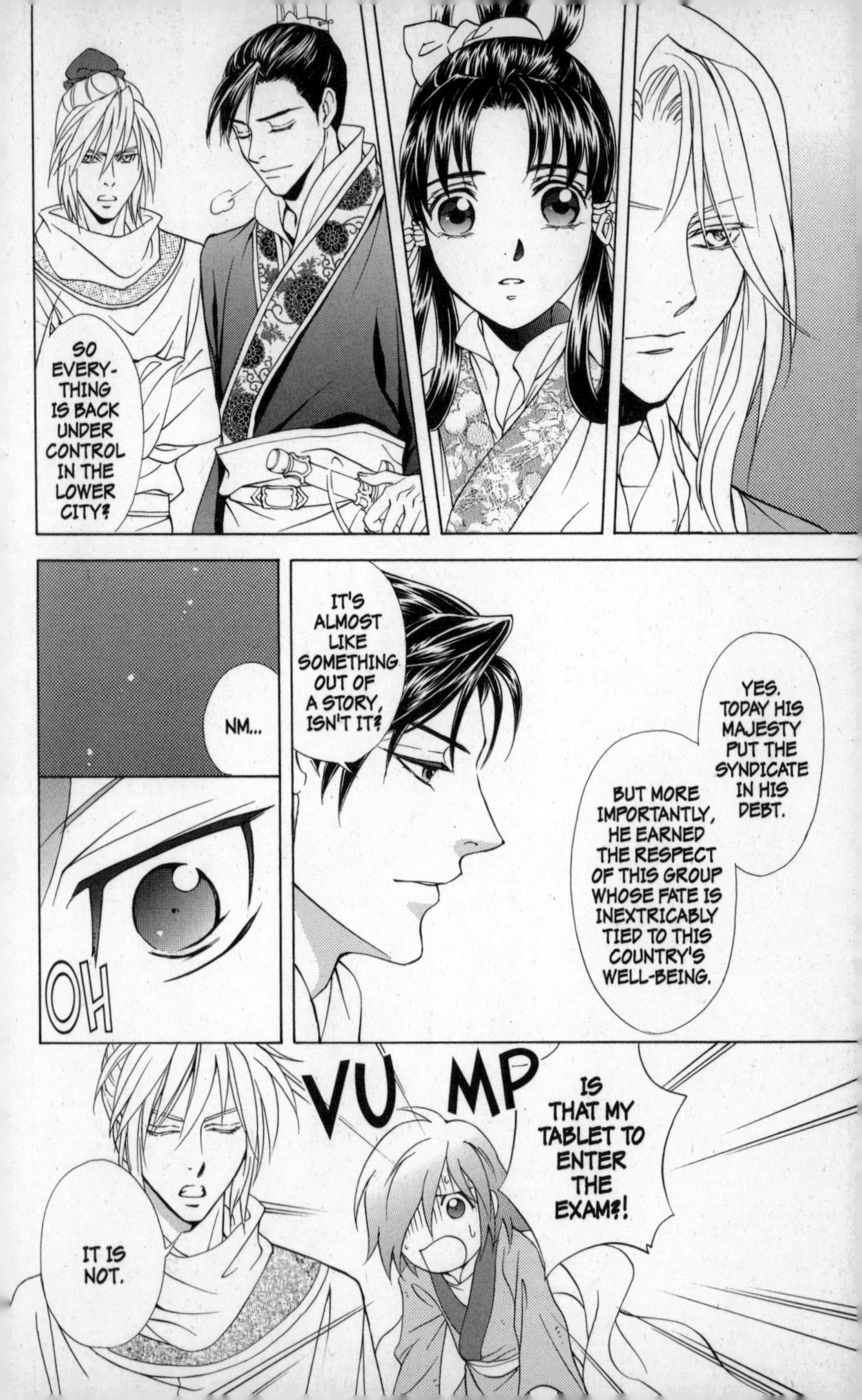
SO EVERYTHING IS BACK UNDER CONTROL IN THE LOWER CITY?
YES. TODAY HIS MAJESTY PUT THE SYNDICATE IN HIS DEBT.
BUT MORE IMPORTANTLY, HE EARNED THE RESPECT OF THIS GROUP WHOSE FATE IS INEXTRICABLY TIED TO THIS COUNTRY'S WELL-BEING.
IT'S ALMOST LIKE SOMETHING OUT OF A STORY, ISN'T IT?
NM...
OH
VUMP
IS THAT MY TABLET TO ENTER THE EXAM?!
IT IS NOT.

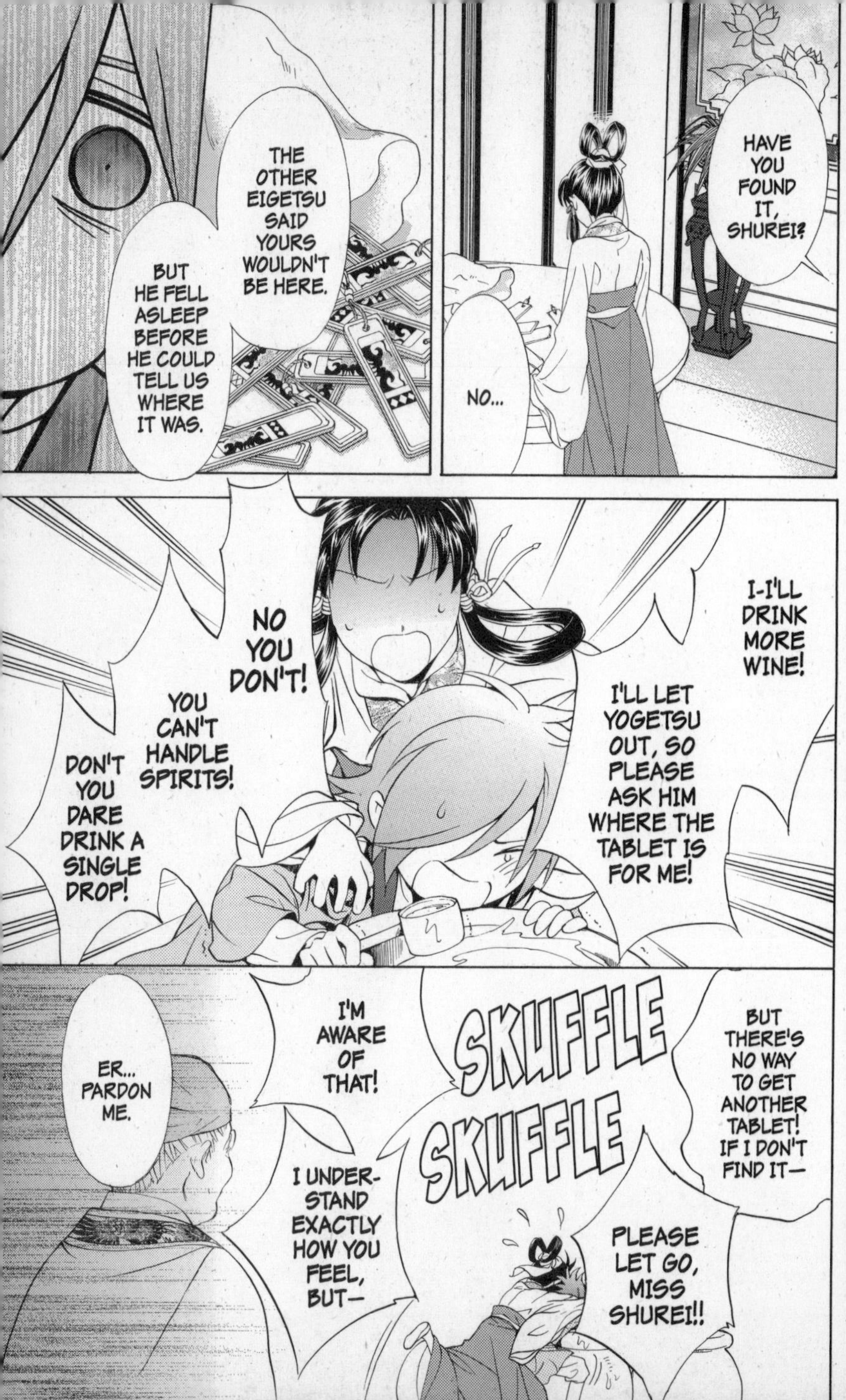
HAVE YOU FOUND IT, SHUREI?
NO...
THE OTHER EIGETSU SAID YOURS WOULDN'T BE HERE.
BUT HE FELL ASLEEP BEFORE HE COULD TELL US WHERE IT WAS.
I-I'LL DRINK MORE WINE!
I'LL LET YOGETSU OUT, SO PLEASE ASK HIM WHERE THE TABLET IS FOR ME!
NO YOU DON'T!
YOU CAN'T HANDLE SPIRITS!
DON'T YOU DARE DRINK A SINGLE DROP!
BUT THERE'S NO WAY TO GET ANOTHER TABLET! IF I DON'T FIND IT—
SKUFFLE
SKUFFLE
PLEASE LET GO, MISS SHUREI!!
I'M AWARE OF THAT!
I UNDER-STAND EXACTLY HOW YOU FEEL, BUT—
ER... PARDON ME.

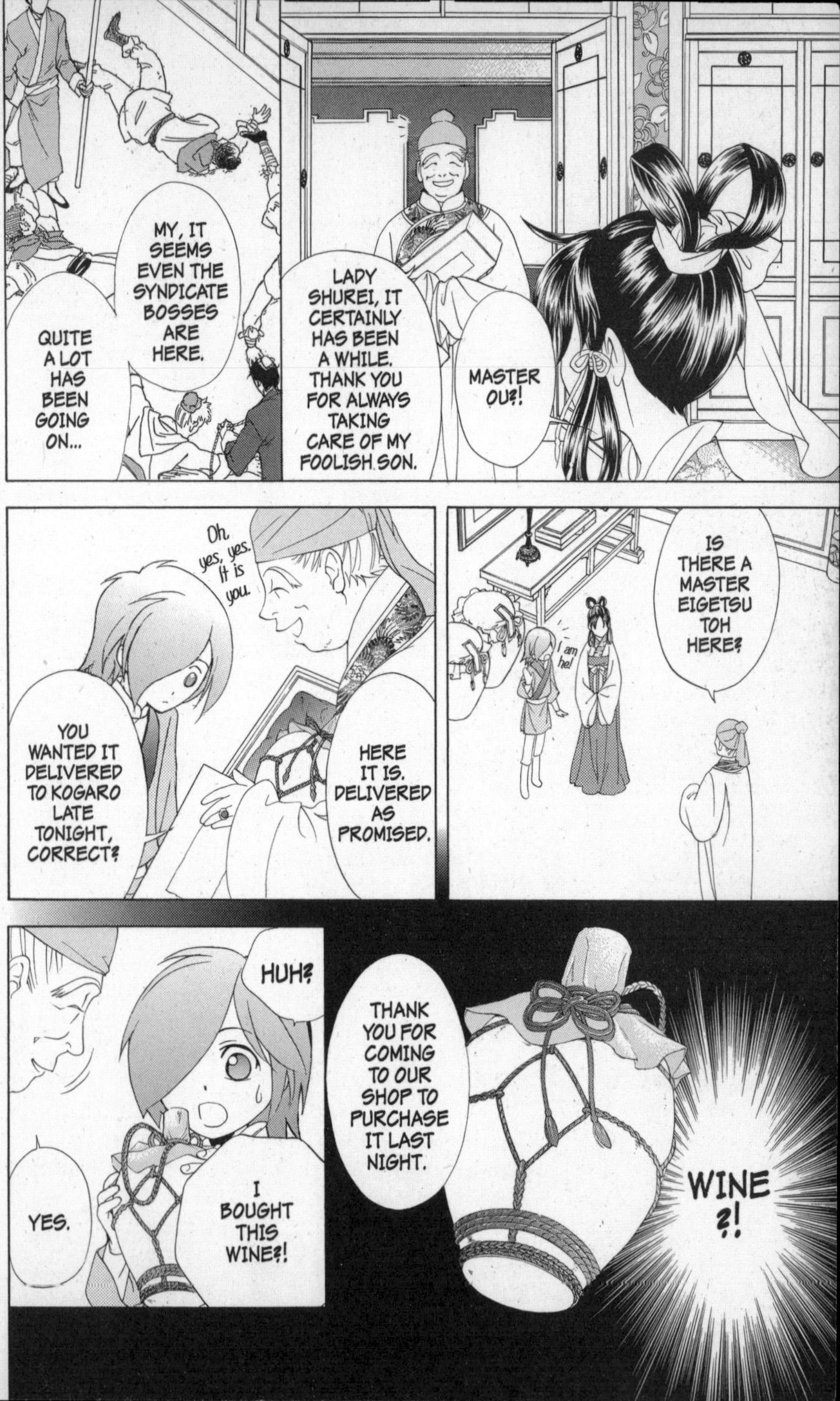
MASTER OU?!
LADY SHUREI, IT CERTAINLY HAS BEEN A WHILE. THANK YOU FOR ALWAYS TAKING CARE OF MY FOOLISH SON.
MY, IT SEEMS EVEN THE SYNDICATE BOSSES ARE HERE.
QUITE A LOT HAS BEEN GOING ON...
IS THERE A MASTER EIGETSU TOH HERE?
I am he!
Oh, yes, yes. It is you.
HERE IT IS. DELIVERED AS PROMISED.
YOU WANTED IT DELIVERED TO KOGARO LATE TONIGHT, CORRECT?
WINE?!
THANK YOU FOR COMING TO OUR SHOP TO PURCHASE IT LAST NIGHT.
HUH?
I BOUGHT THIS WINE?!
YES.

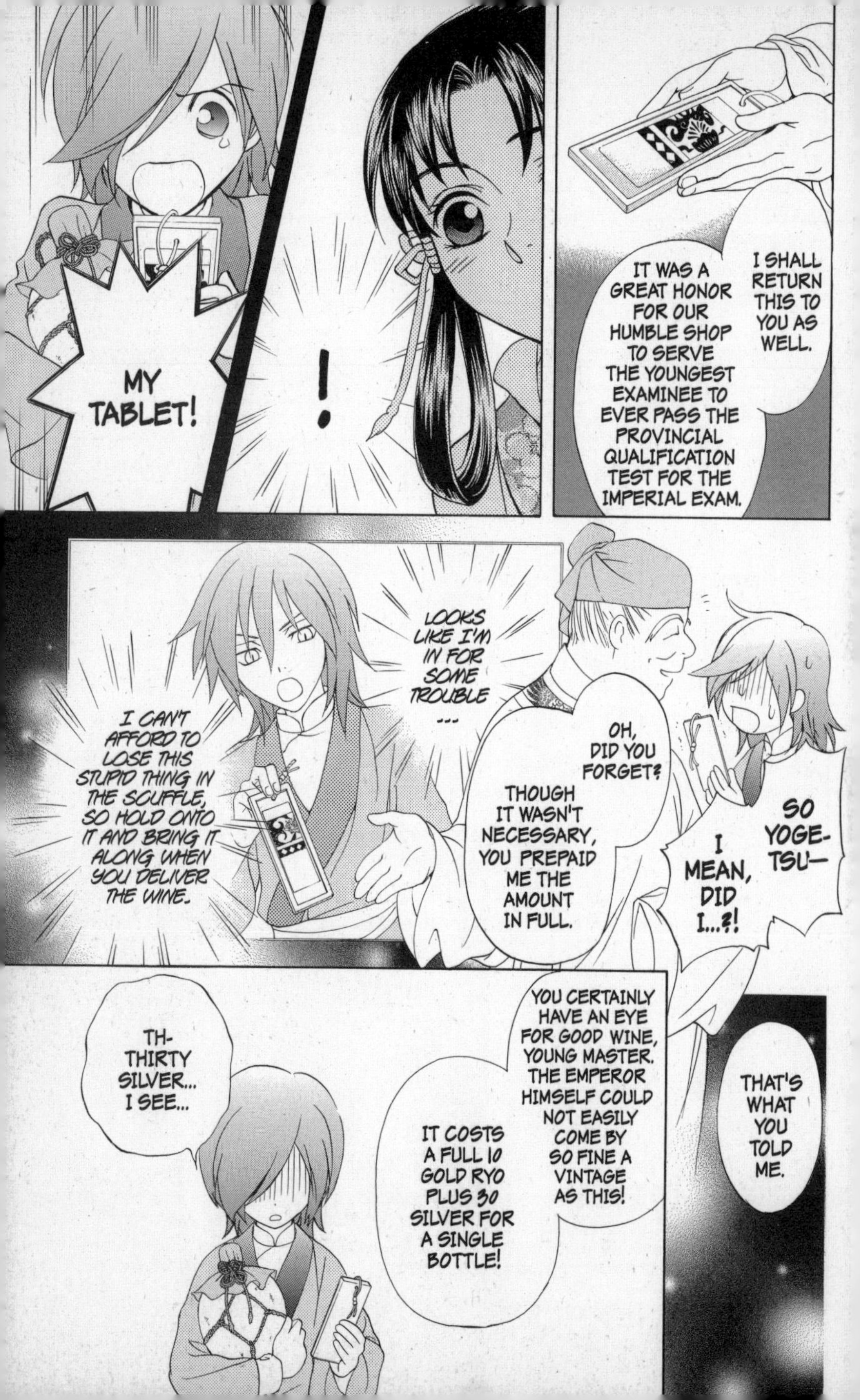
I SHALL RETURN THIS TO YOU AS WELL.
IT WAS A GREAT HONOR FOR OUR HUMBLE SHOP TO SERVE THE YOUNGEST EXAMINEE TO EVER PASS THE PROVINCIAL QUALIFICATION TEST FOR THE IMPERIAL EXAM.
!
MY TABLET!
SO YOGE-TSU—
I MEAN, DID I...?!
OH, DID YOU FORGET?
THOUGH IT WASN'T NECESSARY, YOU PREPAID ME THE AMOUNT IN FULL.
LOOKS LIKE I'M IN FOR SOME TROUBLE...
I CAN'T AFFORD TO LOSE THIS STUPID THING IN THE SCUFFLE, SO HOLD ONTO IT AND BRING IT ALONG WHEN YOU DELIVER THE WINE.
THAT'S WHAT YOU TOLD ME.
YOU CERTAINLY HAVE AN EYE FOR GOOD WINE, YOUNG MASTER. THE EMPEROR HIMSELF COULD NOT EASILY COME BY SO FINE A VINTAGE AS THIS!
IT COSTS A FULL 10 GOLD RYO PLUS 30 SILVER FOR A SINGLE BOTTLE!
TH-THIRTY SILVER... I SEE...

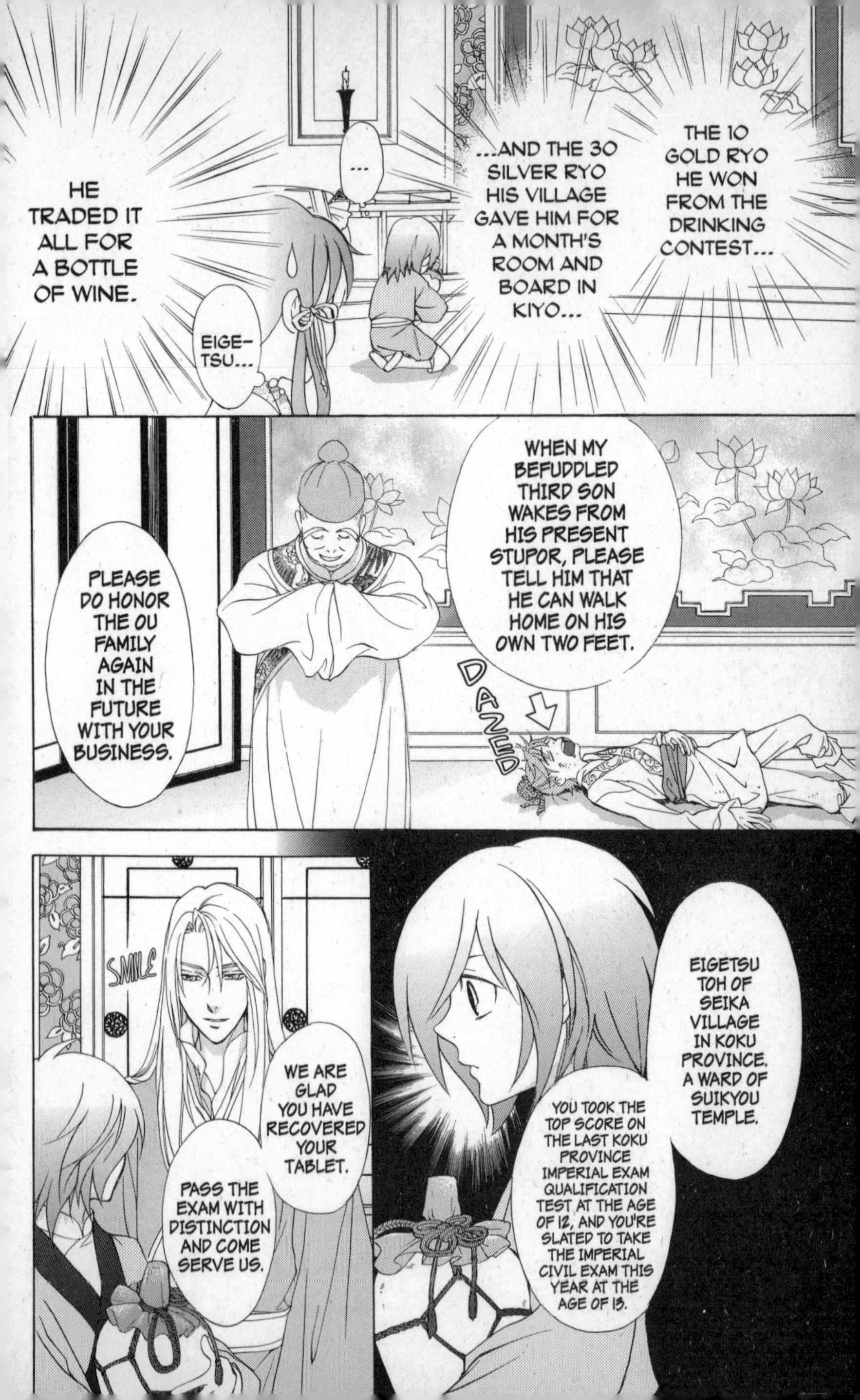
THE 10 GOLD RYO HE WON FROM THE DRINKING CONTEST...
...AND THE 30 SILVER RYO HIS VILLAGE GAVE HIM FOR A MONTH'S ROOM AND BOARD IN KIYO...
...
HE TRADED IT ALL FOR A BOTTLE OF WINE.
EIGE-TSU...
WHEN MY BEFUDDLED THIRD SON WAKES FROM HIS PRESENT STUPOR, PLEASE TELL HIM THAT HE CAN WALK HOME ON HIS OWN TWO FEET.
PLEASE DO HONOR THE OU FAMILY AGAIN IN THE FUTURE WITH YOUR BUSINESS.
DAZED
EIGETSU TOH OF SEIKA VILLAGE IN KOKU PROVINCE. A WARD OF SUIKYOU TEMPLE.
YOU TOOK THE TOP SCORE ON THE LAST KOKU PROVINCE IMPERIAL EXAM QUALIFICATION TEST AT THE AGE OF 12, AND YOU'RE SLATED TO TAKE THE IMPERIAL CIVIL EXAM THIS YEAR AT THE AGE OF 13.
SMILE
WE ARE GLAD YOU HAVE RECOVERED YOUR TABLET.
PASS THE EXAM WITH DISTINCTION AND COME SERVE US.

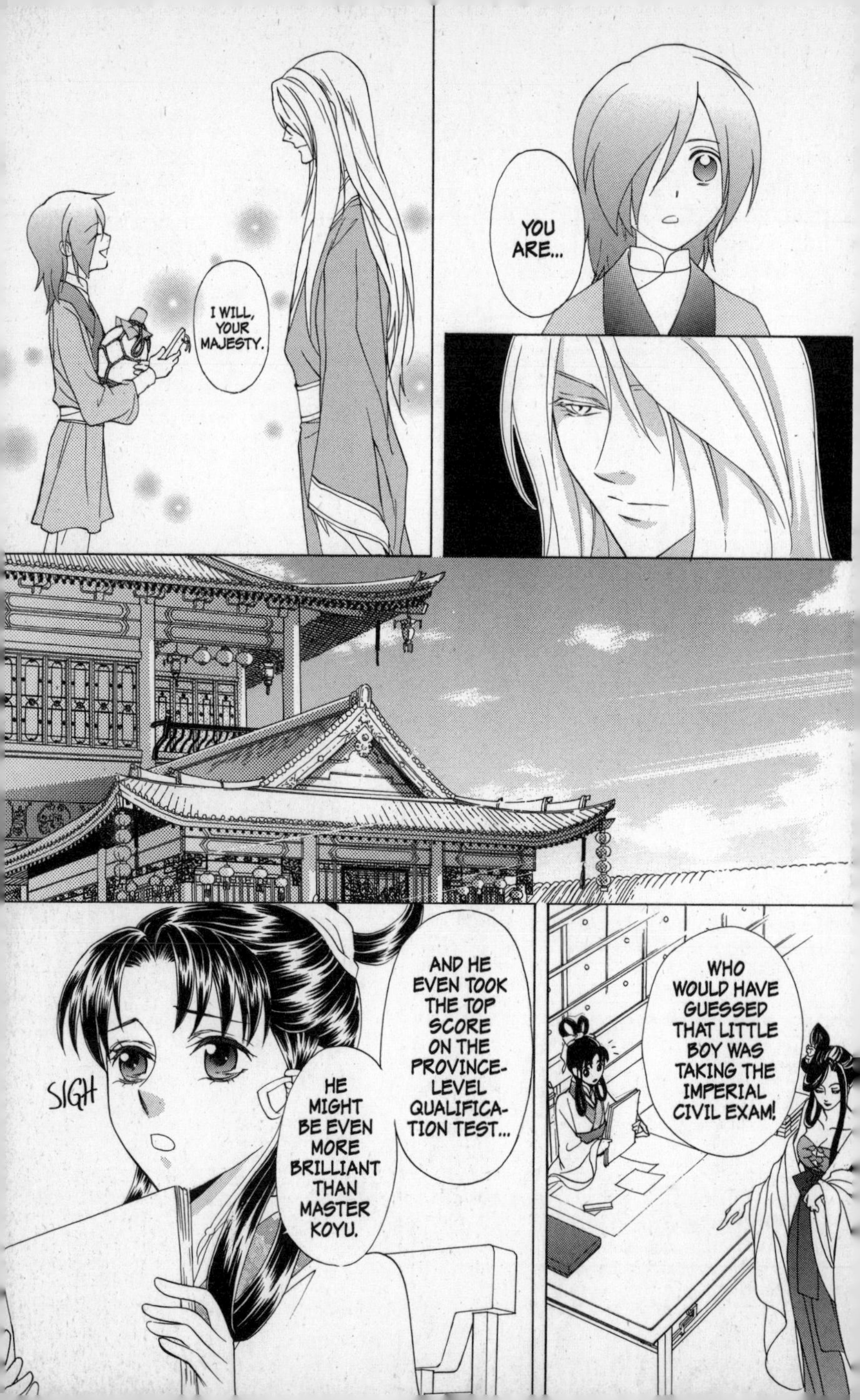
YOU ARE...
I WILL, YOUR MAJESTY.
WHO WOULD HAVE GUESSED THAT LITTLE BOY WAS TAKING THE IMPERIAL CIVIL EXAM!
AND HE EVEN TOOK THE TOP SCORE ON THE PROVINCE-LEVEL QUALIFICATION TEST...
HE MIGHT BE EVEN MORE BRILLIANT THAN MASTER KOYU.
SIGH

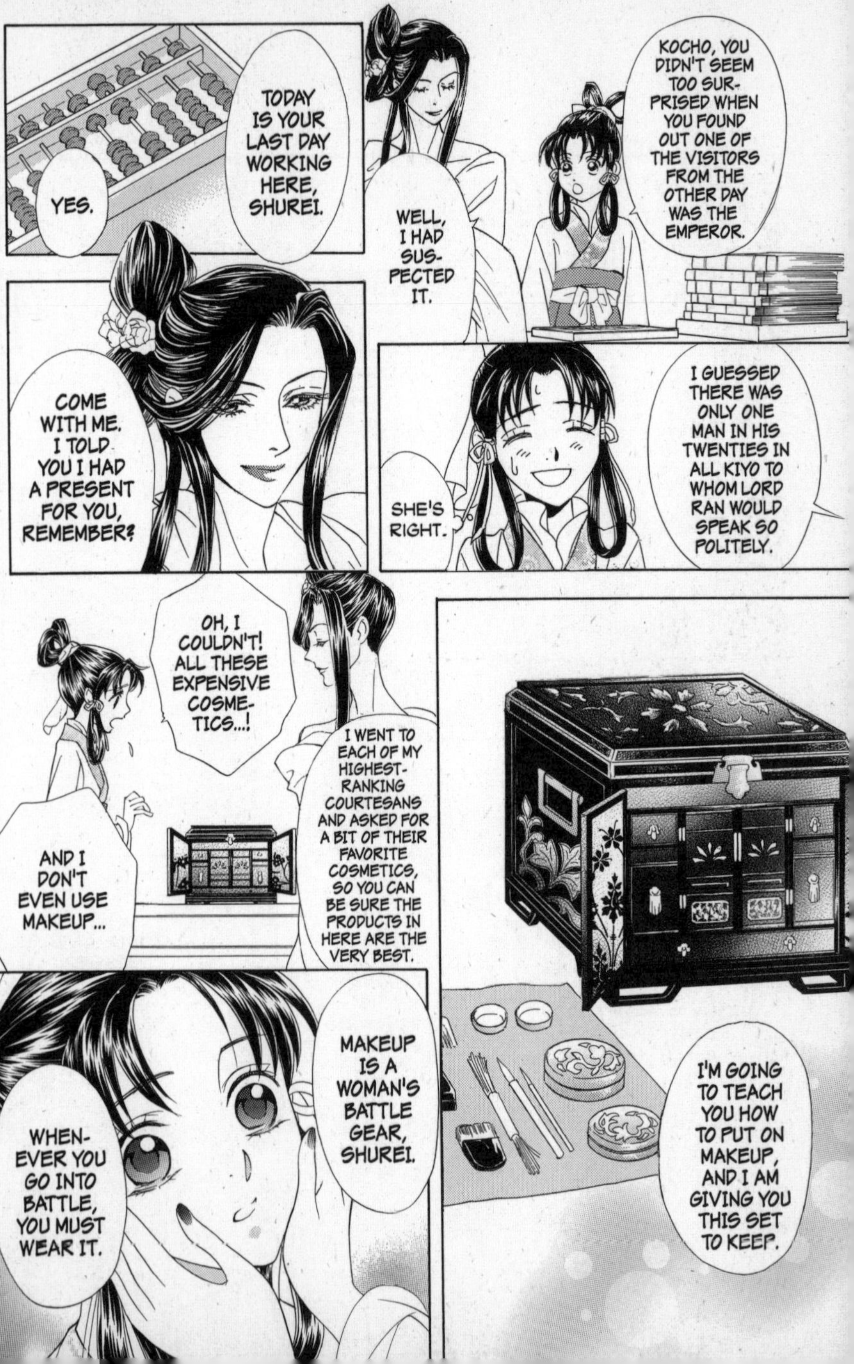
KOCHO, YOU DIDN'T SEEM TOO SUR-PRISED WHEN YOU FOUND OUT ONE OF THE VISITORS FROM THE OTHER DAY WAS THE EMPEROR.
WELL, I HAD SUS-PECTED IT.
TODAY IS YOUR LAST DAY WORKING HERE, SHUREI.
YES.
I GUESSED THERE WAS ONLY ONE MAN IN HIS TWENTIES IN ALL KIYO TO WHOM LORD RAN WOULD SPEAK SO POLITELY.
SHE'S RIGHT.
COME WITH ME. I TOLD YOU I HAD A PRESENT FOR YOU, REMEMBER?
I'M GOING TO TEACH YOU HOW TO PUT ON MAKEUP, AND I AM GIVING YOU THIS SET TO KEEP.
OH, I COULDN'T! ALL THESE EXPENSIVE COSME-TICS...!
I WENT TO EACH OF MY HIGHEST-RANKING COURTESANS AND ASKED FOR A BIT OF THEIR FAVORITE COSMETICS, SO YOU CAN BE SURE THE PRODUCTS IN HERE ARE THE VERY BEST.
AND I DON'T EVEN USE MAKEUP...
MAKEUP IS A WOMAN'S BATTLE GEAR, SHUREI.
WHEN-EVER YOU GO INTO BATTLE, YOU MUST WEAR IT.

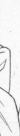

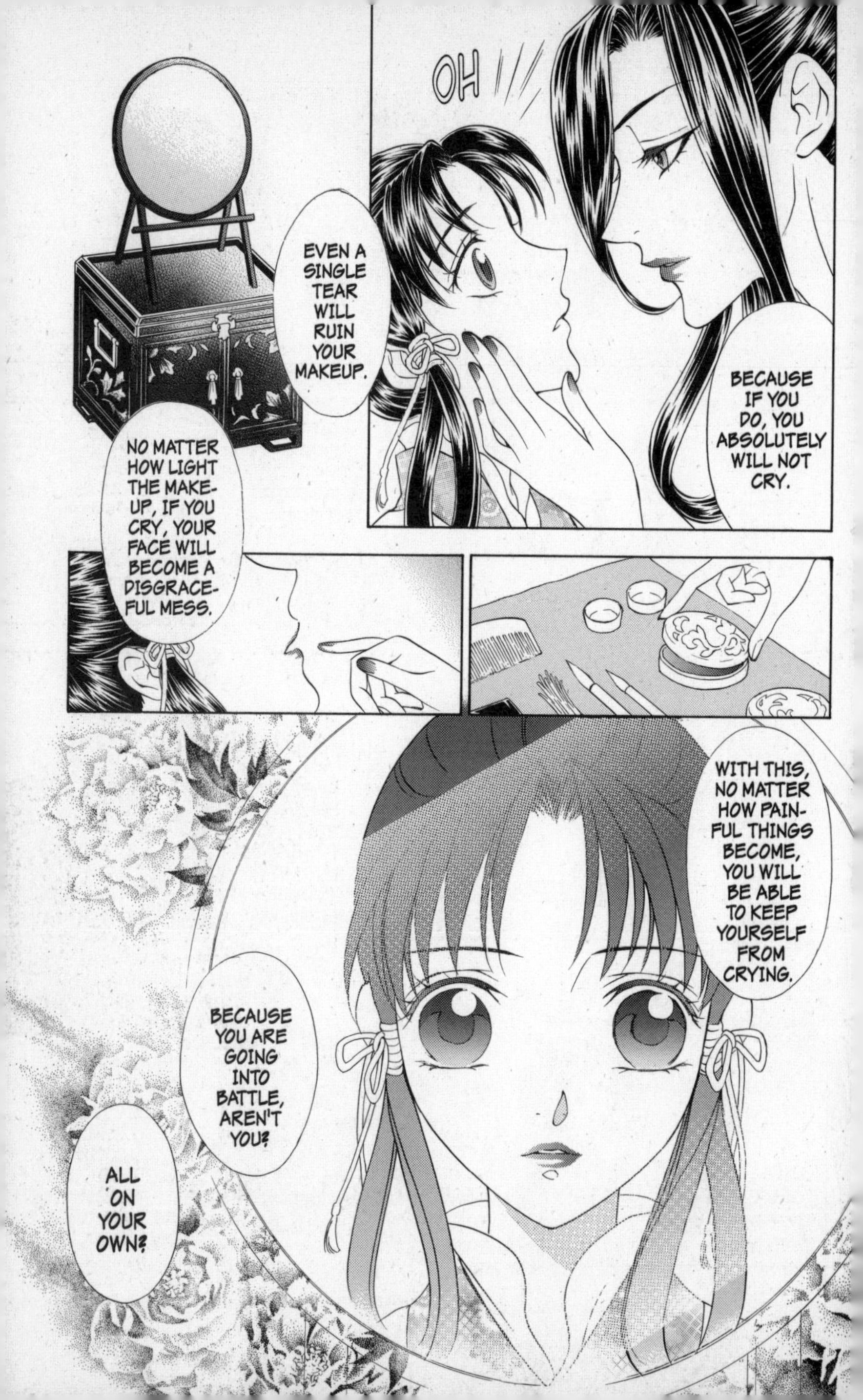
OH
EVEN A SINGLE TEAR WILL RUIN YOUR MAKEUP.
BECAUSE IF YOU DO, YOU ABSOLUTELY WILL NOT CRY.
NO MATTER HOW LIGHT THE MAKE-UP, IF YOU CRY, YOUR FACE WILL BECOME A DISGRACE-FUL MESS.
WITH THIS, NO MATTER HOW PAIN-FUL THINGS BECOME, YOU WILL BE ABLE TO KEEP YOURSELF FROM CRYING.
BECAUSE YOU ARE GOING INTO BATTLE, AREN'T YOU?
ALL ON YOUR OWN?

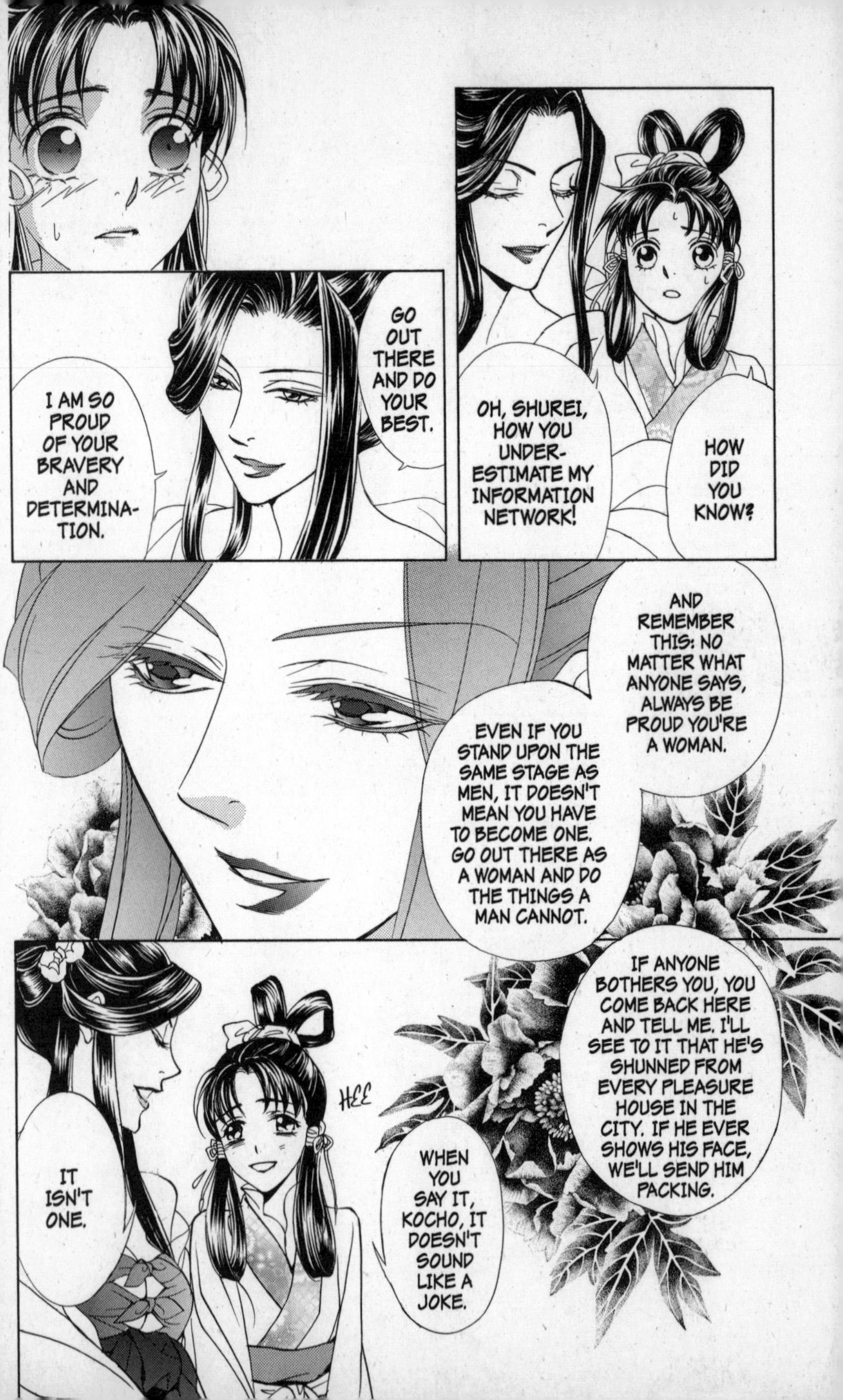
HOW DID YOU KNOW?
OH, SHUREI, HOW YOU UNDER-ESTIMATE MY INFORMATION NETWORK!
GO OUT THERE AND DO YOUR BEST.
I AM SO PROUD OF YOUR BRAVERY AND DETERMINA-TION.
AND REMEMBER THIS: NO MATTER WHAT ANYONE SAYS, ALWAYS BE PROUD YOU'RE A WOMAN.
EVEN IF YOU STAND UPON THE SAME STAGE AS MEN, IT DOESN'T MEAN YOU HAVE TO BECOME ONE. GO OUT THERE AS A WOMAN AND DO THE THINGS A MAN CANNOT.
IF ANYONE BOTHERS YOU, YOU COME BACK HERE AND TELL ME. I'LL SEE TO IT THAT HE'S SHUNNED FROM EVERY PLEASURE HOUSE IN THE CITY. IF HE EVER SHOWS HIS FACE, WE'LL SEND HIM PACKING.
HEE
WHEN YOU SAY IT, KOCHO, IT DOESN'T SOUND LIKE A JOKE.
IT ISN'T ONE.

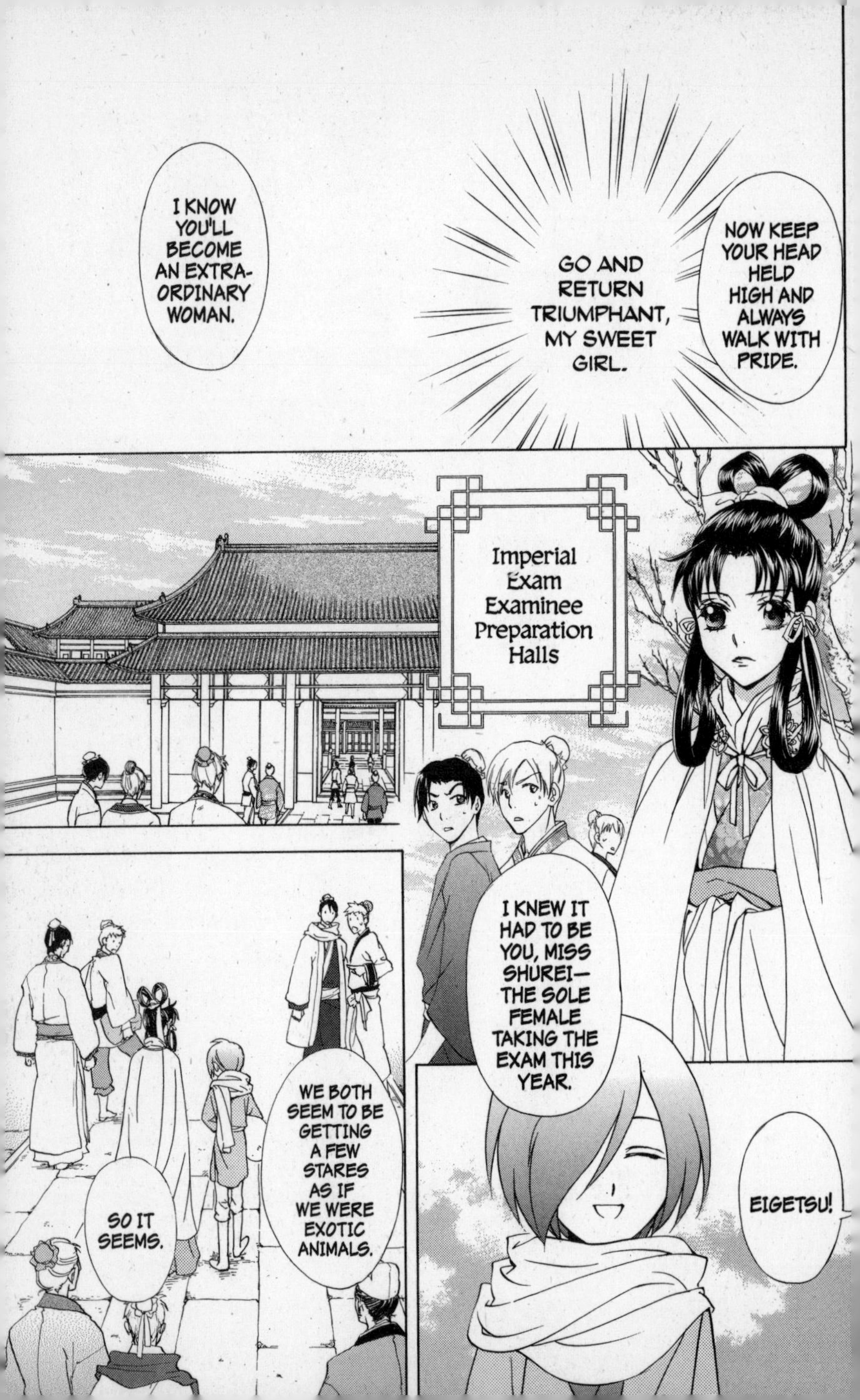
NOW KEEP YOUR HEAD HELD HIGH AND ALWAYS WALK WITH PRIDE.
GO AND RETURN TRIUMPHANT, MY SWEET GIRL.
I KNOW YOU'LL BECOME AN EXTRA-ORDINARY WOMAN.
Imperial Exam Examinee Preparation Halls
I KNEW IT HAD TO BE YOU, MISS SHUREI—THE SOLE FEMALE TAKING THE EXAM THIS YEAR.
EIGETSU!
WE BOTH SEEM TO BE GETTING A FEW STARES AS IF WE WERE EXOTIC ANIMALS.
SO IT SEEMS.

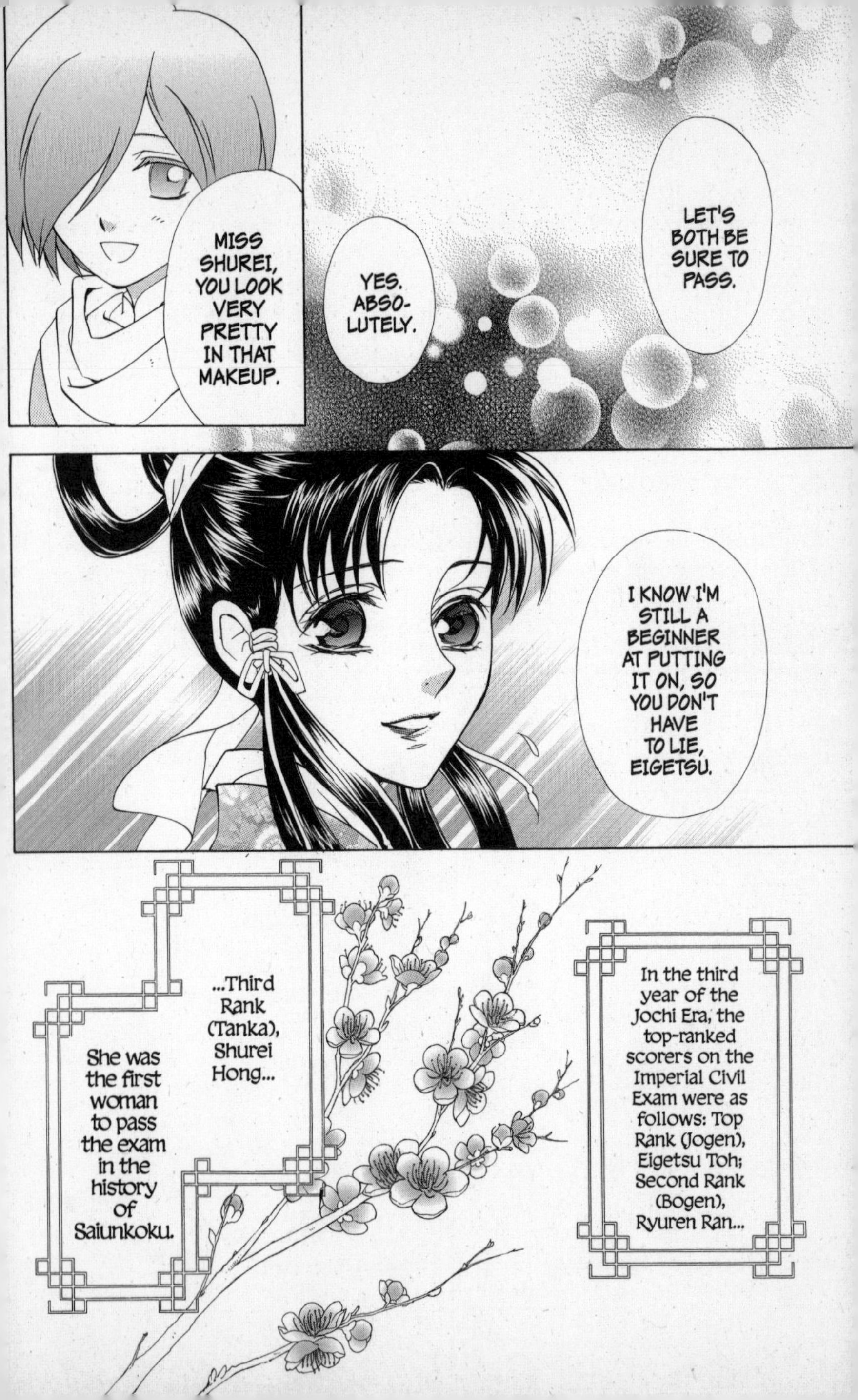
LET'S BOTH BE SURE TO PASS.
YES. ABSOLUTELY.
MISS SHUREI, YOU LOOK VERY PRETTY IN THAT MAKEUP.
I KNOW I'M STILL A BEGINNER AT PUTTING IT ON, SO YOU DON'T HAVE TO LIE, EIGETSU.
In the third year of the Jochi Era, the top-ranked scorers on the Imperial Civil Exam were as follows: Top Rank (Jogen), Eigetsu Toh; Second Rank (Bogen), Ryuren Ran...
...Third Rank (Tanka), Shurei Hong...
She was the first woman to pass the exam in the history of Saiunkoku.

The Story of
SAIUNKOKU

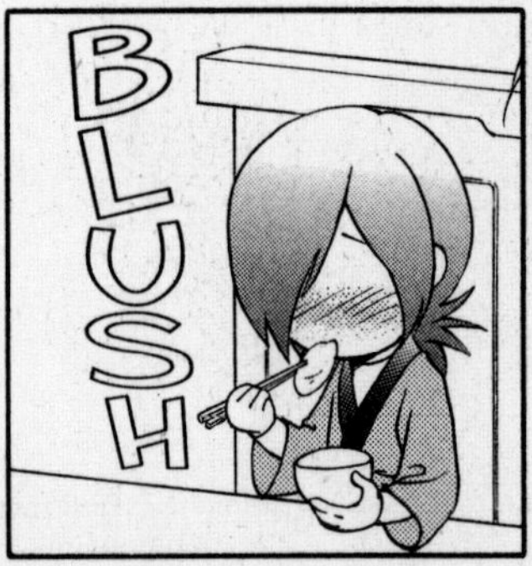
BLUSH

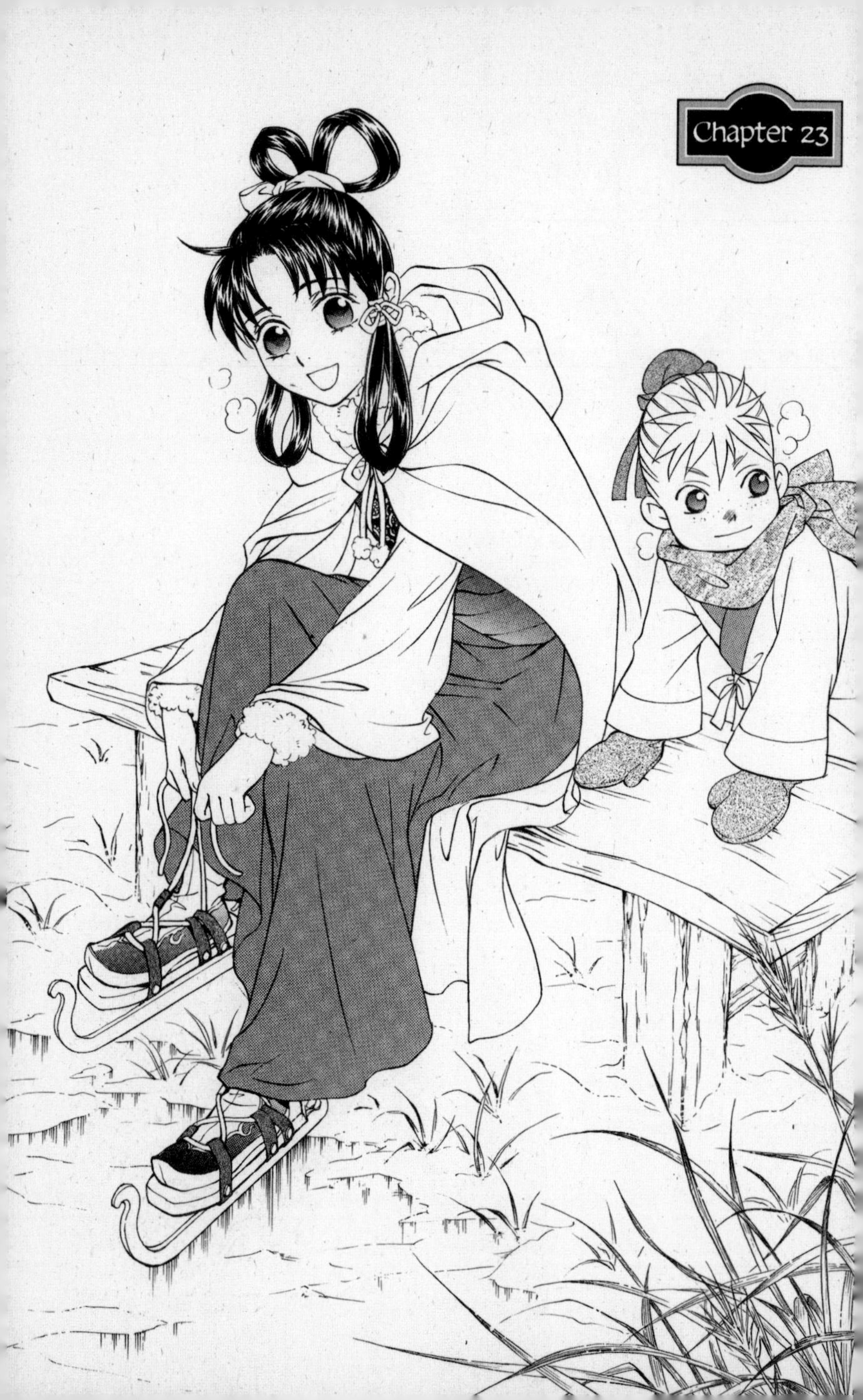
Chapter 23

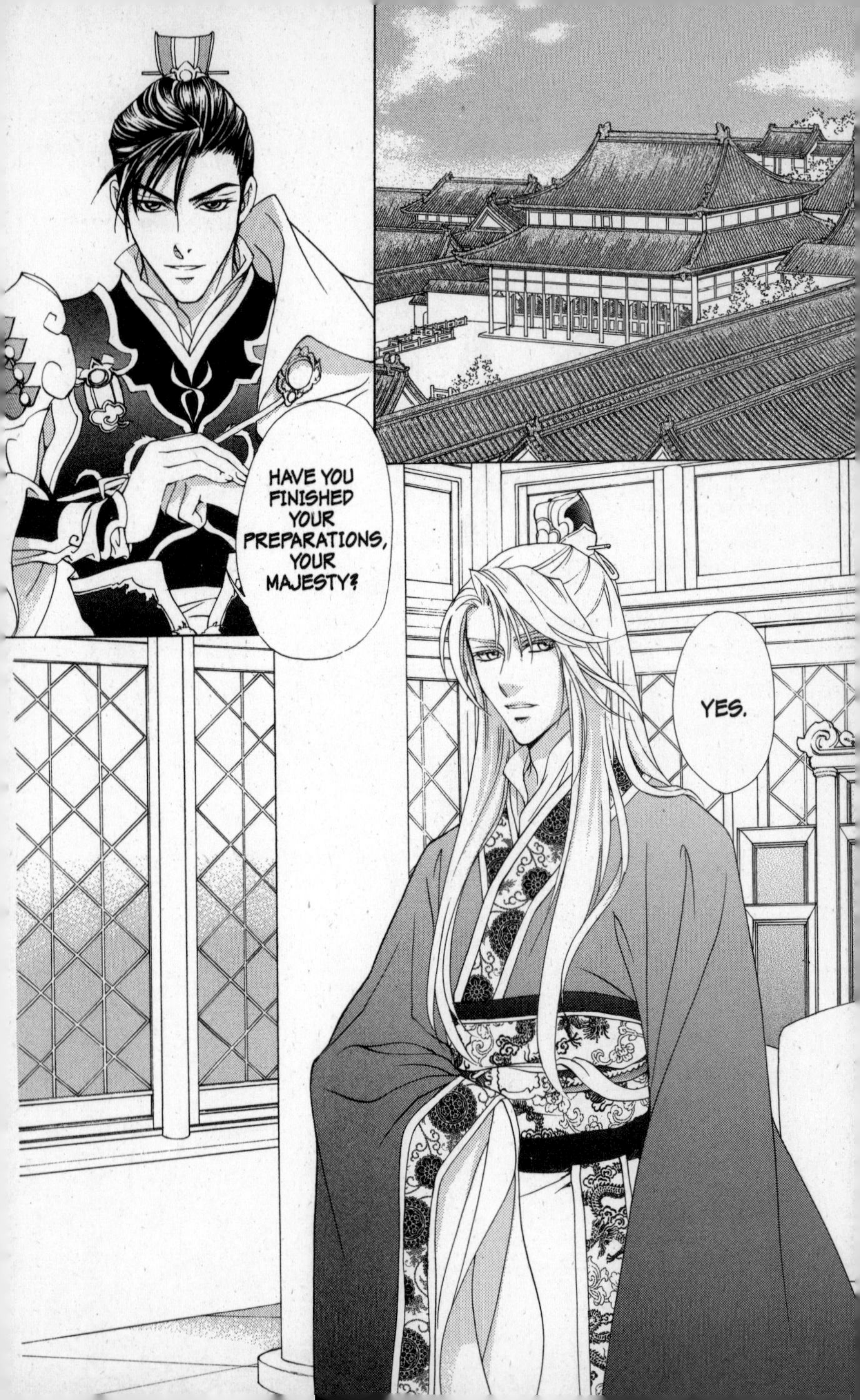
HAVE YOU FINISHED YOUR PREPARATIONS, YOUR MAJESTY?
YES.

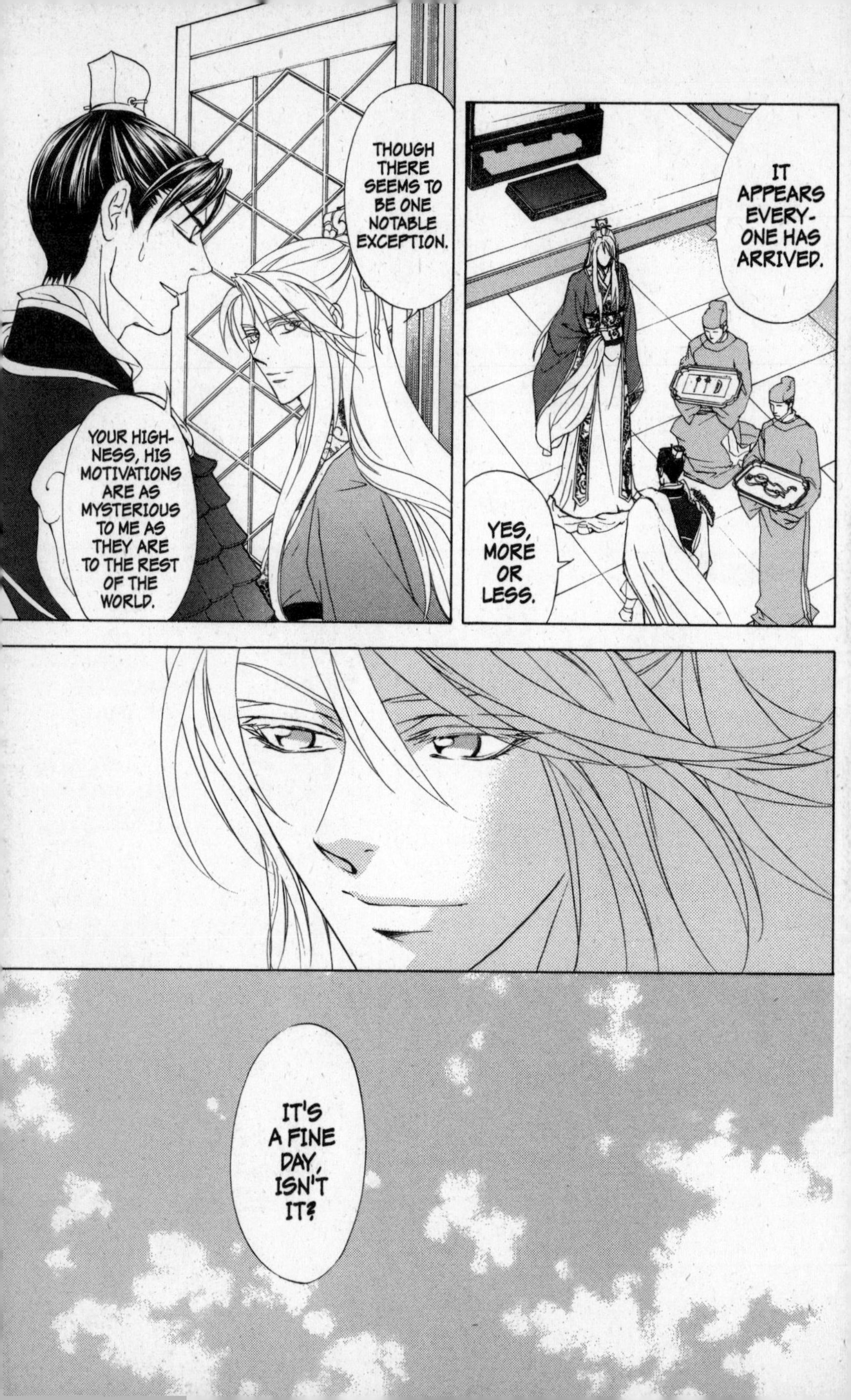
IT APPEARS EVERY-ONE HAS ARRIVED.
YES, MORE OR LESS.
THOUGH THERE SEEMS TO BE ONE NOTABLE EXCEPTION.
YOUR HIGH-NESS, HIS MOTIVATIONS ARE AS MYSTERIOUS TO ME AS THEY ARE TO THE REST OF THE WORLD.
IT'S A FINE DAY, ISN'T IT?

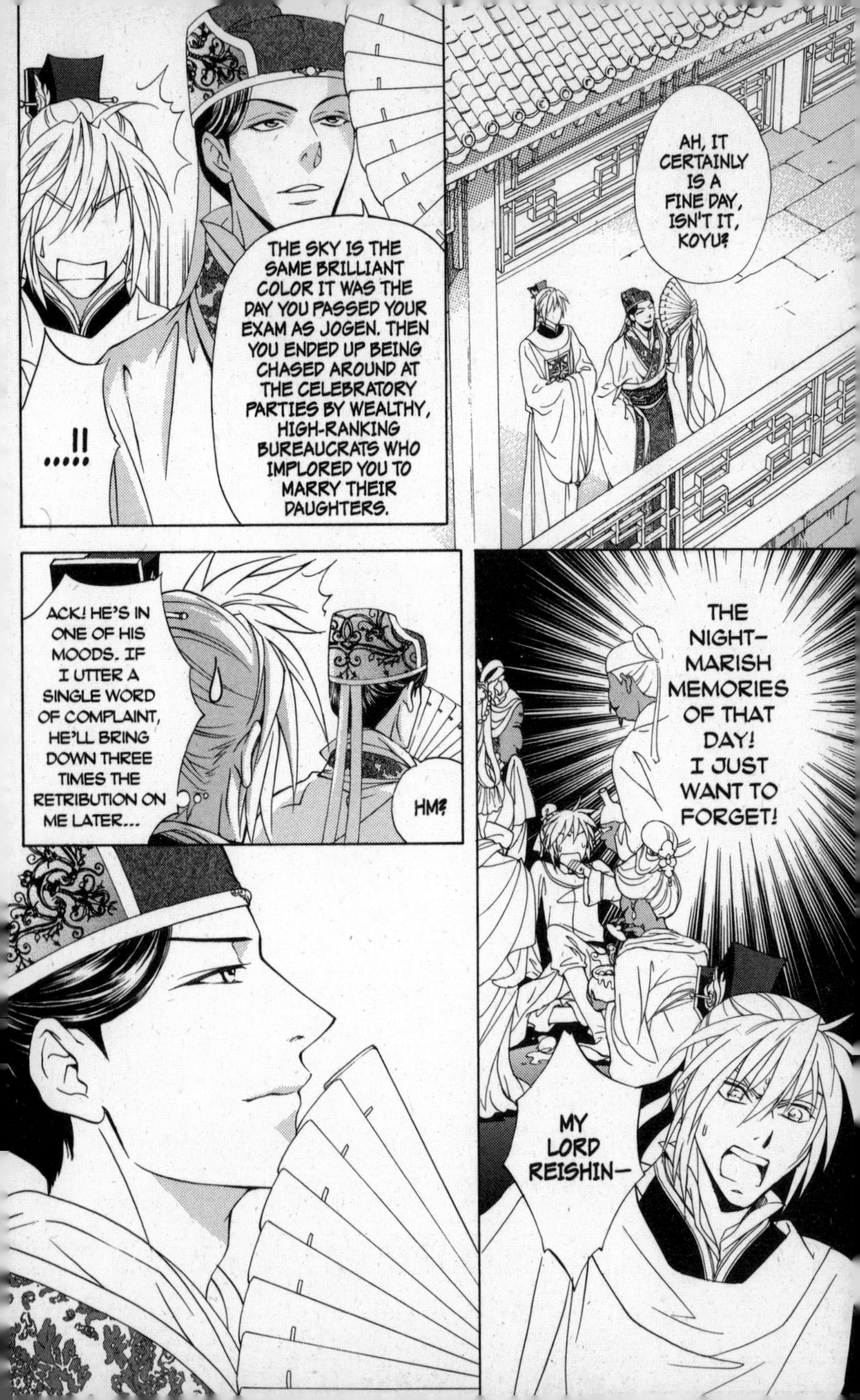
AH, IT CERTAINLY IS A FINE DAY, ISN'T IT, KOYU?
THE SKY IS THE SAME BRILLIANT COLOR IT WAS THE DAY YOU PASSED YOUR EXAM AS JOGEN. THEN YOU ENDED UP BEING CHASED AROUND AT THE CELEBRATORY PARTIES BY WEALTHY, HIGH-RANKING BUREAUCRATS WHO IMPLORED YOU TO MARRY THEIR DAUGHTERS.
......!!
THE NIGHT-MARISH MEMORIES OF THAT DAY! I JUST WANT TO FORGET!
MY LORD REISHIN—
ACK! HE'S IN ONE OF HIS MOODS. IF I UTTER A SINGLE WORD OF COMPLAINT, HE'LL BRING DOWN THREE TIMES THE RETRIBUTION ON ME LATER...
HM?

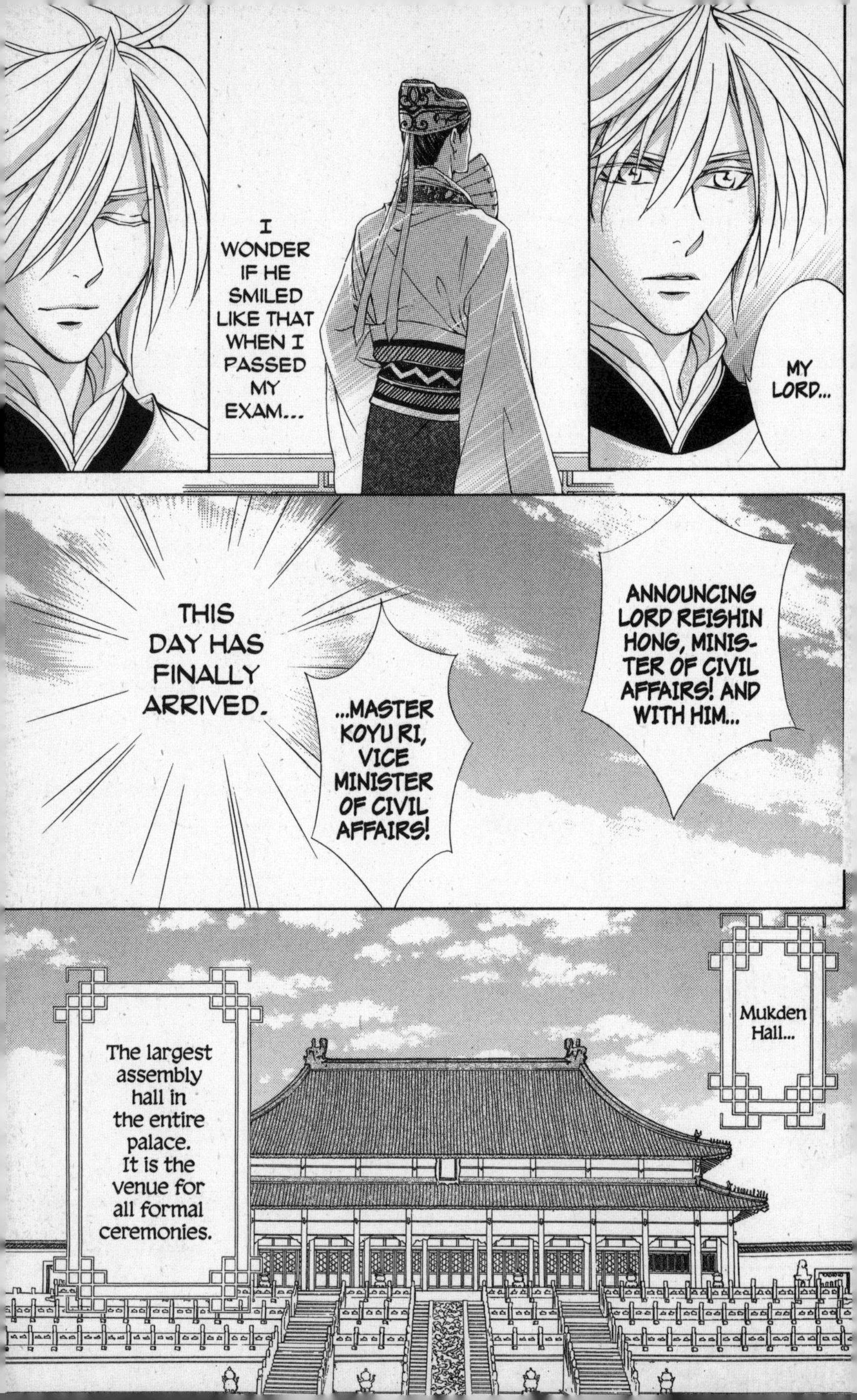
MY LORD...
I WONDER IF HE SMILED LIKE THAT WHEN I PASSED MY EXAM...
ANNOUNCING LORD REISHIN HONG, MINISTER OF CIVIL AFFAIRS! AND WITH HIM...
...MASTER KOYU RI, VICE MINISTER OF CIVIL AFFAIRS!
THIS DAY HAS FINALLY ARRIVED.
Mukden Hall...
The largest assembly hall in the entire palace. It is the venue for all formal ceremonies.

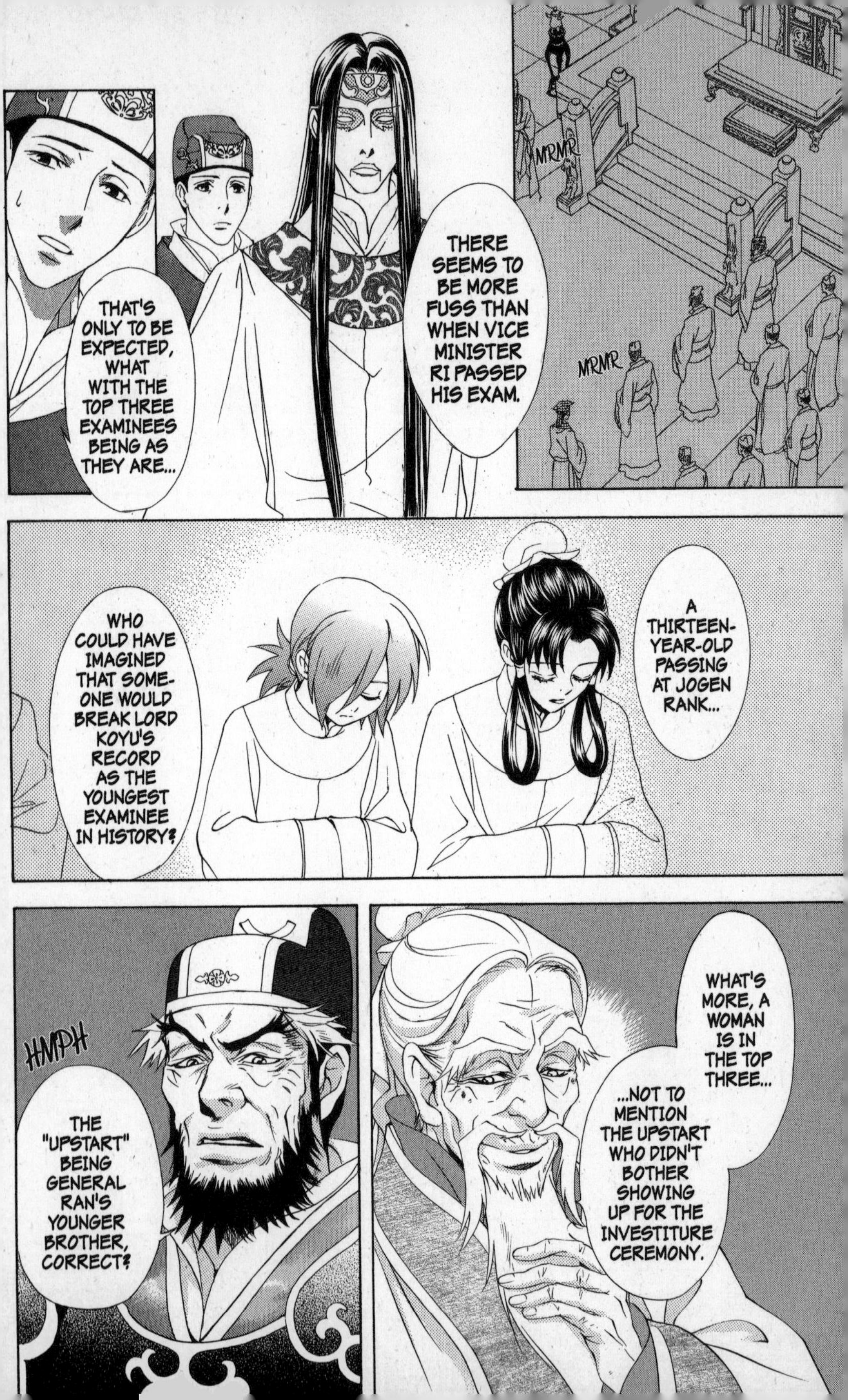
MRMR
MRMR
THERE SEEMS TO BE MORE FUSS THAN WHEN VICE MINISTER RI PASSED HIS EXAM.
THAT'S ONLY TO BE EXPECTED, WHAT WITH THE TOP THREE EXAMINEES BEING AS THEY ARE...
A THIRTEEN-YEAR-OLD PASSING AT JOGEN RANK...
WHO COULD HAVE IMAGINED THAT SOME-ONE WOULD BREAK LORD KOYU'S RECORD AS THE YOUNGEST EXAMINEE IN HISTORY?
WHAT'S MORE, A WOMAN IS IN THE TOP THREE...
...NOT TO MENTION THE UPSTART WHO DIDN'T BOTHER SHOWING UP FOR THE INVESTITURE CEREMONY.
HMPH
THE "UPSTART" BEING GENERAL RAN'S YOUNGER BROTHER, CORRECT?

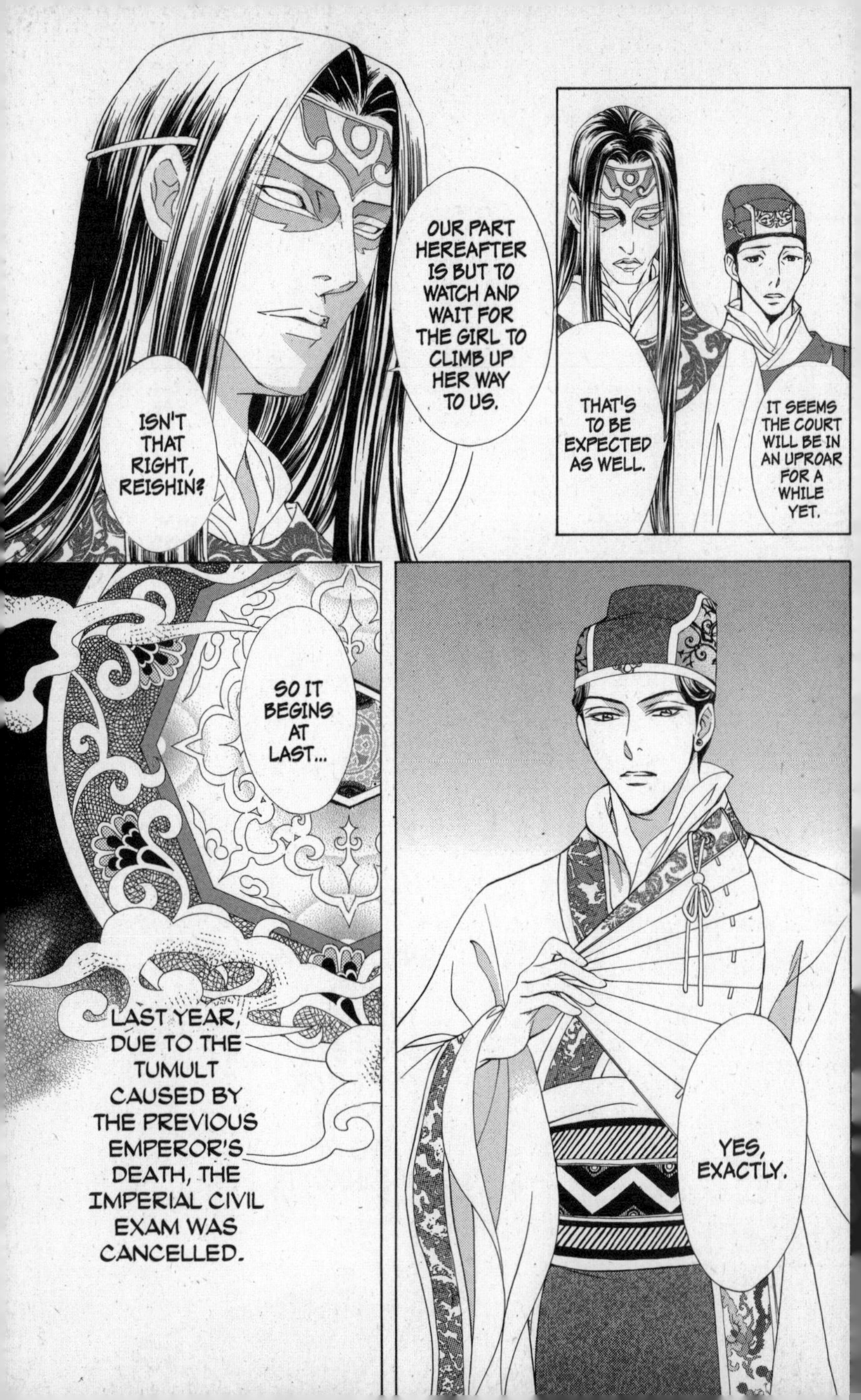
IT SEEMS THE COURT WILL BE IN AN UPROAR FOR A WHILE YET.
THAT'S TO BE EXPECTED AS WELL.
OUR PART HEREAFTER IS BUT TO WATCH AND WAIT FOR THE GIRL TO CLIMB UP HER WAY TO US.
ISN'T THAT RIGHT, REISHIN?
YES, EXACTLY.
SO IT BEGINS AT LAST...
LAST YEAR, DUE TO THE TUMULT CAUSED BY THE PREVIOUS EMPEROR'S DEATH, THE IMPERIAL CIVIL EXAM WAS CANCELLED.

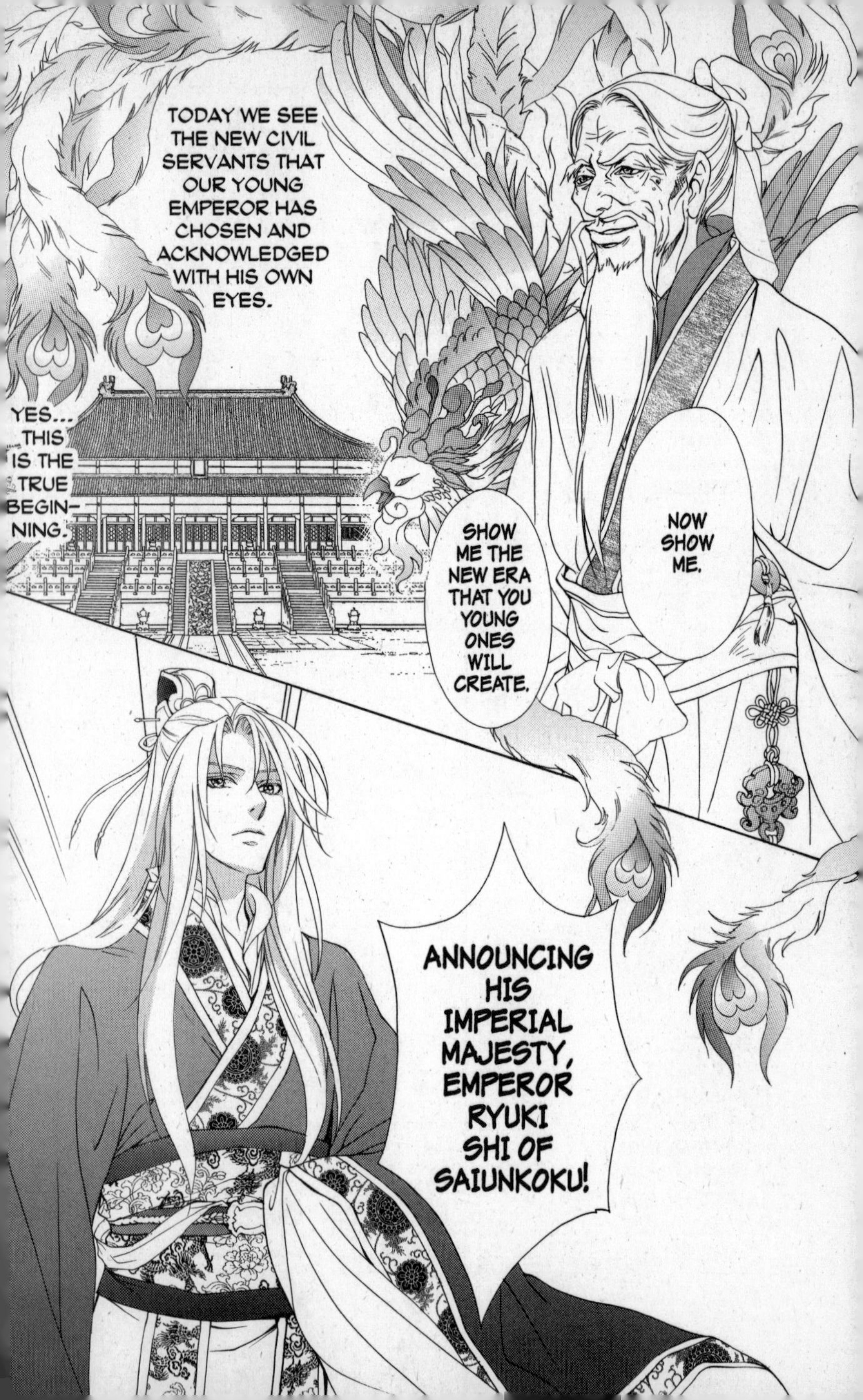
TODAY WE SEE THE NEW CIVIL SERVANTS THAT OUR YOUNG EMPEROR HAS CHOSEN AND ACKNOWLEDGED WITH HIS OWN EYES.
YES... THIS IS THE TRUE BEGINNING.
NOW SHOW ME.
SHOW ME THE NEW ERA THAT YOU YOUNG ONES WILL CREATE.
ANNOUNCING HIS IMPERIAL MAJESTY, EMPEROR RYUKI SHI OF SAIUNKOKU!

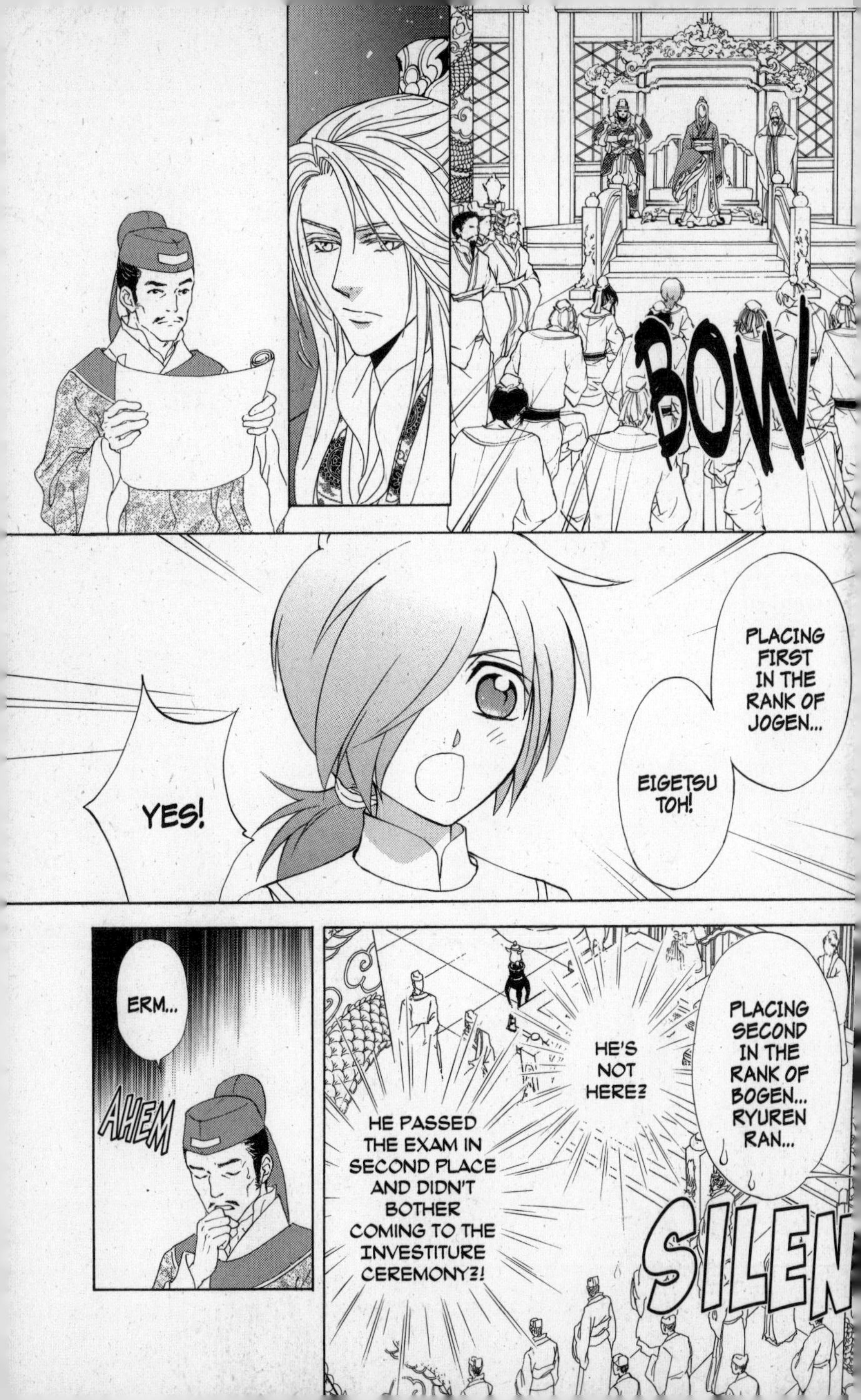
BOW
PLACING FIRST IN THE RANK OF JOGEN...
EIGETSU TOH!
YES!
PLACING SECOND IN THE RANK OF BOGEN... RYUREN RAN...
SILEN
HE'S NOT HERE?
HE PASSED THE EXAM IN SECOND PLACE AND DIDN'T BOTHER COMING TO THE INVESTITURE CEREMONY?!
ERM...
AHEM

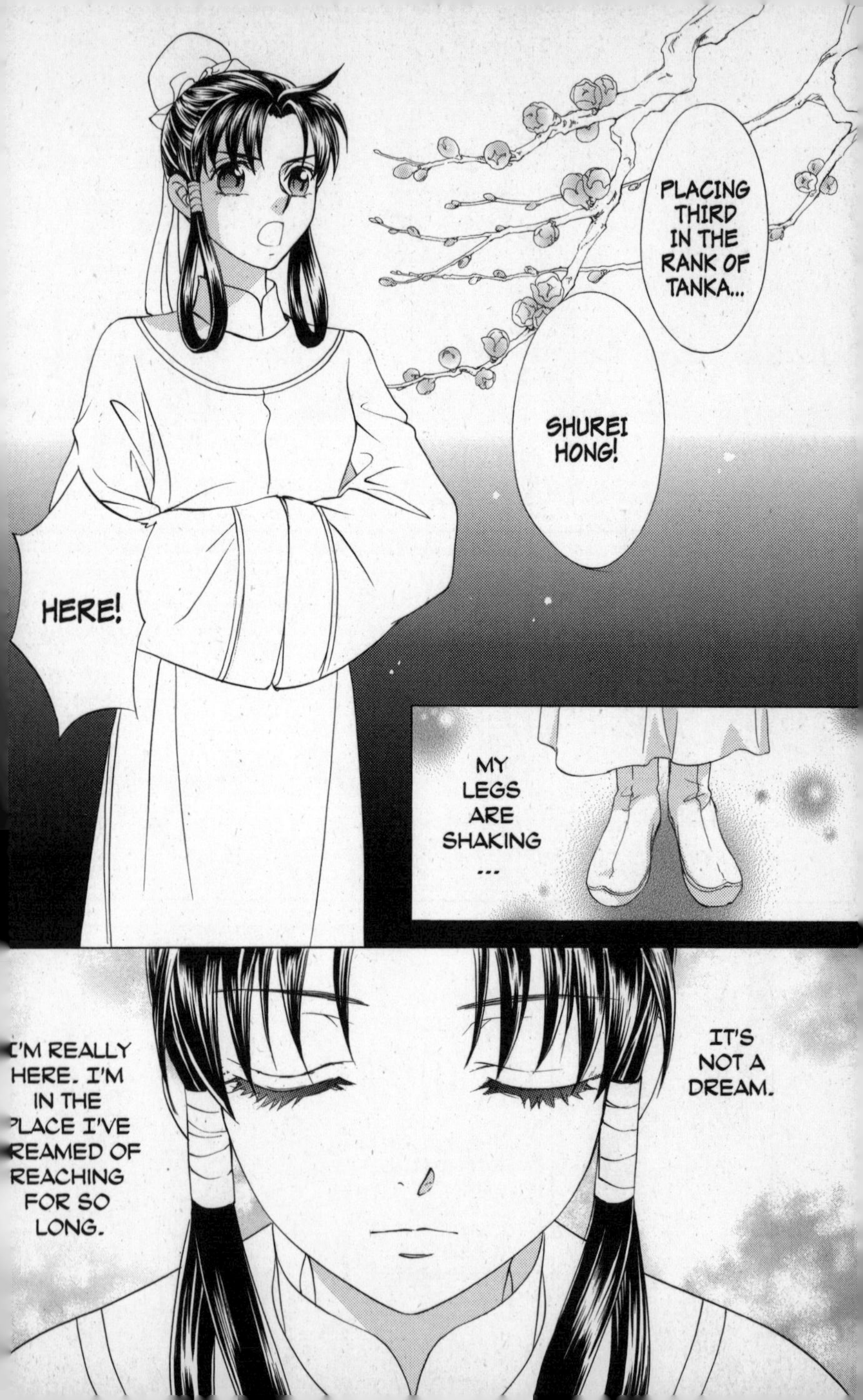
PLACING THIRD IN THE RANK OF TANKA...
SHUREI HONG!
HERE!
MY LEGS ARE SHAKING ...
IT'S NOT A DREAM.
I'M REALLY HERE. I'M IN THE PLACE I'VE REAMED OF REACHING FOR SO LONG.

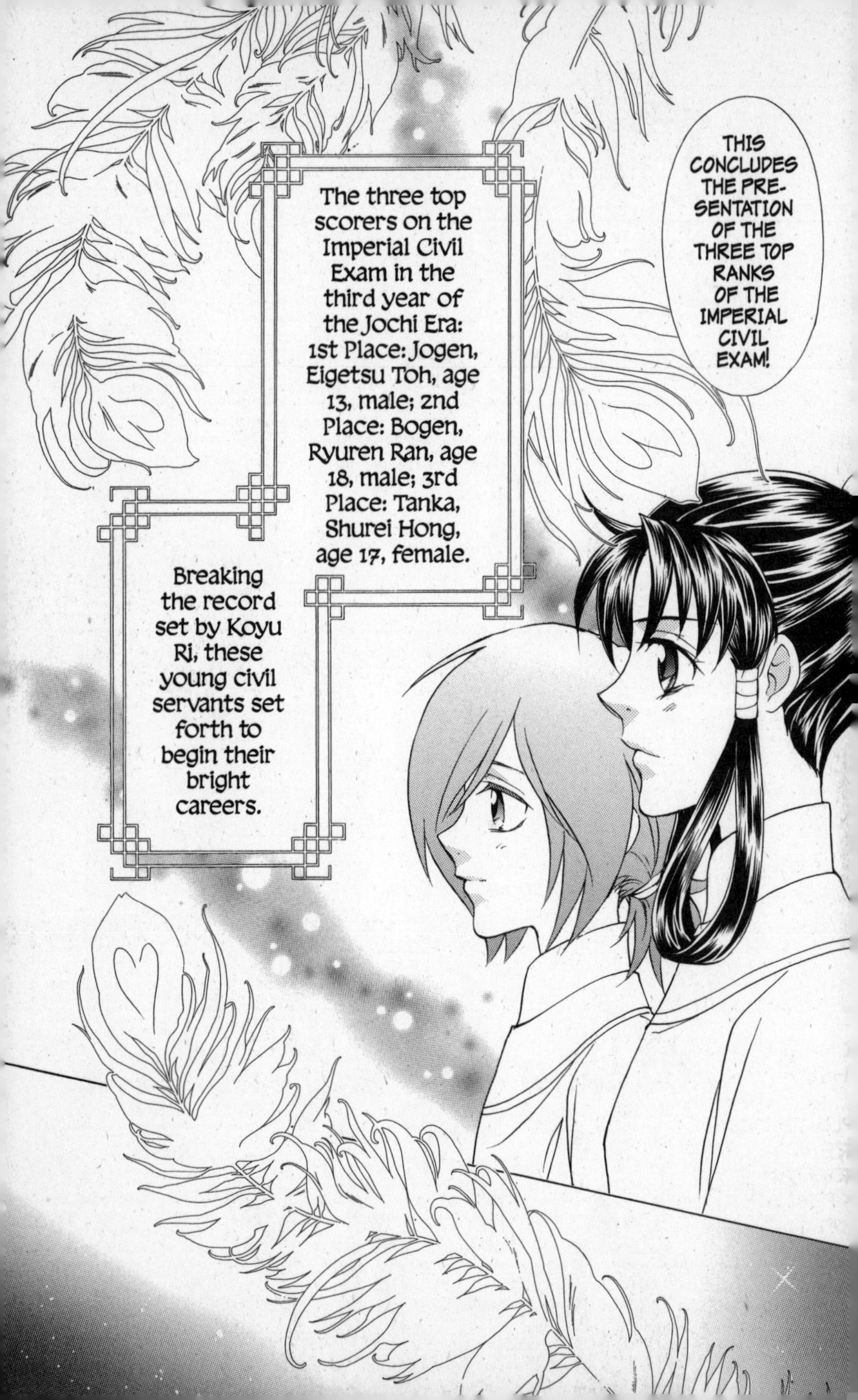
THIS CONCLUDES THE PRE-SENTATION OF THE THREE TOP RANKS OF THE IMPERIAL CIVIL EXAM!
The three top scorers on the Imperial Civil Exam in the third year of the Jochi Era: 1st Place: Jogen, Eigetsu Toh, age 13, male; 2nd Place: Bogen, Ryuren Ran, age 18, male; 3rd Place: Tanka, Shurei Hong, age 17, female.
Breaking the record set by Koyu Ri, these young civil servants set forth to begin their bright careers.

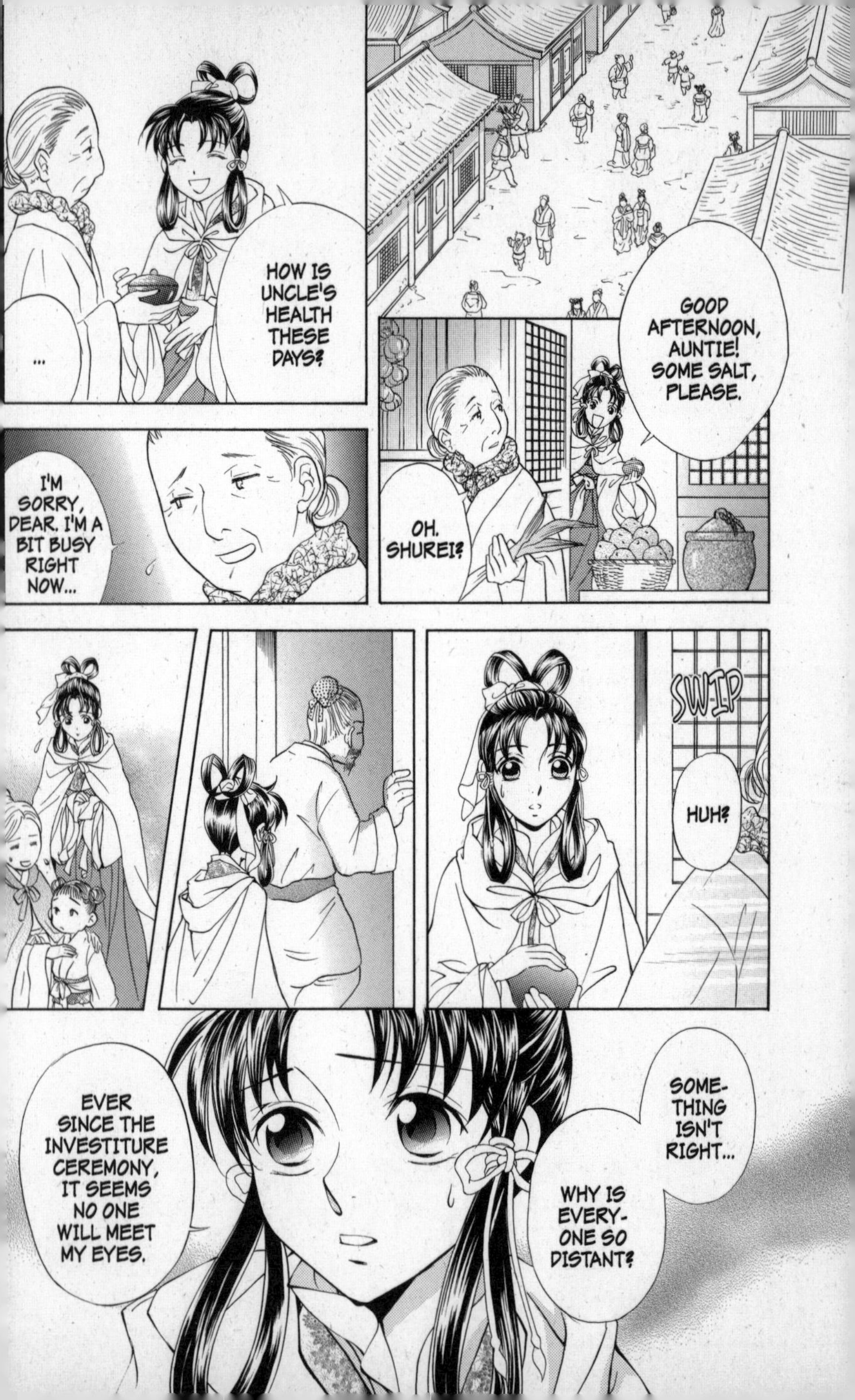
HOW IS UNCLE'S HEALTH THESE DAYS?
...
GOOD AFTERNOON, AUNTIE! SOME SALT, PLEASE.
OH. SHUREI?
I'M SORRY, DEAR. I'M A BIT BUSY RIGHT NOW...
SWIP
HUH?
SOME-THING ISN'T RIGHT...
WHY IS EVERY-ONE SO DISTANT?
EVER SINCE THE INVESTITURE CEREMONY, IT SEEMS NO ONE WILL MEET MY EYES.

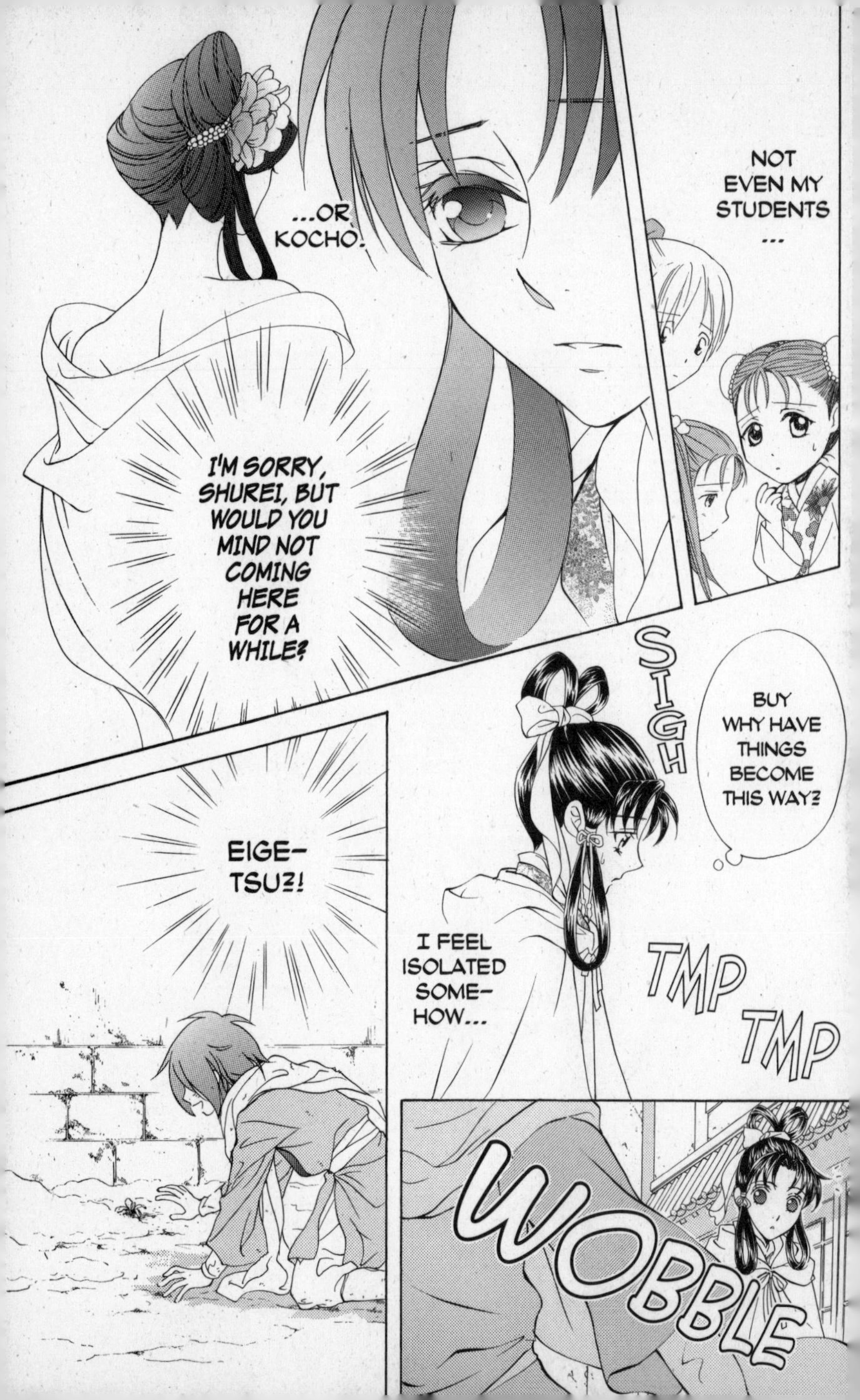
NOT EVEN MY STUDENTS ...
...OR KOCHO.
I'M SORRY, SHUREI, BUT WOULD YOU MIND NOT COMING HERE FOR A WHILE?
SIGH
BUY WHY HAVE THINGS BECOME THIS WAY?
I FEEL ISOLATED SOME-HOW...
TMP TMP
EIGE-TSU?!
WOBBLE

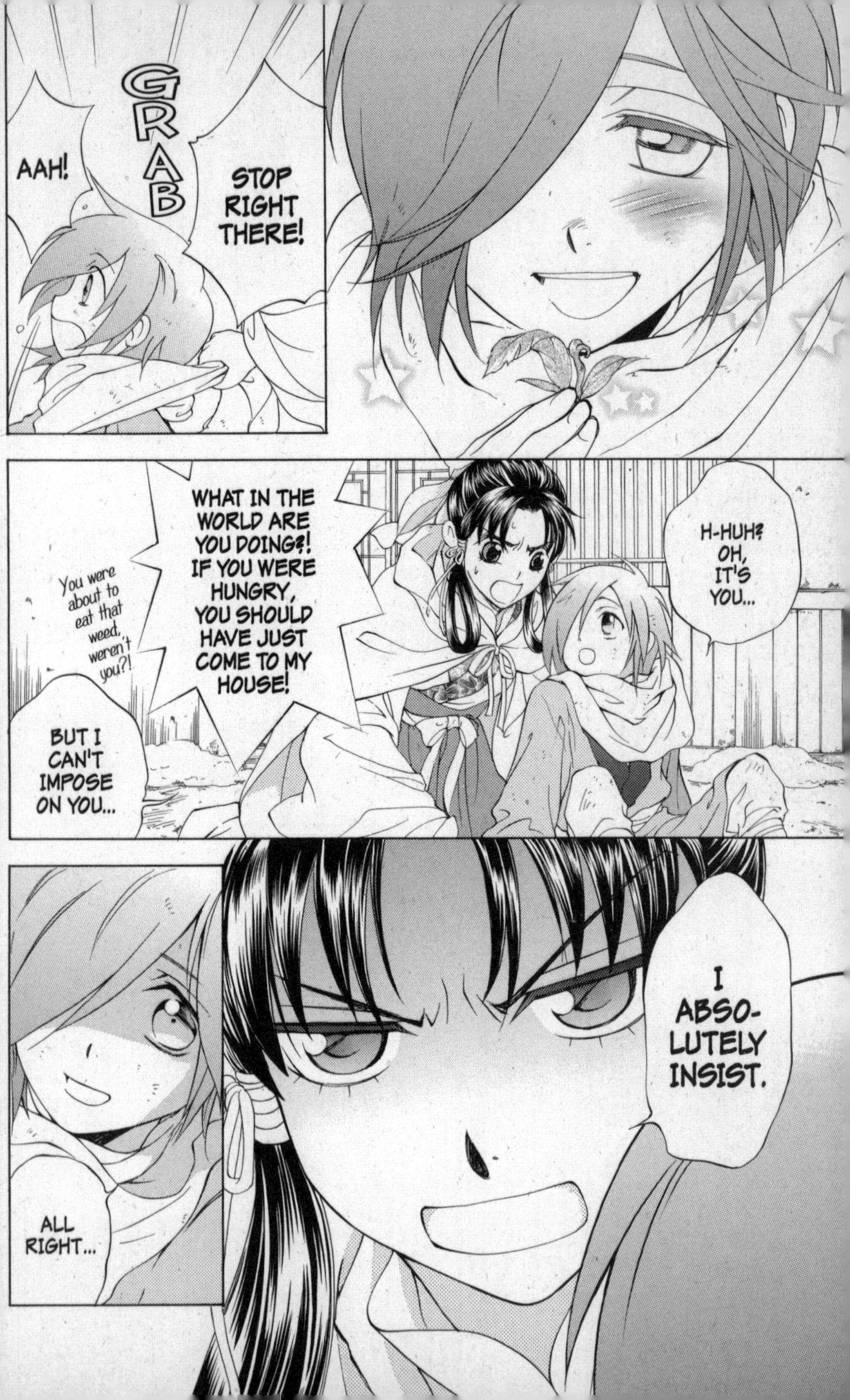
GRAB
STOP RIGHT THERE!
AAH!
H-HUH? OH, IT'S YOU...
WHAT IN THE WORLD ARE YOU DOING?! IF YOU WERE HUNGRY, YOU SHOULD HAVE JUST COME TO MY HOUSE!
You were about to eat that weed, weren't you?!
BUT I CAN'T IMPOSE ON YOU...
I ABSO-LUTELY INSIST.
ALL RIGHT...

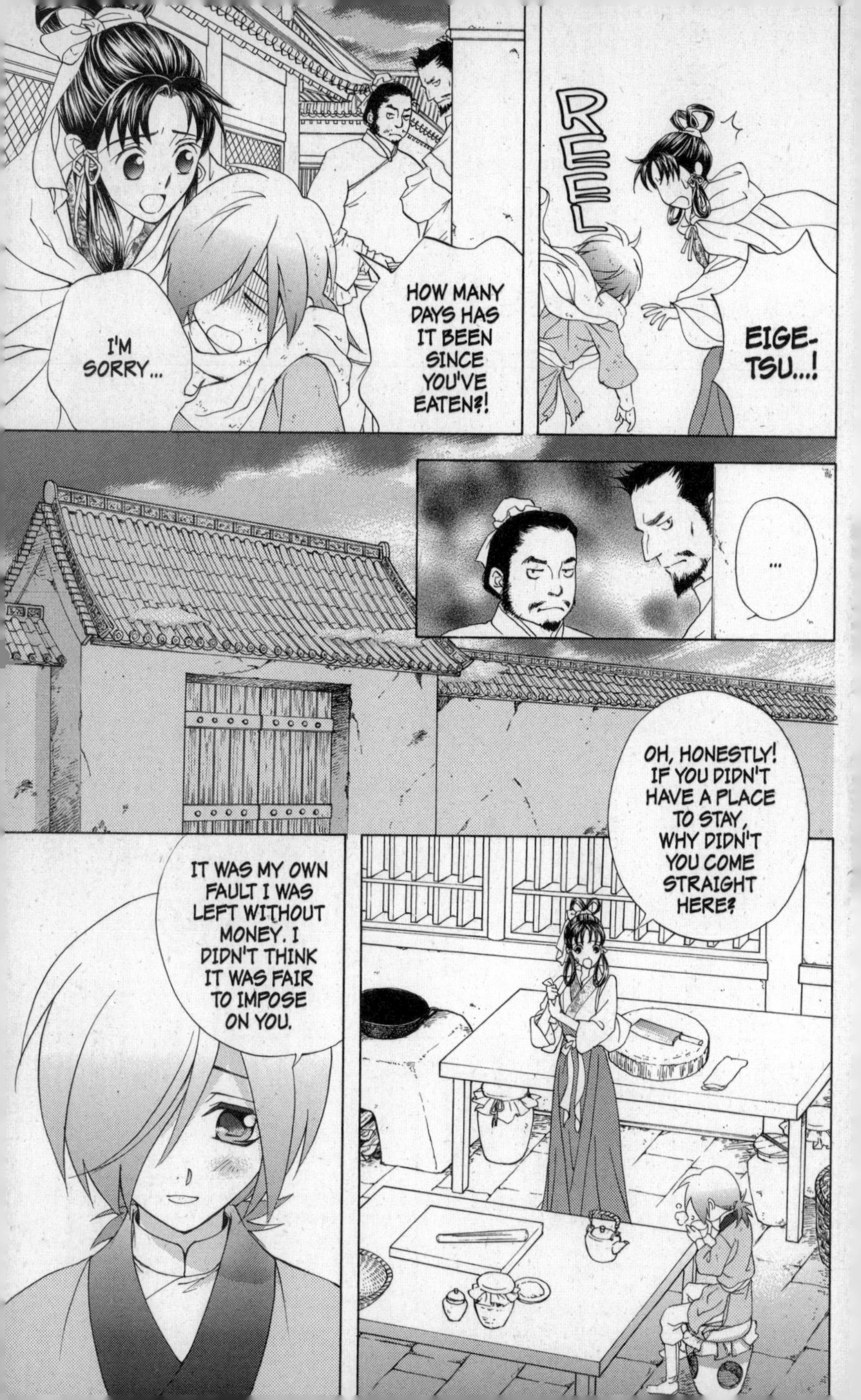
REEL
EIGE-TSU...!
HOW MANY DAYS HAS IT BEEN SINCE YOU'VE EATEN?!
I'M SORRY...
...
OH, HONESTLY! IF YOU DIDN'T HAVE A PLACE TO STAY, WHY DIDN'T YOU COME STRAIGHT HERE?
IT WAS MY OWN FAULT I WAS LEFT WITHOUT MONEY. I DIDN'T THINK IT WAS FAIR TO IMPOSE ON YOU.

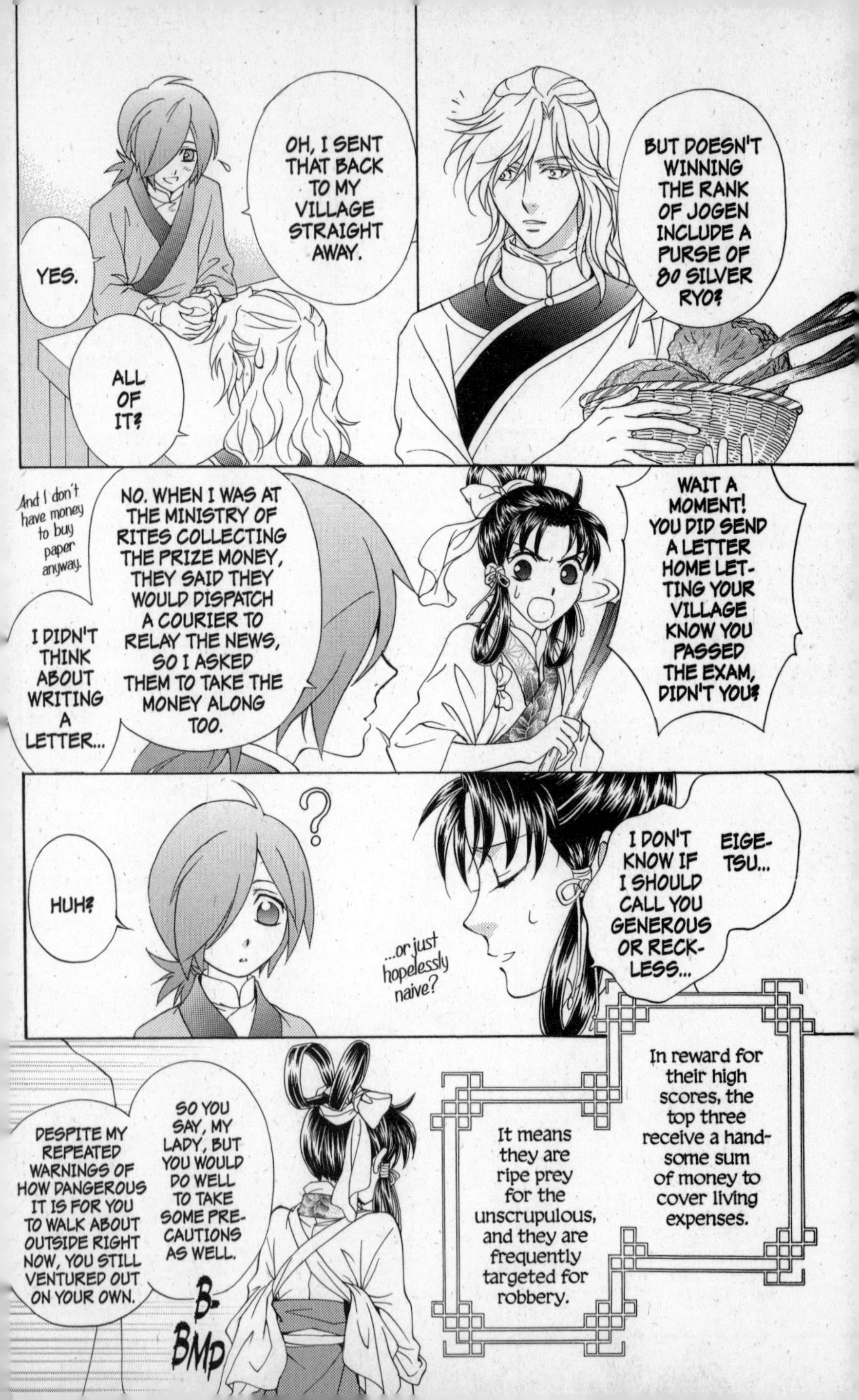
BUT DOESN'T WINNING THE RANK OF JOGEN INCLUDE A PURSE OF 80 SILVER RYO?
OH, I SENT THAT BACK TO MY VILLAGE STRAIGHT AWAY.
ALL OF IT?
YES.
WAIT A MOMENT! YOU DID SEND A LETTER HOME LETTING YOUR VILLAGE KNOW YOU PASSED THE EXAM, DIDN'T YOU?
NO. WHEN I WAS AT THE MINISTRY OF RITES COLLECTING THE PRIZE MONEY, THEY SAID THEY WOULD DISPATCH A COURIER TO RELAY THE NEWS, SO I ASKED THEM TO TAKE THE MONEY ALONG TOO.
I DIDN'T THINK ABOUT WRITING A LETTER...
And I don't have money to buy paper anyway.
EIGETSU...
I DON'T KNOW IF I SHOULD CALL YOU GENEROUS OR RECKLESS...
...or just hopelessly naive?
?
HUH?
In reward for their high scores, the top three receive a handsome sum of money to cover living expenses.
It means they are ripe prey for the unscrupulous, and they are frequently targeted for robbery.
SO YOU SAY, MY LADY, BUT YOU WOULD DO WELL TO TAKE SOME PRECAUTIONS AS WELL.
DESPITE MY REPEATED WARNINGS OF HOW DANGEROUS IT IS FOR YOU TO WALK ABOUT OUTSIDE RIGHT NOW, YOU STILL VENTURED OUT ON YOUR OWN.
B-BMP

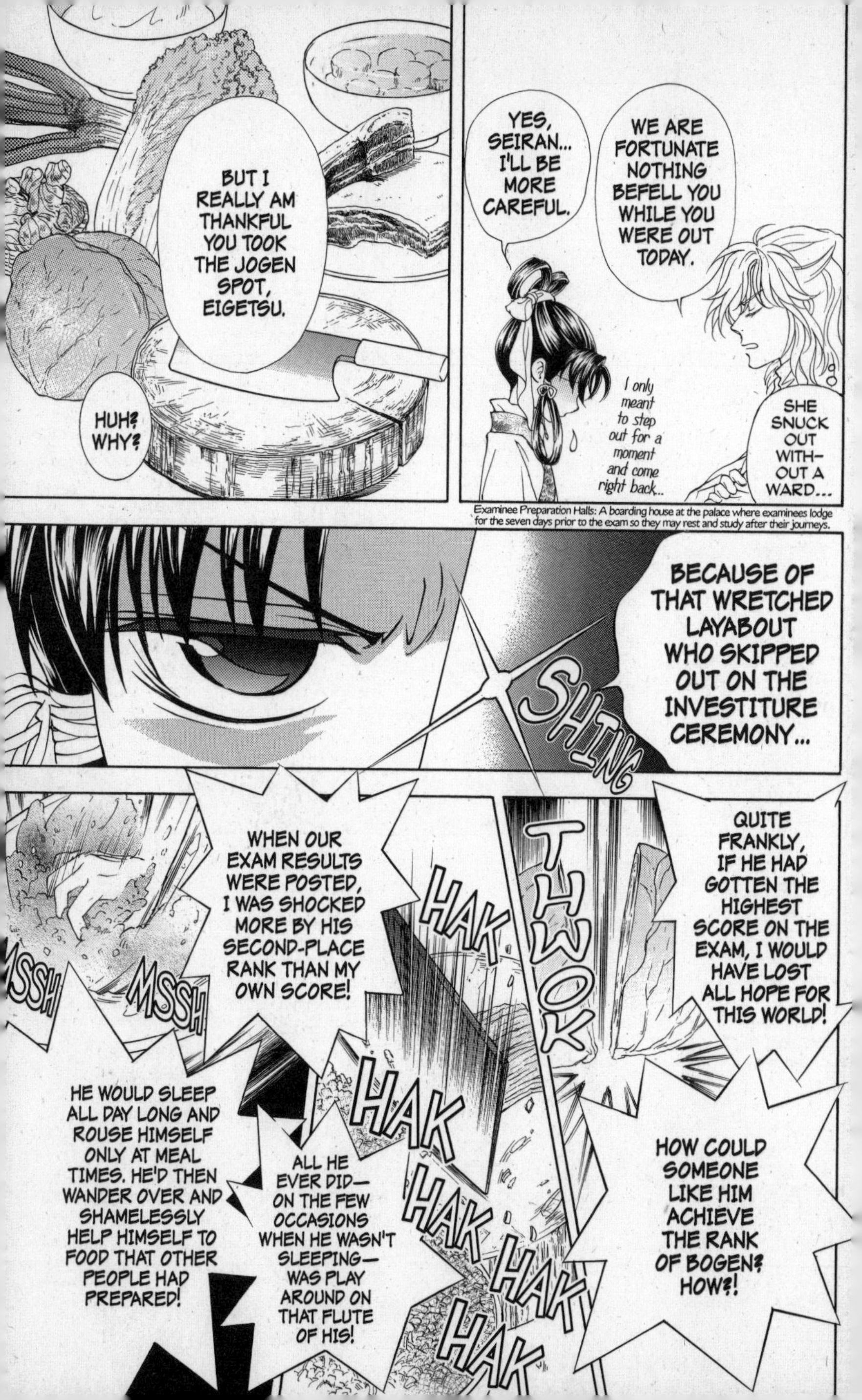
WE ARE FORTUNATE NOTHING BEFELL YOU WHILE YOU WERE OUT TODAY.
YES, SEIRAN... I'LL BE MORE CAREFUL.
SHE SNUCK OUT WITH-OUT A WARD...
I only meant to step out for a moment and come right back...
BUT I REALLY AM THANKFUL YOU TOOK THE JOGEN SPOT, EIGETSU.
HUH? WHY?
Examinee Preparation Halls: A boarding house at the palace where examinees lodge for the seven days prior to the exam so they may rest and study after their journeys.
BECAUSE OF THAT WRETCHED LAYABOUT WHO SKIPPED OUT ON THE INVESTITURE CEREMONY...
SHING
QUITE FRANKLY, IF HE HAD GOTTEN THE HIGHEST SCORE ON THE EXAM, I WOULD HAVE LOST ALL HOPE FOR THIS WORLD!
THWOK
WHEN OUR EXAM RESULTS WERE POSTED, I WAS SHOCKED MORE BY HIS SECOND-PLACE RANK THAN MY OWN SCORE!
HAK
MSSH
MSSH
HOW COULD SOMEONE LIKE HIM ACHIEVE THE RANK OF BOGEN? HOW?!
HAK
HAK
HAK
HAK
HAK
ALL HE EVER DID—ON THE FEW OCCASIONS WHEN HE WASN'T SLEEPING—WAS PLAY AROUND ON THAT FLUTE OF HIS!
HE WOULD SLEEP ALL DAY LONG AND ROUSE HIMSELF ONLY AT MEAL TIMES. HE'D THEN WANDER OVER AND SHAMELESSLY HELP HIMSELF TO FOOD THAT OTHER PEOPLE HAD PREPARED!

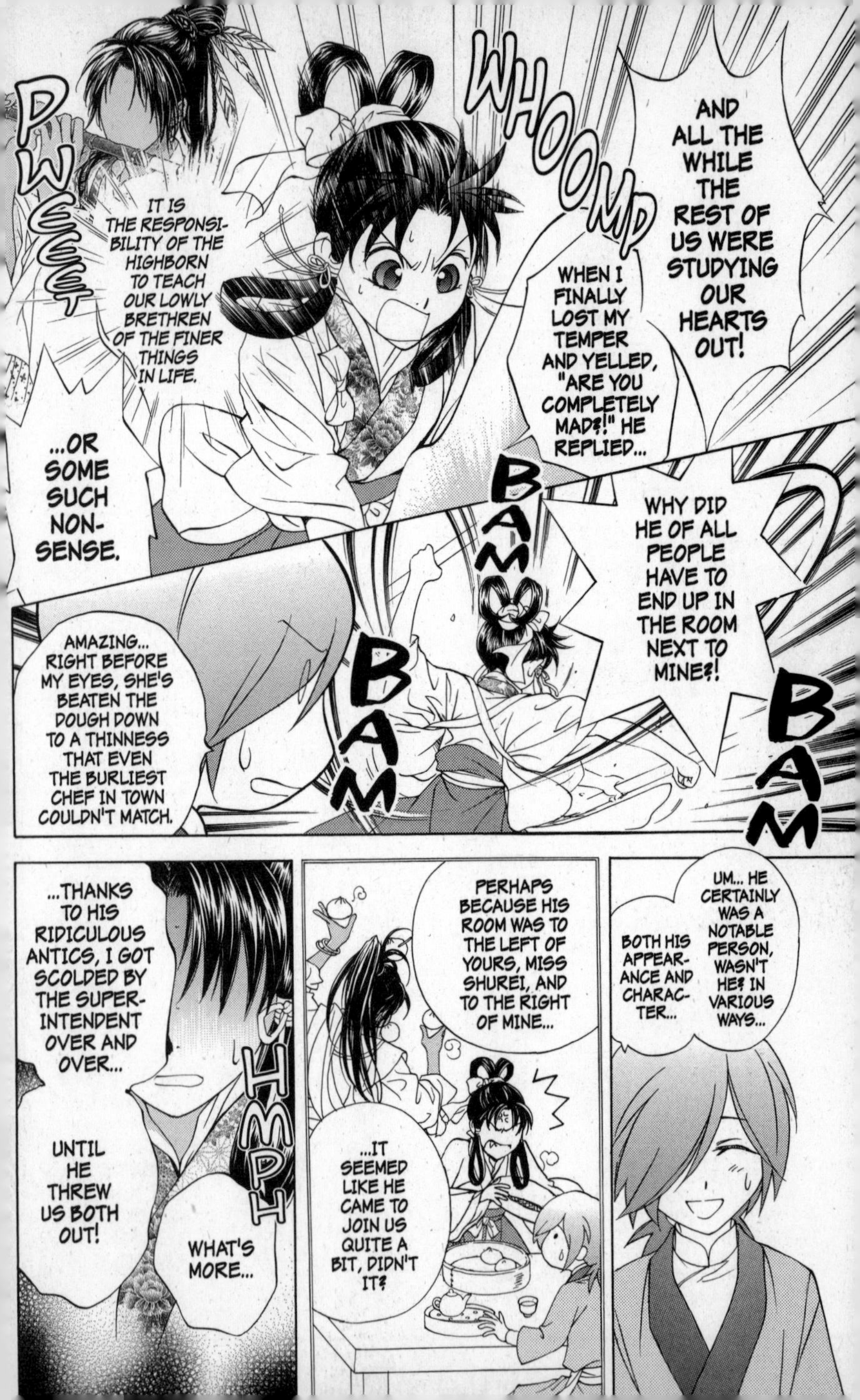
AND ALL THE WHILE THE REST OF US WERE STUDYING OUR HEARTS OUT!
WHEN I FINALLY LOST MY TEMPER AND YELLED, "ARE YOU COMPLETELY MAD?!" HE REPLIED...
WHOOMP
IT IS THE RESPONSIBILITY OF THE HIGHBORN TO TEACH OUR LOWLY BRETHREN OF THE FINER THINGS IN LIFE.
PWEEEE
...OR SOME SUCH NONSENSE.
WHY DID HE OF ALL PEOPLE HAVE TO END UP IN THE ROOM NEXT TO MINE?!
BAM
BAM
BAM
AMAZING... RIGHT BEFORE MY EYES, SHE'S BEATEN THE DOUGH DOWN TO A THINNESS THAT EVEN THE BURLIEST CHEF IN TOWN COULDN'T MATCH.
UM... HE CERTAINLY WAS A NOTABLE PERSON, WASN'T HE? IN VARIOUS WAYS...
BOTH HIS APPEARANCE AND CHARACTER...
PERHAPS BECAUSE HIS ROOM WAS TO THE LEFT OF YOURS, MISS SHUREI, AND TO THE RIGHT OF MINE...
...IT SEEMED LIKE HE CAME TO JOIN US QUITE A BIT, DIDN'T IT?
...THANKS TO HIS RIDICULOUS ANTICS, I GOT SCOLDED BY THE SUPERINTENDENT OVER AND OVER...
UNTIL HE THREW US BOTH OUT!
HMPH
WHAT'S MORE...

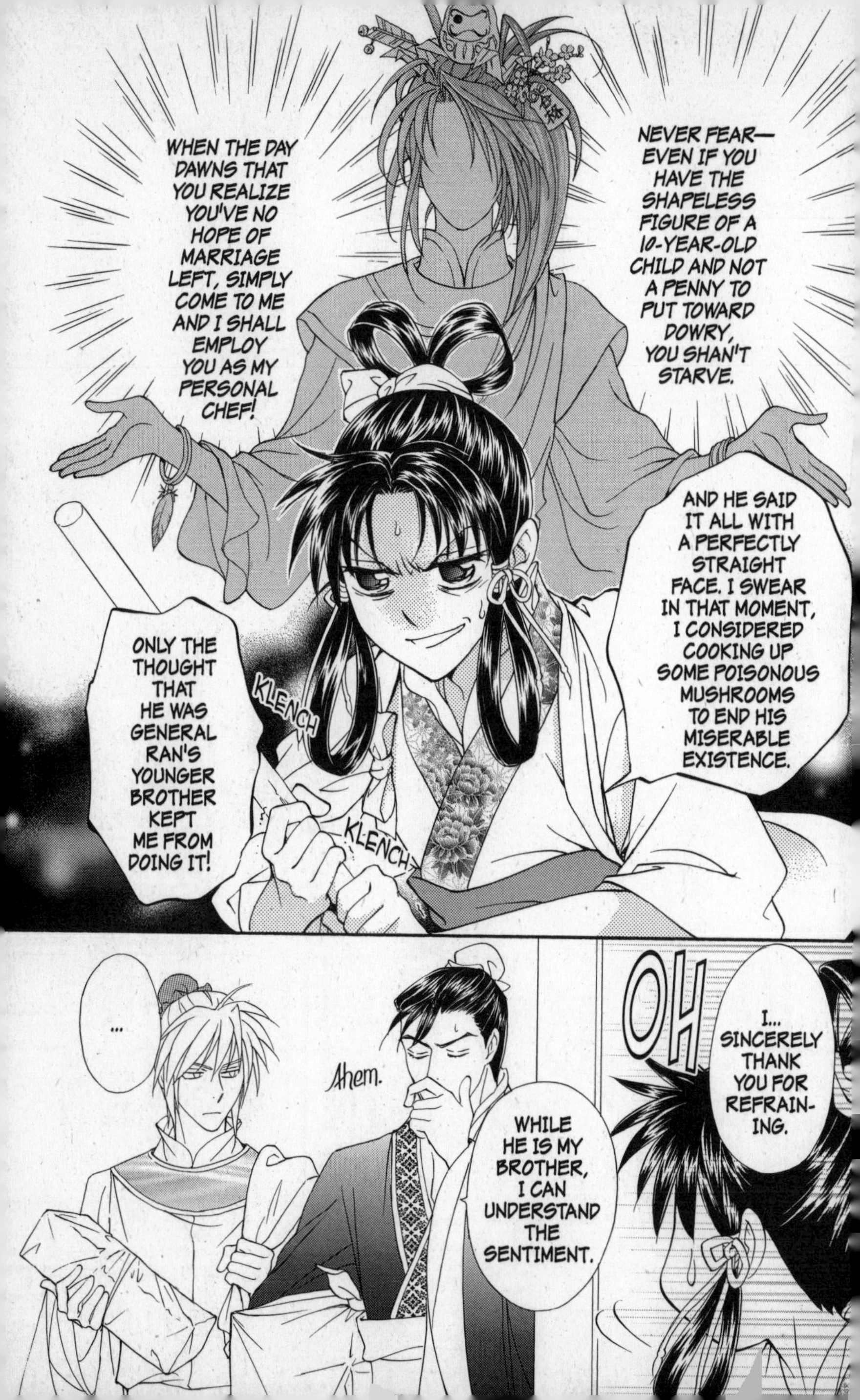
NEVER FEAR—EVEN IF YOU HAVE THE SHAPELESS FIGURE OF A 10-YEAR-OLD CHILD AND NOT A PENNY TO PUT TOWARD DOWRY, YOU SHAN'T STARVE.
WHEN THE DAY DAWNS THAT YOU REALIZE YOU'VE NO HOPE OF MARRIAGE LEFT, SIMPLY COME TO ME AND I SHALL EMPLOY YOU AS MY PERSONAL CHEF!
AND HE SAID IT ALL WITH A PERFECTLY STRAIGHT FACE. I SWEAR IN THAT MOMENT, I CONSIDERED COOKING UP SOME POISONOUS MUSHROOMS TO END HIS MISERABLE EXISTENCE.
KLENCH
KLENCH
ONLY THE THOUGHT THAT HE WAS GENERAL RAN'S YOUNGER BROTHER KEPT ME FROM DOING IT!
OH
I... SINCERELY THANK YOU FOR REFRAIN-ING.
WHILE HE IS MY BROTHER, I CAN UNDERSTAND THE SENTIMENT.
Ahem.
...

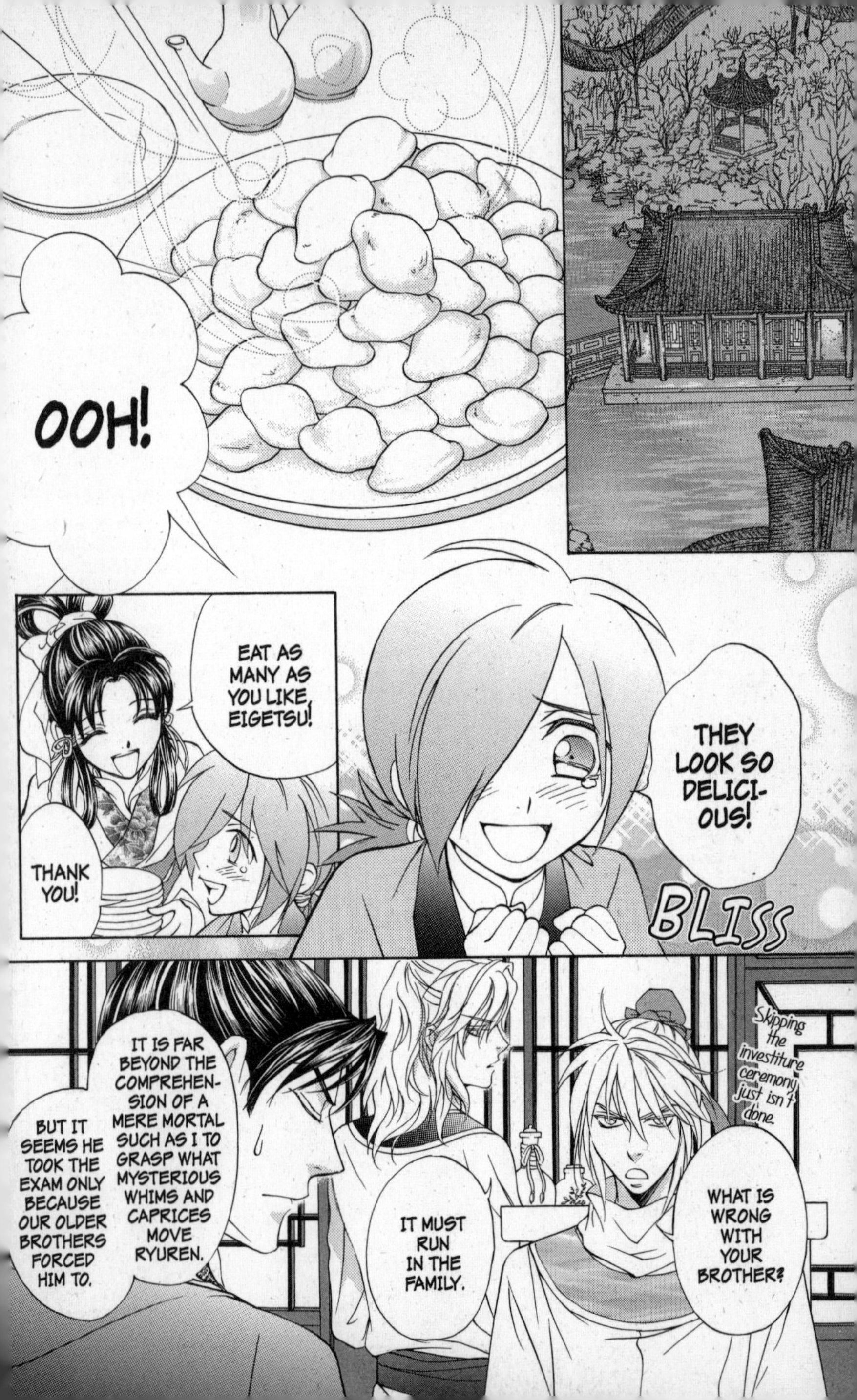
OOH!
THEY LOOK SO DELICI-OUS!
BLISS
EAT AS MANY AS YOU LIKE, EIGETSU!
THANK YOU!
Skipping the investiture ceremony just isn't done.
WHAT IS WRONG WITH YOUR BROTHER?
IT MUST RUN IN THE FAMILY.
IT IS FAR BEYOND THE COMPREHEN-SION OF A MERE MORTAL SUCH AS I TO GRASP WHAT MYSTERIOUS WHIMS AND CAPRICES MOVE RYUREN.
BUT IT SEEMS HE TOOK THE EXAM ONLY BECAUSE OUR OLDER BROTHERS FORCED HIM TO.

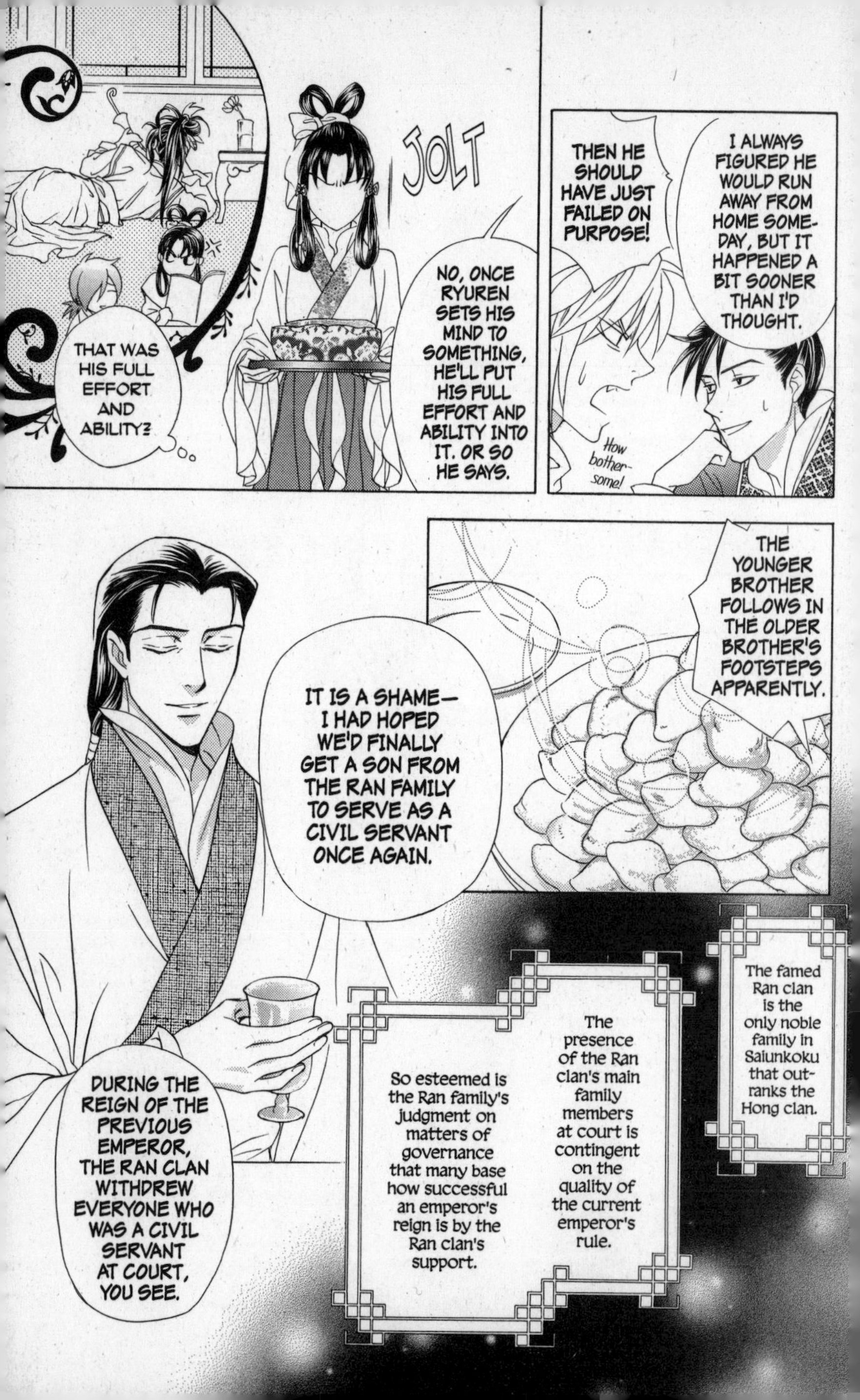
I ALWAYS FIGURED HE WOULD RUN AWAY FROM HOME SOME-DAY, BUT IT HAPPENED A BIT SOONER THAN I'D THOUGHT.
THEN HE SHOULD HAVE JUST FAILED ON PURPOSE!
How bother-some!
JOLT
NO, ONCE RYUREN SETS HIS MIND TO SOMETHING, HE'LL PUT HIS FULL EFFORT AND ABILITY INTO IT. OR SO HE SAYS.
THAT WAS HIS FULL EFFORT AND ABILITY?!
THE YOUNGER BROTHER FOLLOWS IN THE OLDER BROTHER'S FOOTSTEPS APPARENTLY.
IT IS A SHAME—I HAD HOPED WE'D FINALLY GET A SON FROM THE RAN FAMILY TO SERVE AS A CIVIL SERVANT ONCE AGAIN.
The famed Ran clan is the only noble family in Saiunkoku that out-ranks the Hong clan.
The presence of the Ran clan's main family members at court is contingent on the quality of the current emperor's rule.
So esteemed is the Ran family's judgment on matters of governance that many base how successful an emperor's reign is by the Ran clan's support.
DURING THE REIGN OF THE PREVIOUS EMPEROR, THE RAN CLAN WITHDREW EVERYONE WHO WAS A CIVIL SERVANT AT COURT, YOU SEE.

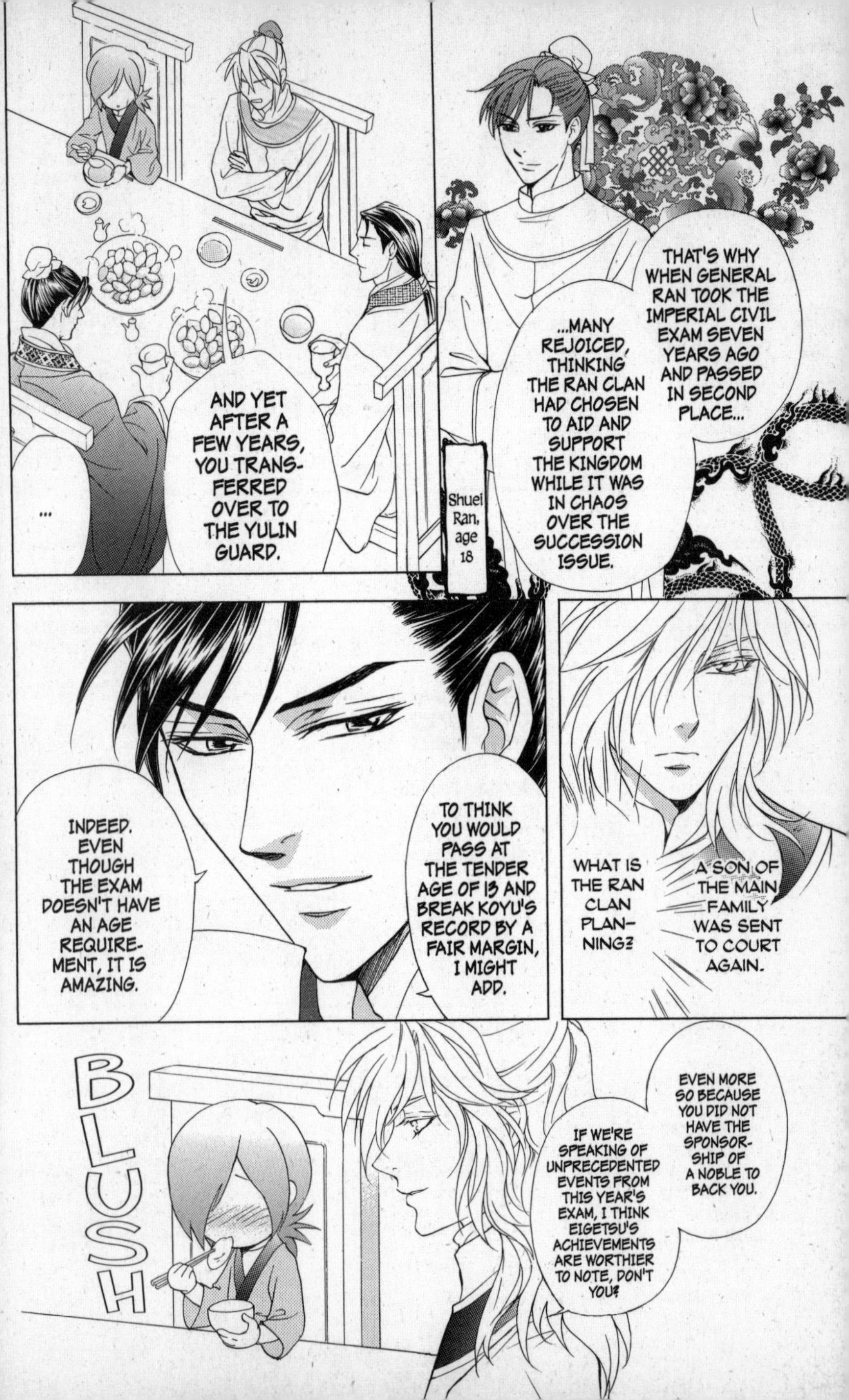
THAT'S WHY WHEN GENERAL RAN TOOK THE IMPERIAL CIVIL EXAM SEVEN YEARS AGO AND PASSED IN SECOND PLACE...
...MANY REJOICED, THINKING THE RAN CLAN HAD CHOSEN TO AID AND SUPPORT THE KINGDOM WHILE IT WAS IN CHAOS OVER THE SUCCESSION ISSUE.
Shuei Ran, age 18
AND YET AFTER A FEW YEARS, YOU TRANSFERRED OVER TO THE YULIN GUARD.
...
A SON OF THE MAIN FAMILY WAS SENT TO COURT AGAIN.
WHAT IS THE RAN CLAN PLANNING?
TO THINK YOU WOULD PASS AT THE TENDER AGE OF 13 AND BREAK KOYU'S RECORD BY A FAIR MARGIN, I MIGHT ADD.
INDEED. EVEN THOUGH THE EXAM DOESN'T HAVE AN AGE REQUIREMENT, IT IS AMAZING.
EVEN MORE SO BECAUSE YOU DID NOT HAVE THE SPONSORSHIP OF A NOBLE TO BACK YOU.
IF WE'RE SPEAKING OF UNPRECEDENTED EVENTS FROM THIS YEAR'S EXAM, I THINK EIGETSU'S ACHIEVEMENTS ARE WORTHIER TO NOTE, DON'T YOU?
BLUSH

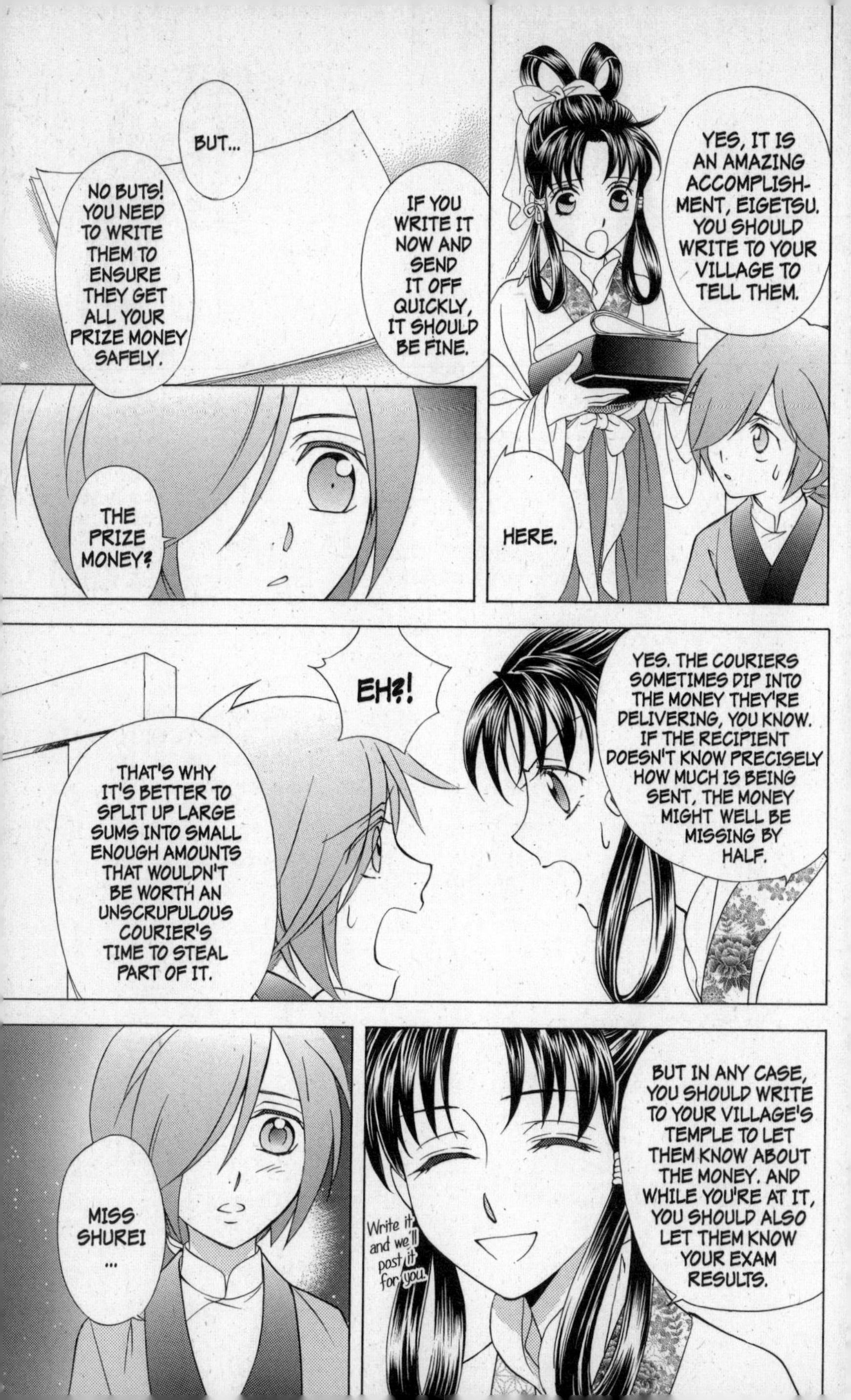
YES, IT IS AN AMAZING ACCOMPLISH-MENT, EIGETSU. YOU SHOULD WRITE TO YOUR VILLAGE TO TELL THEM.
HERE.
IF YOU WRITE IT NOW AND SEND IT OFF QUICKLY, IT SHOULD BE FINE.
BUT...
NO BUTS! YOU NEED TO WRITE THEM TO ENSURE THEY GET ALL YOUR PRIZE MONEY SAFELY.
THE PRIZE MONEY?
YES. THE COURIERS SOMETIMES DIP INTO THE MONEY THEY'RE DELIVERING, YOU KNOW. IF THE RECIPIENT DOESN'T KNOW PRECISELY HOW MUCH IS BEING SENT, THE MONEY MIGHT WELL BE MISSING BY HALF.
EH?!
THAT'S WHY IT'S BETTER TO SPLIT UP LARGE SUMS INTO SMALL ENOUGH AMOUNTS THAT WOULDN'T BE WORTH AN UNSCRUPULOUS COURIER'S TIME TO STEAL PART OF IT.
BUT IN ANY CASE, YOU SHOULD WRITE TO YOUR VILLAGE'S TEMPLE TO LET THEM KNOW ABOUT THE MONEY. AND WHILE YOU'RE AT IT, YOU SHOULD ALSO LET THEM KNOW YOUR EXAM RESULTS.
Write it and we'll post it for you.
MISS SHUREI ...

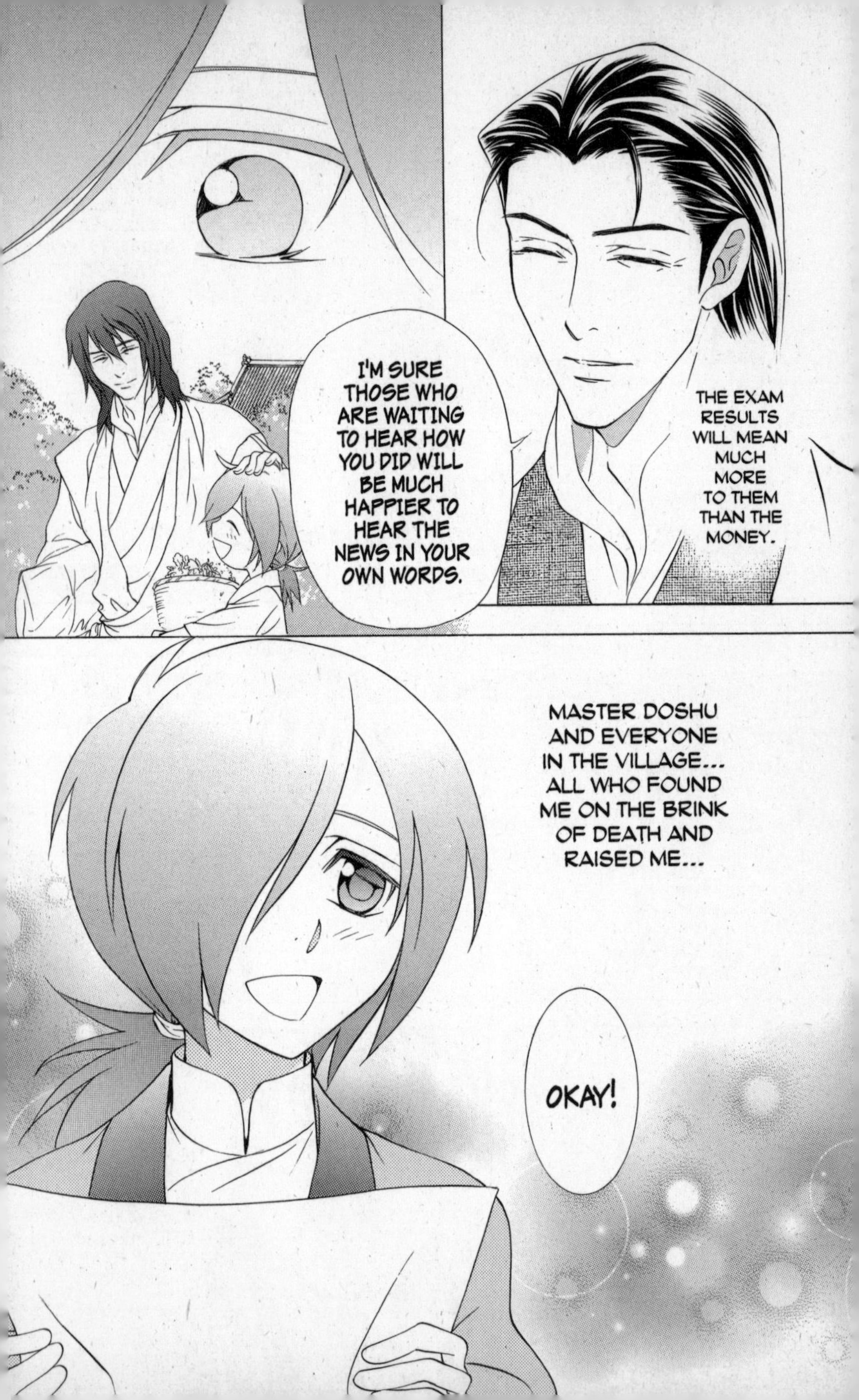
THE EXAM RESULTS WILL MEAN MUCH MORE TO THEM THAN THE MONEY.
I'M SURE THOSE WHO ARE WAITING TO HEAR HOW YOU DID WILL BE MUCH HAPPIER TO HEAR THE NEWS IN YOUR OWN WORDS.
MASTER DOSHU AND EVERYONE IN THE VILLAGE... ALL WHO FOUND ME ON THE BRINK OF DEATH AND RAISED ME...
OKAY!

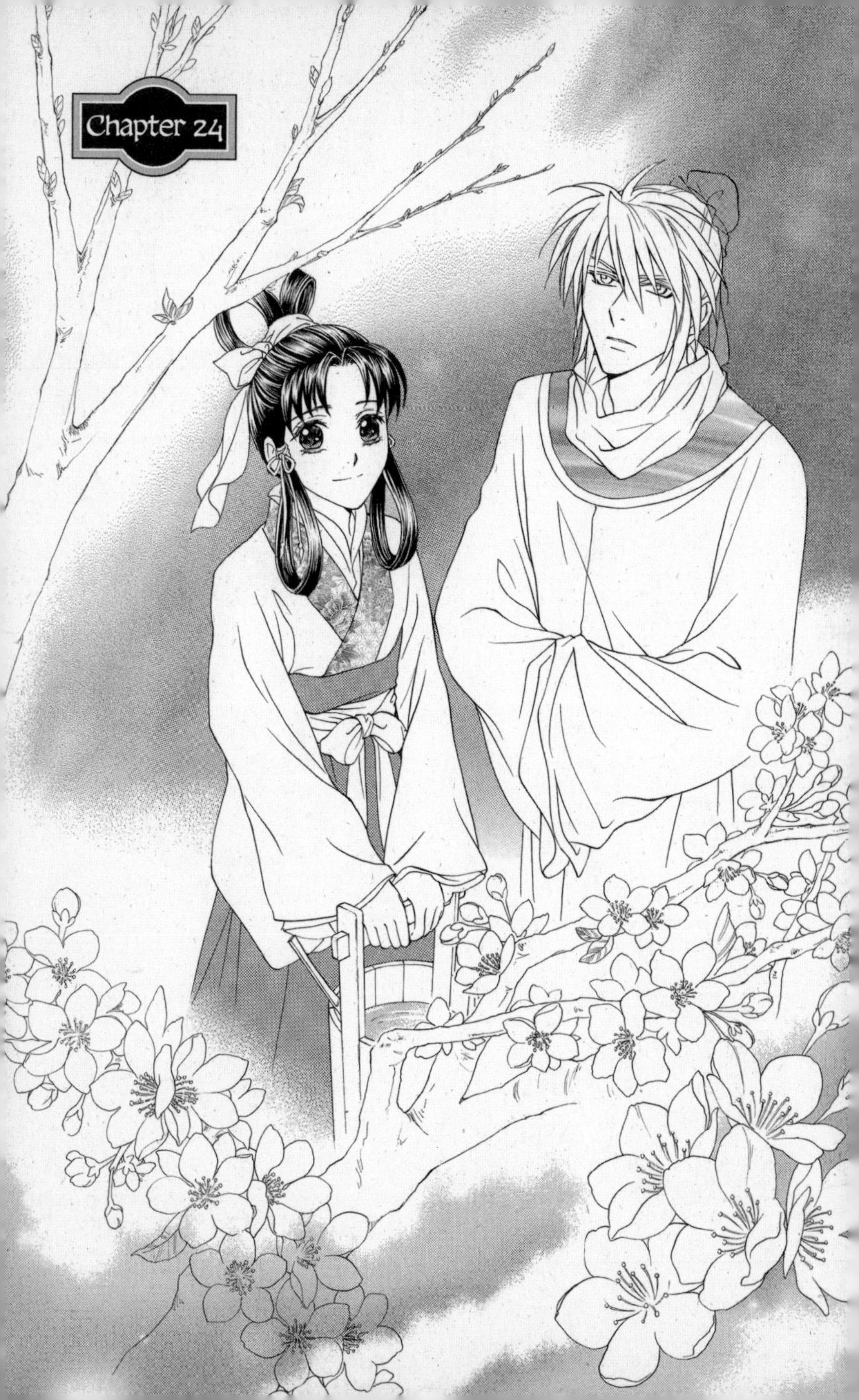
Chapter 24

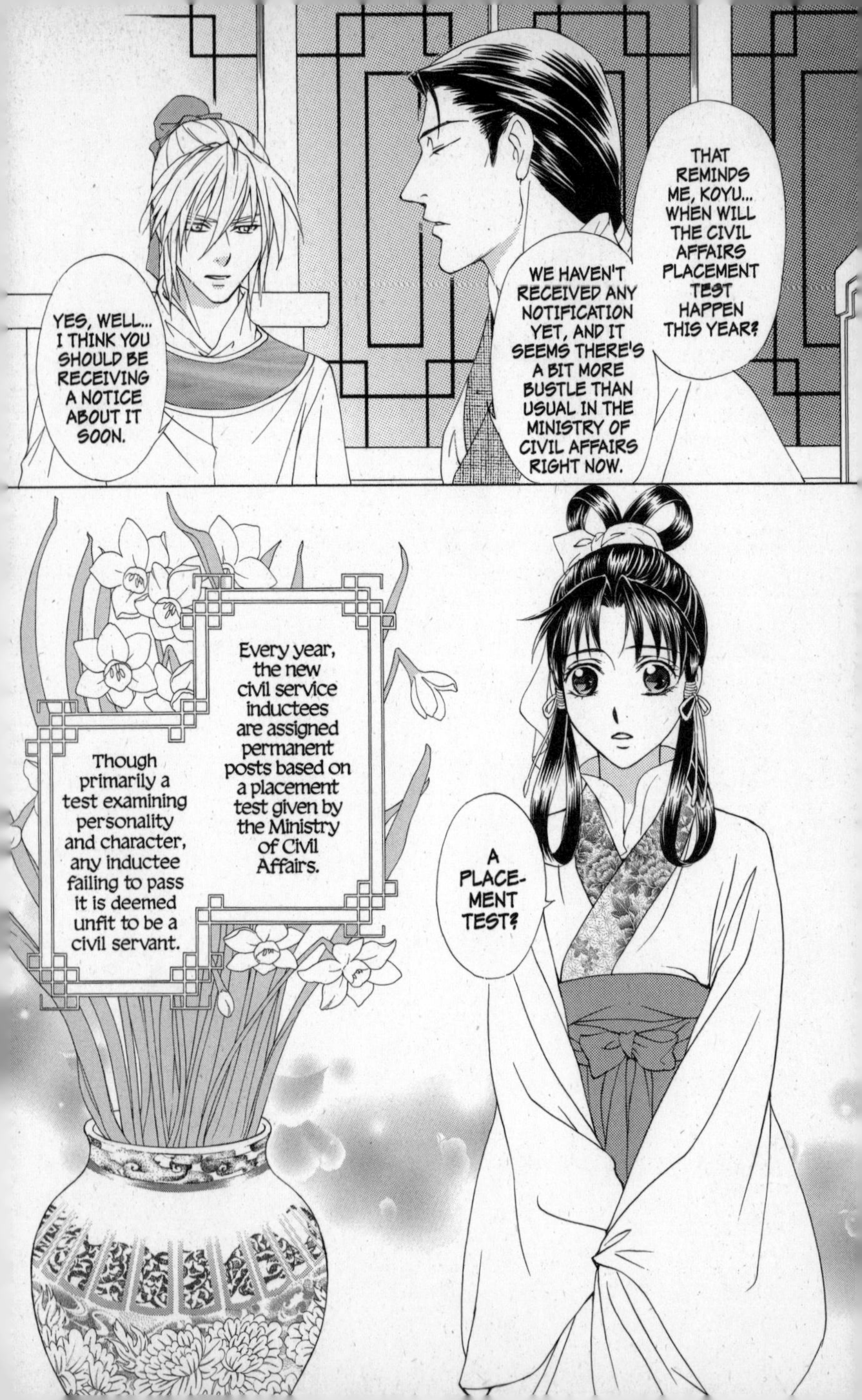
THAT REMINDS ME, KOYU... WHEN WILL THE CIVIL AFFAIRS PLACEMENT TEST HAPPEN THIS YEAR?
WE HAVEN'T RECEIVED ANY NOTIFICATION YET, AND IT SEEMS THERE'S A BIT MORE BUSTLE THAN USUAL IN THE MINISTRY OF CIVIL AFFAIRS RIGHT NOW.
YES, WELL... I THINK YOU SHOULD BE RECEIVING A NOTICE ABOUT IT SOON.
A PLACE-MENT TEST?
Every year, the new civil service inductees are assigned permanent posts based on a placement test given by the Ministry of Civil Affairs.
Though primarily a test examining personality and character, any inductee failing to pass it is deemed unfit to be a civil servant.

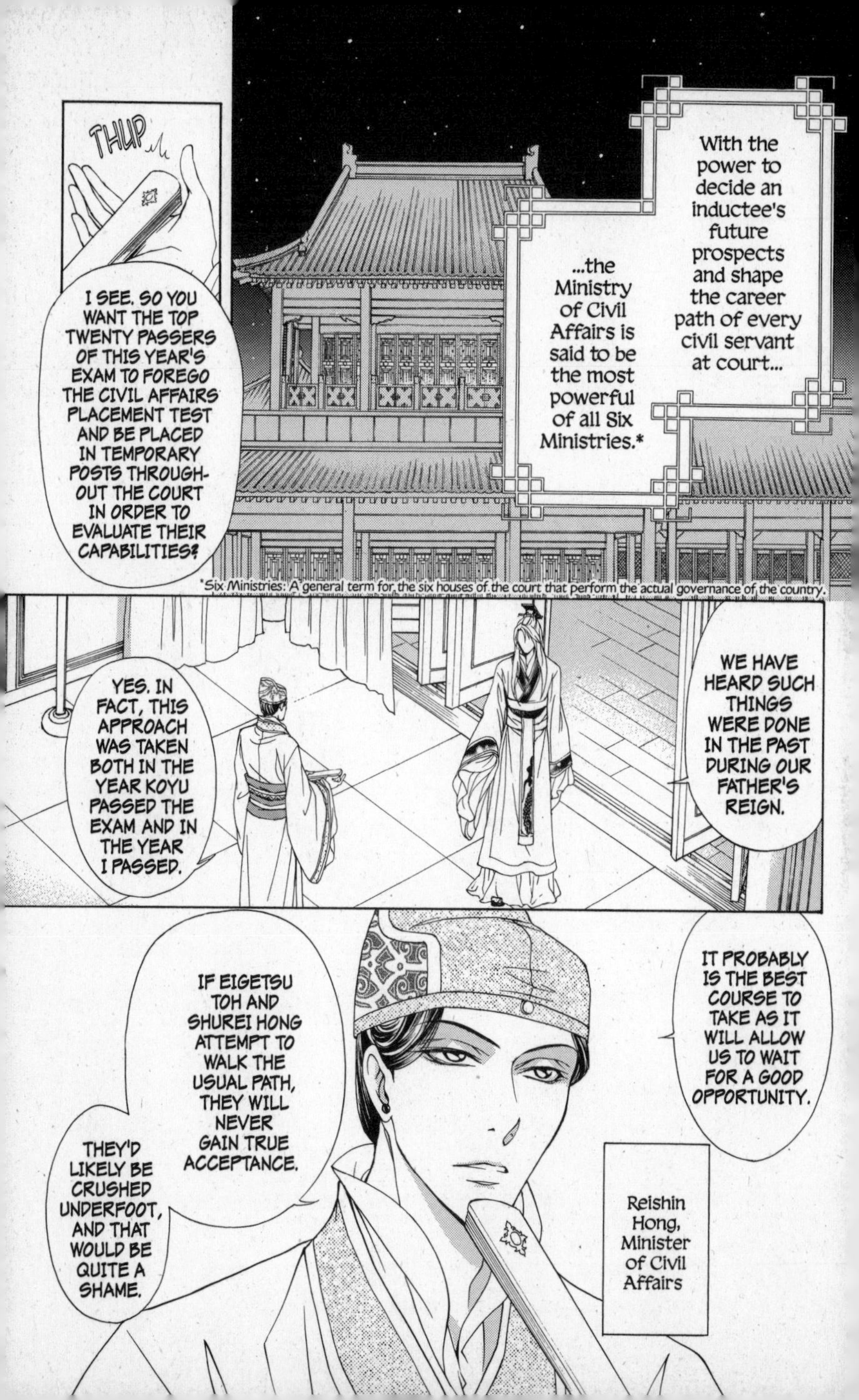
With the power to decide an inductee's future prospects and shape the career path of every civil servant at court...
...the Ministry of Civil Affairs is said to be the most powerful of all Six Ministries.*
THUP
I SEE. SO YOU WANT THE TOP TWENTY PASSERS OF THIS YEAR'S EXAM TO FOREGO THE CIVIL AFFAIRS PLACEMENT TEST AND BE PLACED IN TEMPORARY POSTS THROUGH-OUT THE COURT IN ORDER TO EVALUATE THEIR CAPABILITIES?
WE HAVE HEARD SUCH THINGS WERE DONE IN THE PAST DURING OUR FATHER'S REIGN.
YES. IN FACT, THIS APPROACH WAS TAKEN BOTH IN THE YEAR KOYU PASSED THE EXAM AND IN THE YEAR I PASSED.
IT PROBABLY IS THE BEST COURSE TO TAKE AS IT WILL ALLOW US TO WAIT FOR A GOOD OPPORTUNITY.
Reishin Hong, Minister of Civil Affairs
IF EIGETSU TOH AND SHUREI HONG ATTEMPT TO WALK THE USUAL PATH, THEY WILL NEVER GAIN TRUE ACCEPTANCE.
THEY'D LIKELY BE CRUSHED UNDERFOOT, AND THAT WOULD BE QUITE A SHAME.

*Six Ministries: A general term for the six houses of the court that perform the actual governance of the country.

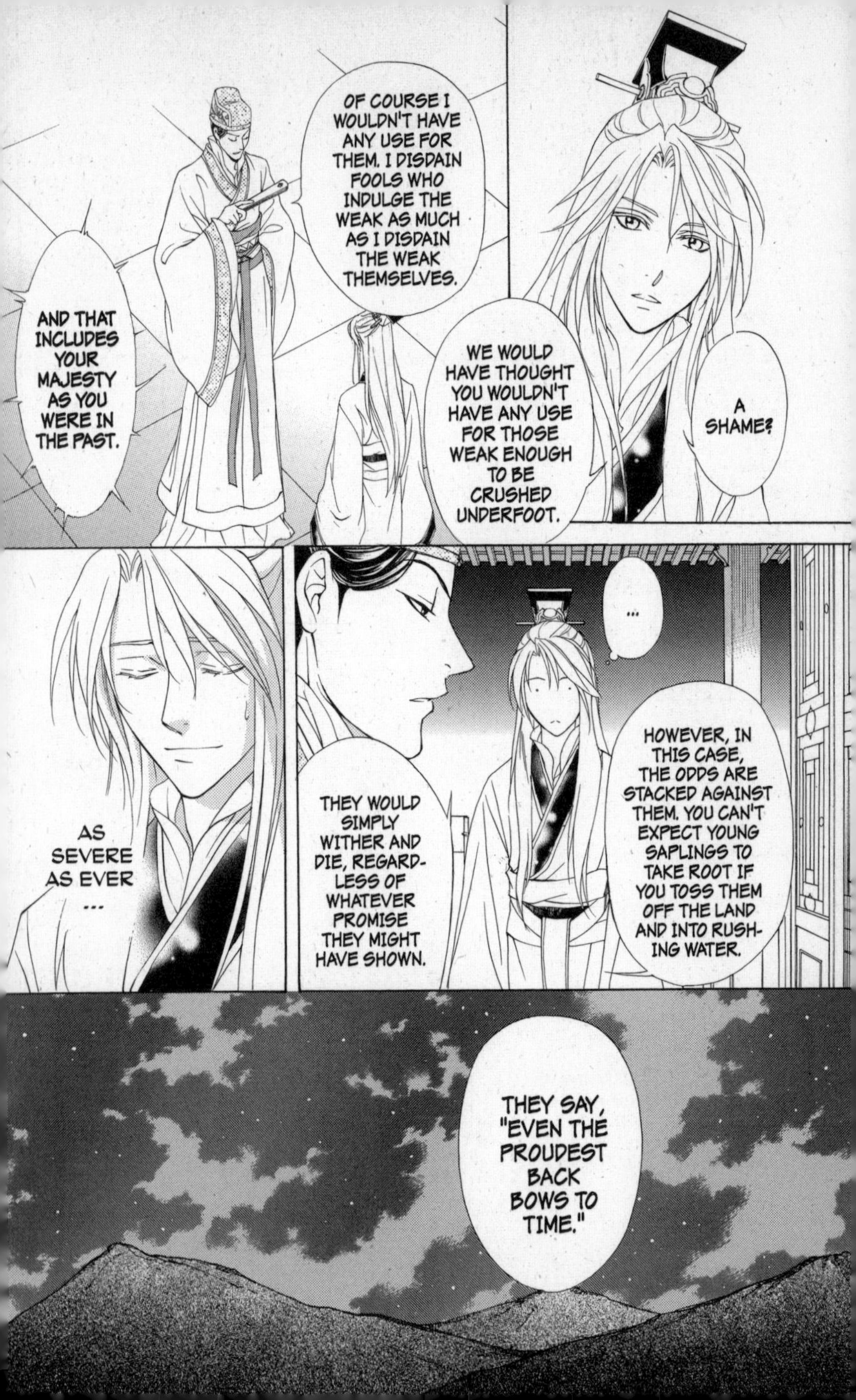
A SHAME?
WE WOULD HAVE THOUGHT YOU WOULDN'T HAVE ANY USE FOR THOSE WEAK ENOUGH TO BE CRUSHED UNDERFOOT.
OF COURSE I WOULDN'T HAVE ANY USE FOR THEM. I DISDAIN FOOLS WHO INDULGE THE WEAK AS MUCH AS I DISDAIN THE WEAK THEMSELVES.
AND THAT INCLUDES YOUR MAJESTY AS YOU WERE IN THE PAST.
...
HOWEVER, IN THIS CASE, THE ODDS ARE STACKED AGAINST THEM. YOU CAN'T EXPECT YOUNG SAPLINGS TO TAKE ROOT IF YOU TOSS THEM OFF THE LAND AND INTO RUSHING WATER.
THEY WOULD SIMPLY WITHER AND DIE, REGARDLESS OF WHATEVER PROMISE THEY MIGHT HAVE SHOWN.
AS SEVERE AS EVER ...
THEY SAY, "EVEN THE PROUDEST BACK BOWS TO TIME."

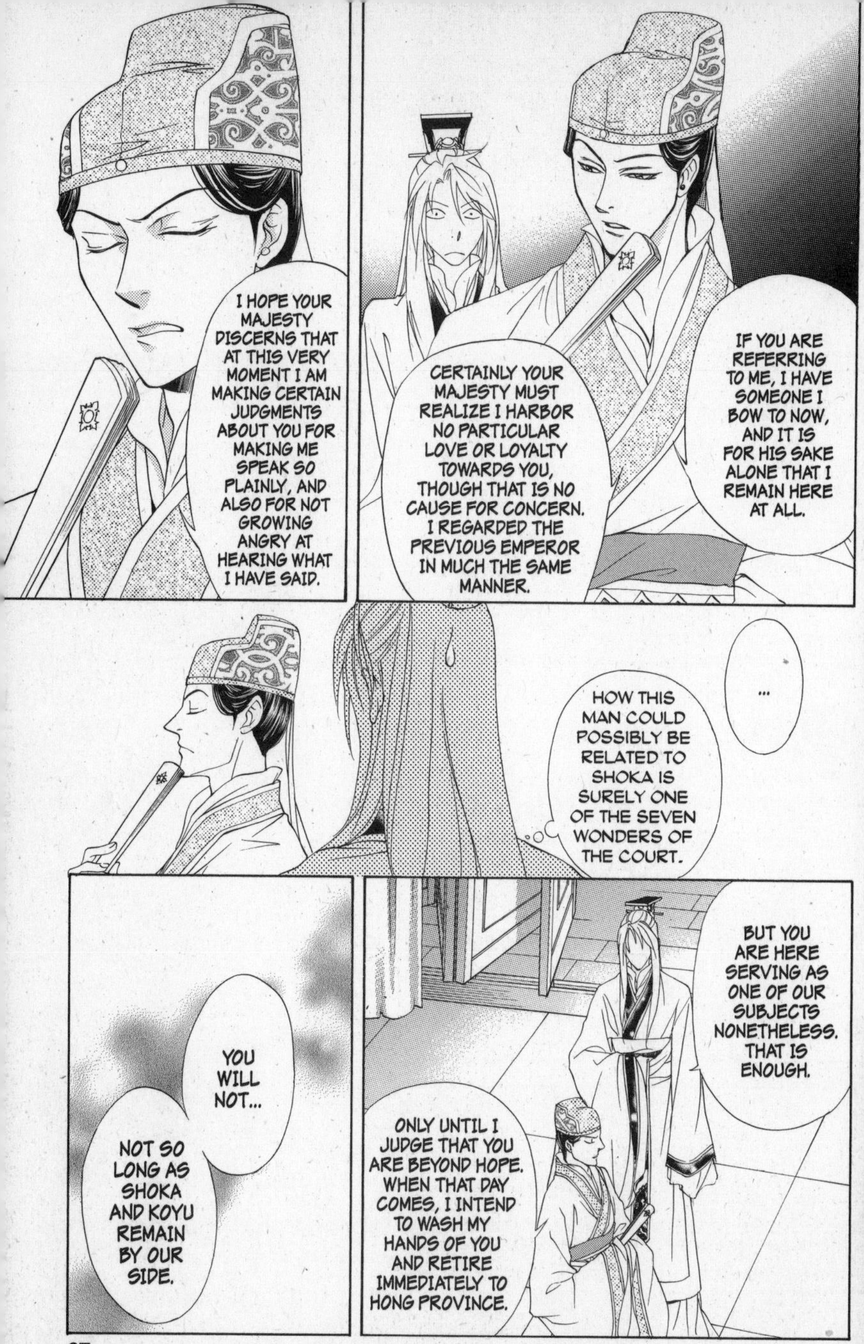
IF YOU ARE REFERRING TO ME, I HAVE SOMEONE I BOW TO NOW, AND IT IS FOR HIS SAKE ALONE THAT I REMAIN HERE AT ALL.
CERTAINLY YOUR MAJESTY MUST REALIZE I HARBOR NO PARTICULAR LOVE OR LOYALTY TOWARDS YOU, THOUGH THAT IS NO CAUSE FOR CONCERN. I REGARDED THE PREVIOUS EMPEROR IN MUCH THE SAME MANNER.
I HOPE YOUR MAJESTY DISCERNS THAT AT THIS VERY MOMENT I AM MAKING CERTAIN JUDGMENTS ABOUT YOU FOR MAKING ME SPEAK SO PLAINLY, AND ALSO FOR NOT GROWING ANGRY AT HEARING WHAT I HAVE SAID.
...
HOW THIS MAN COULD POSSIBLY BE RELATED TO SHOKA IS SURELY ONE OF THE SEVEN WONDERS OF THE COURT.
BUT YOU ARE HERE SERVING AS ONE OF OUR SUBJECTS NONETHELESS. THAT IS ENOUGH.
ONLY UNTIL I JUDGE THAT YOU ARE BEYOND HOPE. WHEN THAT DAY COMES, I INTEND TO WASH MY HANDS OF YOU AND RETIRE IMMEDIATELY TO HONG PROVINCE.
YOU WILL NOT...
NOT SO LONG AS SHOKA AND KOYU REMAIN BY OUR SIDE.

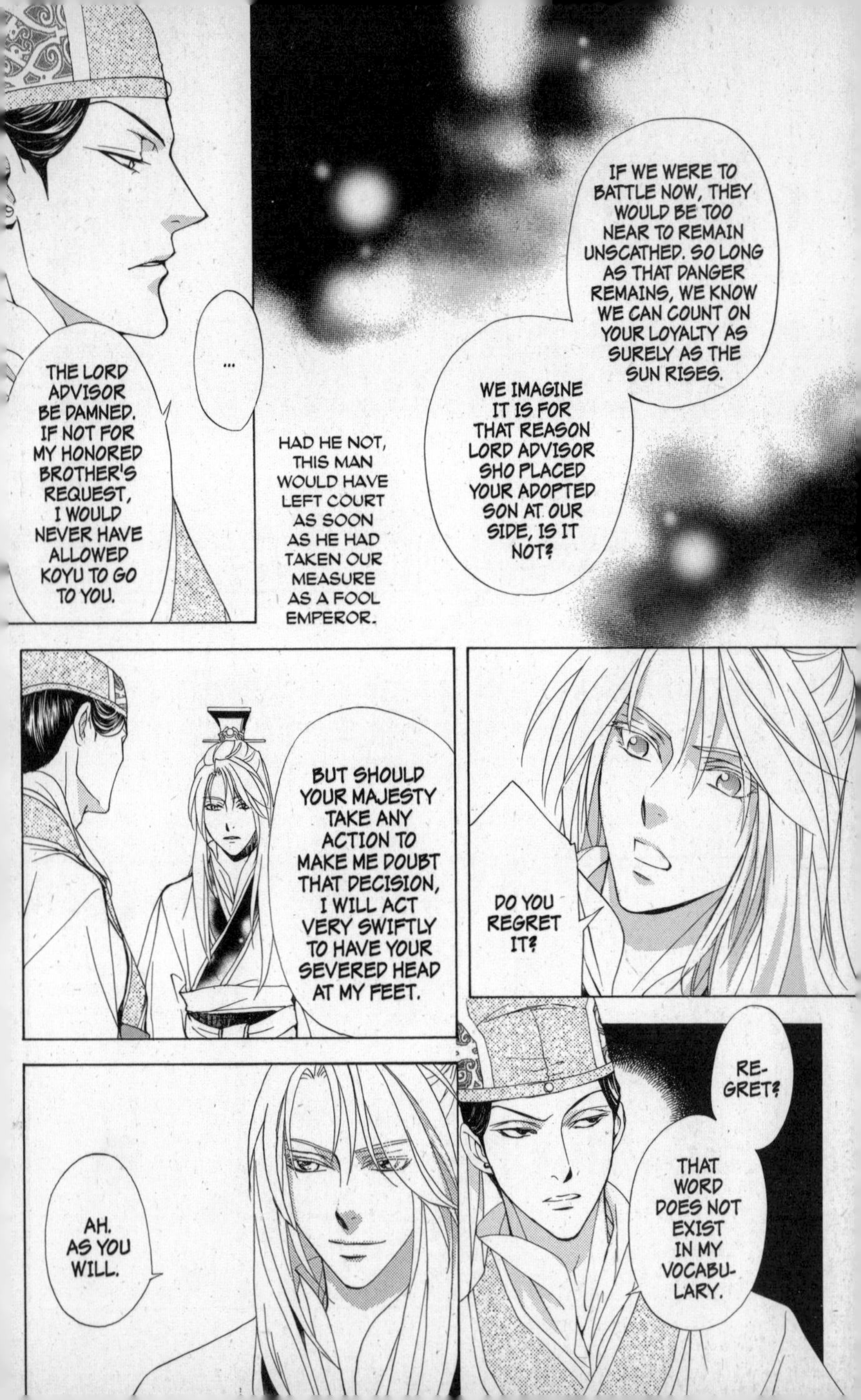
IF WE WERE TO BATTLE NOW, THEY WOULD BE TOO NEAR TO REMAIN UNSCATHED. SO LONG AS THAT DANGER REMAINS, WE KNOW WE CAN COUNT ON YOUR LOYALTY AS SURELY AS THE SUN RISES.
WE IMAGINE IT IS FOR THAT REASON LORD ADVISOR SHO PLACED YOUR ADOPTED SON AT OUR SIDE, IS IT NOT?
HAD HE NOT, THIS MAN WOULD HAVE LEFT COURT AS SOON AS HE HAD TAKEN OUR MEASURE AS A FOOL EMPEROR.
...
THE LORD ADVISOR BE DAMNED. IF NOT FOR MY HONORED BROTHER'S REQUEST, I WOULD NEVER HAVE ALLOWED KOYU TO GO TO YOU.
DO YOU REGRET IT?
BUT SHOULD YOUR MAJESTY TAKE ANY ACTION TO MAKE ME DOUBT THAT DECISION, I WILL ACT VERY SWIFTLY TO HAVE YOUR SEVERED HEAD AT MY FEET.
RE-GRET?
THAT WORD DOES NOT EXIST IN MY VOCABU-LARY.
AH. AS YOU WILL.

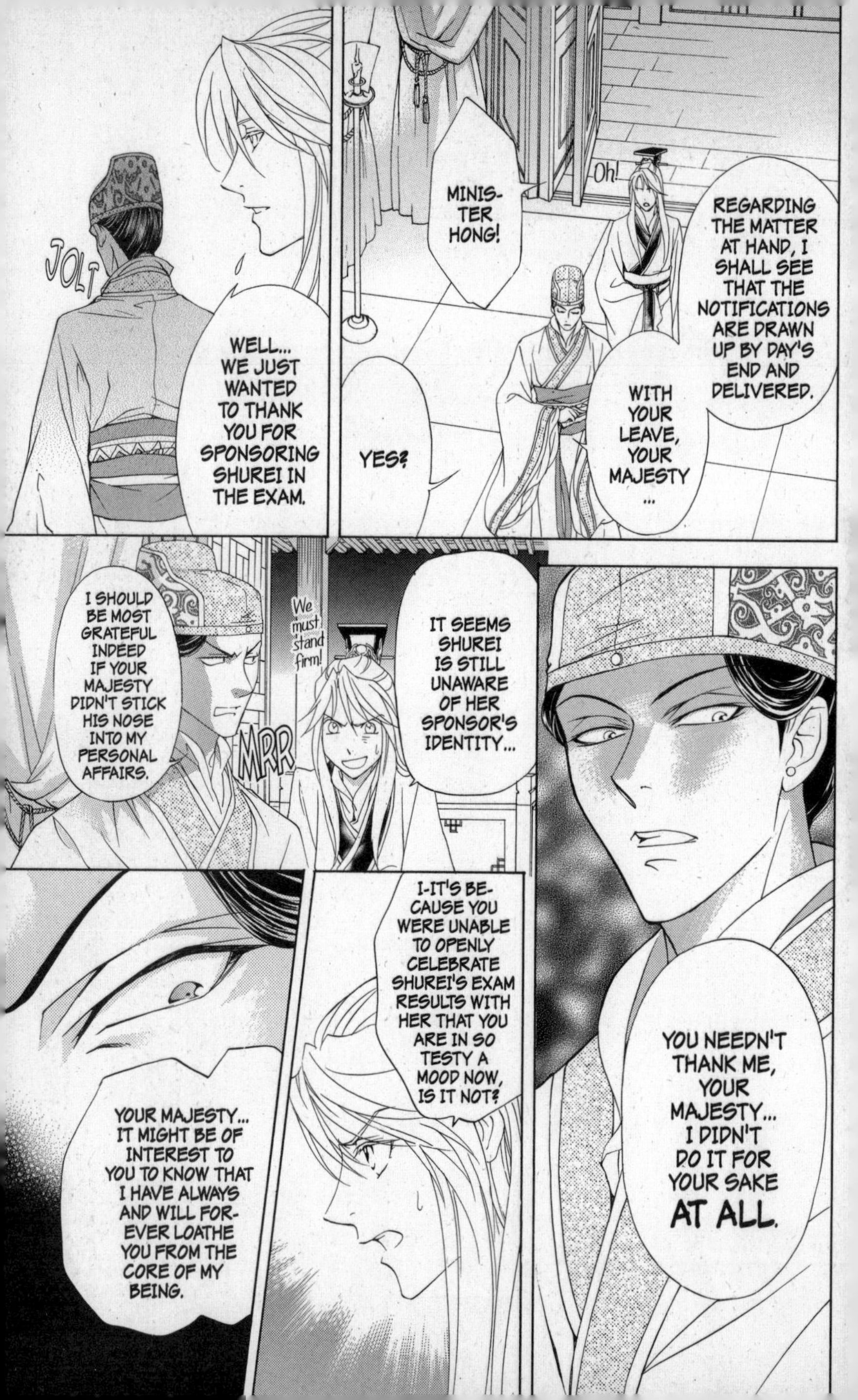
Oh!
REGARDING THE MATTER AT HAND, I SHALL SEE THAT THE NOTIFICATIONS ARE DRAWN UP BY DAY'S END AND DELIVERED.
WITH YOUR LEAVE, YOUR MAJESTY...
MINISTER HONG!
YES?
JOLT
WELL... WE JUST WANTED TO THANK YOU FOR SPONSORING SHUREI IN THE EXAM.
YOU NEEDN'T THANK ME, YOUR MAJESTY... I DIDN'T DO IT FOR YOUR SAKE AT ALL.
IT SEEMS SHUREI IS STILL UNAWARE OF HER SPONSOR'S IDENTITY...
We must stand firm!
MRR
I SHOULD BE MOST GRATEFUL INDEED IF YOUR MAJESTY DIDN'T STICK HIS NOSE INTO MY PERSONAL AFFAIRS.
I-IT'S BECAUSE YOU WERE UNABLE TO OPENLY CELEBRATE SHUREI'S EXAM RESULTS WITH HER THAT YOU ARE IN SO TESTY A MOOD NOW, IS IT NOT?
YOUR MAJESTY... IT MIGHT BE OF INTEREST TO YOU TO KNOW THAT I HAVE ALWAYS AND WILL FOREVER LOATHE YOU FROM THE CORE OF MY BEING.

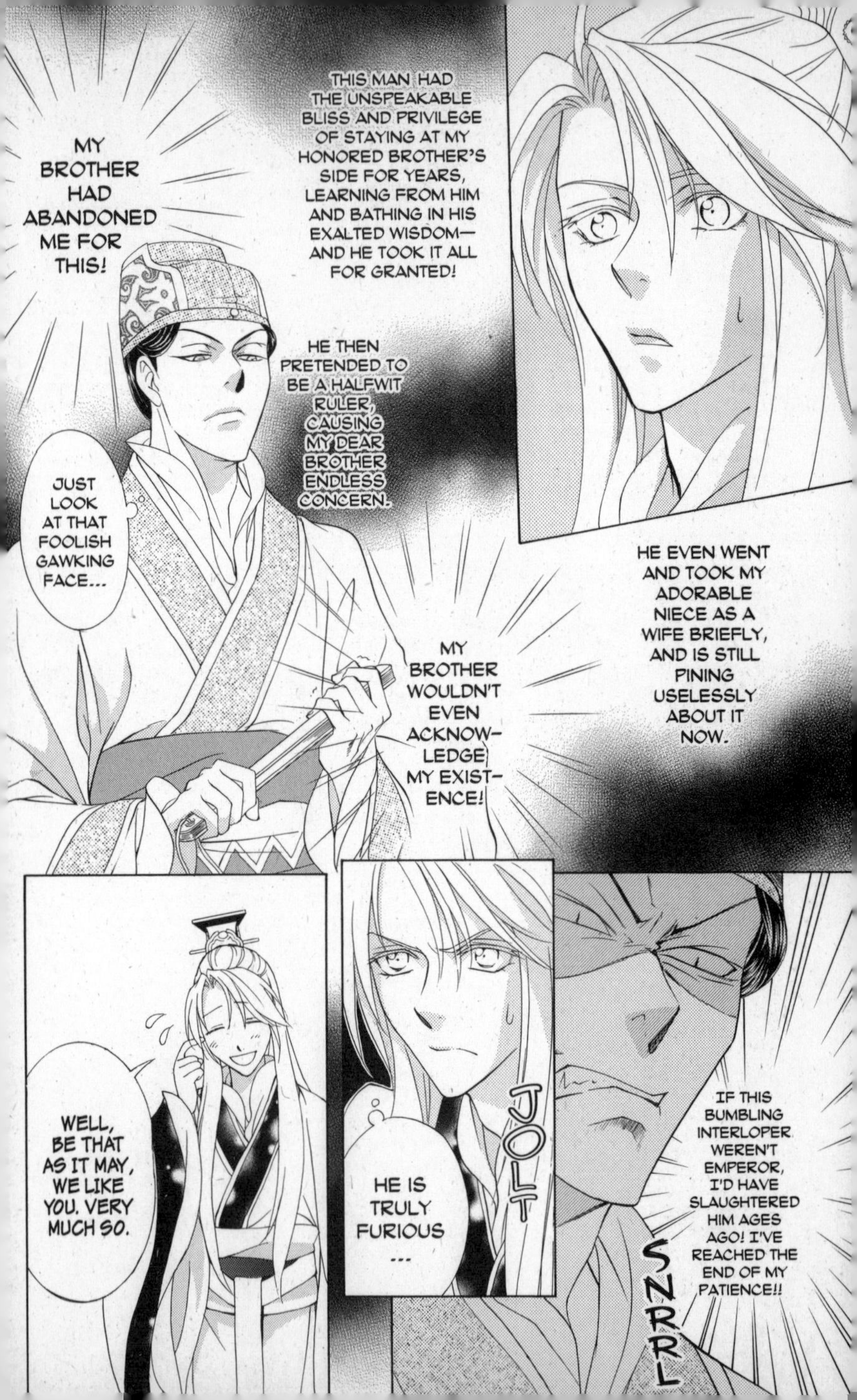
THIS MAN HAD THE UNSPEAKABLE BLISS AND PRIVILEGE OF STAYING AT MY HONORED BROTHER'S SIDE FOR YEARS, LEARNING FROM HIM AND BATHING IN HIS EXALTED WISDOM— AND HE TOOK IT ALL FOR GRANTED!
MY BROTHER HAD ABANDONED ME FOR THIS!
HE THEN PRETENDED TO BE A HALFWIT RULER, CAUSING MY DEAR BROTHER ENDLESS CONCERN.
JUST LOOK AT THAT FOOLISH GAWKING FACE...
HE EVEN WENT AND TOOK MY ADORABLE NIECE AS A WIFE BRIEFLY, AND IS STILL PINING USELESSLY ABOUT IT NOW.
MY BROTHER WOULDN'T EVEN ACKNOW- LEDGE MY EXIST- ENCE!
IF THIS BUMBLING INTERLOPER WEREN'T EMPEROR, I'D HAVE SLAUGHTERED HIM AGES AGO! I'VE REACHED THE END OF MY PATIENCE!!
SNRRL
JOLT
HE IS TRULY FURIOUS ...
WELL, BE THAT AS IT MAY, WE LIKE YOU. VERY MUCH SO.

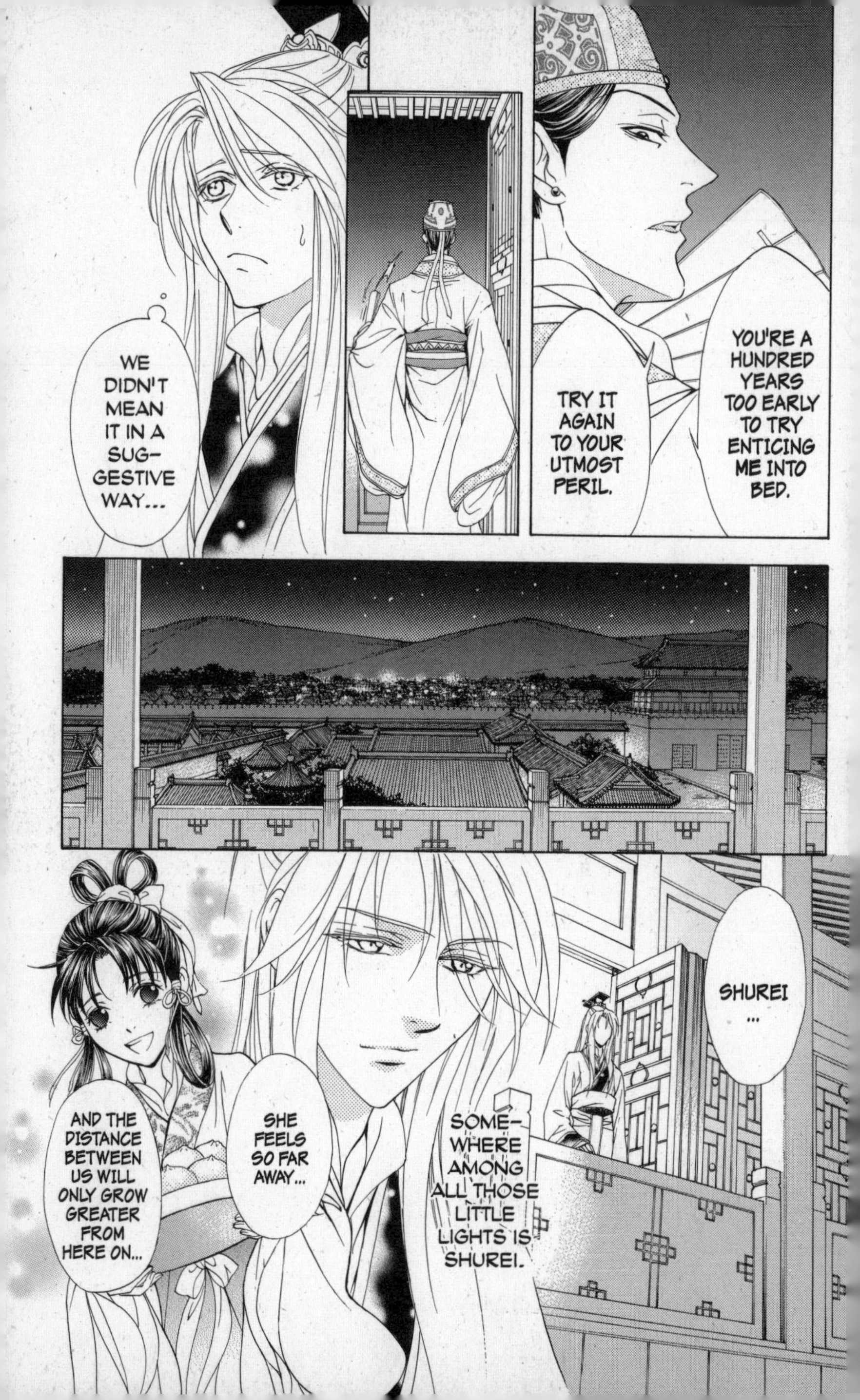
YOU'RE A HUNDRED YEARS TOO EARLY TO TRY ENTICING ME INTO BED.
TRY IT AGAIN TO YOUR UTMOST PERIL.
WE DIDN'T MEAN IT IN A SUG-GESTIVE WAY...
SHUREI ...
SOME-WHERE AMONG ALL THOSE LITTLE LIGHTS IS SHUREI.
SHE FEELS SO FAR AWAY...
AND THE DISTANCE BETWEEN US WILL ONLY GROW GREATER FROM HERE ON...

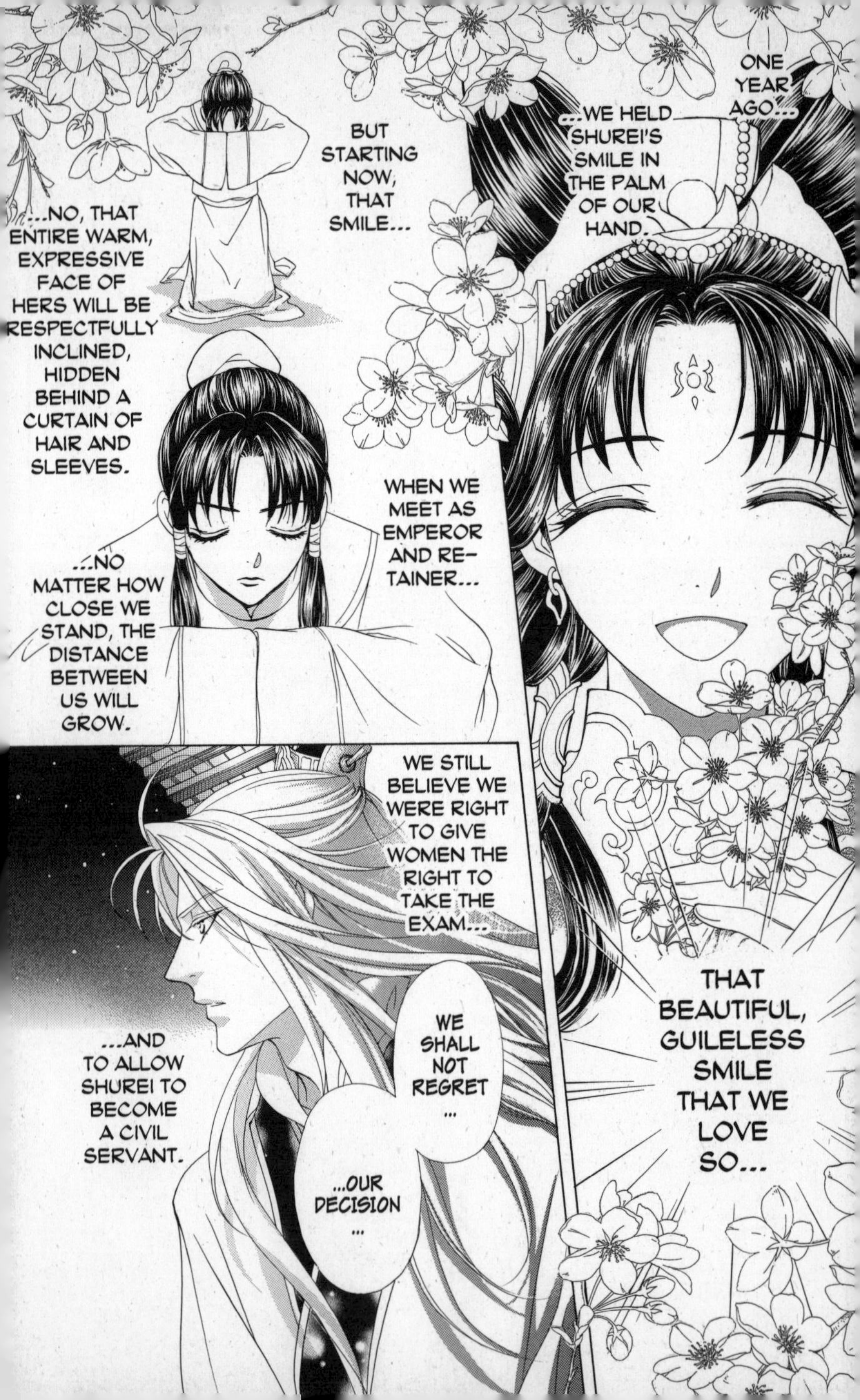
ONE YEAR AGO...
...WE HELD SHUREI'S SMILE IN THE PALM OF OUR HAND.
THAT BEAUTIFUL, GUILELESS SMILE THAT WE LOVE SO...
BUT STARTING NOW, THAT SMILE...
...NO, THAT ENTIRE WARM, EXPRESSIVE FACE OF HERS WILL BE RESPECTFULLY INCLINED, HIDDEN BEHIND A CURTAIN OF HAIR AND SLEEVES.
WHEN WE MEET AS EMPEROR AND RE-TAINER...
...NO MATTER HOW CLOSE WE STAND, THE DISTANCE BETWEEN US WILL GROW.
WE STILL BELIEVE WE WERE RIGHT TO GIVE WOMEN THE RIGHT TO TAKE THE EXAM...
...AND TO ALLOW SHUREI TO BECOME A CIVIL SERVANT.
WE SHALL NOT REGRET...
...OUR DECISION...

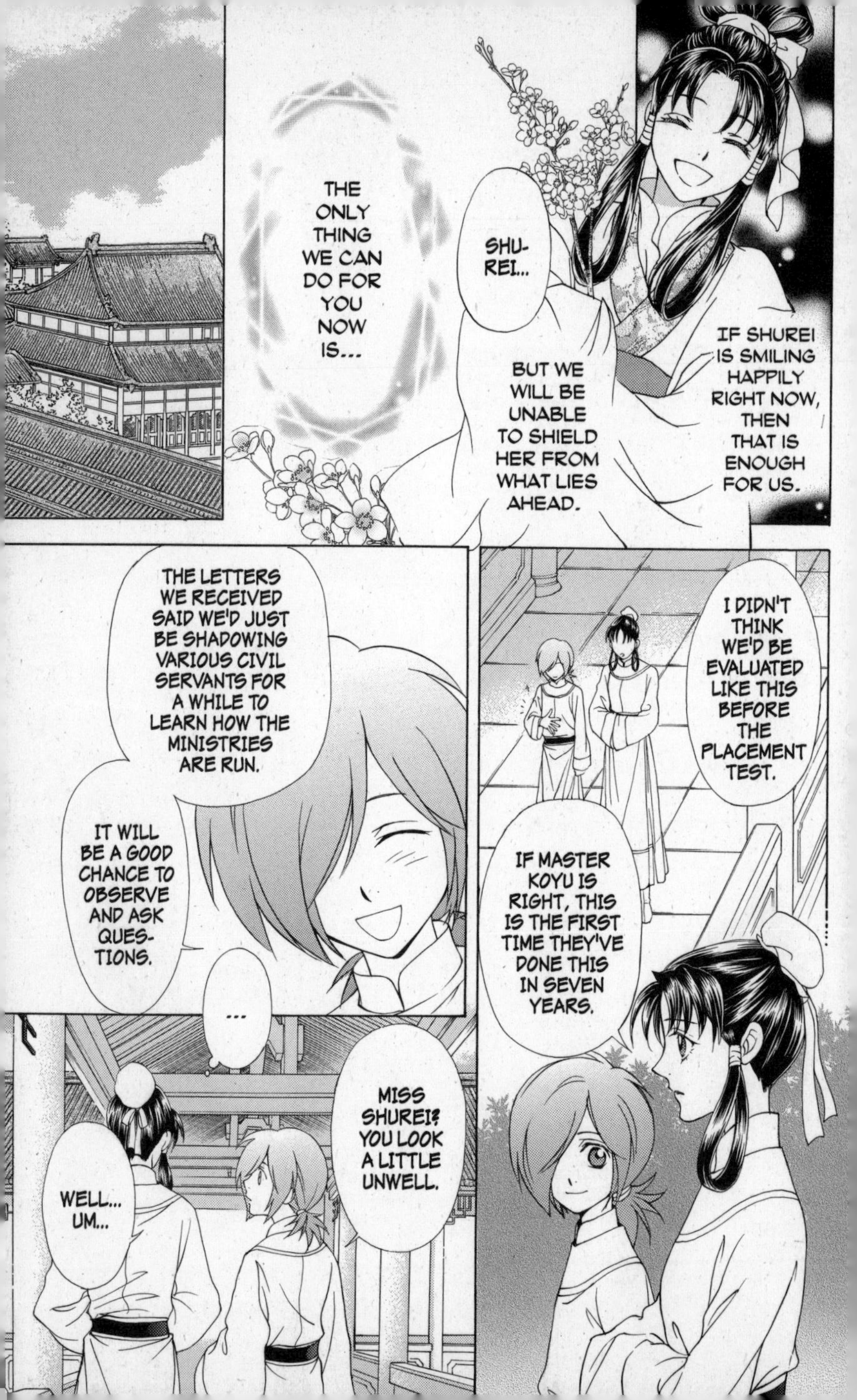
IF SHUREI IS SMILING HAPPILY RIGHT NOW, THEN THAT IS ENOUGH FOR US.
SHU-REI...
BUT WE WILL BE UNABLE TO SHIELD HER FROM WHAT LIES AHEAD.
THE ONLY THING WE CAN DO FOR YOU NOW IS...
I DIDN'T THINK WE'D BE EVALUATED LIKE THIS BEFORE THE PLACEMENT TEST.
IF MASTER KOYU IS RIGHT, THIS IS THE FIRST TIME THEY'VE DONE THIS IN SEVEN YEARS.
THE LETTERS WE RECEIVED SAID WE'D JUST BE SHADOWING VARIOUS CIVIL SERVANTS FOR A WHILE TO LEARN HOW THE MINISTRIES ARE RUN.
IT WILL BE A GOOD CHANCE TO OBSERVE AND ASK QUES-TIONS.
...
MISS SHUREI? YOU LOOK A LITTLE UNWELL.
WELL... UM...

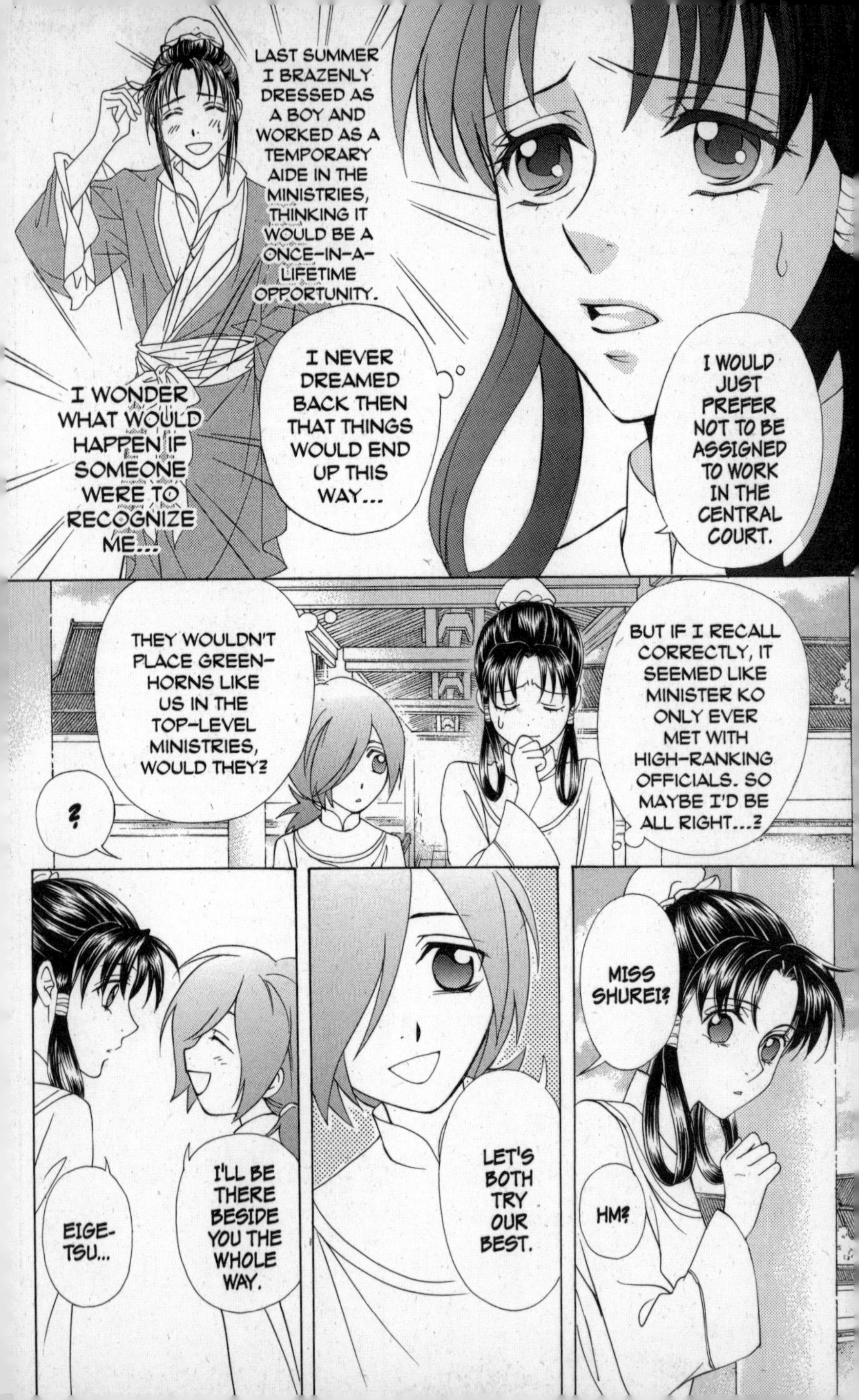
I WOULD JUST PREFER NOT TO BE ASSIGNED TO WORK IN THE CENTRAL COURT.
LAST SUMMER I BRAZENLY DRESSED AS A BOY AND WORKED AS A TEMPORARY AIDE IN THE MINISTRIES, THINKING IT WOULD BE A ONCE-IN-A-LIFETIME OPPORTUNITY.
I NEVER DREAMED BACK THEN THAT THINGS WOULD END UP THIS WAY...
I WONDER WHAT WOULD HAPPEN IF SOMEONE WERE TO RECOGNIZE ME...
BUT IF I RECALL CORRECTLY, IT SEEMED LIKE MINISTER KO ONLY EVER MET WITH HIGH-RANKING OFFICIALS. SO MAYBE I'D BE ALL RIGHT...?
THEY WOULDN'T PLACE GREENHORNS LIKE US IN THE TOP-LEVEL MINISTRIES, WOULD THEY?
?
MISS SHUREI?
HM?
LET'S BOTH TRY OUR BEST.
I'LL BE THERE BESIDE YOU THE WHOLE WAY.
EIGETSU...

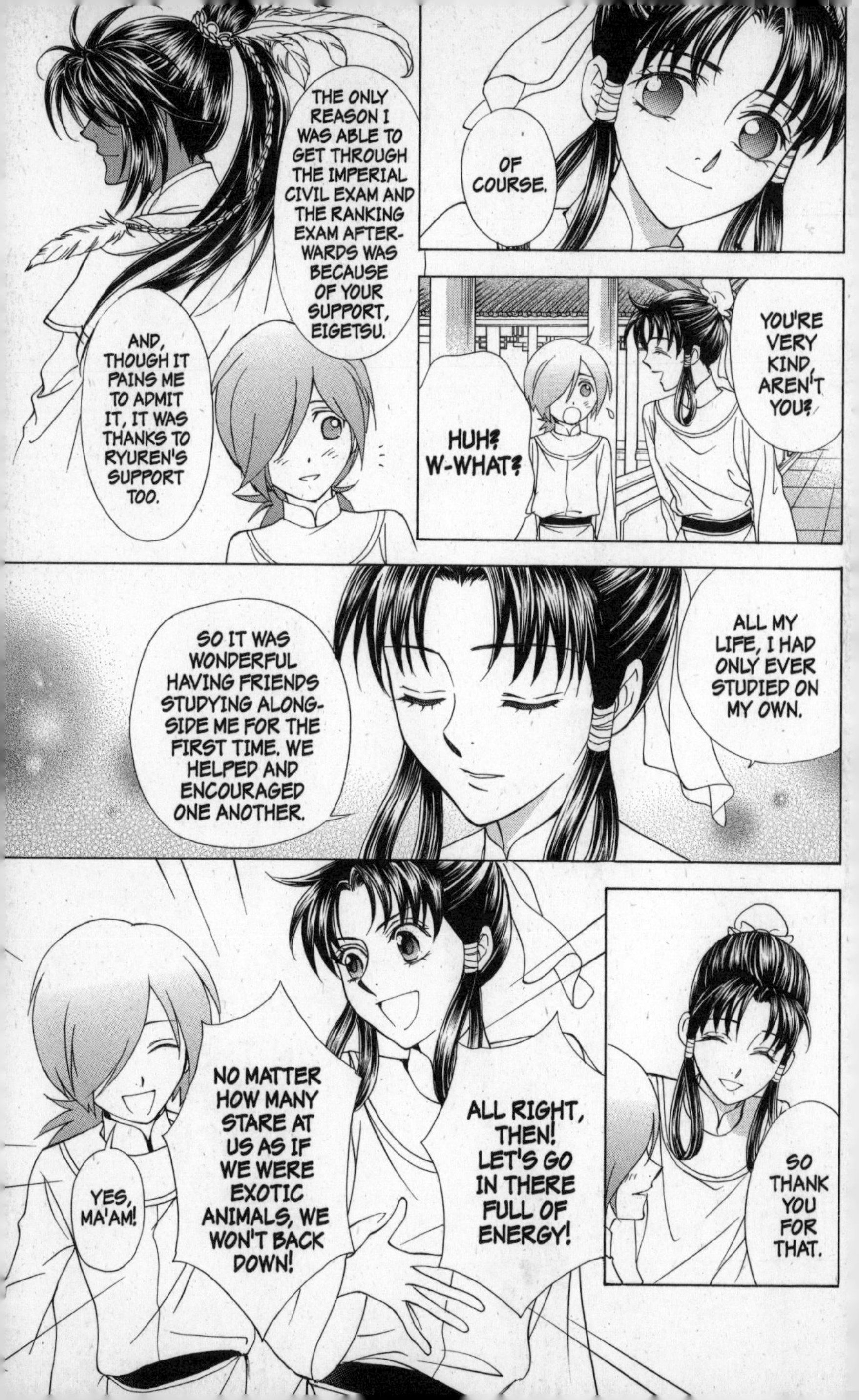
OF COURSE.
YOU'RE VERY KIND, AREN'T YOU?
HUH? W-WHAT?
THE ONLY REASON I WAS ABLE TO GET THROUGH THE IMPERIAL CIVIL EXAM AND THE RANKING EXAM AFTER-WARDS WAS BECAUSE OF YOUR SUPPORT, EIGETSU.
AND, THOUGH IT PAINS ME TO ADMIT IT, IT WAS THANKS TO RYUREN'S SUPPORT TOO.
ALL MY LIFE, I HAD ONLY EVER STUDIED ON MY OWN.
SO IT WAS WONDERFUL HAVING FRIENDS STUDYING ALONG-SIDE ME FOR THE FIRST TIME. WE HELPED AND ENCOURAGED ONE ANOTHER.
SO THANK YOU FOR THAT.
ALL RIGHT, THEN! LET'S GO IN THERE FULL OF ENERGY!
NO MATTER HOW MANY STARE AT US AS IF WE WERE EXOTIC ANIMALS, WE WON'T BACK DOWN!
YES, MA'AM!

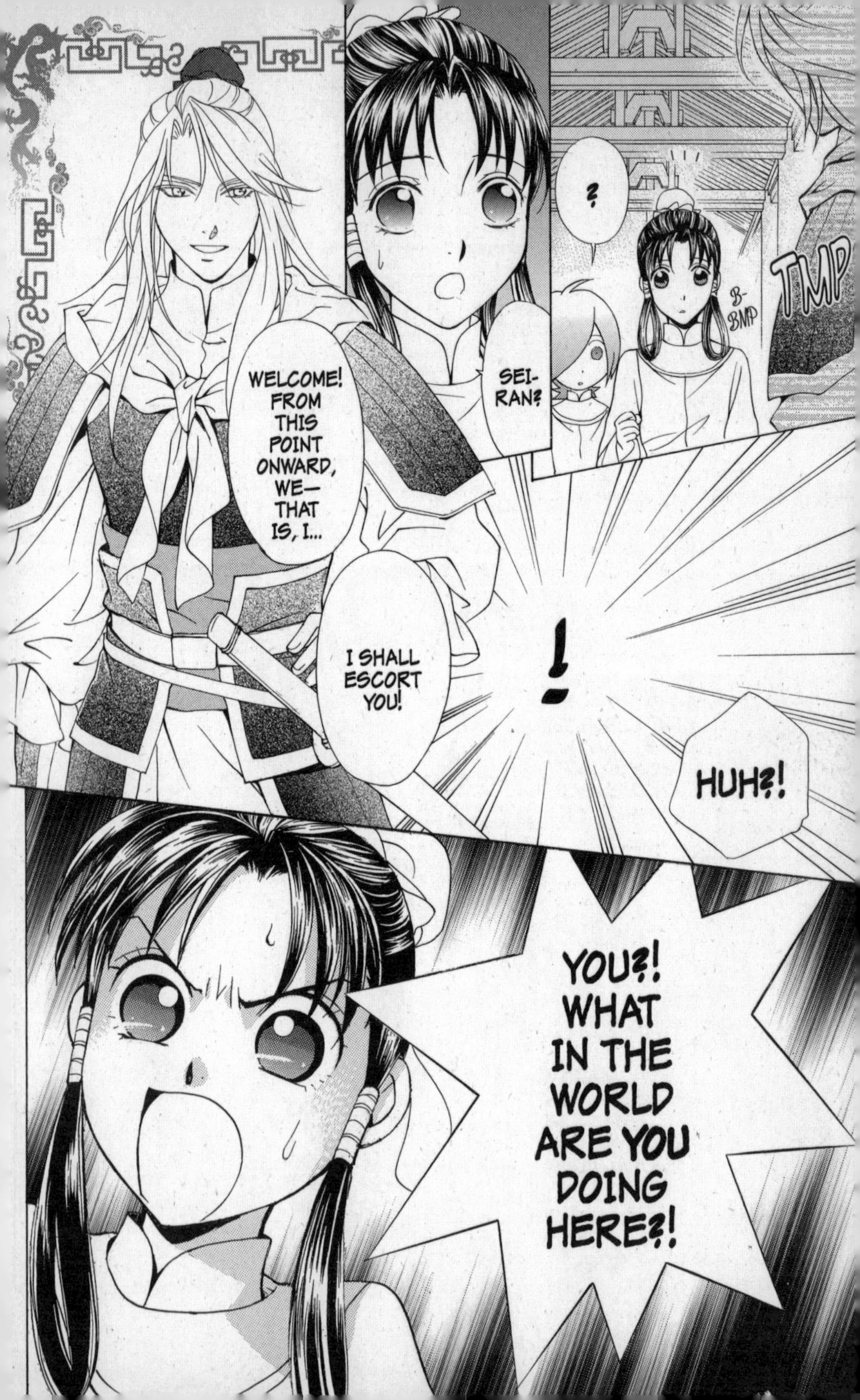
TMP
B-BMP
?
SEI-RAN?
WELCOME! FROM THIS POINT ONWARD, WE—THAT IS, I...
I SHALL ESCORT YOU!
!
HUH?!
YOU?! WHAT IN THE WORLD ARE YOU DOING HERE?!

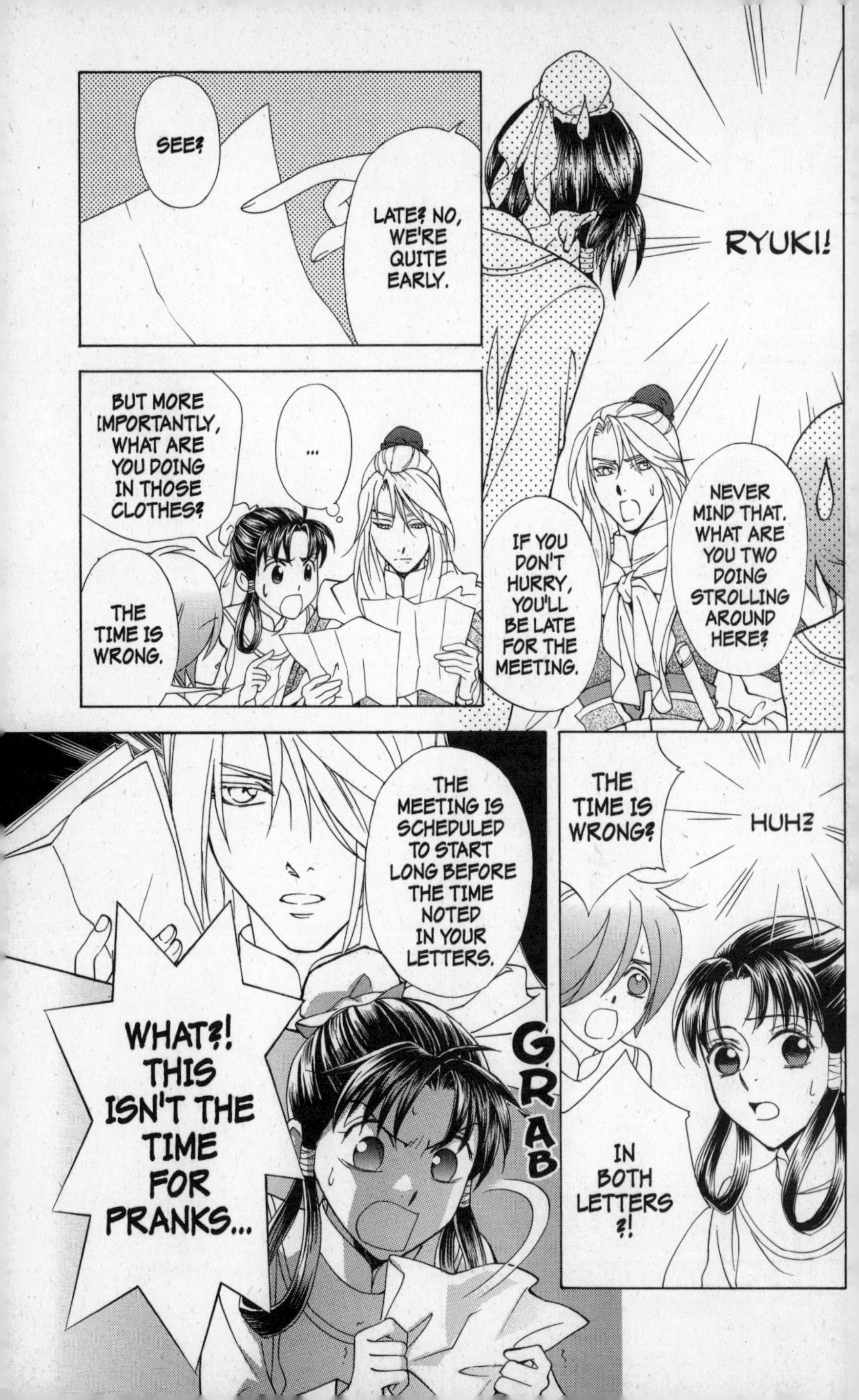
RYUKI!
NEVER MIND THAT. WHAT ARE YOU TWO DOING STROLLING AROUND HERE?
IF YOU DON'T HURRY, YOU'LL BE LATE FOR THE MEETING.
LATE? NO, WE'RE QUITE EARLY.
SEE?
...
BUT MORE IMPORTANTLY, WHAT ARE YOU DOING IN THOSE CLOTHES?
THE TIME IS WRONG.
HUH?
THE TIME IS WRONG?
IN BOTH LETTERS?!
THE MEETING IS SCHEDULED TO START LONG BEFORE THE TIME NOTED IN YOUR LETTERS.
GRAB
WHAT?! THIS ISN'T THE TIME FOR PRANKS...

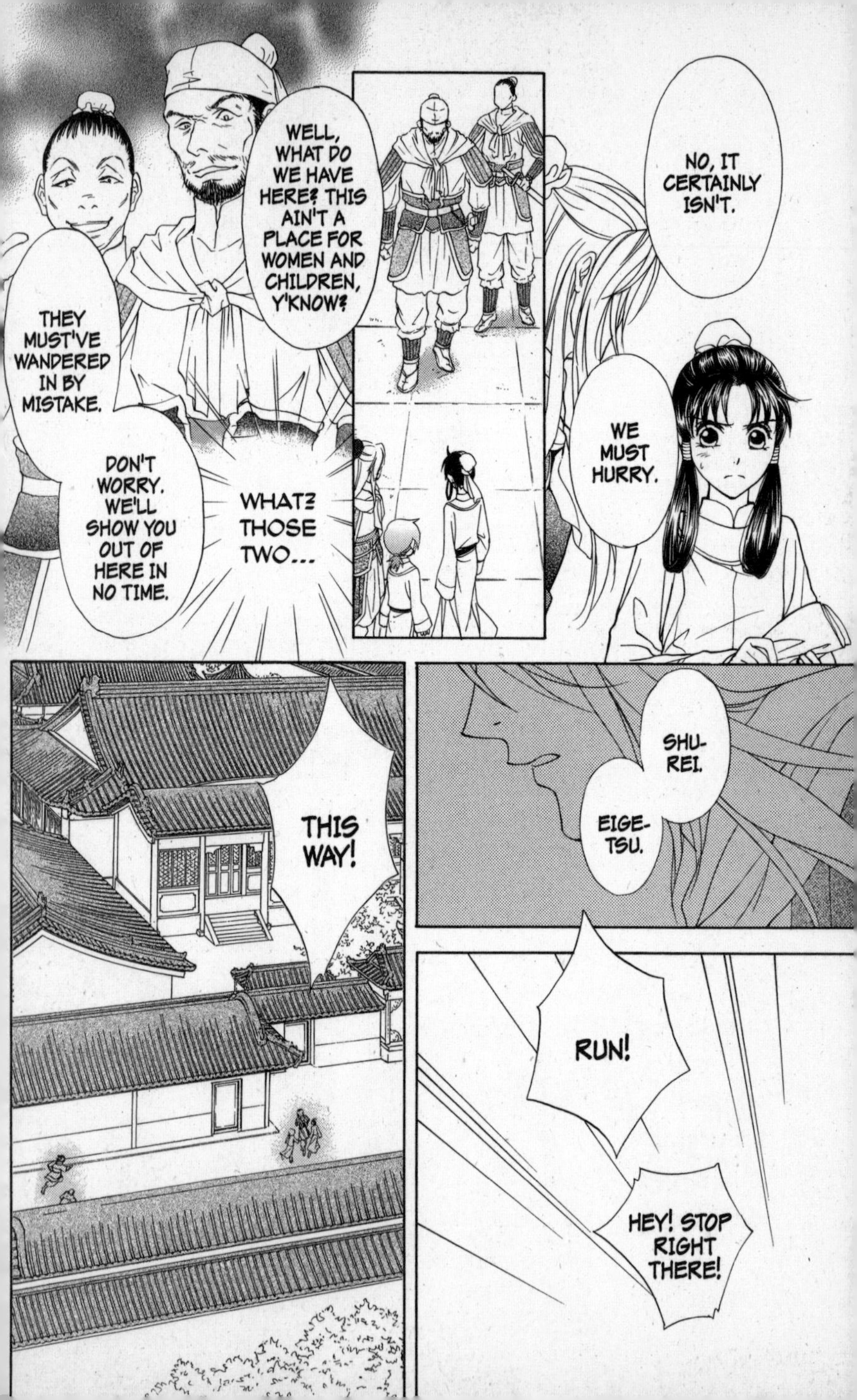
NO, IT CERTAINLY ISN'T.
WE MUST HURRY.
WELL, WHAT DO WE HAVE HERE? THIS AIN'T A PLACE FOR WOMEN AND CHILDREN, Y'KNOW?
WHAT? THOSE TWO...
THEY MUST'VE WANDERED IN BY MISTAKE.
DON'T WORRY. WE'LL SHOW YOU OUT OF HERE IN NO TIME.
SHU-REI.
EIGE-TSU.
RUN!
HEY! STOP RIGHT THERE!
THIS WAY!

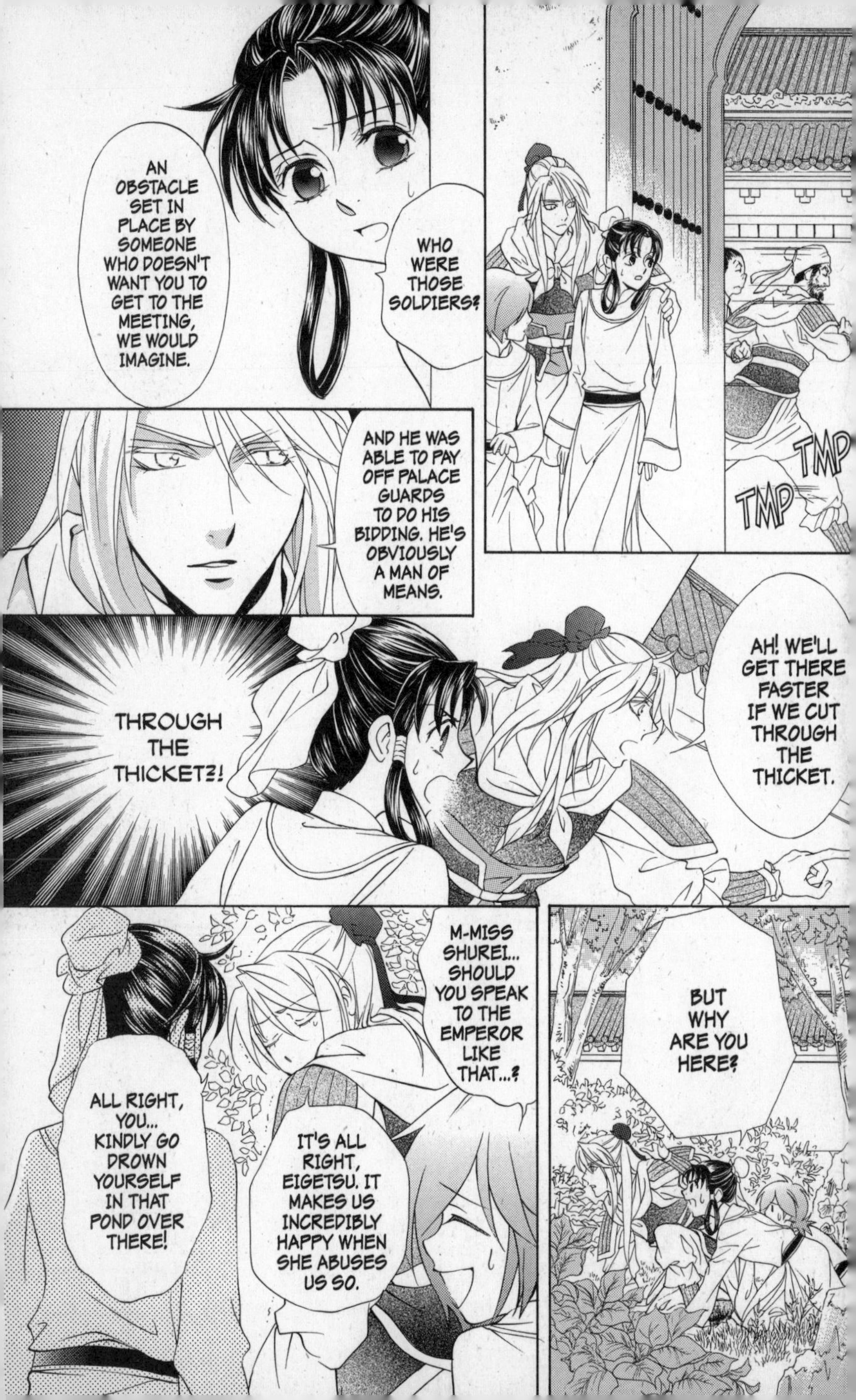
TMP
TMP
WHO WERE THOSE SOLDIERS?
AN OBSTACLE SET IN PLACE BY SOMEONE WHO DOESN'T WANT YOU TO GET TO THE MEETING, WE WOULD IMAGINE.
AND HE WAS ABLE TO PAY OFF PALACE GUARDS TO DO HIS BIDDING. HE'S OBVIOUSLY A MAN OF MEANS.
AH! WE'LL GET THERE FASTER IF WE CUT THROUGH THE THICKET.
THROUGH THE THICKET?!
BUT WHY ARE YOU HERE?
M-MISS SHUREI... SHOULD YOU SPEAK TO THE EMPEROR LIKE THAT...?
IT'S ALL RIGHT, EIGETSU. IT MAKES US INCREDIBLY HAPPY WHEN SHE ABUSES US SO.
ALL RIGHT, YOU... KINDLY GO DROWN YOURSELF IN THAT POND OVER THERE!

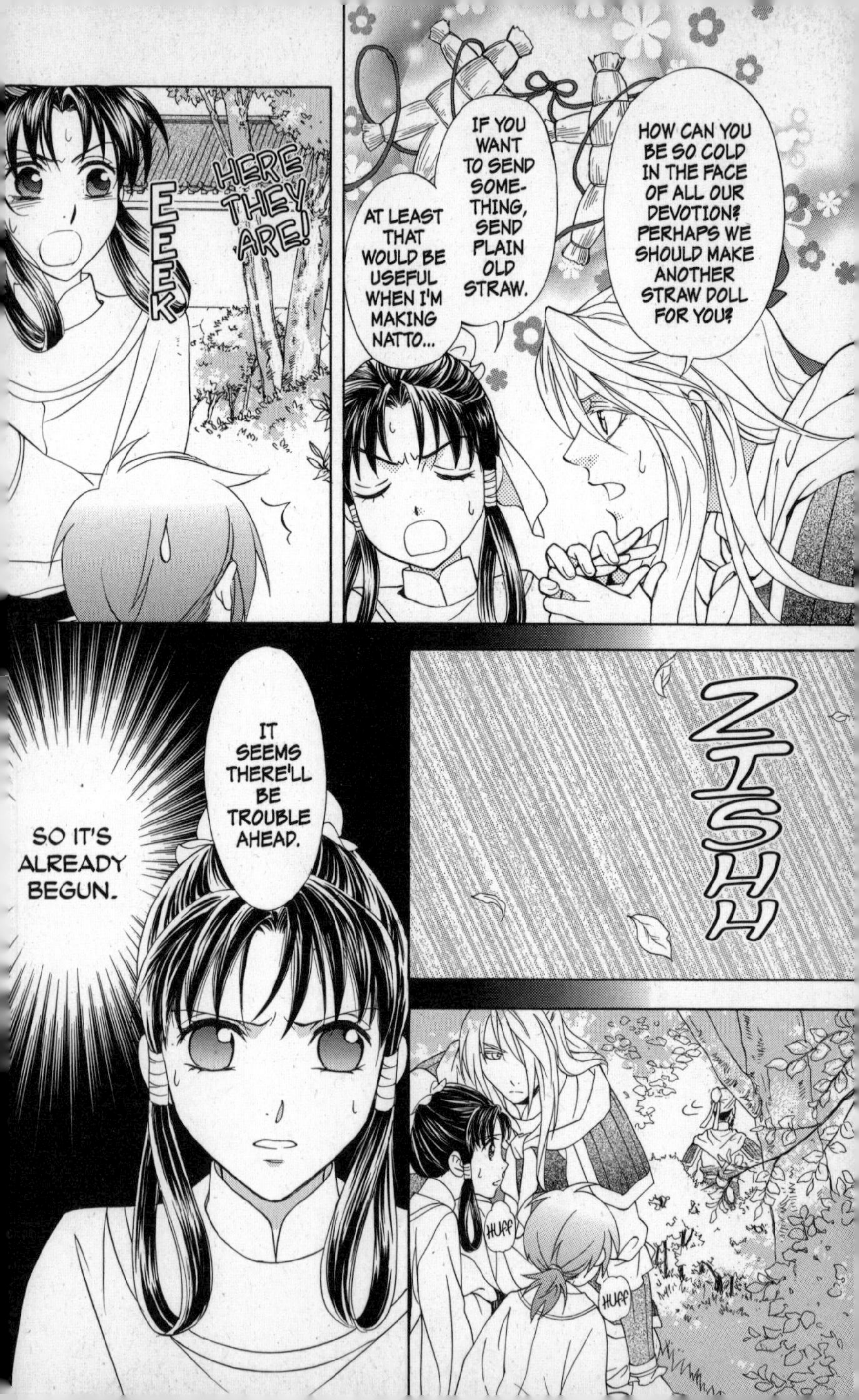
HOW CAN YOU BE SO COLD IN THE FACE OF ALL OUR DEVOTION? PERHAPS WE SHOULD MAKE ANOTHER STRAW DOLL FOR YOU?
IF YOU WANT TO SEND SOME-THING, SEND PLAIN OLD STRAW.
AT LEAST THAT WOULD BE USEFUL WHEN I'M MAKING NATTO...
HERE THEY ARE!
EEEK
ZISHH
HUFF
HUFF
IT SEEMS THERE'LL BE TROUBLE AHEAD.
SO IT'S ALREADY BEGUN.

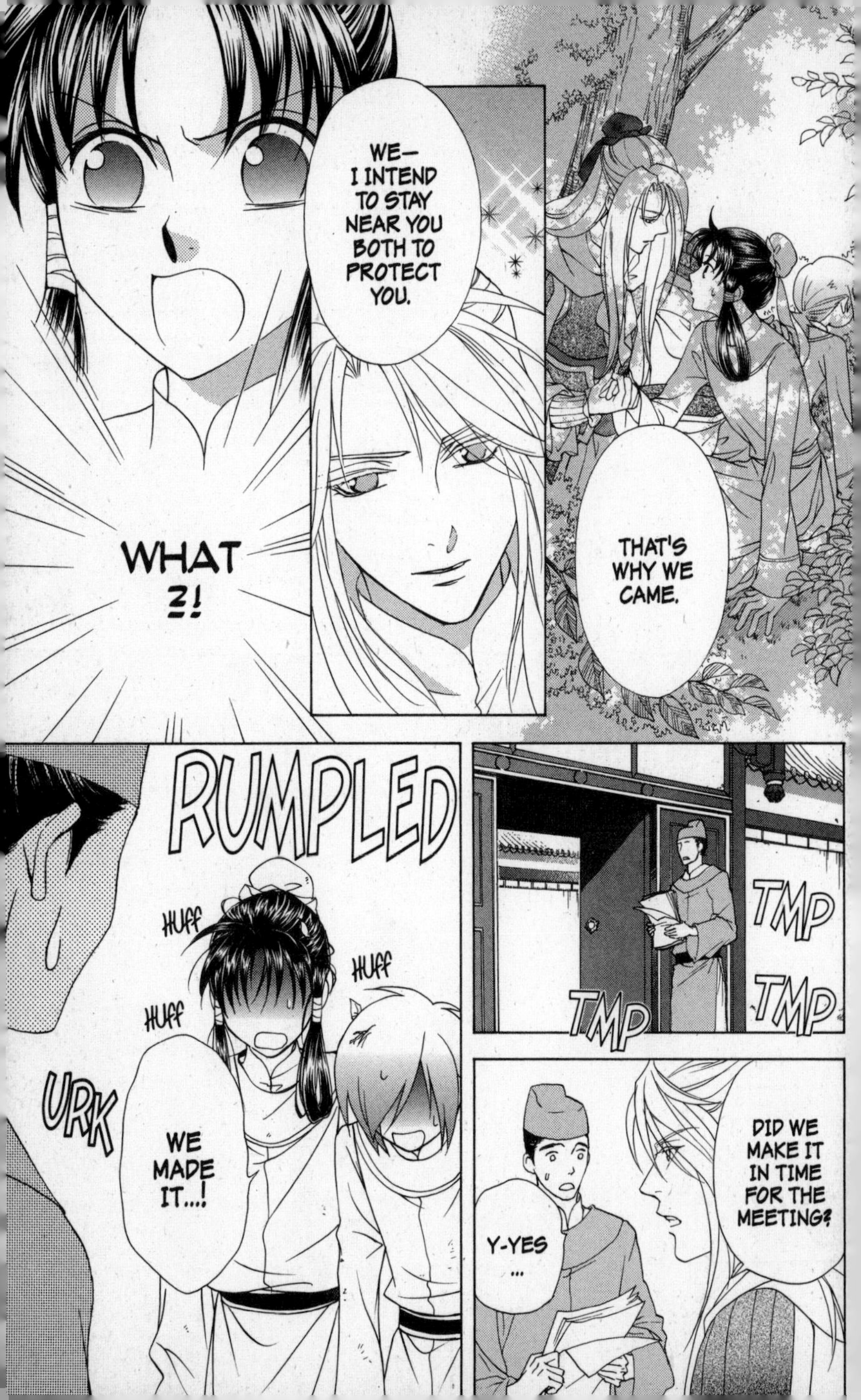

WE— I INTEND TO STAY NEAR YOU BOTH TO PROTECT YOU.
THAT'S WHY WE CAME.
WHAT ?!
TMP
TMP
TMP
DID WE MAKE IT IN TIME FOR THE MEETING?
Y-YES ...
RUMPLED
HUFF
HUFF
HUFF
WE MADE IT...!
URK

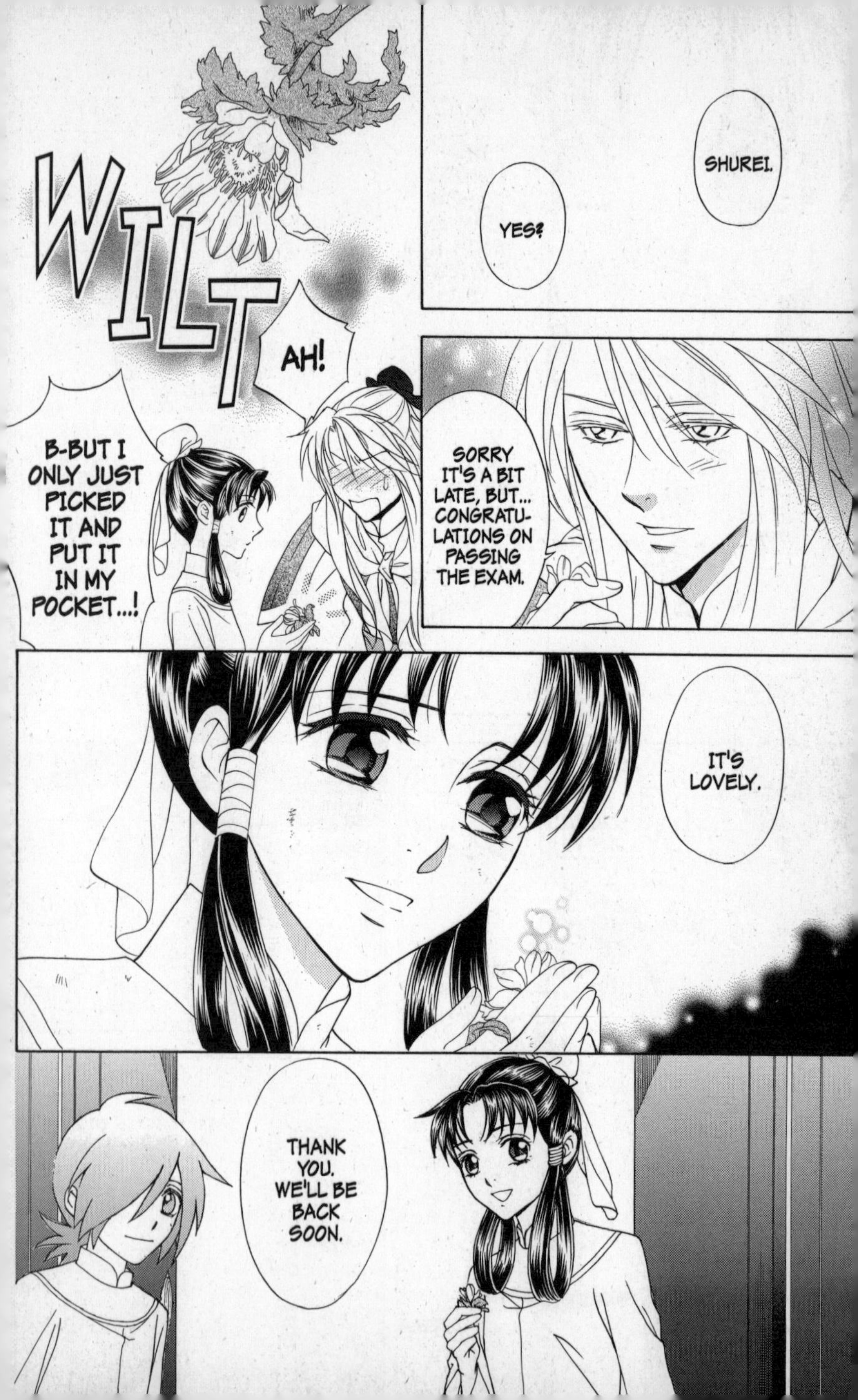
SHUREI.
YES?
SORRY IT'S A BIT LATE, BUT... CONGRATULATIONS ON PASSING THE EXAM.
WILT
AH!
B-BUT I ONLY JUST PICKED IT AND PUT IT IN MY POCKET...!
IT'S LOVELY.
THANK YOU. WE'LL BE BACK SOON.

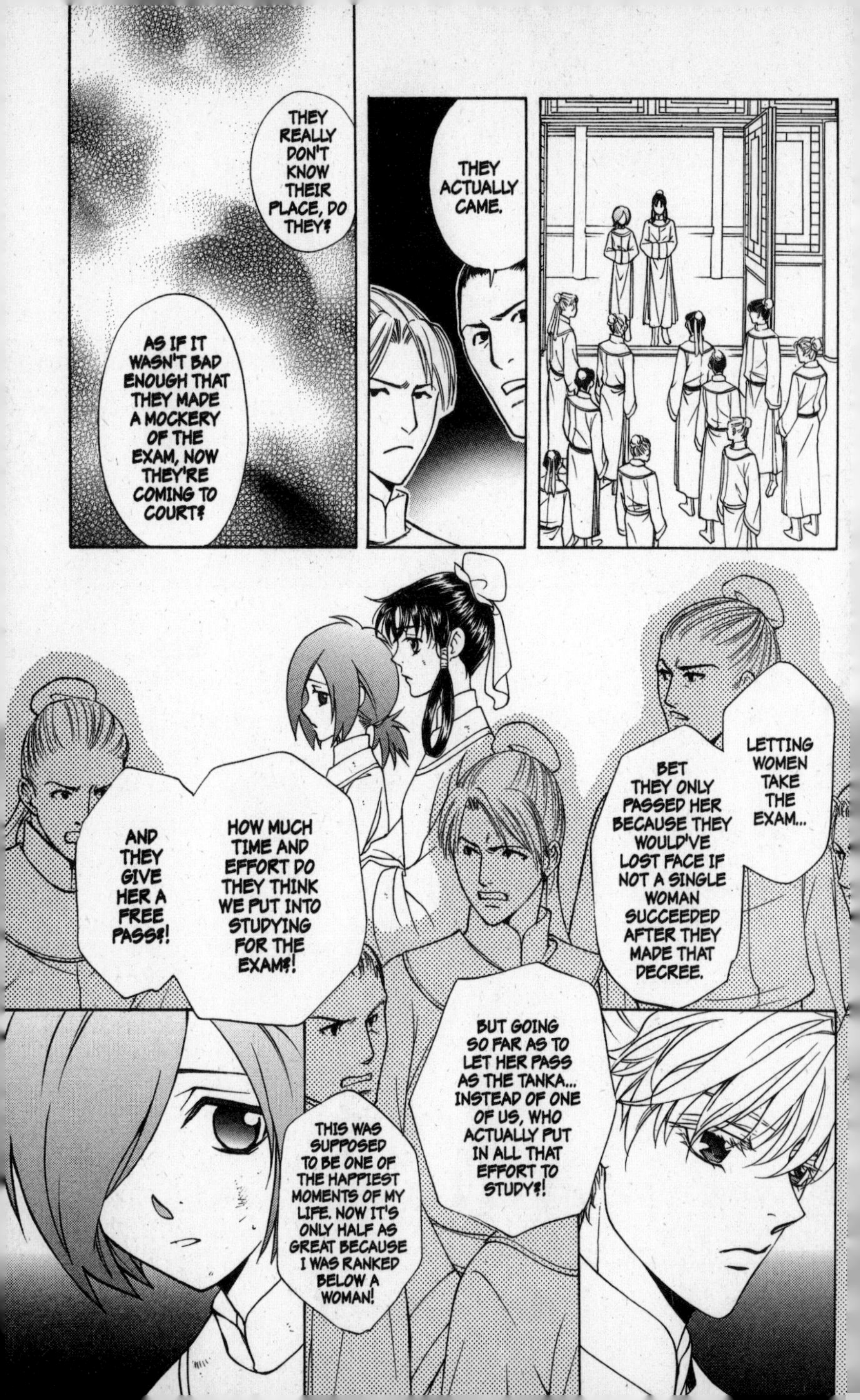
THEY ACTUALLY CAME.
THEY REALLY DON'T KNOW THEIR PLACE, DO THEY?
AS IF IT WASN'T BAD ENOUGH THAT THEY MADE A MOCKERY OF THE EXAM, NOW THEY'RE COMING TO COURT?
LETTING WOMEN TAKE THE EXAM...
BET THEY ONLY PASSED HER BECAUSE THEY WOULD'VE LOST FACE IF NOT A SINGLE WOMAN SUCCEEDED AFTER THEY MADE THAT DECREE.
HOW MUCH TIME AND EFFORT DO THEY THINK WE PUT INTO STUDYING FOR THE EXAM?!
AND THEY GIVE HER A FREE PASS?!
BUT GOING SO FAR AS TO LET HER PASS AS THE TANKA... INSTEAD OF ONE OF US, WHO ACTUALLY PUT IN ALL THAT EFFORT TO STUDY?!
THIS WAS SUPPOSED TO BE ONE OF THE HAPPIEST MOMENTS OF MY LIFE. NOW IT'S ONLY HALF AS GREAT BECAUSE I WAS RANKED BELOW A WOMAN!

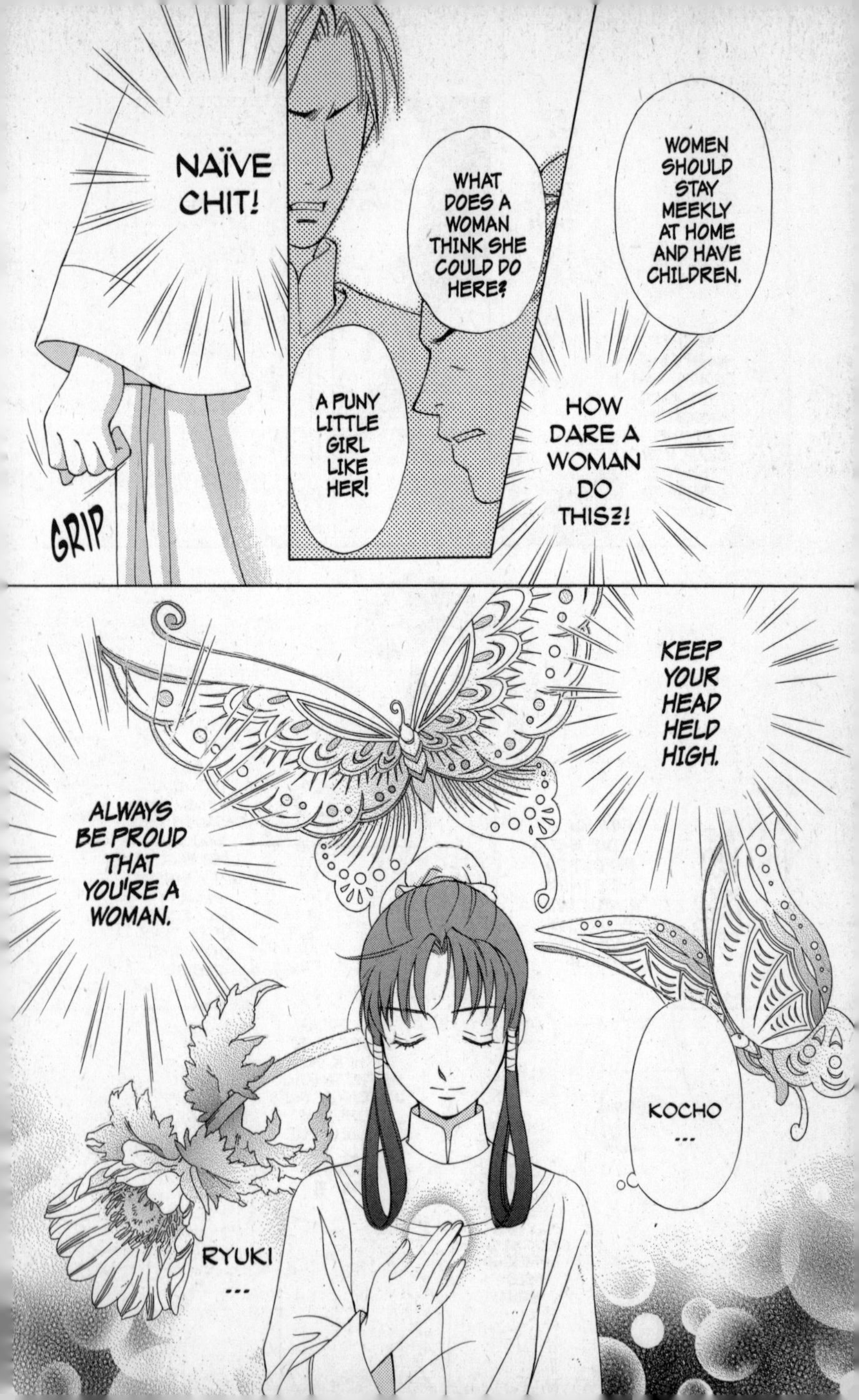
WOMEN SHOULD STAY MEEKLY AT HOME AND HAVE CHILDREN.
HOW DARE A WOMAN DO THIS?!
WHAT DOES A WOMAN THINK SHE COULD DO HERE?
A PUNY LITTLE GIRL LIKE HER!
NAÏVE CHIT!
GRIP
KEEP YOUR HEAD HELD HIGH.
KOCHO ...
ALWAYS BE PROUD THAT YOU'RE A WOMAN.
RYUKI ...

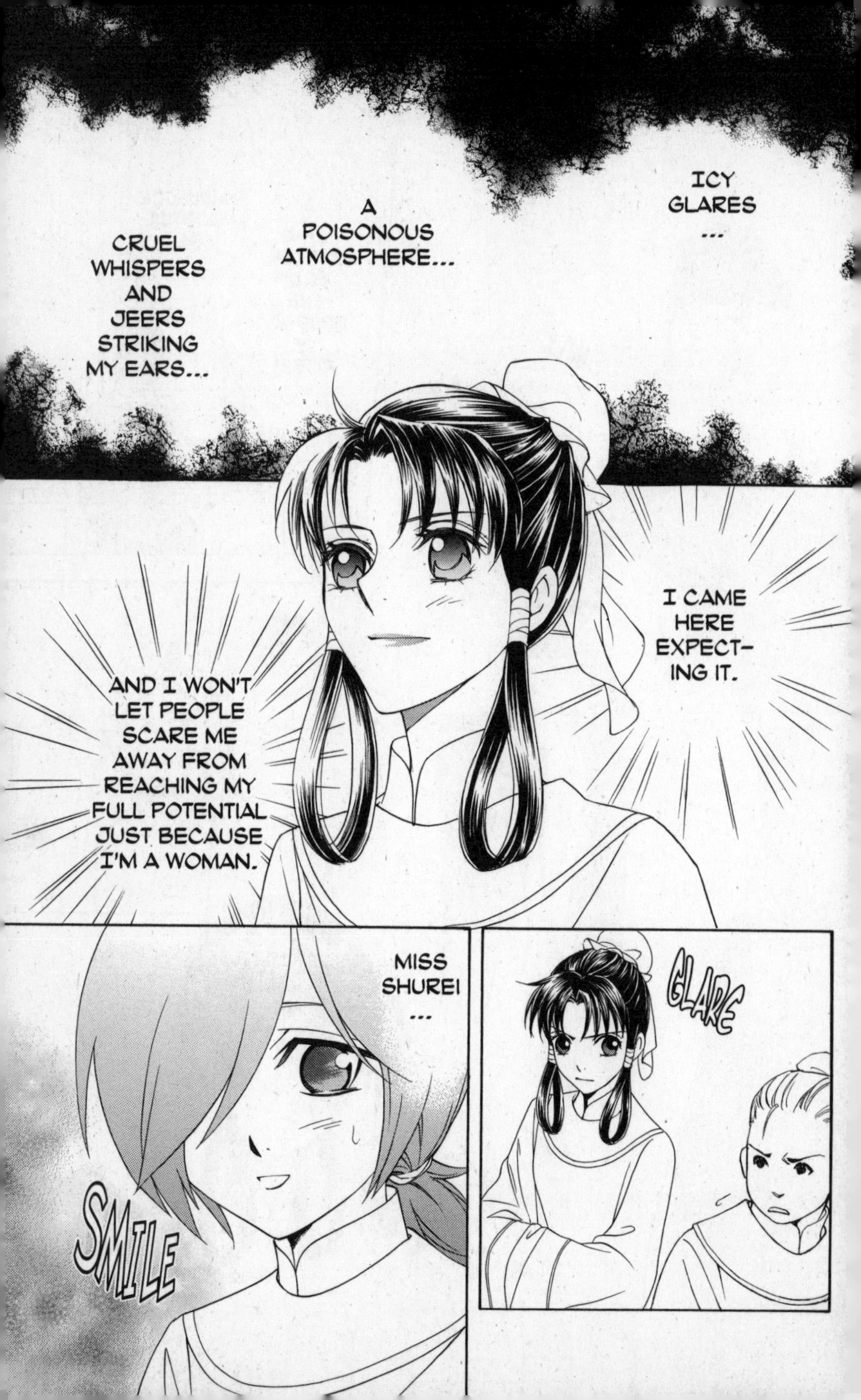
ICY GLARES ...
A POISONOUS ATMOSPHERE...
CRUEL WHISPERS AND JEERS STRIKING MY EARS...
I CAME HERE EXPECT-ING IT.
AND I WON'T LET PEOPLE SCARE ME AWAY FROM REACHING MY FULL POTENTIAL JUST BECAUSE I'M A WOMAN.
GLARE
MISS SHUREI ...
SMILE

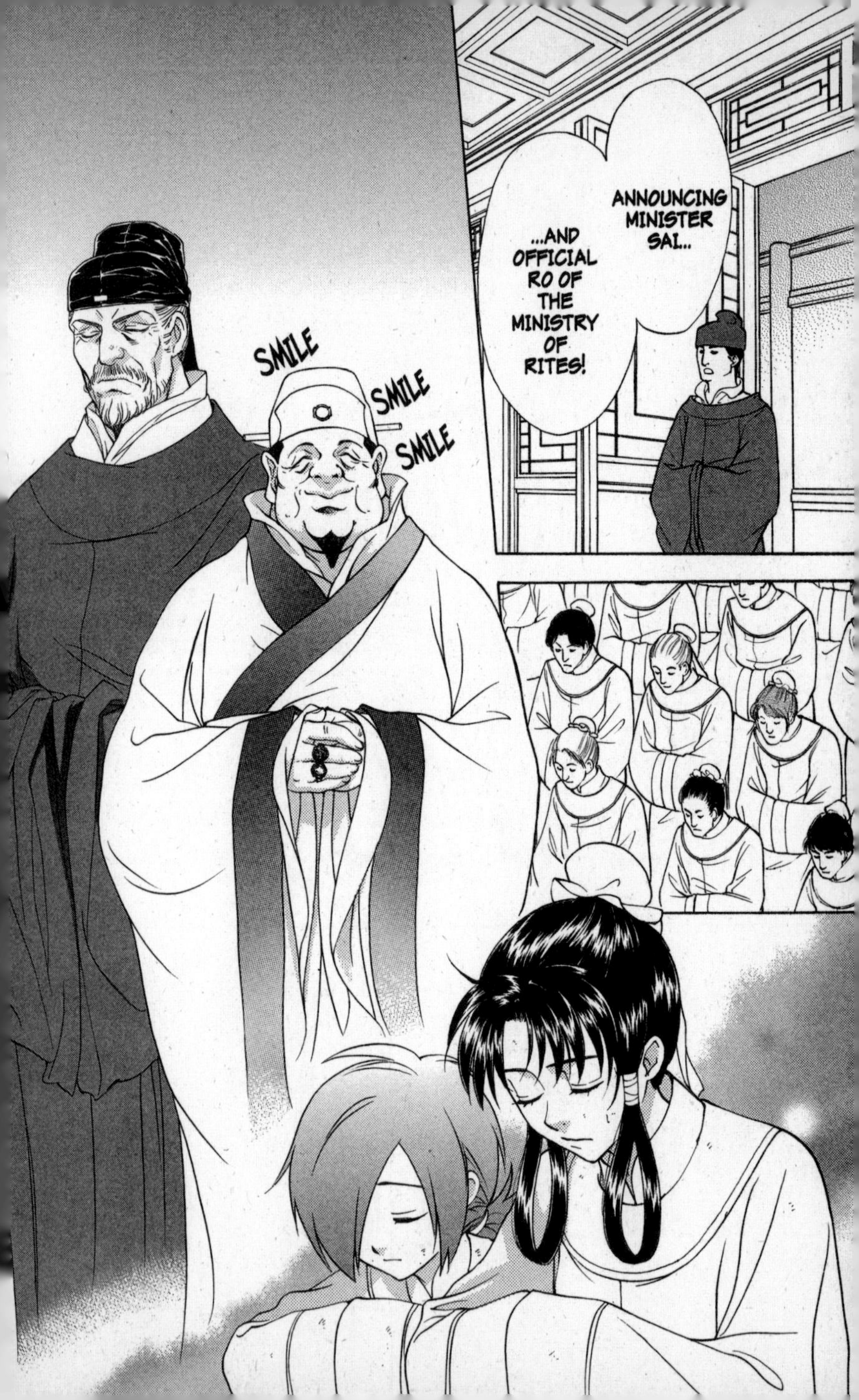
ANNOUNCING MINISTER SAI...
...AND OFFICIAL RO OF THE MINISTRY OF RITES!
SMILE
SMILE
SMILE

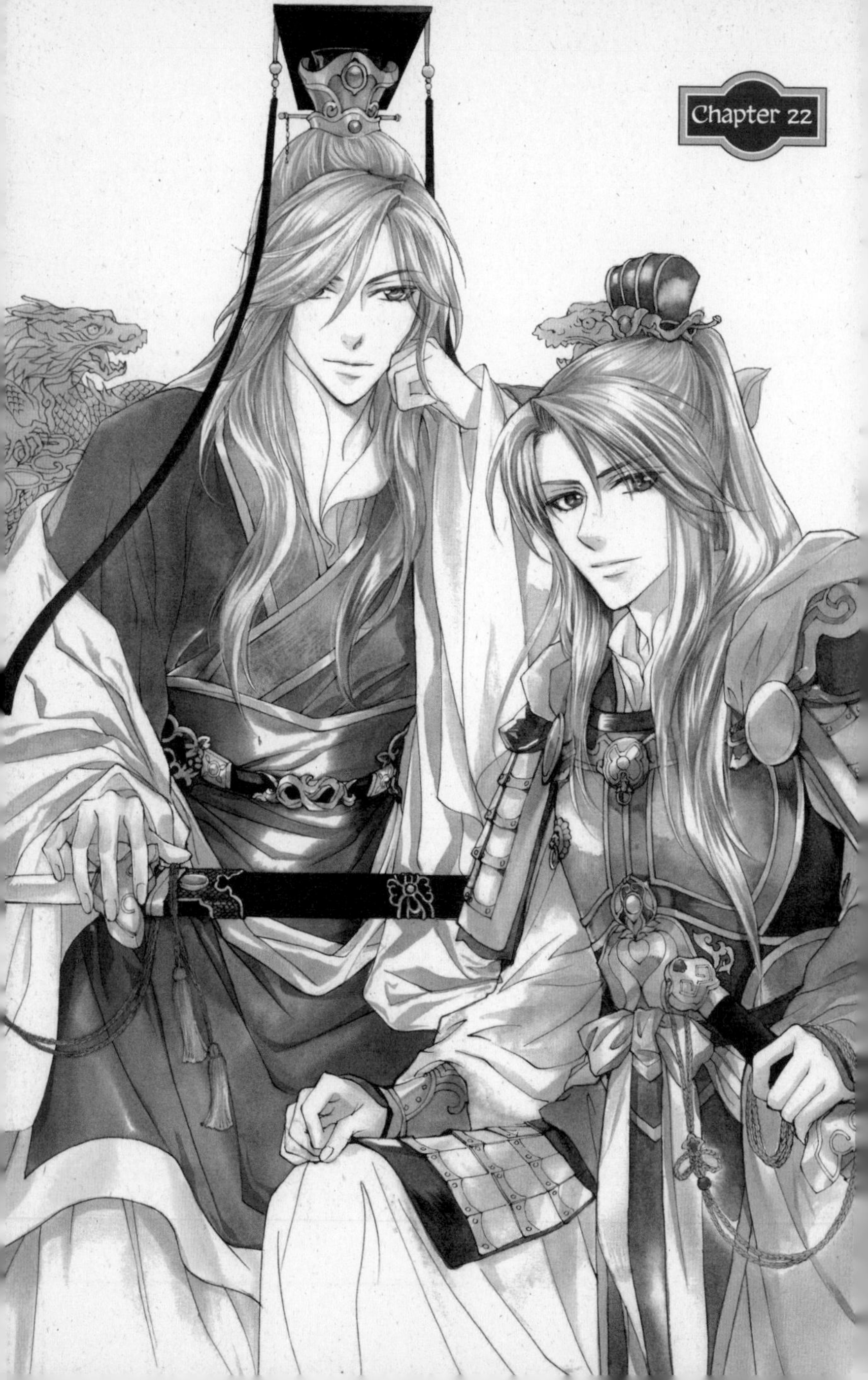
Chapter 22

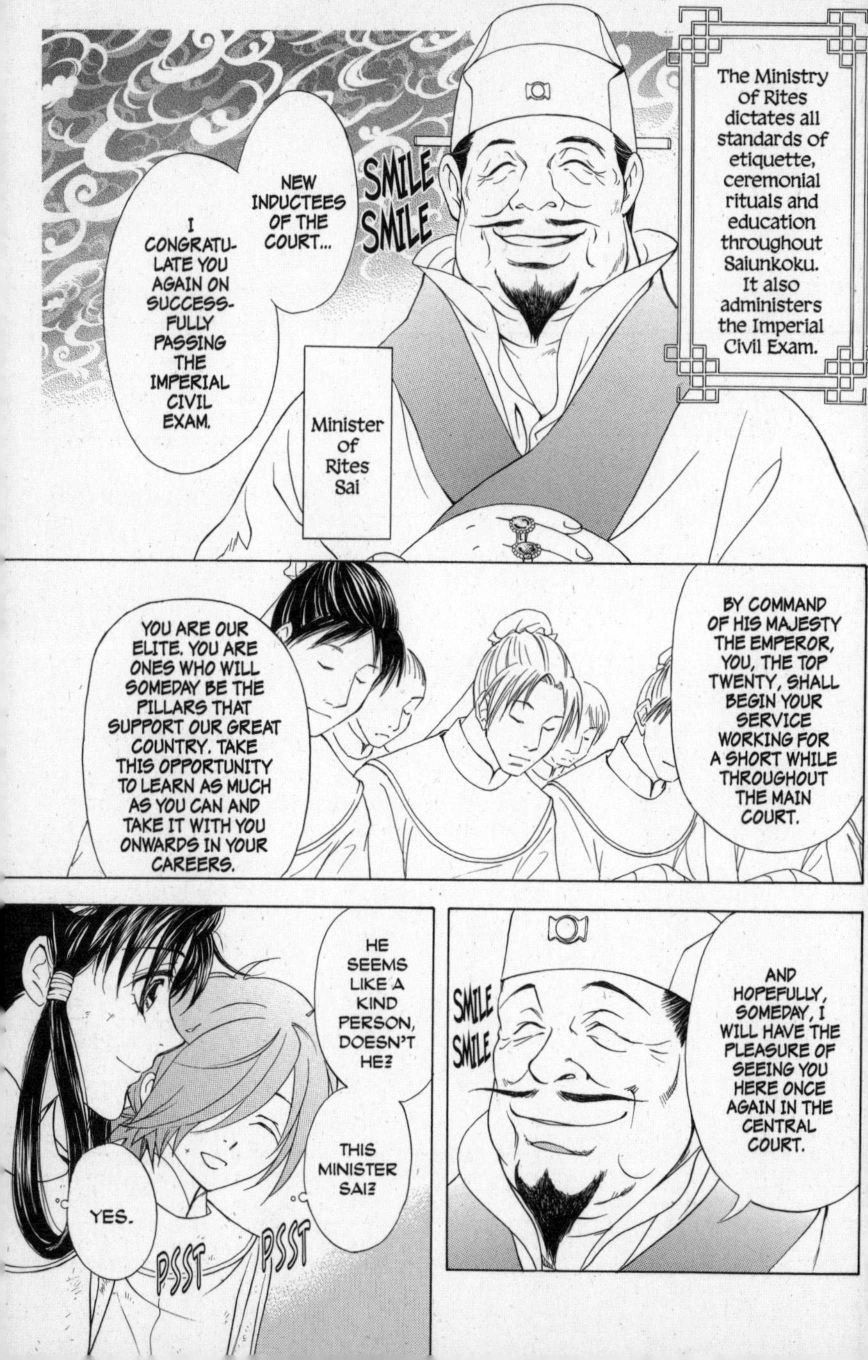
The Ministry of Rites dictates all standards of etiquette, ceremonial rituals and education throughout Saiunkoku. It also administers the Imperial Civil Exam.
SMILE SMILE
NEW INDUCTEES OF THE COURT...
I CONGRATULATE YOU AGAIN ON SUCCESSFULLY PASSING THE IMPERIAL CIVIL EXAM.
Minister of Rites Sai
BY COMMAND OF HIS MAJESTY THE EMPEROR, YOU, THE TOP TWENTY, SHALL BEGIN YOUR SERVICE WORKING FOR A SHORT WHILE THROUGHOUT THE MAIN COURT.
YOU ARE OUR ELITE. YOU ARE ONES WHO WILL SOMEDAY BE THE PILLARS THAT SUPPORT OUR GREAT COUNTRY. TAKE THIS OPPORTUNITY TO LEARN AS MUCH AS YOU CAN AND TAKE IT WITH YOU ONWARDS IN YOUR CAREERS.
SMILE SMILE
AND HOPEFULLY, SOMEDAY, I WILL HAVE THE PLEASURE OF SEEING YOU HERE ONCE AGAIN IN THE CENTRAL COURT.
HE SEEMS LIKE A KIND PERSON, DOESN'T HE?
THIS MINISTER SAI?
YES.
PSST PSST

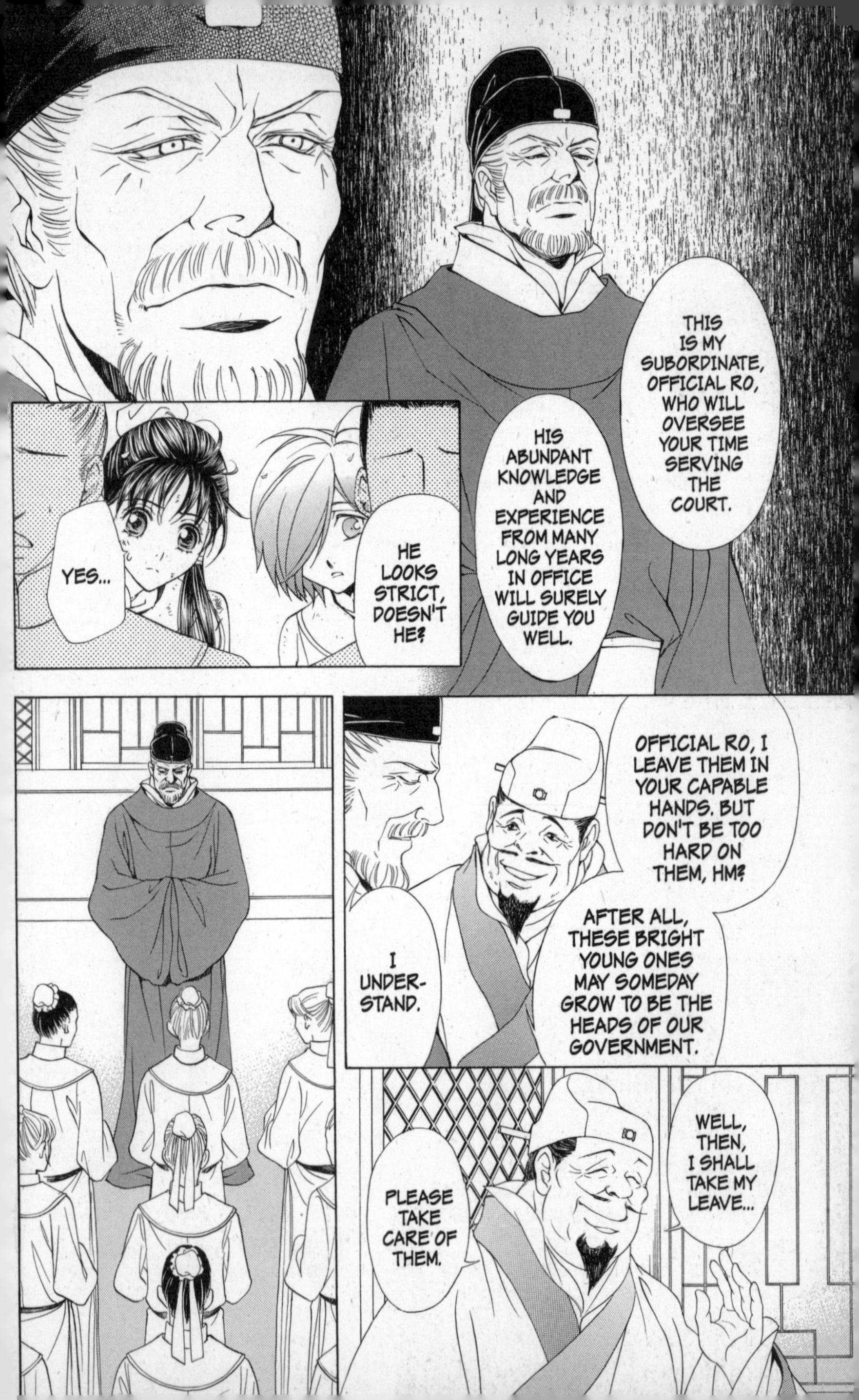
THIS IS MY SUBORDINATE, OFFICIAL RO, WHO WILL OVERSEE YOUR TIME SERVING THE COURT.
HIS ABUNDANT KNOWLEDGE AND EXPERIENCE FROM MANY LONG YEARS IN OFFICE WILL SURELY GUIDE YOU WELL.
HE LOOKS STRICT, DOESN'T HE?
YES...
OFFICIAL RO, I LEAVE THEM IN YOUR CAPABLE HANDS. BUT DON'T BE TOO HARD ON THEM, HM?
AFTER ALL, THESE BRIGHT YOUNG ONES MAY SOMEDAY GROW TO BE THE HEADS OF OUR GOVERNMENT.
I UNDER-STAND.
WELL, THEN, I SHALL TAKE MY LEAVE...
PLEASE TAKE CARE OF THEM.

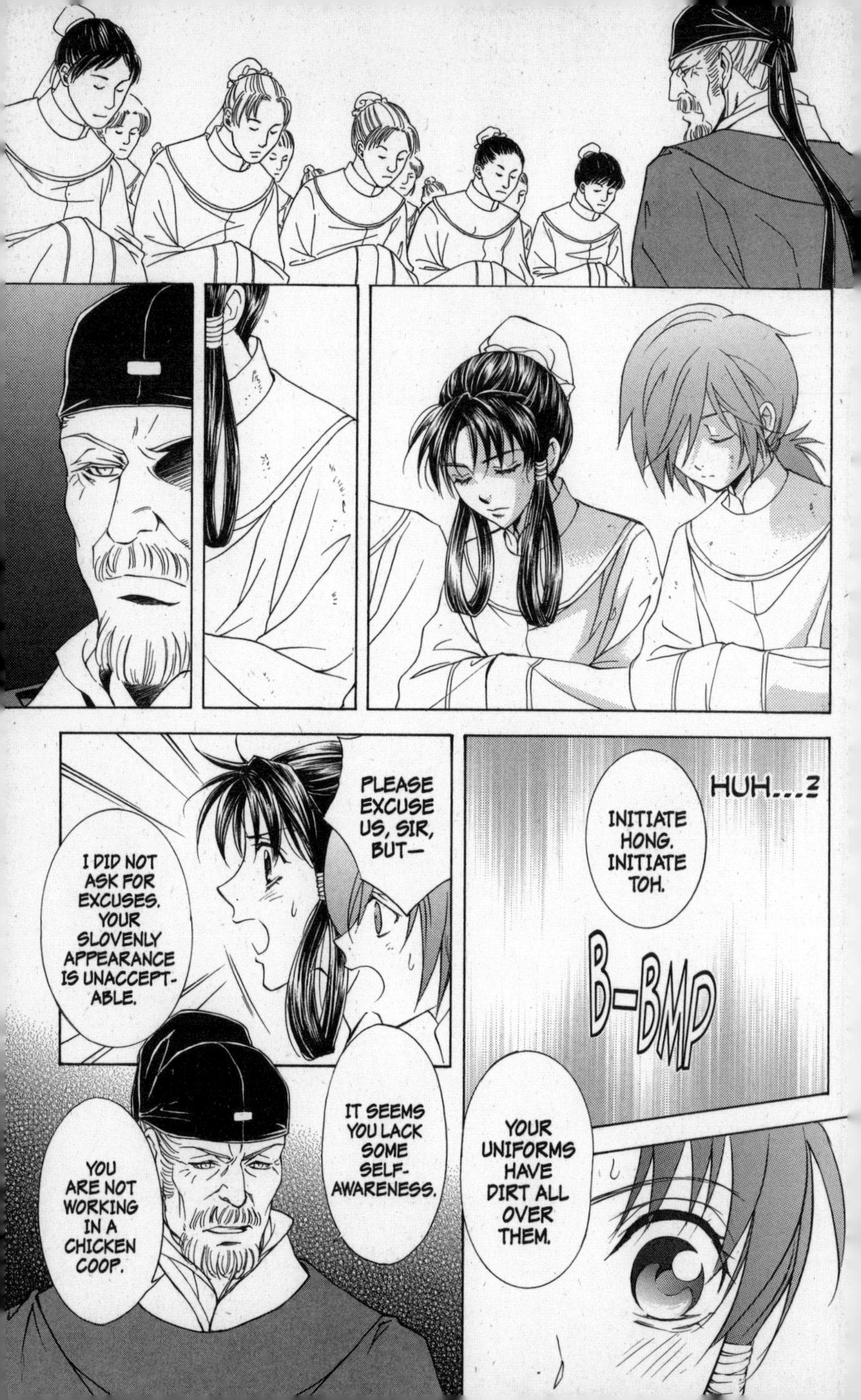
HUH...?
INITIATE HONG. INITIATE TOH.
B-BMP
YOUR UNIFORMS HAVE DIRT ALL OVER THEM.
IT SEEMS YOU LACK SOME SELF-AWARENESS.
YOU ARE NOT WORKING IN A CHICKEN COOP.
PLEASE EXCUSE US, SIR, BUT—
I DID NOT ASK FOR EXCUSES. YOUR SLOVENLY APPEARANCE IS UNACCEPT-ABLE.

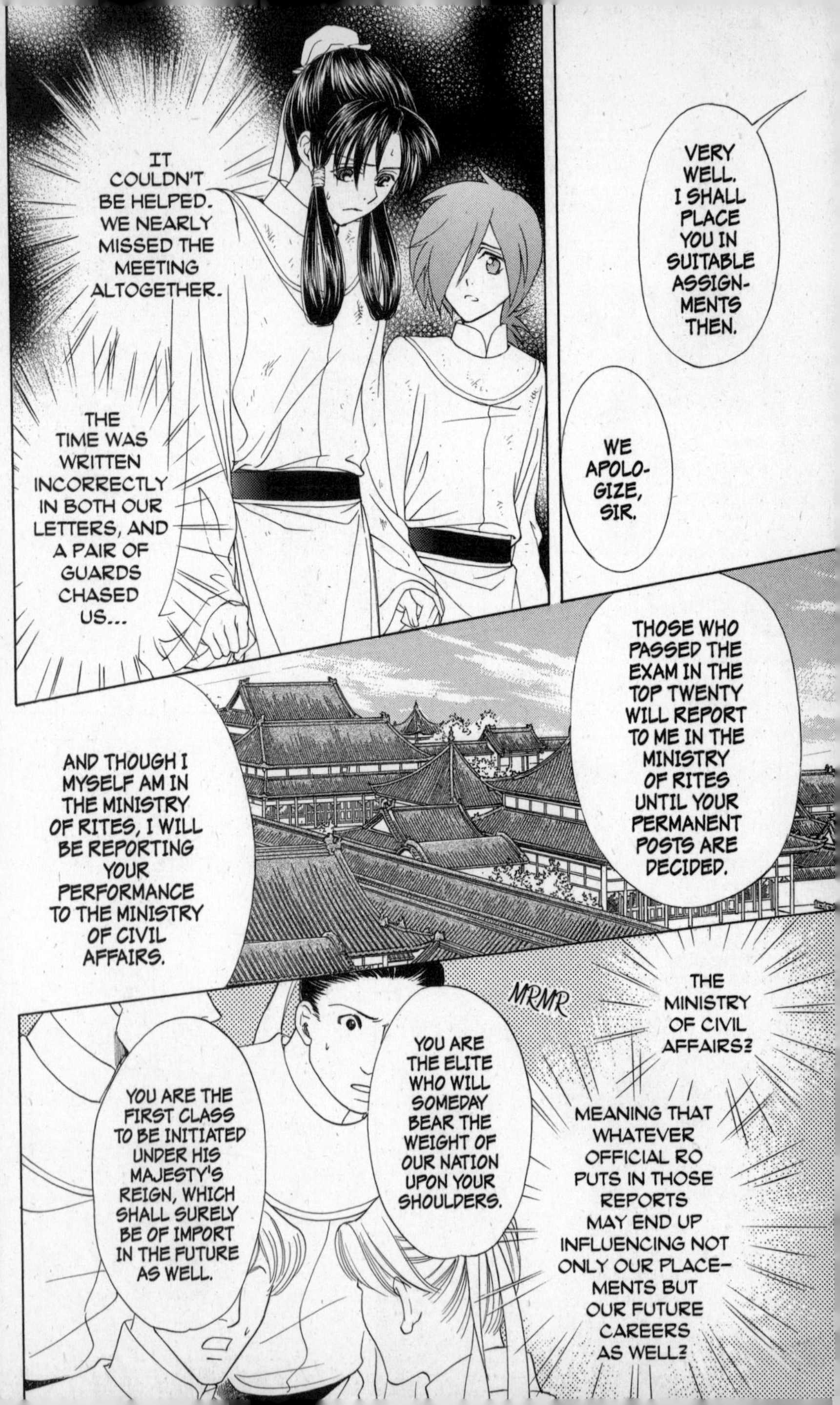
VERY WELL. I SHALL PLACE YOU IN SUITABLE ASSIGNMENTS THEN.
WE APOLOGIZE, SIR.
IT COULDN'T BE HELPED. WE NEARLY MISSED THE MEETING ALTOGETHER.
THE TIME WAS WRITTEN INCORRECTLY IN BOTH OUR LETTERS, AND A PAIR OF GUARDS CHASED US...
THOSE WHO PASSED THE EXAM IN THE TOP TWENTY WILL REPORT TO ME IN THE MINISTRY OF RITES UNTIL YOUR PERMANENT POSTS ARE DECIDED.
AND THOUGH I MYSELF AM IN THE MINISTRY OF RITES, I WILL BE REPORTING YOUR PERFORMANCE TO THE MINISTRY OF CIVIL AFFAIRS.
THE MINISTRY OF CIVIL AFFAIRS?
MEANING THAT WHATEVER OFFICIAL RO PUTS IN THOSE REPORTS MAY END UP INFLUENCING NOT ONLY OUR PLACEMENTS BUT OUR FUTURE CAREERS AS WELL?
MRMR
YOU ARE THE ELITE WHO WILL SOMEDAY BEAR THE WEIGHT OF OUR NATION UPON YOUR SHOULDERS.
YOU ARE THE FIRST CLASS TO BE INITIATED UNDER HIS MAJESTY'S REIGN, WHICH SHALL SURELY BE OF IMPORT IN THE FUTURE AS WELL.

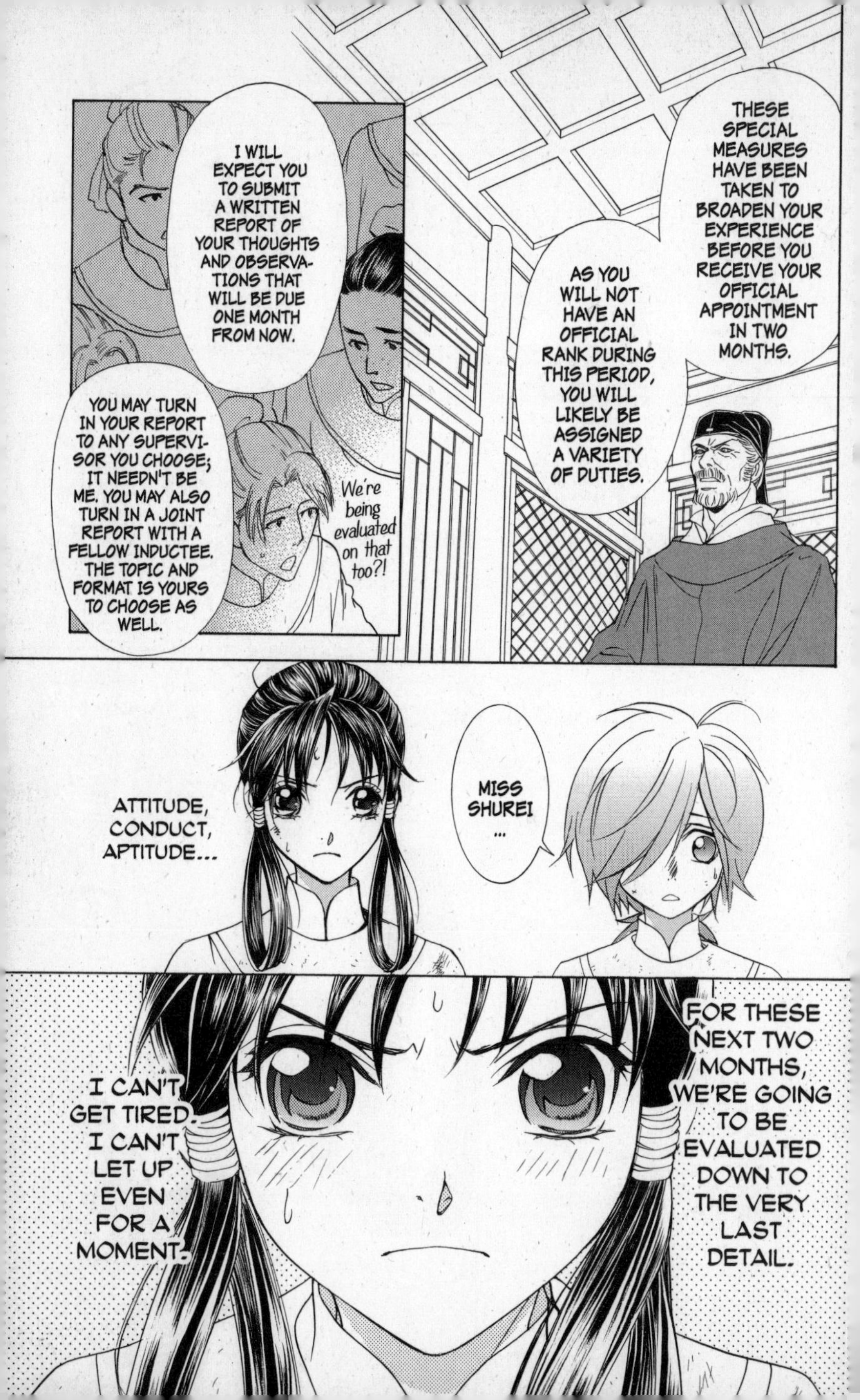
THESE SPECIAL MEASURES HAVE BEEN TAKEN TO BROADEN YOUR EXPERIENCE BEFORE YOU RECEIVE YOUR OFFICIAL APPOINTMENT IN TWO MONTHS.
AS YOU WILL NOT HAVE AN OFFICIAL RANK DURING THIS PERIOD, YOU WILL LIKELY BE ASSIGNED A VARIETY OF DUTIES.
I WILL EXPECT YOU TO SUBMIT A WRITTEN REPORT OF YOUR THOUGHTS AND OBSERVATIONS THAT WILL BE DUE ONE MONTH FROM NOW.
YOU MAY TURN IN YOUR REPORT TO ANY SUPERVISOR YOU CHOOSE; IT NEEDN'T BE ME. YOU MAY ALSO TURN IN A JOINT REPORT WITH A FELLOW INDUCTEE. THE TOPIC AND FORMAT IS YOURS TO CHOOSE AS WELL.
We're being evaluated on that too?!
MISS SHUREI ...
ATTITUDE, CONDUCT, APTITUDE...
FOR THESE NEXT TWO MONTHS, WE'RE GOING TO BE EVALUATED DOWN TO THE VERY LAST DETAIL.
I CAN'T GET TIRED. I CAN'T LET UP EVEN FOR A MOMENT.

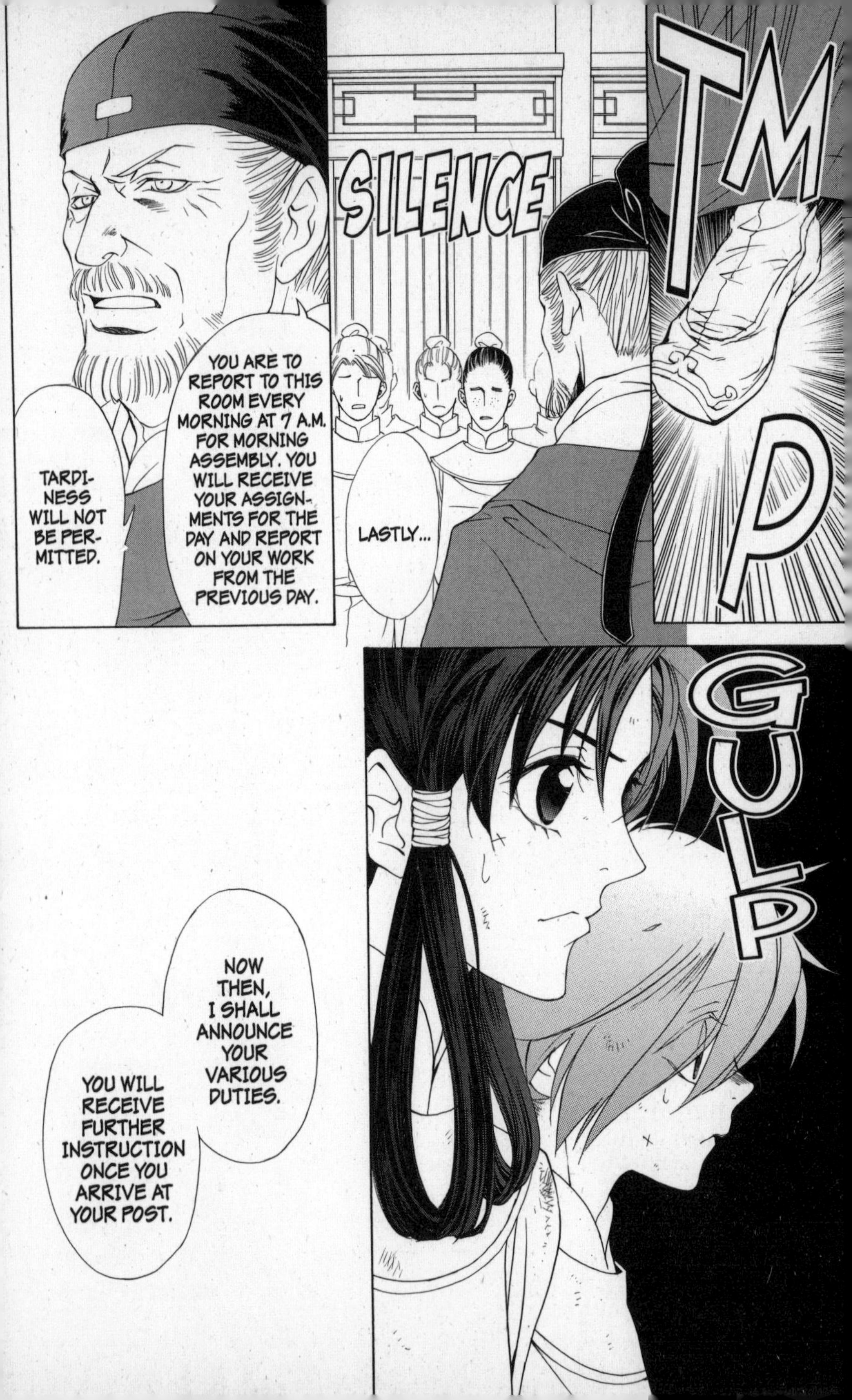
TMP
SILENCE
LASTLY...
YOU ARE TO REPORT TO THIS ROOM EVERY MORNING AT 7 A.M. FOR MORNING ASSEMBLY. YOU WILL RECEIVE YOUR ASSIGN-MENTS FOR THE DAY AND REPORT ON YOUR WORK FROM THE PREVIOUS DAY.
TARDI-NESS WILL NOT BE PER-MITTED.
GULP
NOW THEN, I SHALL ANNOUNCE YOUR VARIOUS DUTIES.
YOU WILL RECEIVE FURTHER INSTRUCTION ONCE YOU ARRIVE AT YOUR POST.

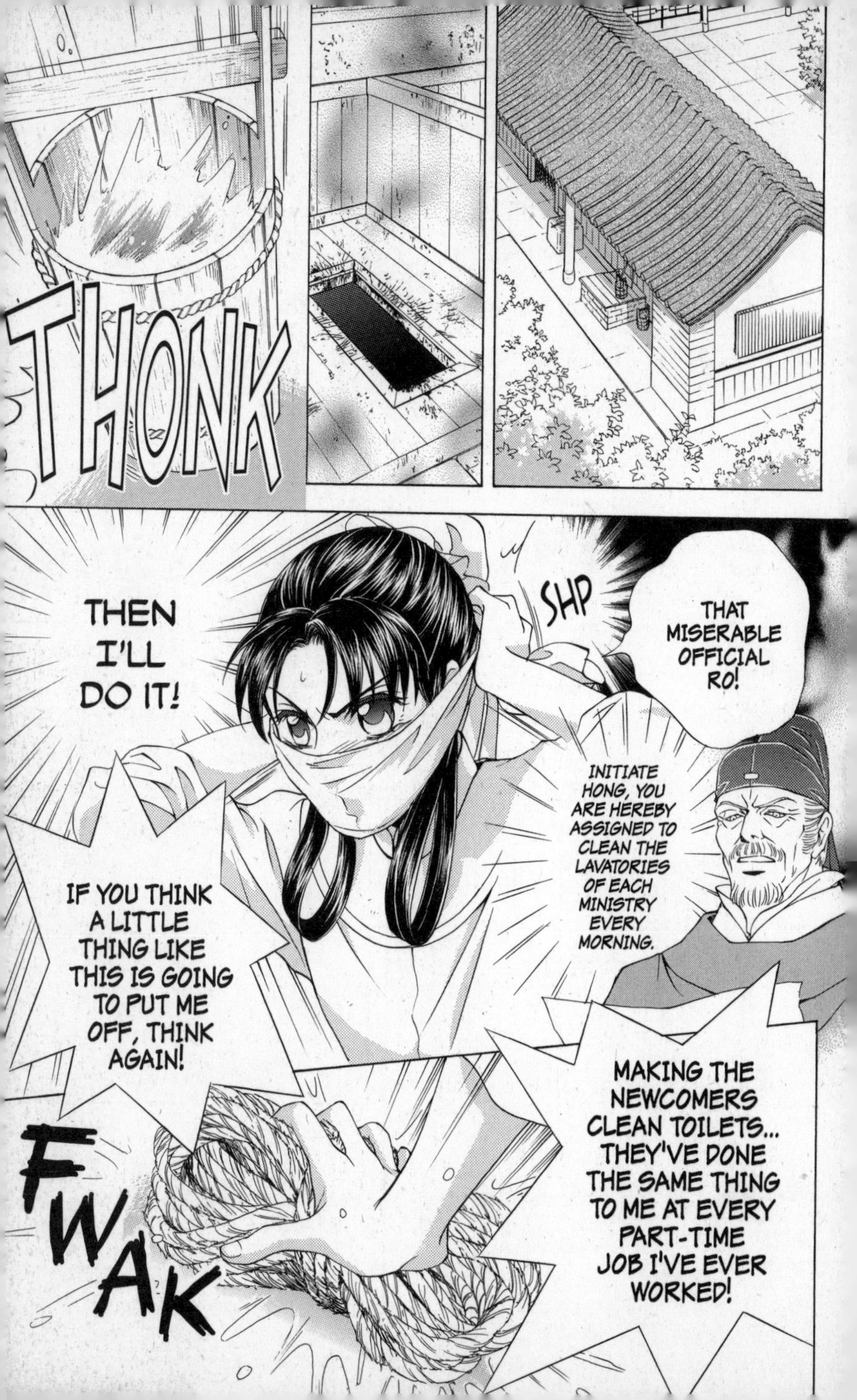
THONK
THAT MISERABLE OFFICIAL RO!
SHP
THEN I'LL DO IT!
INITIATE HONG, YOU ARE HEREBY ASSIGNED TO CLEAN THE LAVATORIES OF EACH MINISTRY EVERY MORNING.
MAKING THE NEWCOMERS CLEAN TOILETS... THEY'VE DONE THE SAME THING TO ME AT EVERY PART-TIME JOB I'VE EVER WORKED!
IF YOU THINK A LITTLE THING LIKE THIS IS GOING TO PUT ME OFF, THINK AGAIN!
FWAK

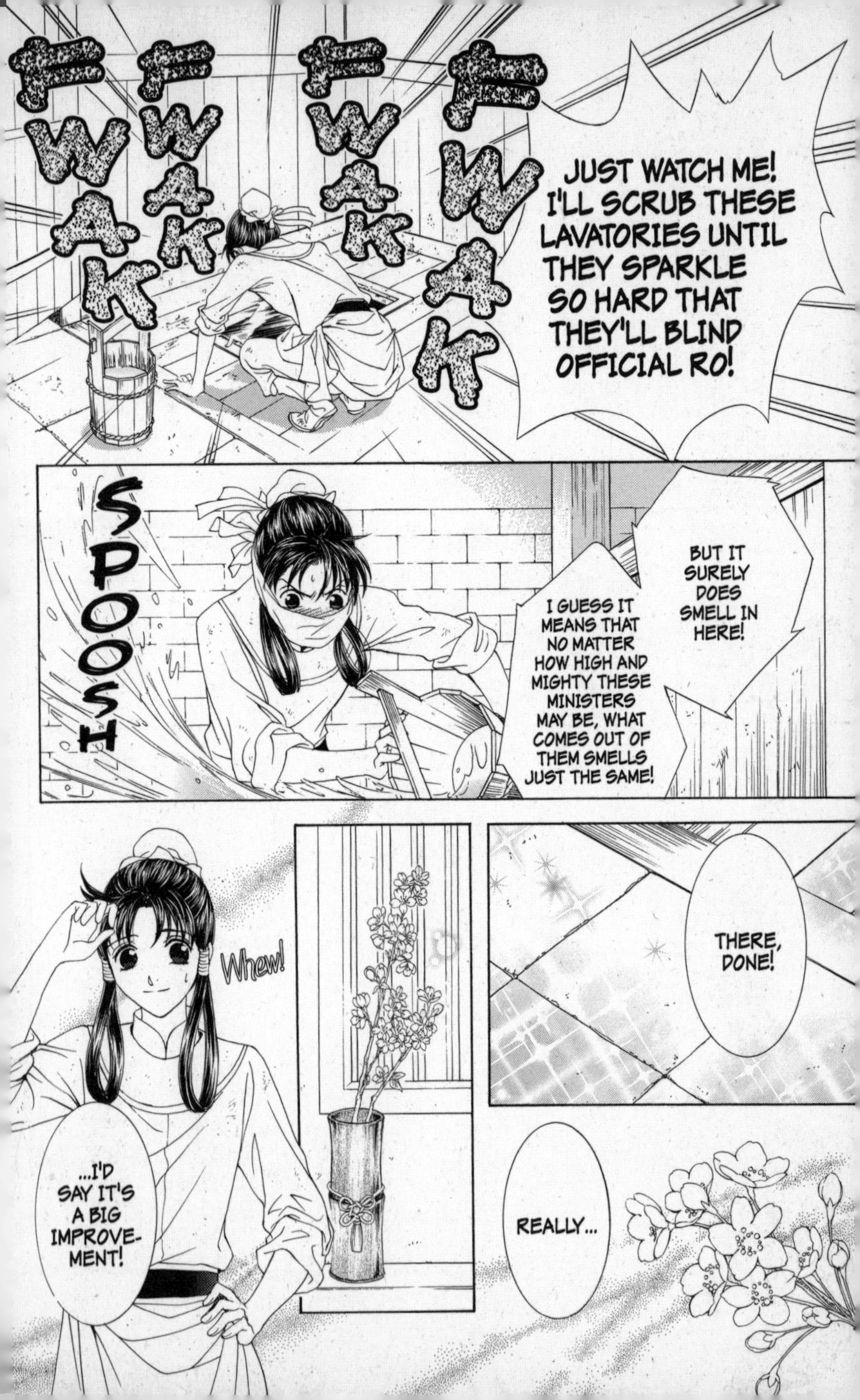
JUST WATCH ME! I'LL SCRUB THESE LAVATORIES UNTIL THEY SPARKLE SO HARD THAT THEY'LL BLIND OFFICIAL RO!
FWAK
FWAK
FWAK
FWAK
BUT IT SURELY DOES SMELL IN HERE!
I GUESS IT MEANS THAT NO MATTER HOW HIGH AND MIGHTY THESE MINISTERS MAY BE, WHAT COMES OUT OF THEM SMELLS JUST THE SAME!
SPOOOSH
THERE, DONE!
REALLY...
Whew!
...I'D SAY IT'S A BIG IMPROVEMENT!

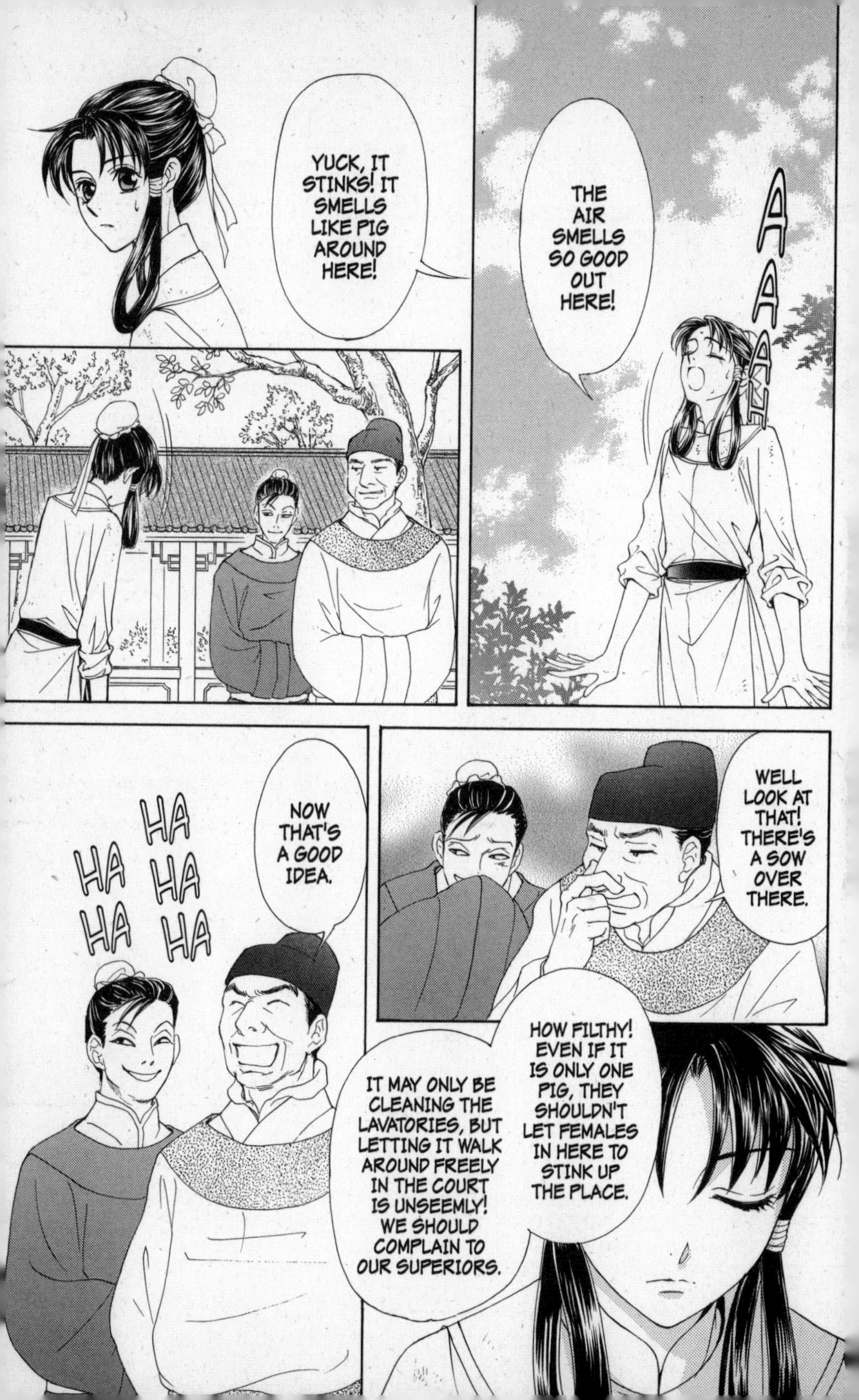
THE AIR SMELLS SO GOOD OUT HERE!
AAAAH
YUCK, IT STINKS! IT SMELLS LIKE PIG AROUND HERE!
WELL LOOK AT THAT! THERE'S A SOW OVER THERE.
HOW FILTHY! EVEN IF IT IS ONLY ONE PIG, THEY SHOULDN'T LET FEMALES IN HERE TO STINK UP THE PLACE.
IT MAY ONLY BE CLEANING THE LAVATORIES, BUT LETTING IT WALK AROUND FREELY IN THE COURT IS UNSEEMLY! WE SHOULD COMPLAIN TO OUR SUPERIORS.
NOW THAT'S A GOOD IDEA.
HA HA HA HA HA HA

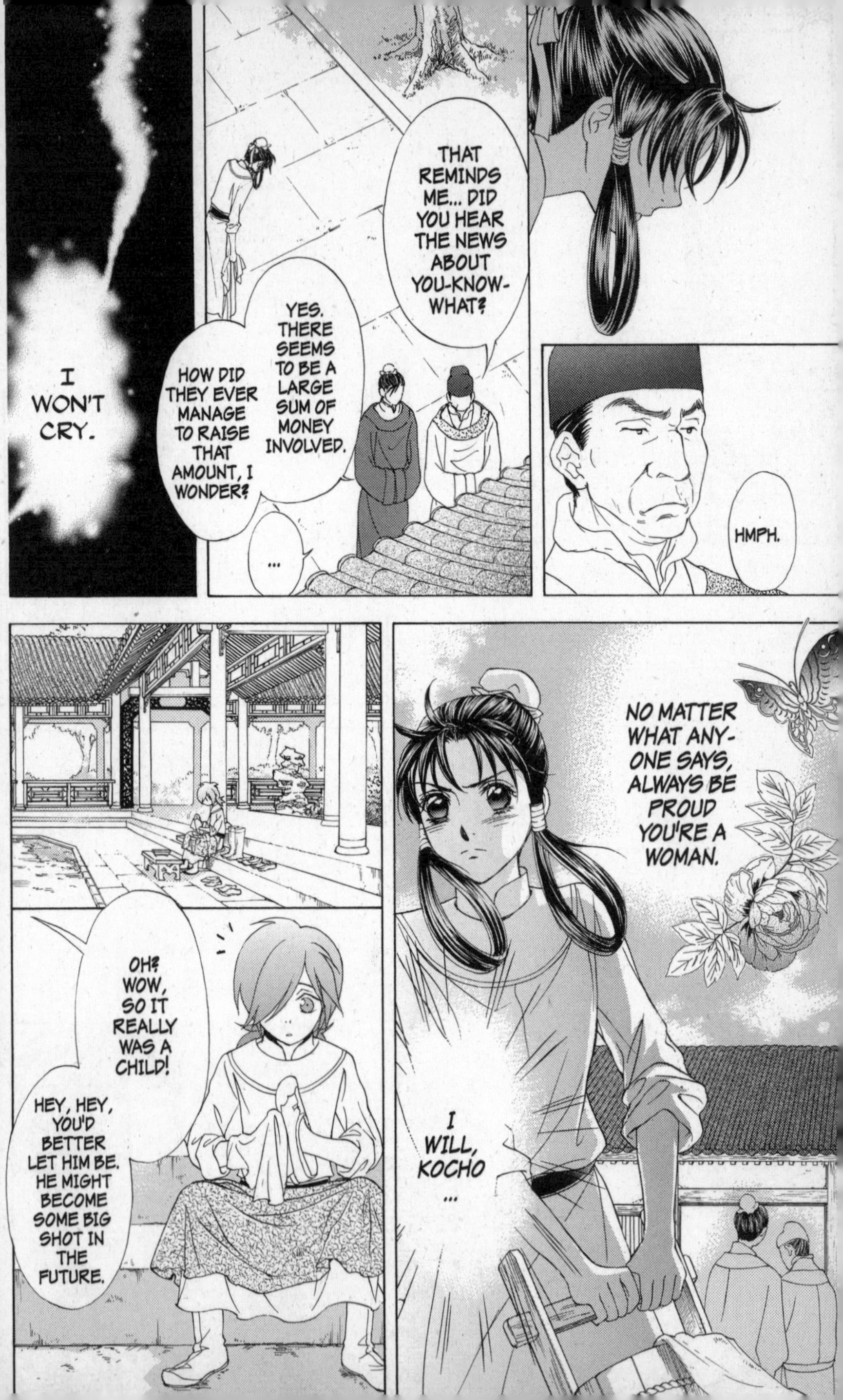
HMPH.
THAT REMINDS ME... DID YOU HEAR THE NEWS ABOUT YOU-KNOW-WHAT?
YES. THERE SEEMS TO BE A LARGE SUM OF MONEY INVOLVED.
HOW DID THEY EVER MANAGE TO RAISE THAT AMOUNT, I WONDER?
...
I WON'T CRY.
NO MATTER WHAT ANY-ONE SAYS, ALWAYS BE PROUD YOU'RE A WOMAN.
I WILL, KOCHO ...
OH? WOW, SO IT REALLY WAS A CHILD!
HEY, HEY, YOU'D BETTER LET HIM BE. HE MIGHT BECOME SOME BIG SHOT IN THE FUTURE.

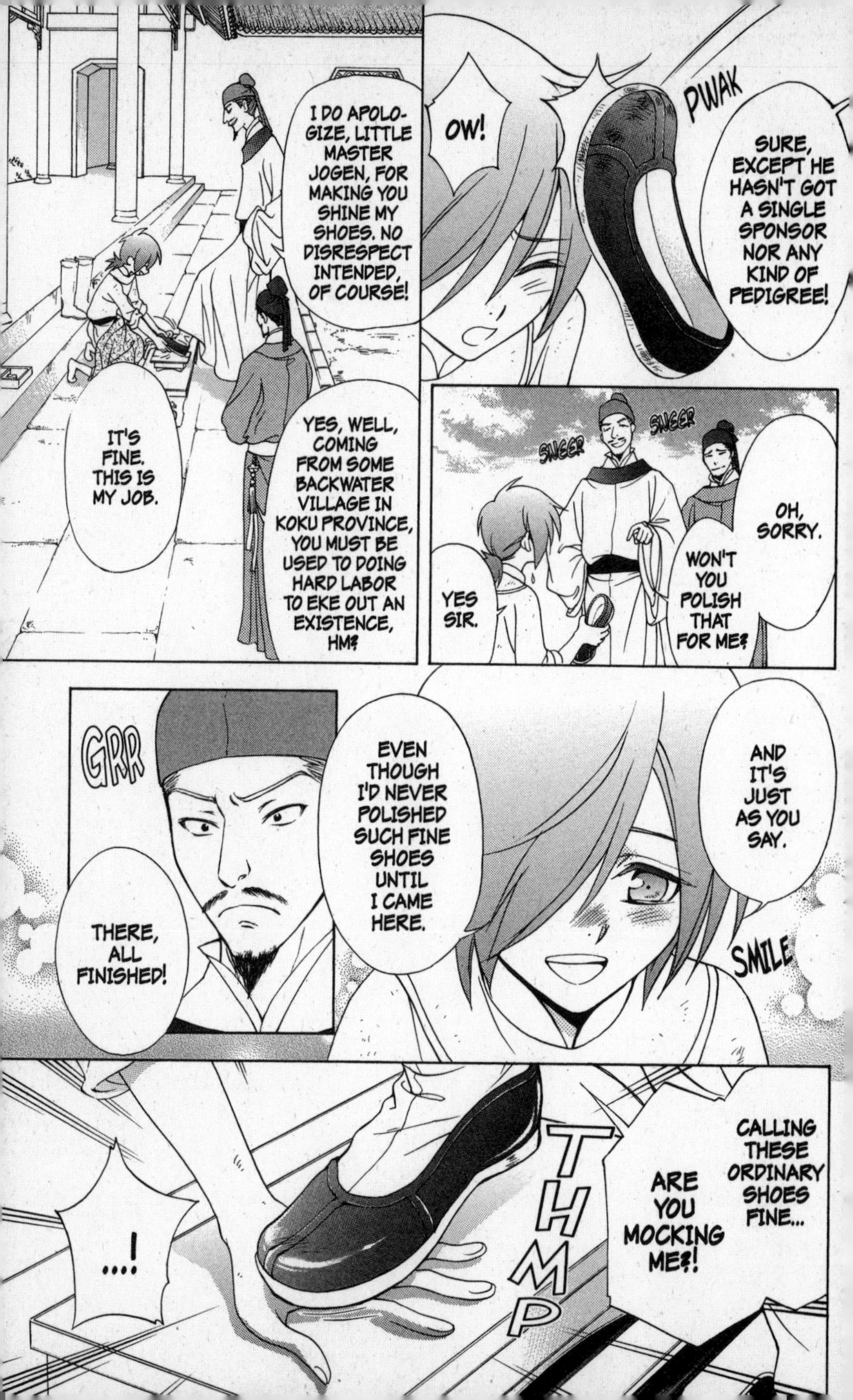
SURE, EXCEPT HE HASN'T GOT A SINGLE SPONSOR NOR ANY KIND OF PEDIGREE!
PWAK
OW!
OH, SORRY.
WON'T YOU POLISH THAT FOR ME?
SNEER
SNEER
YES SIR.
I DO APOLOGIZE, LITTLE MASTER JOGEN, FOR MAKING YOU SHINE MY SHOES. NO DISRESPECT INTENDED, OF COURSE!
YES, WELL, COMING FROM SOME BACKWATER VILLAGE IN KOKU PROVINCE, YOU MUST BE USED TO DOING HARD LABOR TO EKE OUT AN EXISTENCE, HM?
IT'S FINE. THIS IS MY JOB.
AND IT'S JUST AS YOU SAY.
SMILE
EVEN THOUGH I'D NEVER POLISHED SUCH FINE SHOES UNTIL I CAME HERE.
GRR
THERE, ALL FINISHED!
CALLING THESE ORDINARY SHOES FINE...
ARE YOU MOCKING ME?!
THUMP
...!

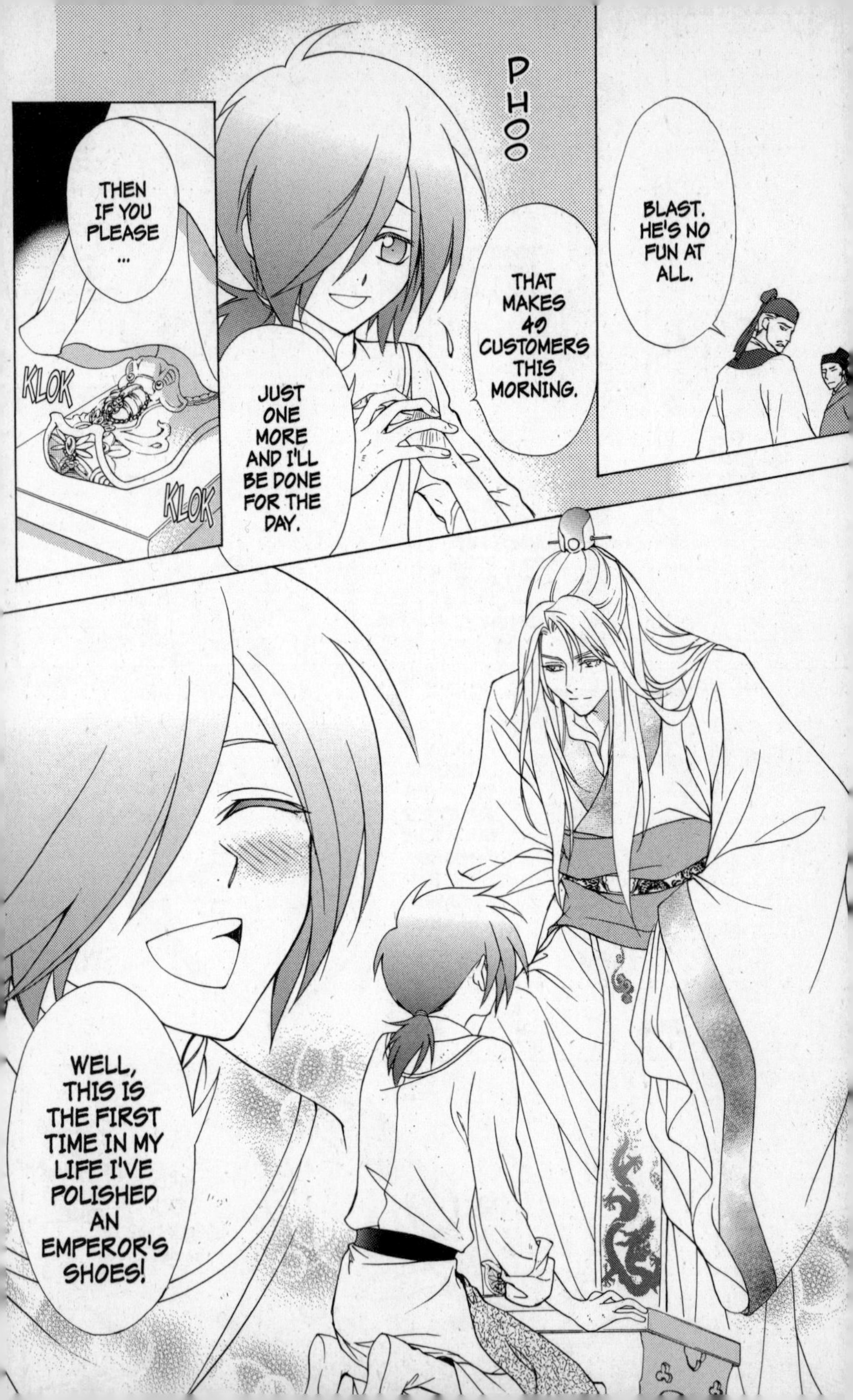
BLAST. HE'S NO FUN AT ALL.
PHOO
THAT MAKES 49 CUSTOMERS THIS MORNING.
JUST ONE MORE AND I'LL BE DONE FOR THE DAY.
THEN IF YOU PLEASE ...
KLOK
KLOK
WELL, THIS IS THE FIRST TIME IN MY LIFE I'VE POLISHED AN EMPEROR'S SHOES!

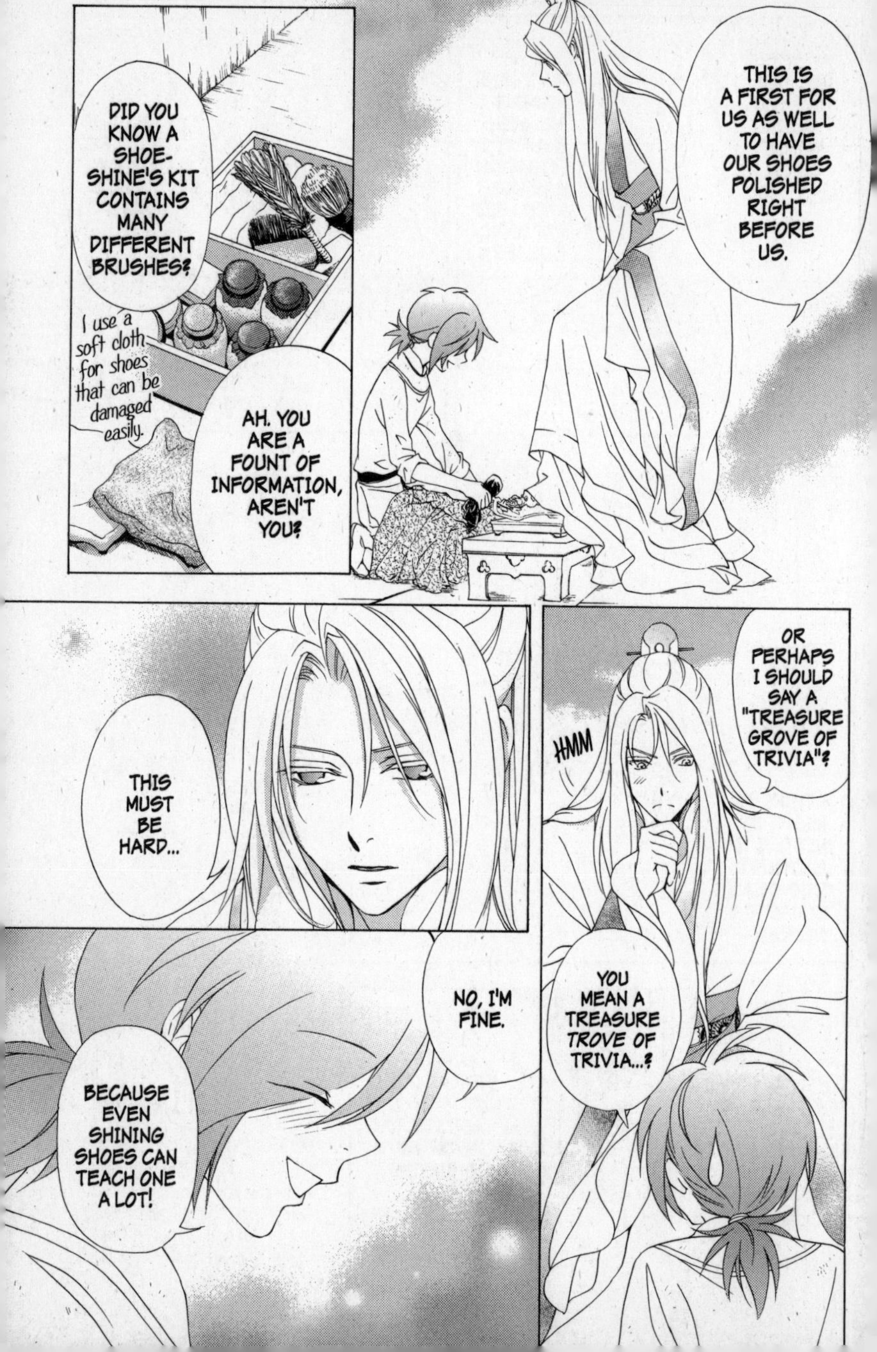
THIS IS A FIRST FOR US AS WELL TO HAVE OUR SHOES POLISHED RIGHT BEFORE US.
DID YOU KNOW A SHOE-SHINE'S KIT CONTAINS MANY DIFFERENT BRUSHES?
I use a soft cloth for shoes that can be damaged easily.
AH. YOU ARE A FOUNT OF INFORMATION, AREN'T YOU?
OR PERHAPS I SHOULD SAY A "TREASURE GROVE OF TRIVIA"?
HMM
YOU MEAN A TREASURE TROVE OF TRIVIA...?
THIS MUST BE HARD...
NO, I'M FINE.
BECAUSE EVEN SHINING SHOES CAN TEACH ONE A LOT!

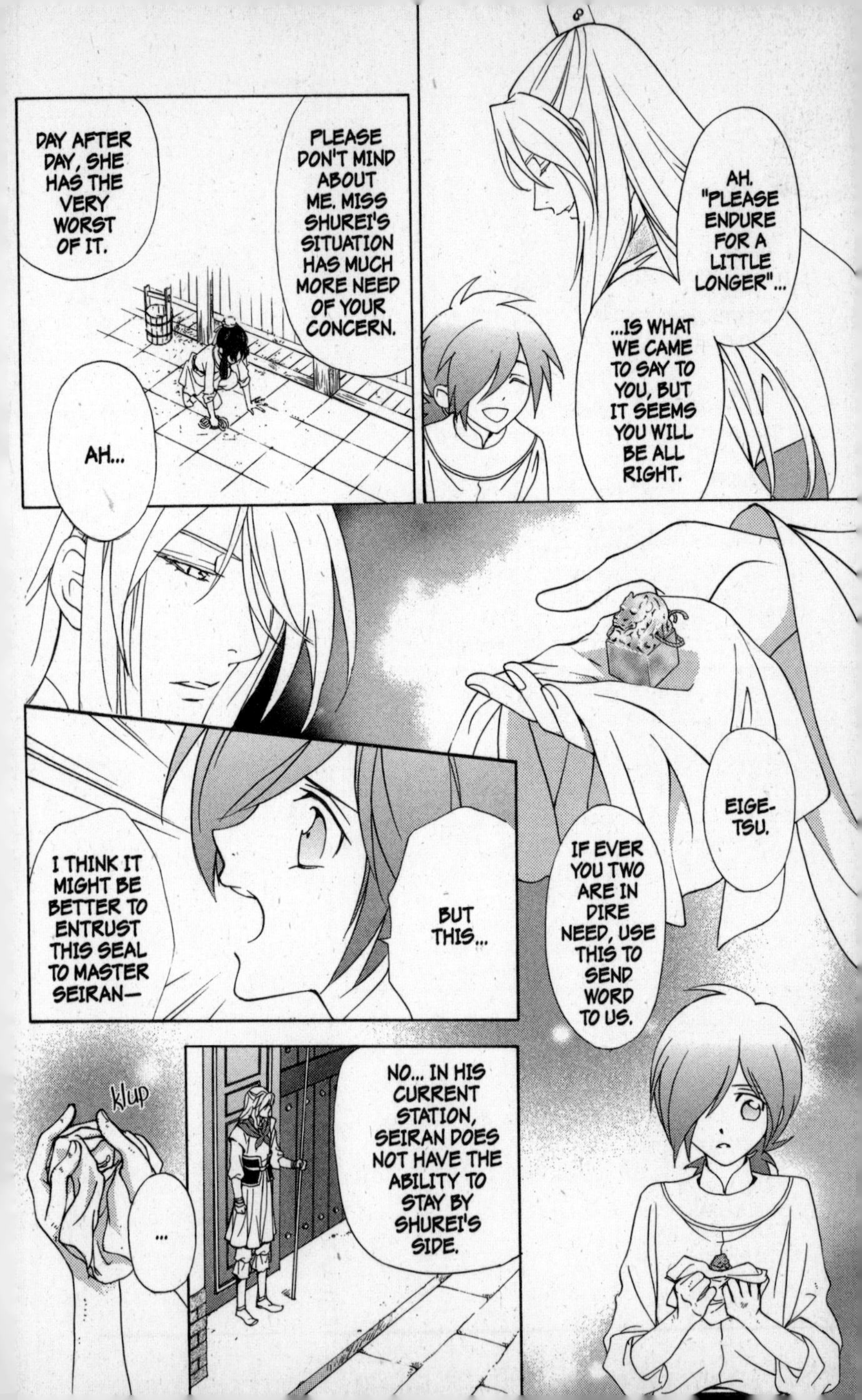
AH. "PLEASE ENDURE FOR A LITTLE LONGER"...
...IS WHAT WE CAME TO SAY TO YOU, BUT IT SEEMS YOU WILL BE ALL RIGHT.
PLEASE DON'T MIND ABOUT ME. MISS SHUREI'S SITUATION HAS MUCH MORE NEED OF YOUR CONCERN.
DAY AFTER DAY, SHE HAS THE VERY WORST OF IT.
AH...
EIGE-TSU.
IF EVER YOU TWO ARE IN DIRE NEED, USE THIS TO SEND WORD TO US.
BUT THIS...
I THINK IT MIGHT BE BETTER TO ENTRUST THIS SEAL TO MASTER SEIRAN—
NO... IN HIS CURRENT STATION, SEIRAN DOES NOT HAVE THE ABILITY TO STAY BY SHUREI'S SIDE.
klup
...

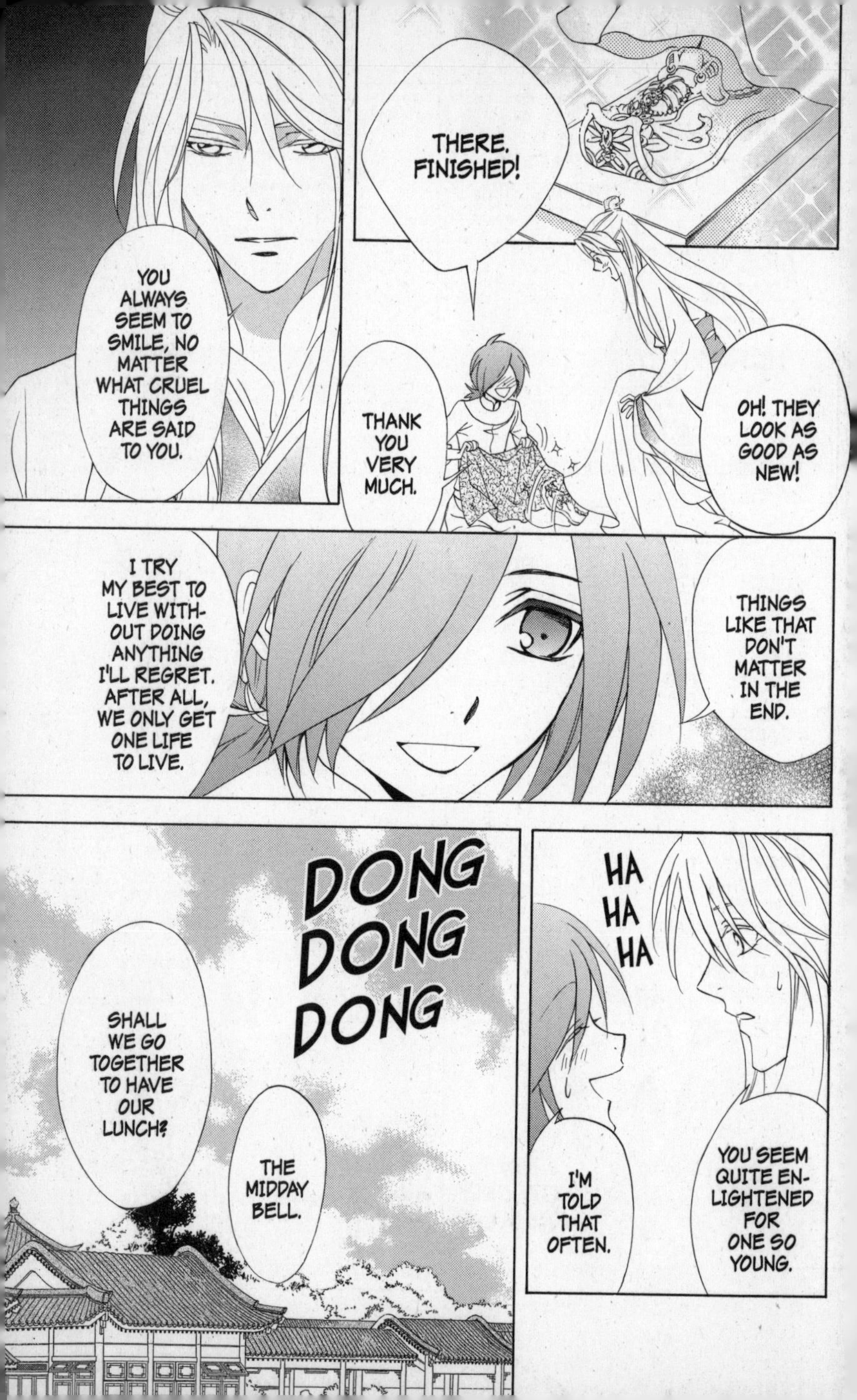
THERE. FINISHED!
OH! THEY LOOK AS GOOD AS NEW!
THANK YOU VERY MUCH.
YOU ALWAYS SEEM TO SMILE, NO MATTER WHAT CRUEL THINGS ARE SAID TO YOU.
THINGS LIKE THAT DON'T MATTER IN THE END.
I TRY MY BEST TO LIVE WITH-OUT DOING ANYTHING I'LL REGRET. AFTER ALL, WE ONLY GET ONE LIFE TO LIVE.
HA HA HA
YOU SEEM QUITE EN-LIGHTENED FOR ONE SO YOUNG.
I'M TOLD THAT OFTEN.
DONG DONG DONG
THE MIDDAY BELL.
SHALL WE GO TOGETHER TO HAVE OUR LUNCH?

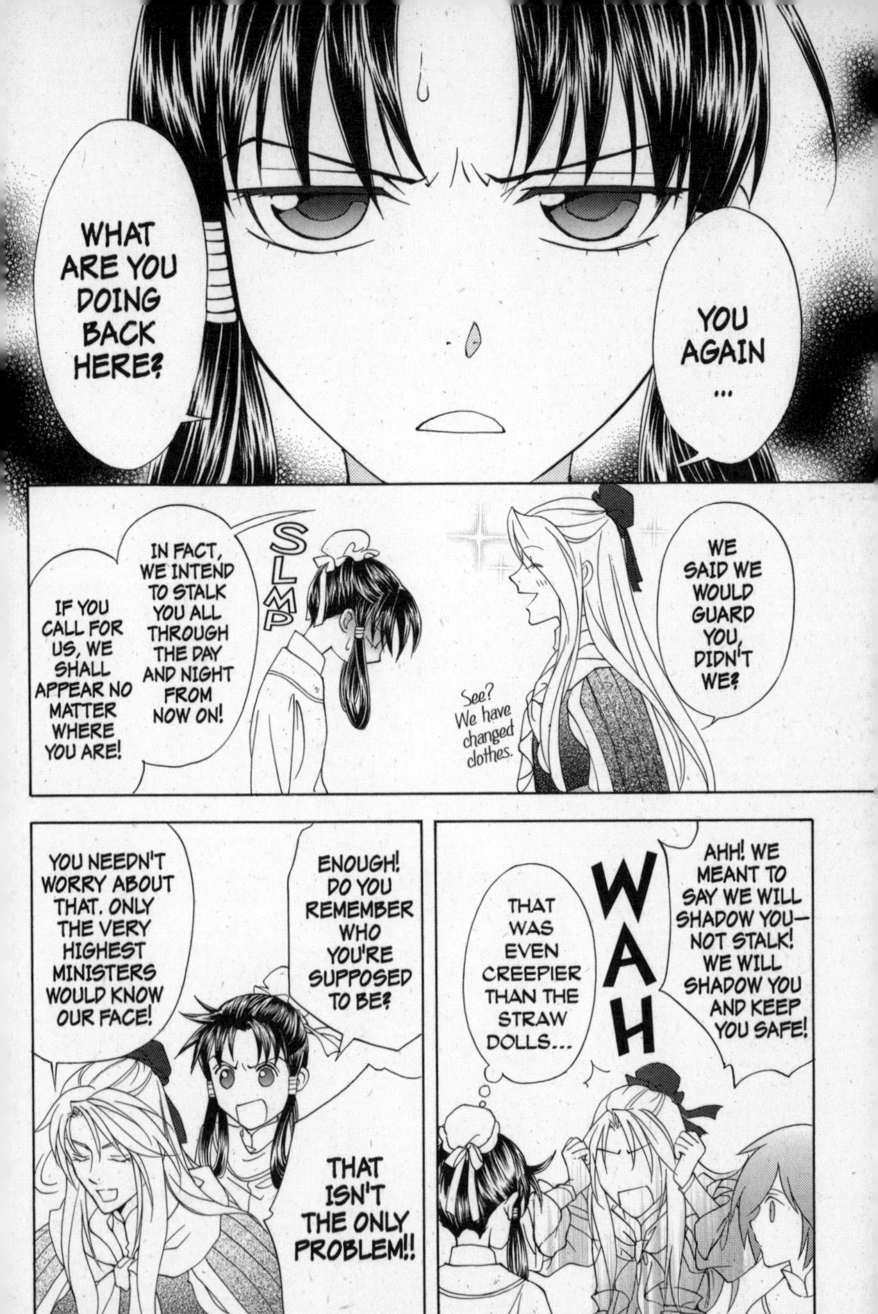
YOU AGAIN ...
WHAT ARE YOU DOING BACK HERE?
WE SAID WE WOULD GUARD YOU, DIDN'T WE?
See? We have changed clothes.
SLMP
IN FACT, WE INTEND TO STALK YOU ALL THROUGH THE DAY AND NIGHT FROM NOW ON!
IF YOU CALL FOR US, WE SHALL APPEAR NO MATTER WHERE YOU ARE!
AHH! WE MEANT TO SAY WE WILL SHADOW YOU— NOT STALK! WE WILL SHADOW YOU AND KEEP YOU SAFE!
WAH
THAT WAS EVEN CREEPIER THAN THE STRAW DOLLS...
ENOUGH! DO YOU REMEMBER WHO YOU'RE SUPPOSED TO BE?
YOU NEEDN'T WORRY ABOUT THAT. ONLY THE VERY HIGHEST MINISTERS WOULD KNOW OUR FACE!
THAT ISN'T THE ONLY PROBLEM!!

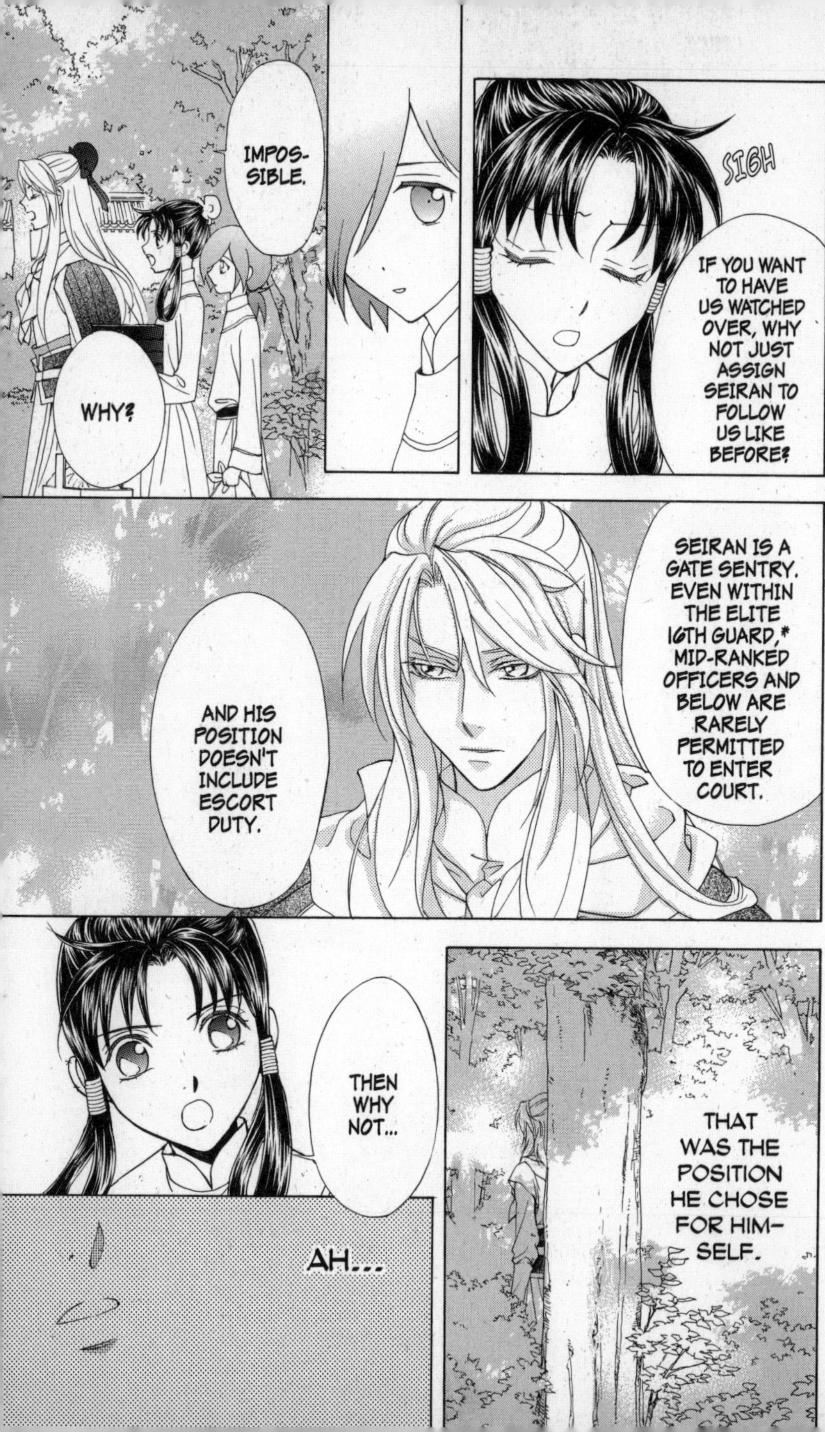
SIGH
IF YOU WANT TO HAVE US WATCHED OVER, WHY NOT JUST ASSIGN SEIRAN TO FOLLOW US LIKE BEFORE?
IMPOS-SIBLE.
WHY?
SEIRAN IS A GATE SENTRY. EVEN WITHIN THE ELITE 16TH GUARD,* MID-RANKED OFFICERS AND BELOW ARE RARELY PERMITTED TO ENTER COURT.
AND HIS POSITION DOESN'T INCLUDE ESCORT DUTY.
THAT WAS THE POSITION HE CHOSE FOR HIM-SELF.
THEN WHY NOT...
AH...

*16th Guard: The squadron of palace guards assigned to protect each ministry and department in the court.

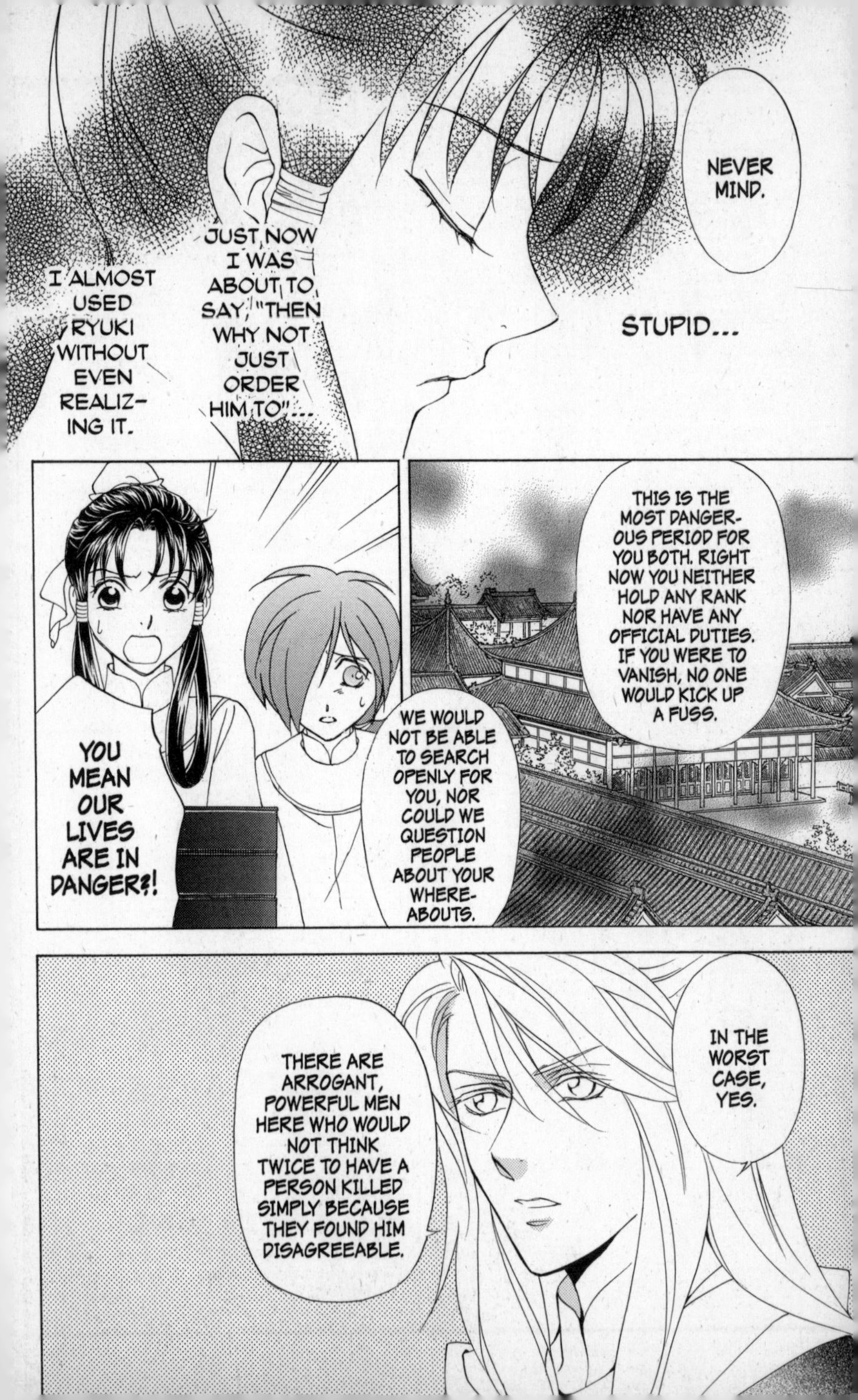
NEVER MIND.
STUPID...
JUST NOW I WAS ABOUT TO SAY, "THEN WHY NOT JUST ORDER HIM TO"...
I ALMOST USED RYUKI WITHOUT EVEN REALIZING IT.
THIS IS THE MOST DANGEROUS PERIOD FOR YOU BOTH. RIGHT NOW YOU NEITHER HOLD ANY RANK NOR HAVE ANY OFFICIAL DUTIES. IF YOU WERE TO VANISH, NO ONE WOULD KICK UP A FUSS.
WE WOULD NOT BE ABLE TO SEARCH OPENLY FOR YOU, NOR COULD WE QUESTION PEOPLE ABOUT YOUR WHEREABOUTS.
YOU MEAN OUR LIVES ARE IN DANGER?!
IN THE WORST CASE, YES.
THERE ARE ARROGANT, POWERFUL MEN HERE WHO WOULD NOT THINK TWICE TO HAVE A PERSON KILLED SIMPLY BECAUSE THEY FOUND HIM DISAGREEABLE.

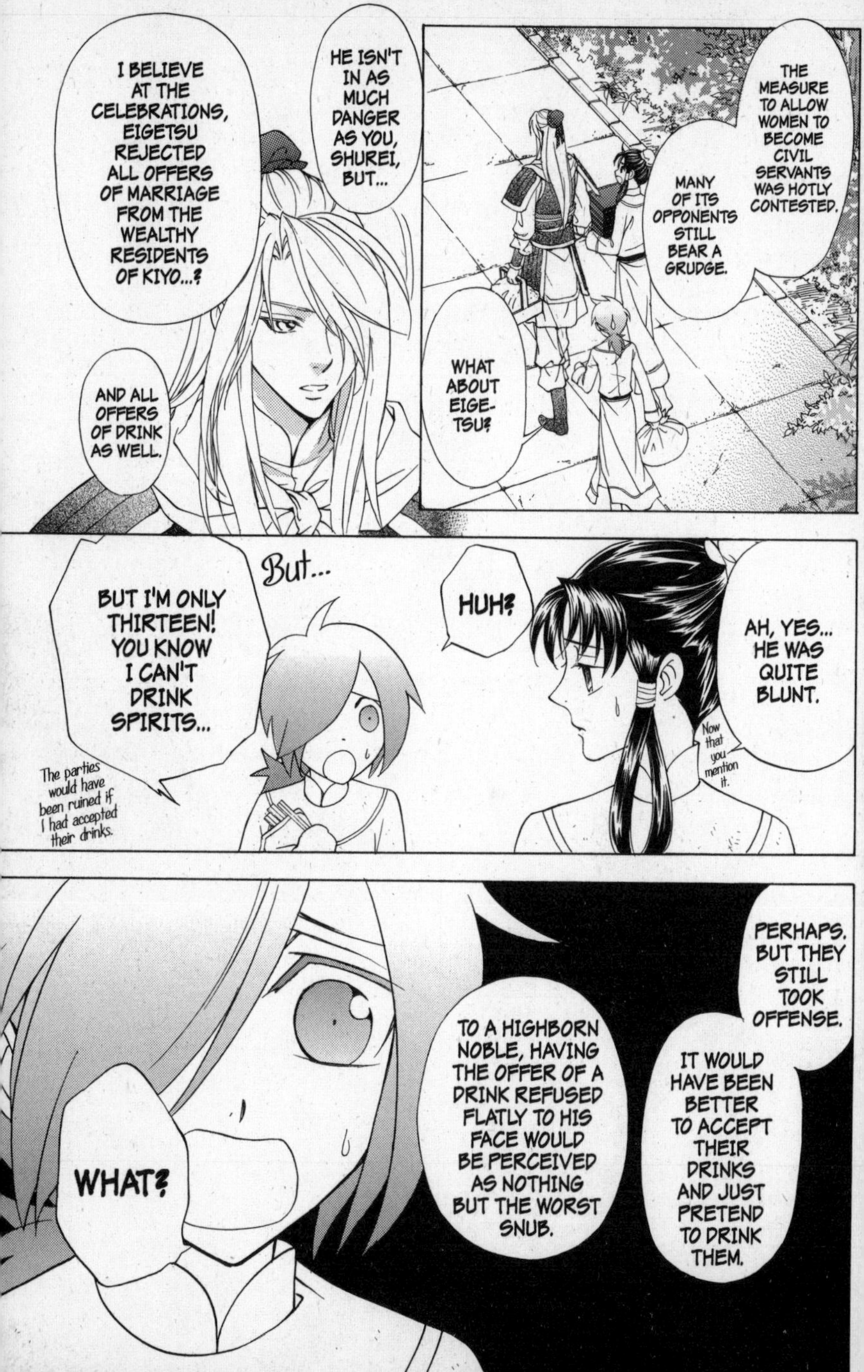
THE MEASURE TO ALLOW WOMEN TO BECOME CIVIL SERVANTS WAS HOTLY CONTESTED.
MANY OF ITS OPPONENTS STILL BEAR A GRUDGE.
WHAT ABOUT EIGE-TSU?
HE ISN'T IN AS MUCH DANGER AS YOU, SHUREI, BUT...
I BELIEVE AT THE CELEBRATIONS, EIGETSU REJECTED ALL OFFERS OF MARRIAGE FROM THE WEALTHY RESIDENTS OF KIYO...?
AND ALL OFFERS OF DRINK AS WELL.
AH, YES... HE WAS QUITE BLUNT.
Now that you mention it.
HUH?
But...
BUT I'M ONLY THIRTEEN! YOU KNOW I CAN'T DRINK SPIRITS...
The parties would have been ruined if I had accepted their drinks.
PERHAPS. BUT THEY STILL TOOK OFFENSE.
IT WOULD HAVE BEEN BETTER TO ACCEPT THEIR DRINKS AND JUST PRETEND TO DRINK THEM.
TO A HIGHBORN NOBLE, HAVING THE OFFER OF A DRINK REFUSED FLATLY TO HIS FACE WOULD BE PERCEIVED AS NOTHING BUT THE WORST SNUB.
WHAT?

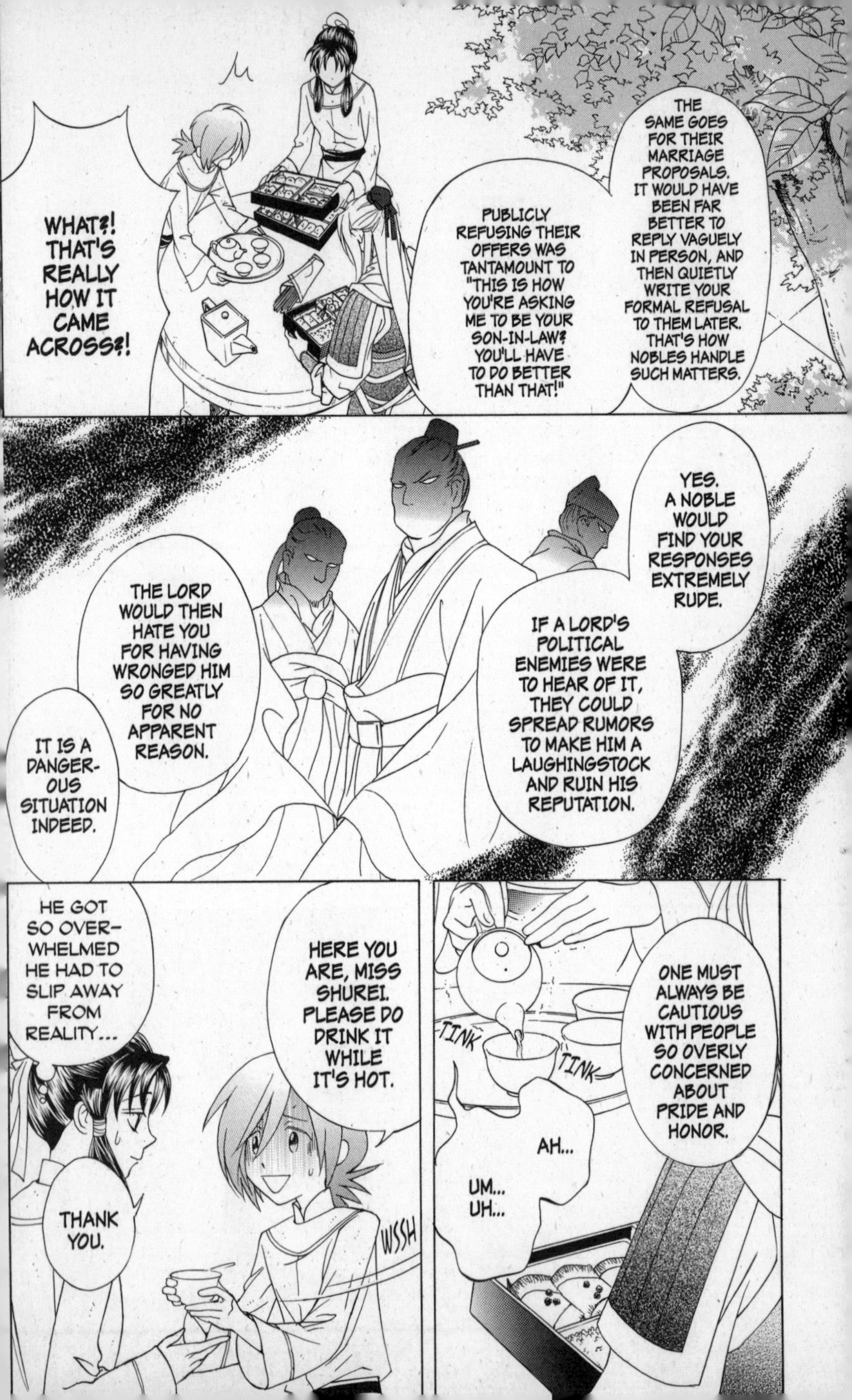
THE SAME GOES FOR THEIR MARRIAGE PROPOSALS. IT WOULD HAVE BEEN FAR BETTER TO REPLY VAGUELY IN PERSON, AND THEN QUIETLY WRITE YOUR FORMAL REFUSAL TO THEM LATER. THAT'S HOW NOBLES HANDLE SUCH MATTERS.
PUBLICLY REFUSING THEIR OFFERS WAS TANTAMOUNT TO "THIS IS HOW YOU'RE ASKING ME TO BE YOUR SON-IN-LAW? YOU'LL HAVE TO DO BETTER THAN THAT!"
WHAT?! THAT'S REALLY HOW IT CAME ACROSS?!
YES. A NOBLE WOULD FIND YOUR RESPONSES EXTREMELY RUDE.
IF A LORD'S POLITICAL ENEMIES WERE TO HEAR OF IT, THEY COULD SPREAD RUMORS TO MAKE HIM A LAUGHINGSTOCK AND RUIN HIS REPUTATION.
THE LORD WOULD THEN HATE YOU FOR HAVING WRONGED HIM SO GREATLY FOR NO APPARENT REASON.
IT IS A DANGER-OUS SITUATION INDEED.
ONE MUST ALWAYS BE CAUTIOUS WITH PEOPLE SO OVERLY CONCERNED ABOUT PRIDE AND HONOR.
TINK
TINK
AH...
UM... UH...
HERE YOU ARE, MISS SHUREI. PLEASE DO DRINK IT WHILE IT'S HOT.
HE GOT SO OVER-WHELMED HE HAD TO SLIP AWAY FROM REALITY...
WSSH
THANK YOU.

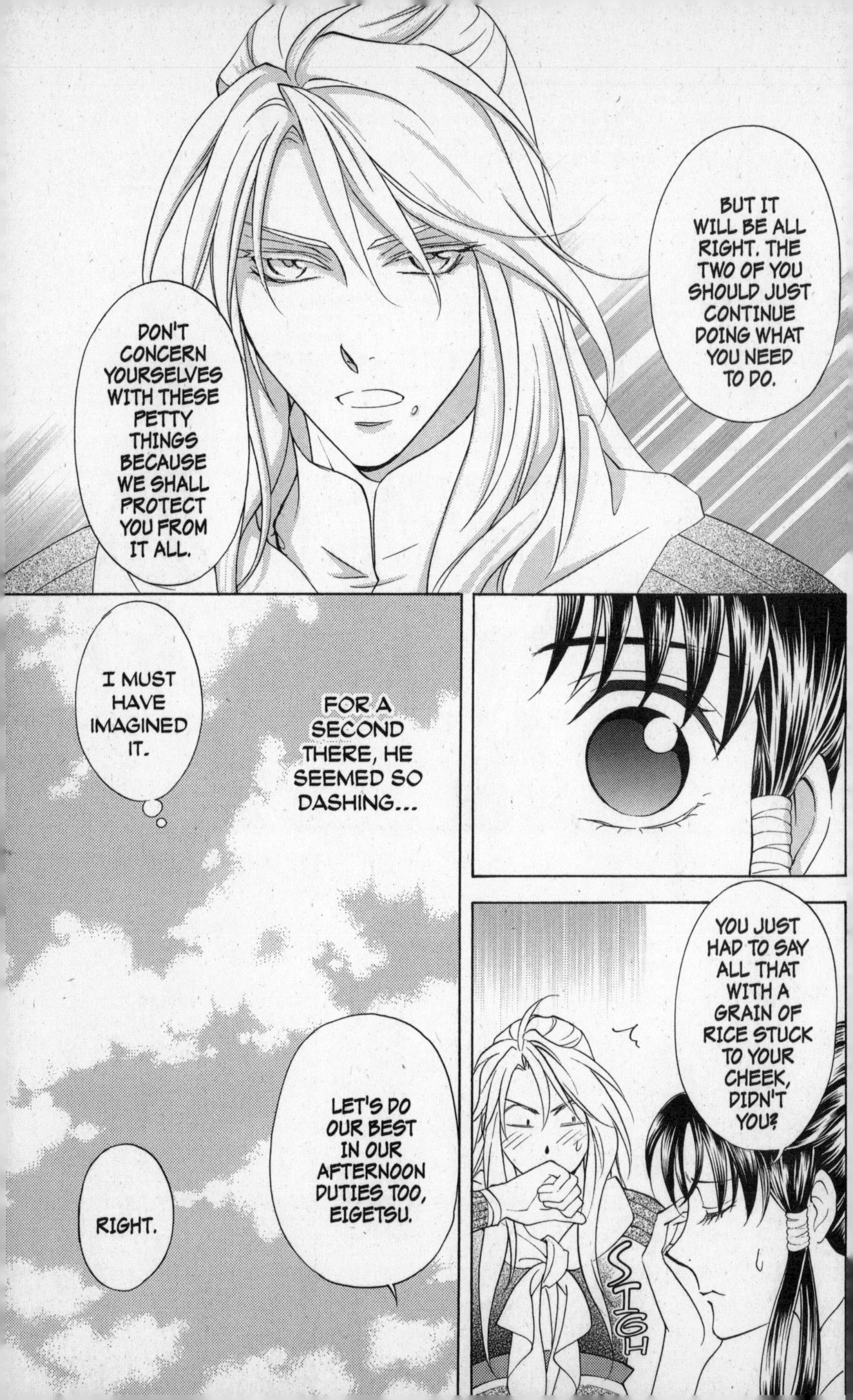
BUT IT WILL BE ALL RIGHT. THE TWO OF YOU SHOULD JUST CONTINUE DOING WHAT YOU NEED TO DO.
DON'T CONCERN YOURSELVES WITH THESE PETTY THINGS BECAUSE WE SHALL PROTECT YOU FROM IT ALL.
YOU JUST HAD TO SAY ALL THAT WITH A GRAIN OF RICE STUCK TO YOUR CHEEK, DIDN'T YOU?
SIGH
FOR A SECOND THERE, HE SEEMED SO DASHING...
I MUST HAVE IMAGINED IT.
LET'S DO OUR BEST IN OUR AFTERNOON DUTIES TOO, EIGETSU.
RIGHT.

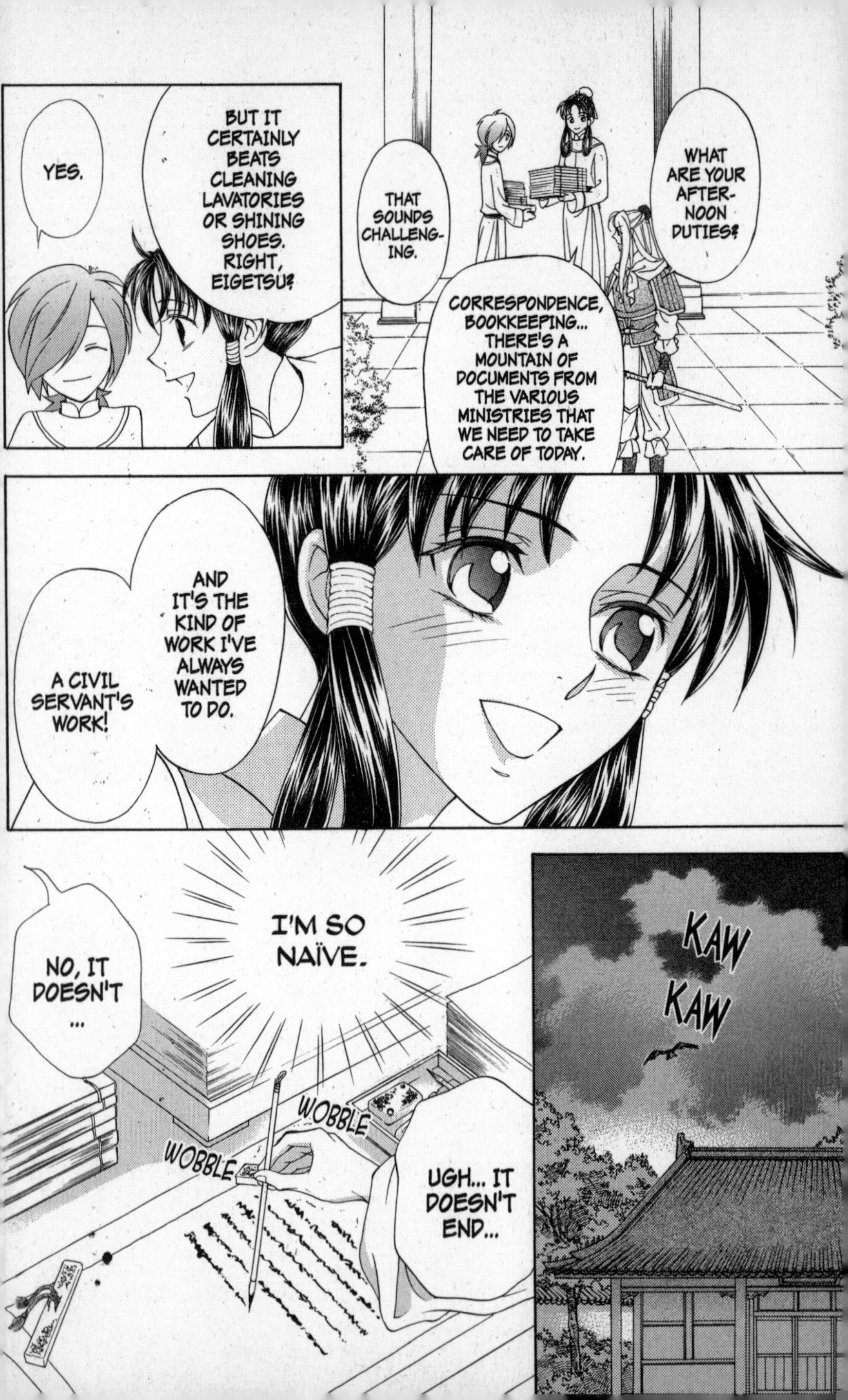
WHAT ARE YOUR AFTERNOON DUTIES?
CORRESPONDENCE, BOOKKEEPING... THERE'S A MOUNTAIN OF DOCUMENTS FROM THE VARIOUS MINISTRIES THAT WE NEED TO TAKE CARE OF TODAY.
THAT SOUNDS CHALLENGING.
BUT IT CERTAINLY BEATS CLEANING LAVATORIES OR SHINING SHOES. RIGHT, EIGETSU?
YES.
AND IT'S THE KIND OF WORK I'VE ALWAYS WANTED TO DO.
A CIVIL SERVANT'S WORK!
KAW
KAW
I'M SO NAÏVE.
NO, IT DOESN'T ...
WOBBLE
UGH... IT DOESN'T END...
WOBBLE

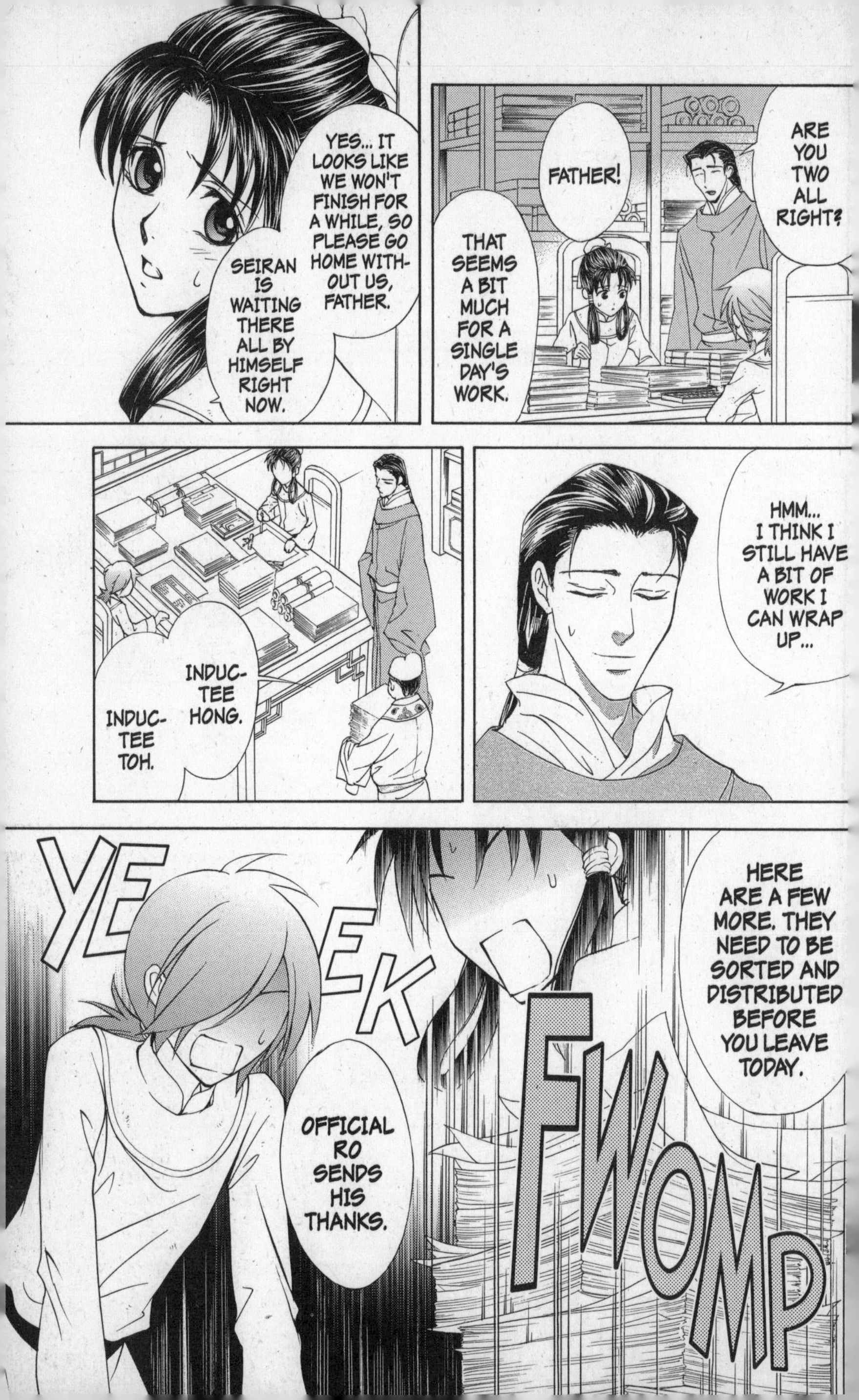
ARE YOU TWO ALL RIGHT?
FATHER!
THAT SEEMS A BIT MUCH FOR A SINGLE DAY'S WORK.
YES... IT LOOKS LIKE WE WON'T FINISH FOR A WHILE, SO PLEASE GO HOME WITHOUT US, FATHER.
SEIRAN IS WAITING THERE ALL BY HIMSELF RIGHT NOW.
HMM... I THINK I STILL HAVE A BIT OF WORK I CAN WRAP UP...
INDUCTEE HONG.
INDUCTEE TOH.
HERE ARE A FEW MORE. THEY NEED TO BE SORTED AND DISTRIBUTED BEFORE YOU LEAVE TODAY.
FWOMP
OFFICIAL RO SENDS HIS THANKS.
YEEK

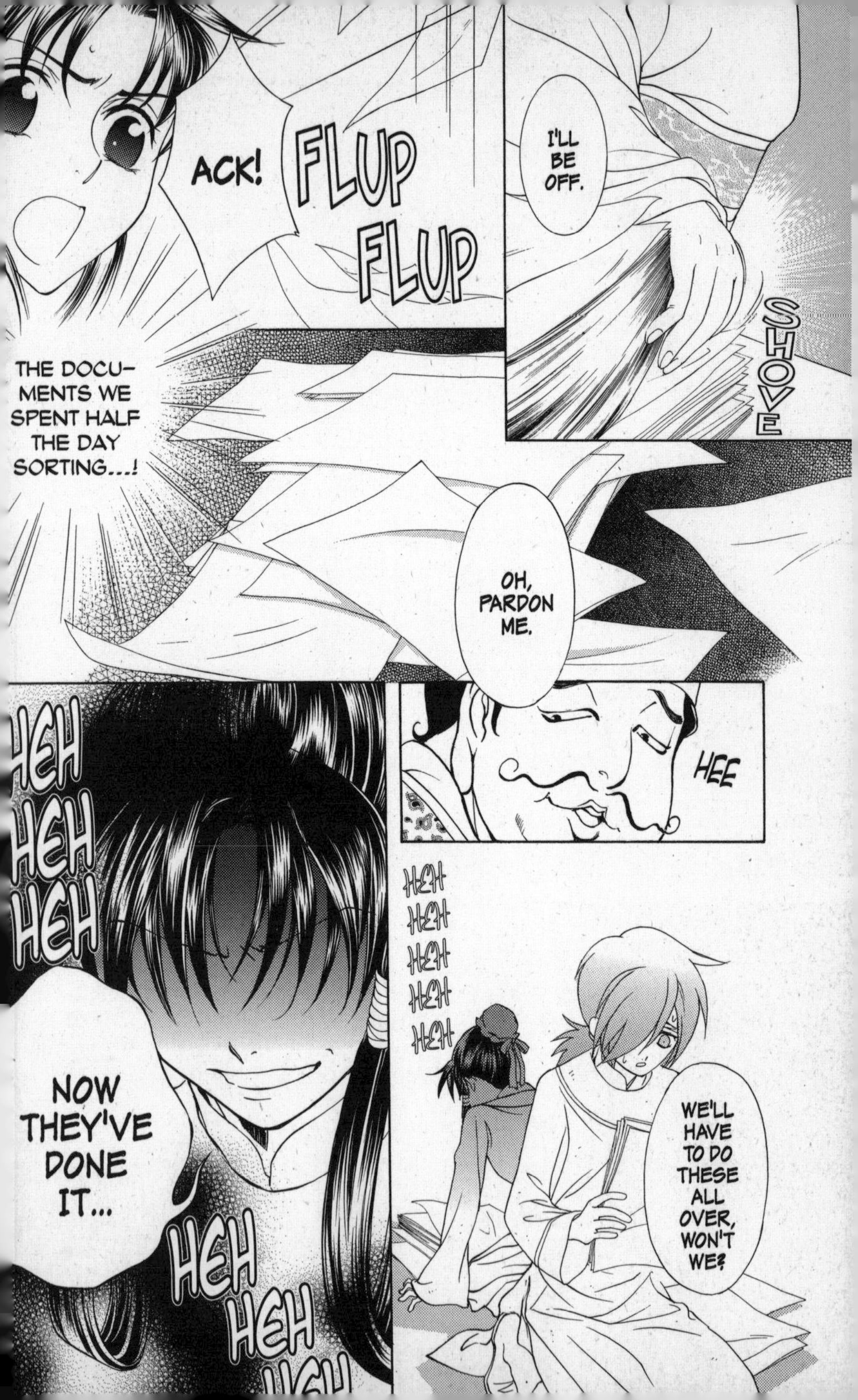
I'LL BE OFF.
SHOVE
ACK!
FLUP FLUP
THE DOCUMENTS WE SPENT HALF THE DAY SORTING...!
OH, PARDON ME.
HEE
HEH HEH HEH HEH HEH
WE'LL HAVE TO DO THESE ALL OVER, WON'T WE?
HEH HEH HEH
NOW THEY'VE DONE IT...
HEH HEH

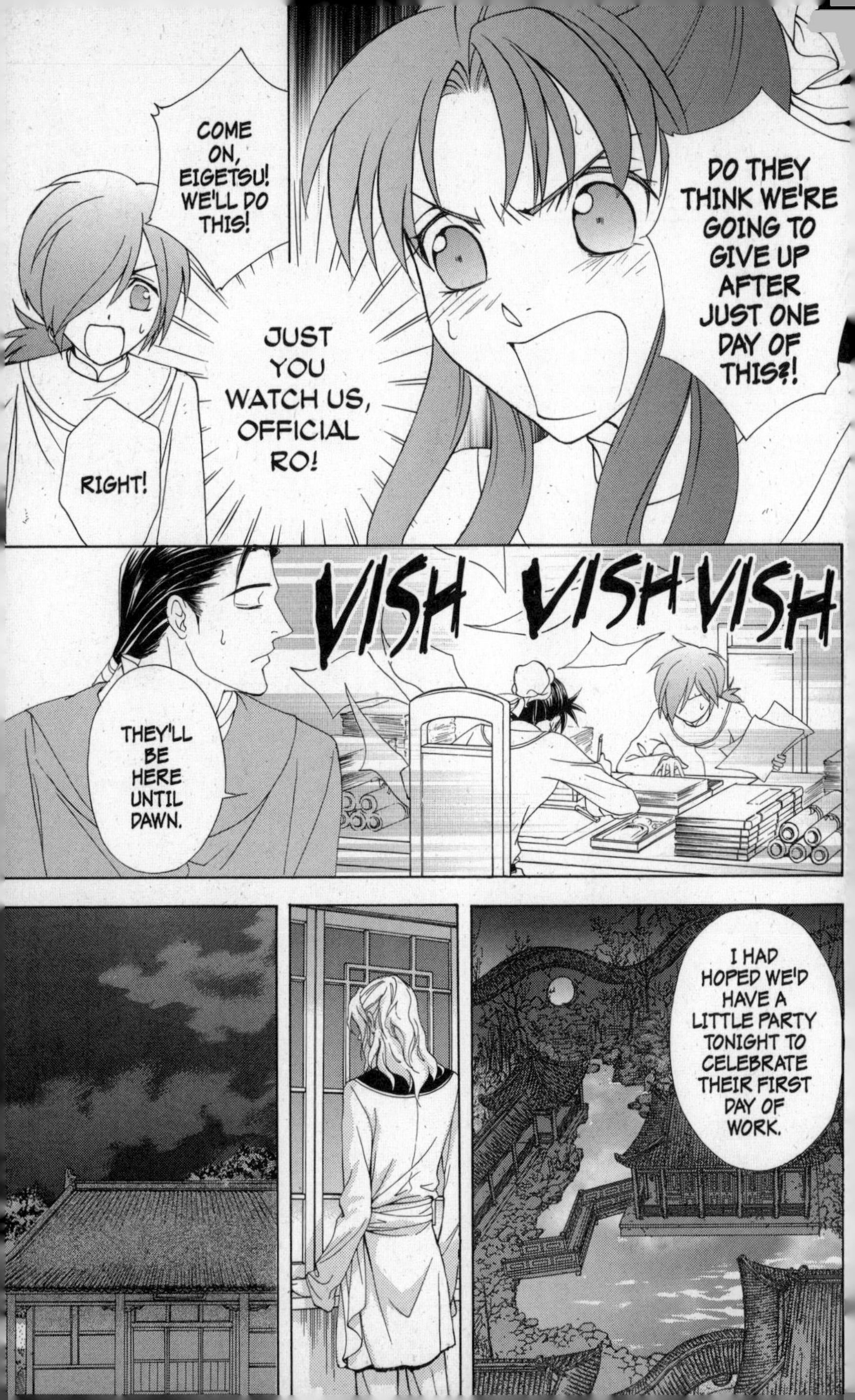
DO THEY THINK WE'RE GOING TO GIVE UP AFTER JUST ONE DAY OF THIS?!
JUST YOU WATCH US, OFFICIAL RO!
COME ON, EIGETSU! WE'LL DO THIS!
RIGHT!
VISH VISH VISH
THEY'LL BE HERE UNTIL DAWN.
I HAD HOPED WE'D HAVE A LITTLE PARTY TONIGHT TO CELEBRATE THEIR FIRST DAY OF WORK.

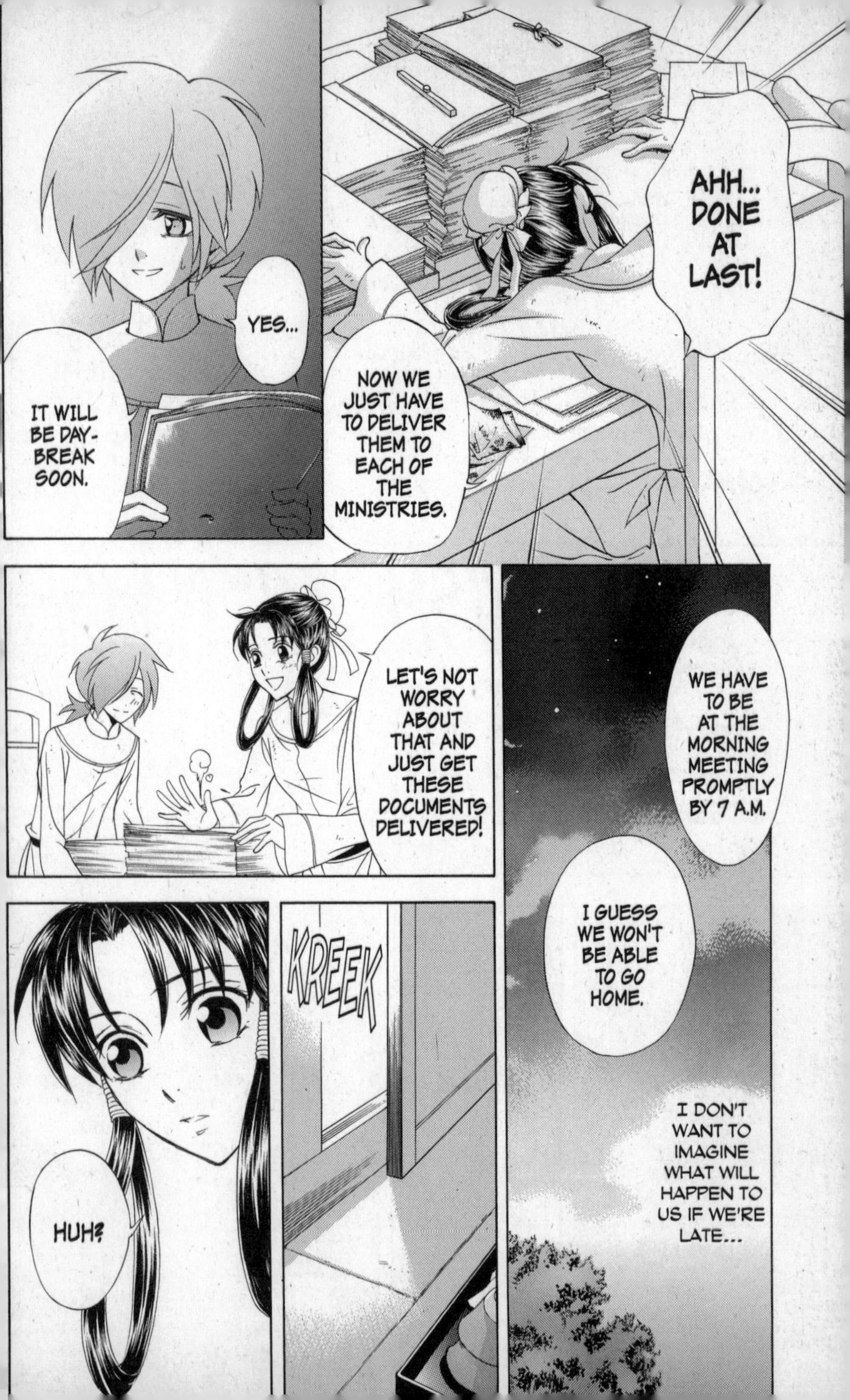
AHH... DONE AT LAST!
NOW WE JUST HAVE TO DELIVER THEM TO EACH OF THE MINISTRIES.
YES...
IT WILL BE DAY-BREAK SOON.
WE HAVE TO BE AT THE MORNING MEETING PROMPTLY BY 7 A.M.
I GUESS WE WON'T BE ABLE TO GO HOME.
I DON'T WANT TO IMAGINE WHAT WILL HAPPEN TO US IF WE'RE LATE...
LET'S NOT WORRY ABOUT THAT AND JUST GET THESE DOCUMENTS DELIVERED!
KREEK
HUH?

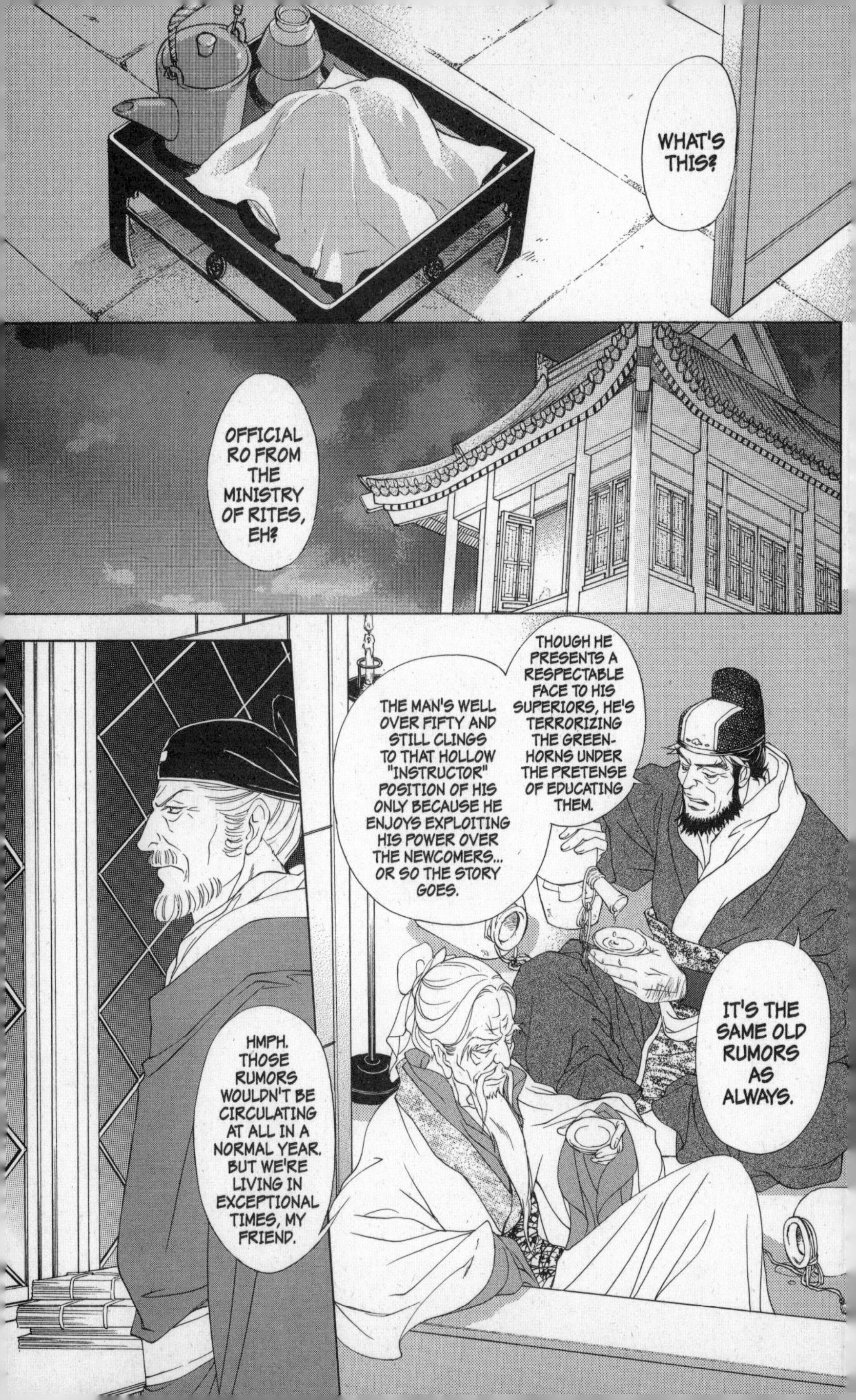
WHAT'S THIS?
OFFICIAL RO FROM THE MINISTRY OF RITES, EH?
THOUGH HE PRESENTS A RESPECTABLE FACE TO HIS SUPERIORS, HE'S TERRORIZING THE GREEN-HORNS UNDER THE PRETENSE OF EDUCATING THEM.
THE MAN'S WELL OVER FIFTY AND STILL CLINGS TO THAT HOLLOW "INSTRUCTOR" POSITION OF HIS ONLY BECAUSE HE ENJOYS EXPLOITING HIS POWER OVER THE NEWCOMERS... OR SO THE STORY GOES.
IT'S THE SAME OLD RUMORS AS ALWAYS.
HMPH. THOSE RUMORS WOULDN'T BE CIRCULATING AT ALL IN A NORMAL YEAR. BUT WE'RE LIVING IN EXCEPTIONAL TIMES, MY FRIEND.

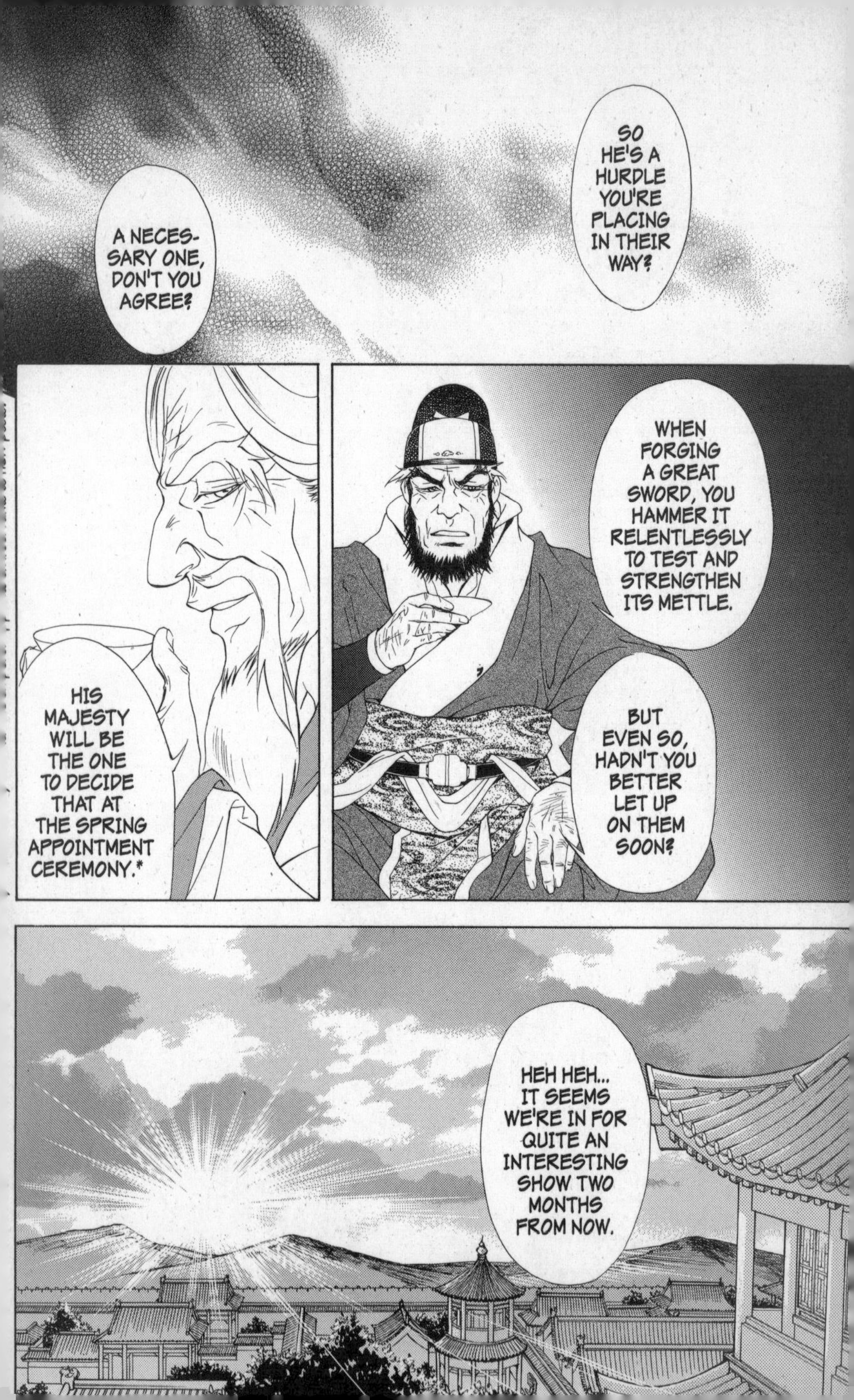
SO HE'S A HURDLE YOU'RE PLACING IN THEIR WAY?
A NECES-SARY ONE, DON'T YOU AGREE?
WHEN FORGING A GREAT SWORD, YOU HAMMER IT RELENTLESSLY TO TEST AND STRENGTHEN ITS METTLE.
BUT EVEN SO, HADN'T YOU BETTER LET UP ON THEM SOON?
HIS MAJESTY WILL BE THE ONE TO DECIDE THAT AT THE SPRING APPOINTMENT CEREMONY.*
HEH HEH... IT SEEMS WE'RE IN FOR QUITE AN INTERESTING SHOW TWO MONTHS FROM NOW.

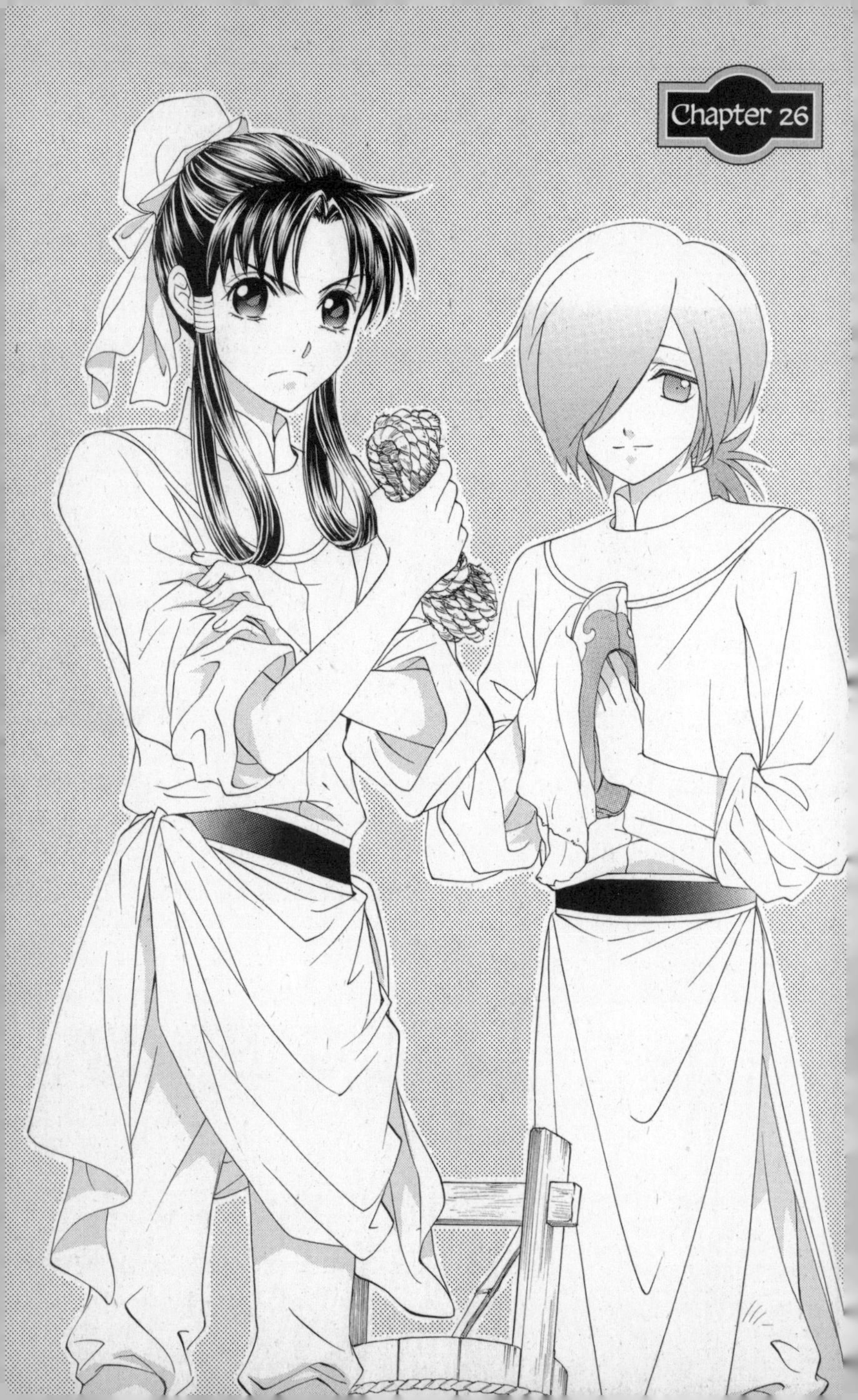
Chapter 26

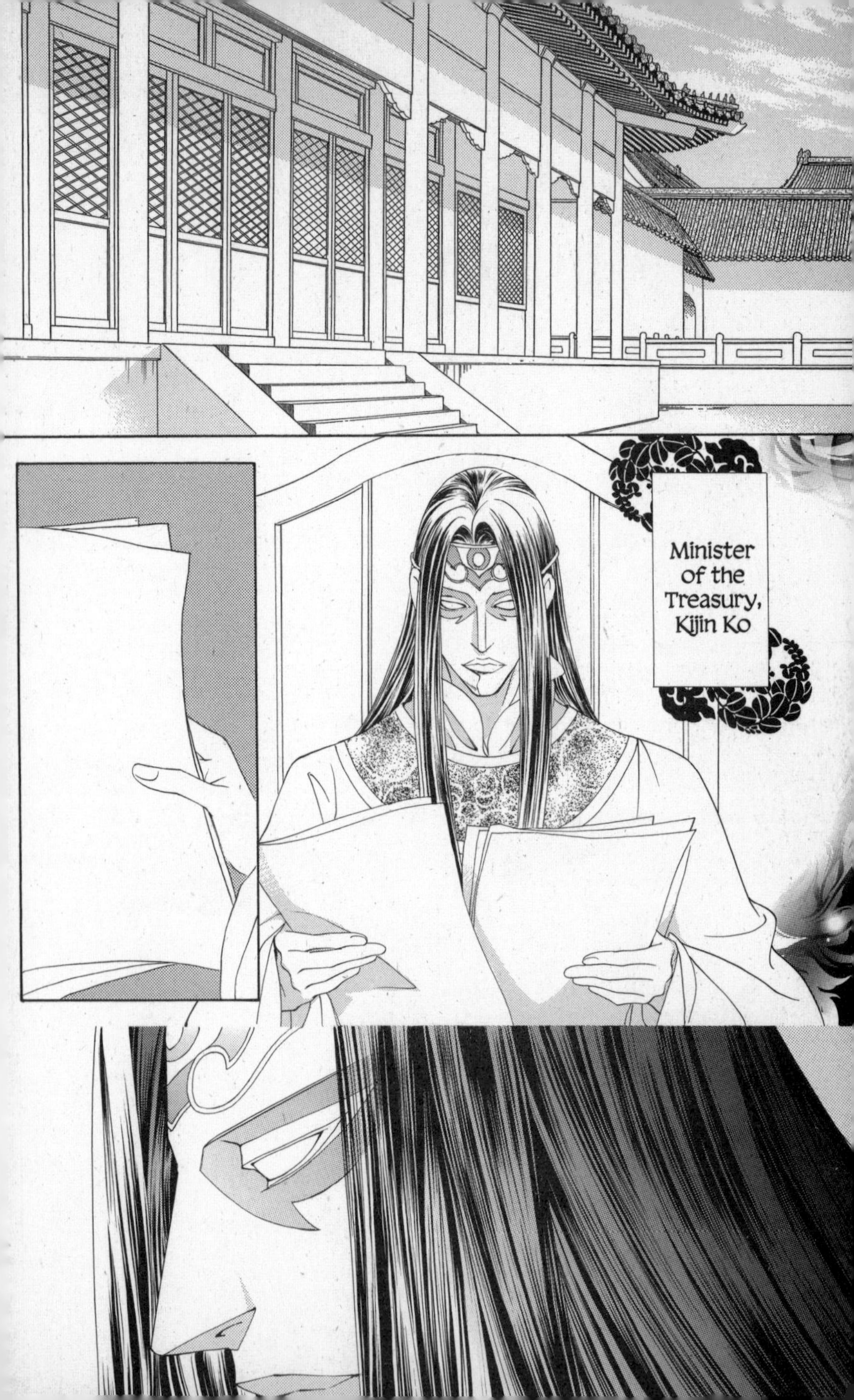
Minister of the Treasury, Kijin Ko

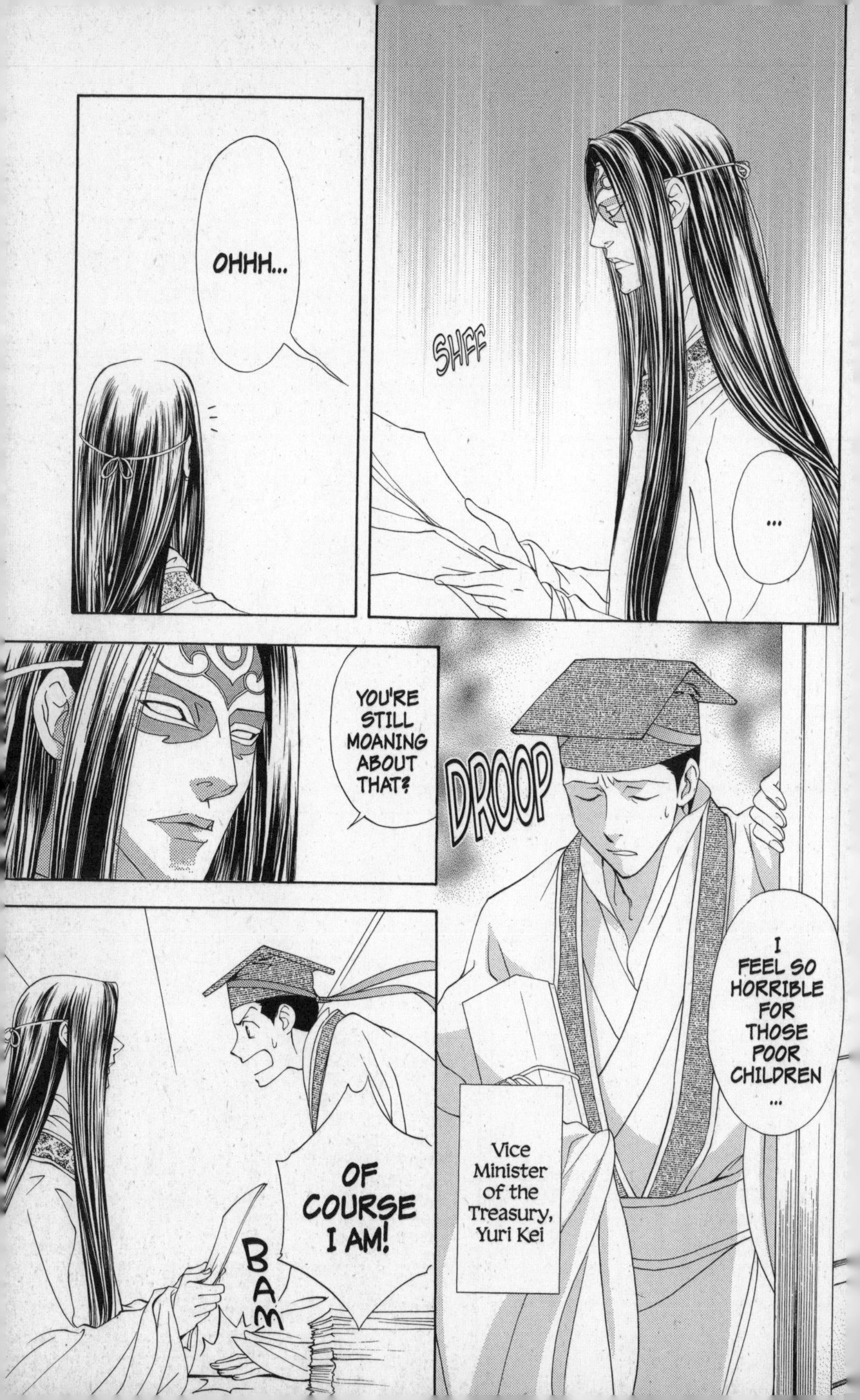
SHFF
...
OHHH...
DROOP
I FEEL SO HORRIBLE FOR THOSE POOR CHILDREN...
Vice Minister of the Treasury, Yuri Kei
YOU'RE STILL MOANING ABOUT THAT?
OF COURSE I AM!
BAM

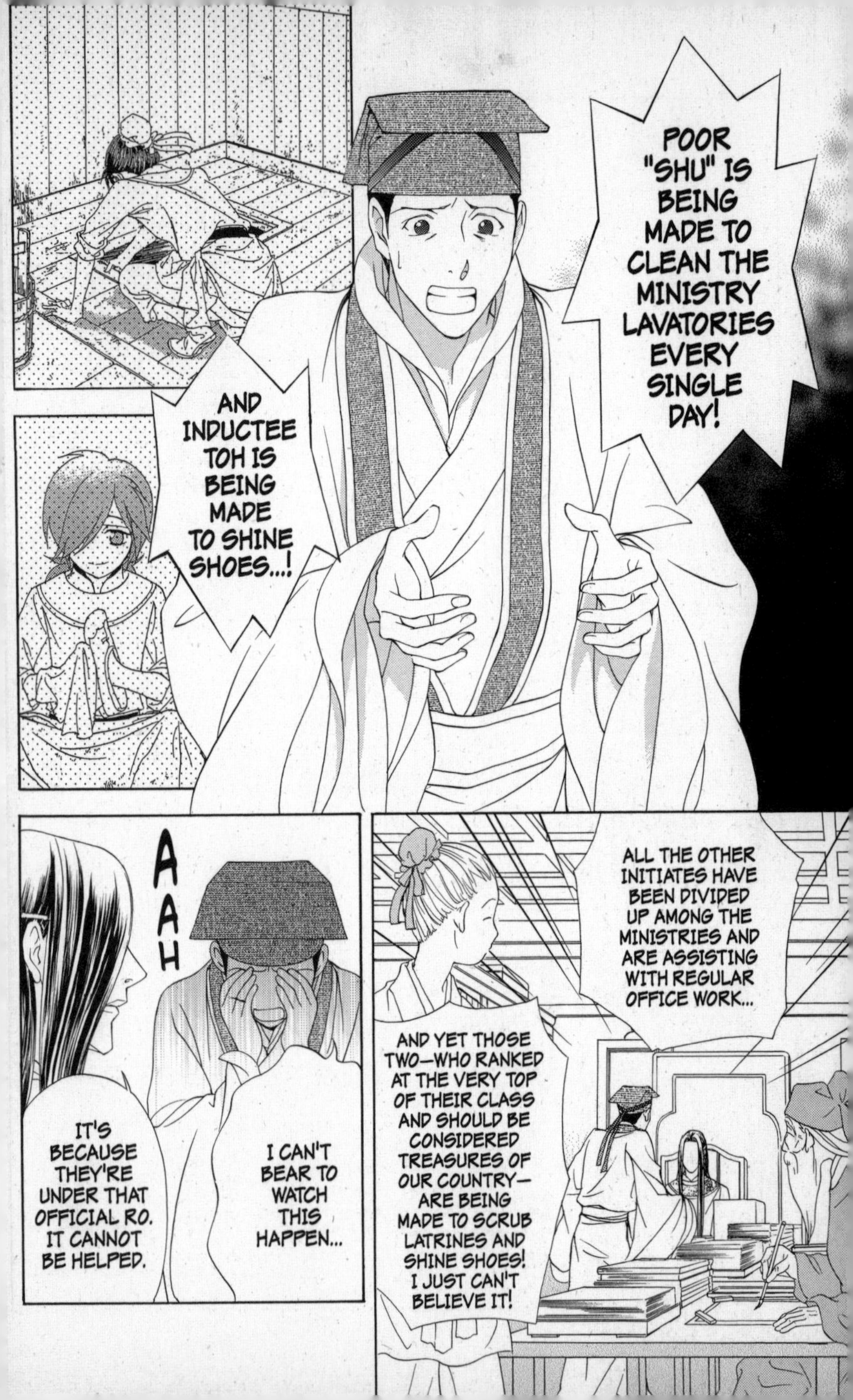
POOR "SHU" IS BEING MADE TO CLEAN THE MINISTRY LAVATORIES EVERY SINGLE DAY!
AND INDUCTEE TOH IS BEING MADE TO SHINE SHOES...!
ALL THE OTHER INITIATES HAVE BEEN DIVIDED UP AMONG THE MINISTRIES AND ARE ASSISTING WITH REGULAR OFFICE WORK...
AND YET THOSE TWO—WHO RANKED AT THE VERY TOP OF THEIR CLASS AND SHOULD BE CONSIDERED TREASURES OF OUR COUNTRY—ARE BEING MADE TO SCRUB LATRINES AND SHINE SHOES! I JUST CAN'T BELIEVE IT!
AAAH
I CAN'T BEAR TO WATCH THIS HAPPEN...
IT'S BECAUSE THEY'RE UNDER THAT OFFICIAL RO. IT CANNOT BE HELPED.

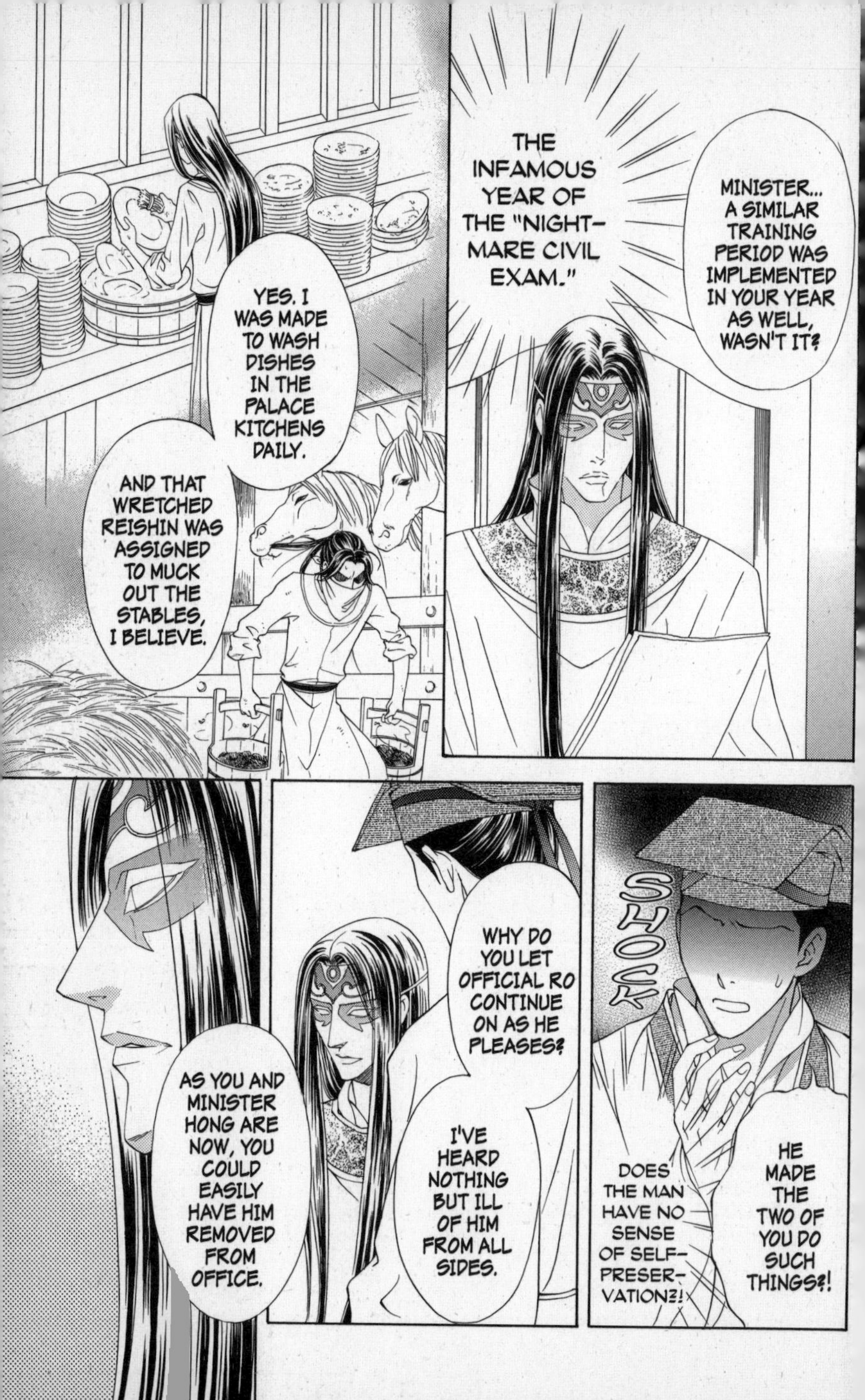
MINISTER... A SIMILAR TRAINING PERIOD WAS IMPLEMENTED IN YOUR YEAR AS WELL, WASN'T IT?
THE INFAMOUS YEAR OF THE "NIGHTMARE CIVIL EXAM."
YES. I WAS MADE TO WASH DISHES IN THE PALACE KITCHENS DAILY.
AND THAT WRETCHED REISHIN WAS ASSIGNED TO MUCK OUT THE STABLES, I BELIEVE.
SHOCK
HE MADE THE TWO OF YOU DO SUCH THINGS?!
DOES THE MAN HAVE NO SENSE OF SELF-PRESERVATION?!
WHY DO YOU LET OFFICIAL RO CONTINUE ON AS HE PLEASES?
I'VE HEARD NOTHING BUT ILL OF HIM FROM ALL SIDES.
AS YOU AND MINISTER HONG ARE NOW, YOU COULD EASILY HAVE HIM REMOVED FROM OFFICE.

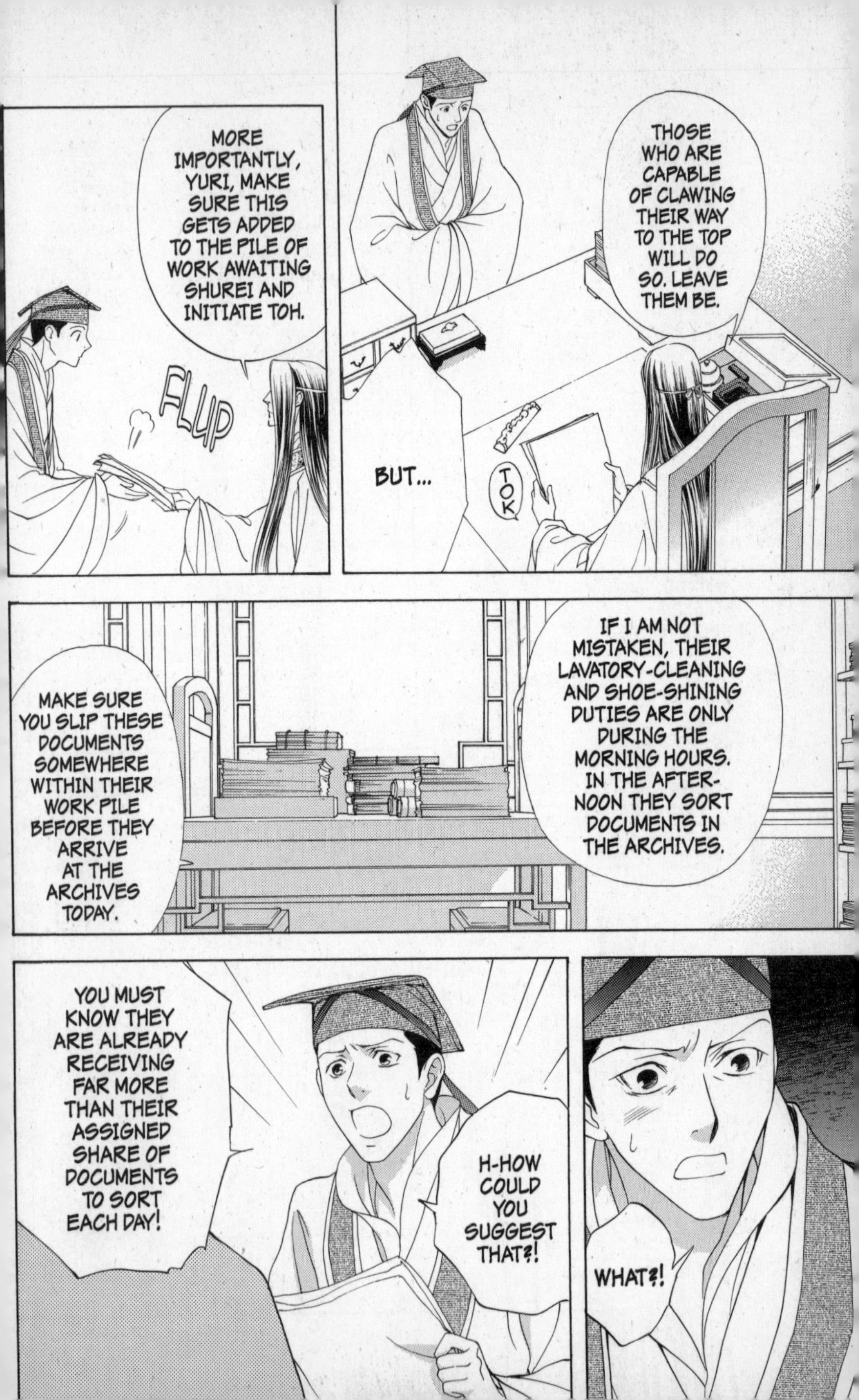
THOSE WHO ARE CAPABLE OF CLAWING THEIR WAY TO THE TOP WILL DO SO. LEAVE THEM BE.
BUT...
TOK
MORE IMPORTANTLY, YURI, MAKE SURE THIS GETS ADDED TO THE PILE OF WORK AWAITING SHUREI AND INITIATE TOH.
FLUP
IF I AM NOT MISTAKEN, THEIR LAVATORY-CLEANING AND SHOE-SHINING DUTIES ARE ONLY DURING THE MORNING HOURS. IN THE AFTER-NOON THEY SORT DOCUMENTS IN THE ARCHIVES.
MAKE SURE YOU SLIP THESE DOCUMENTS SOMEWHERE WITHIN THEIR WORK PILE BEFORE THEY ARRIVE AT THE ARCHIVES TODAY.
WHAT?!
H-HOW COULD YOU SUGGEST THAT?!
YOU MUST KNOW THEY ARE ALREADY RECEIVING FAR MORE THAN THEIR ASSIGNED SHARE OF DOCUMENTS TO SORT EACH DAY!

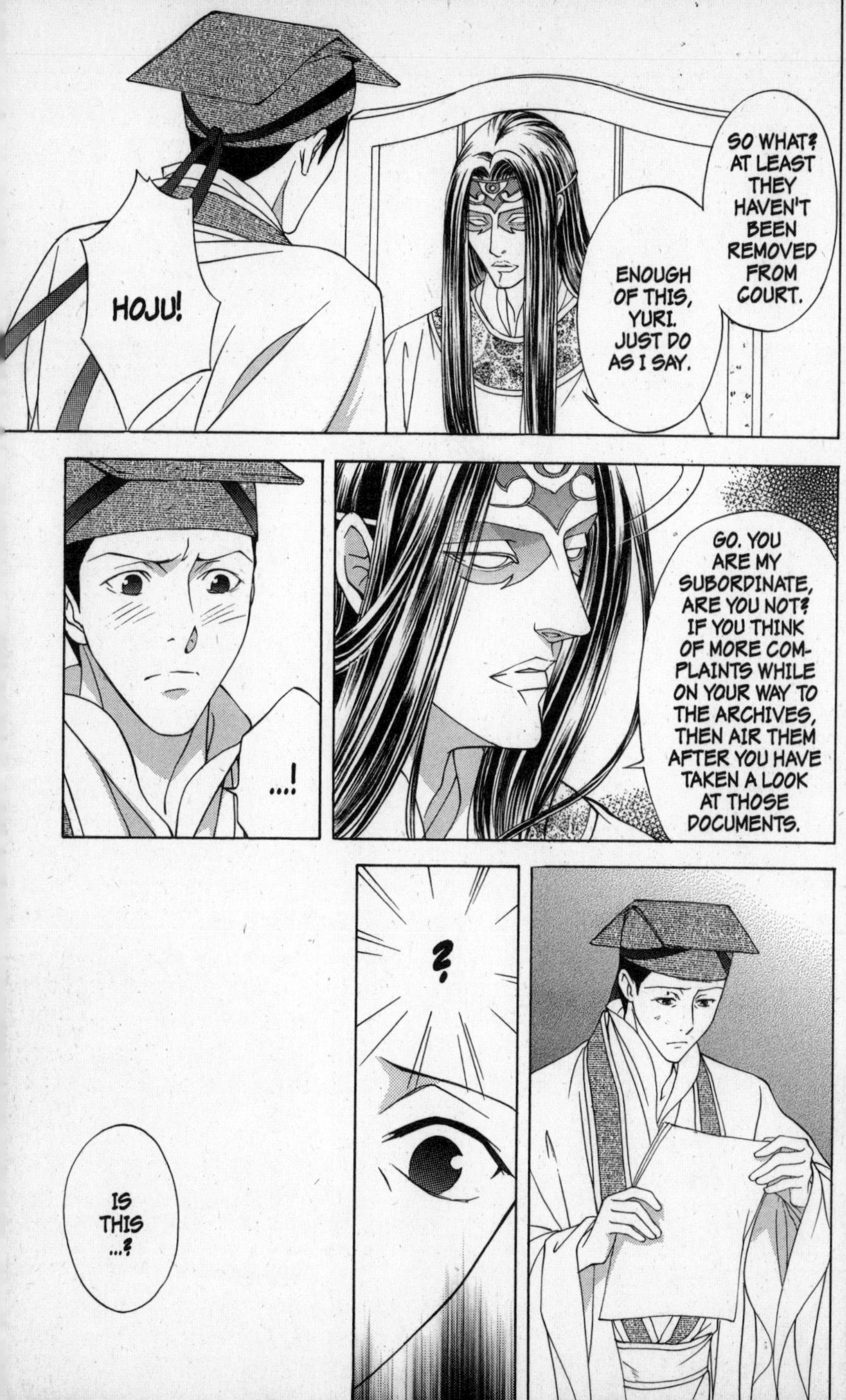
SO WHAT? AT LEAST THEY HAVEN'T BEEN REMOVED FROM COURT.
ENOUGH OF THIS, YURI. JUST DO AS I SAY.
HOJU!
GO. YOU ARE MY SUBORDINATE, ARE YOU NOT? IF YOU THINK OF MORE COMPLAINTS WHILE ON YOUR WAY TO THE ARCHIVES, THEN AIR THEM AFTER YOU HAVE TAKEN A LOOK AT THOSE DOCUMENTS.
...!
?
IS THIS ...?

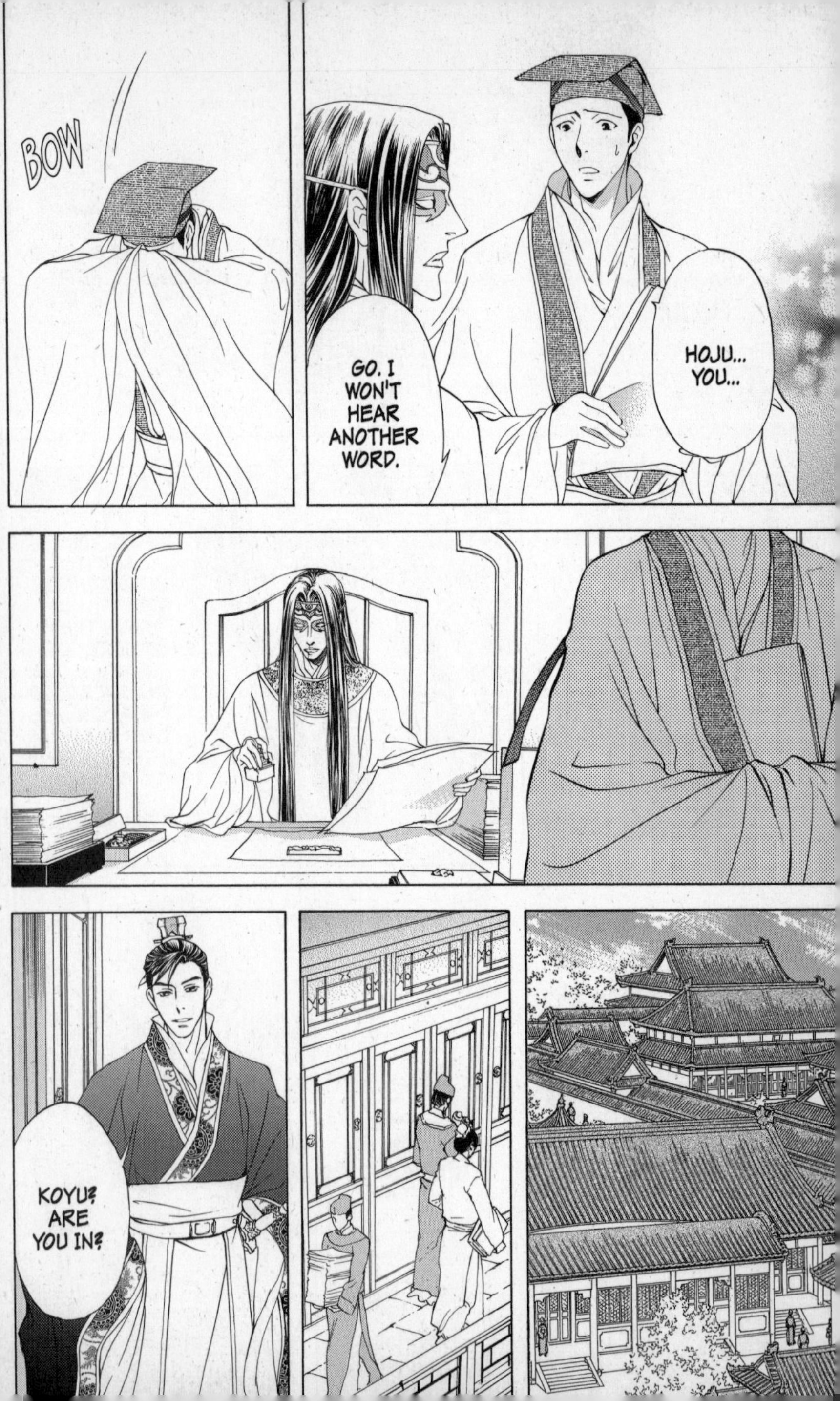
HOJU... YOU...
GO. I WON'T HEAR ANOTHER WORD.
BOW
KOYU? ARE YOU IN?

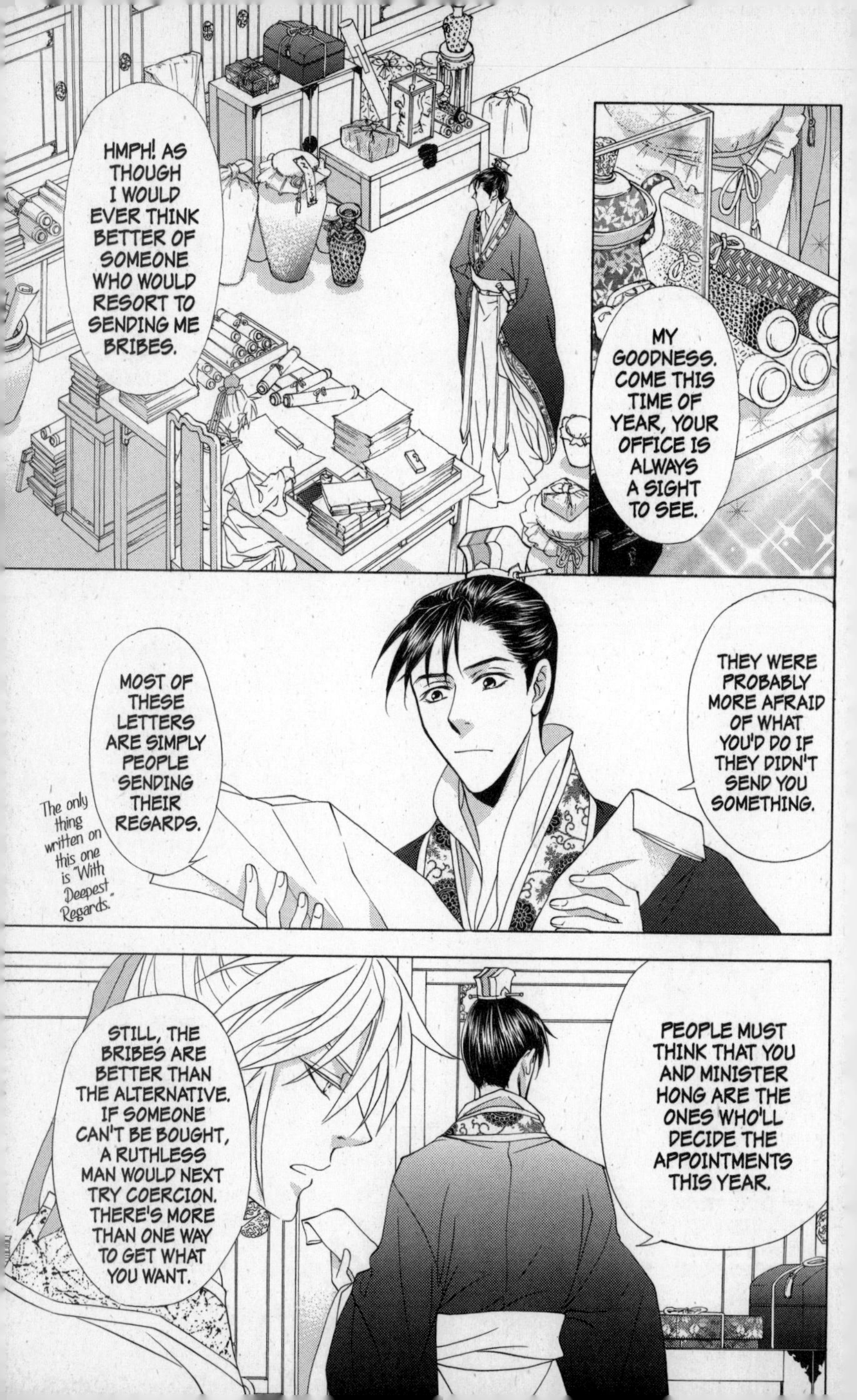
MY GOODNESS. COME THIS TIME OF YEAR, YOUR OFFICE IS ALWAYS A SIGHT TO SEE.
HMPH! AS THOUGH I WOULD EVER THINK BETTER OF SOMEONE WHO WOULD RESORT TO SENDING ME BRIBES.
THEY WERE PROBABLY MORE AFRAID OF WHAT YOU'D DO IF THEY DIDN'T SEND YOU SOMETHING.
MOST OF THESE LETTERS ARE SIMPLY PEOPLE SENDING THEIR REGARDS.
The only thing written on this one is "With Deepest Regards."
PEOPLE MUST THINK THAT YOU AND MINISTER HONG ARE THE ONES WHO'LL DECIDE THE APPOINTMENTS THIS YEAR.
STILL, THE BRIBES ARE BETTER THAN THE ALTERNATIVE. IF SOMEONE CAN'T BE BOUGHT, A RUTHLESS MAN WOULD NEXT TRY COERCION. THERE'S MORE THAN ONE WAY TO GET WHAT YOU WANT.

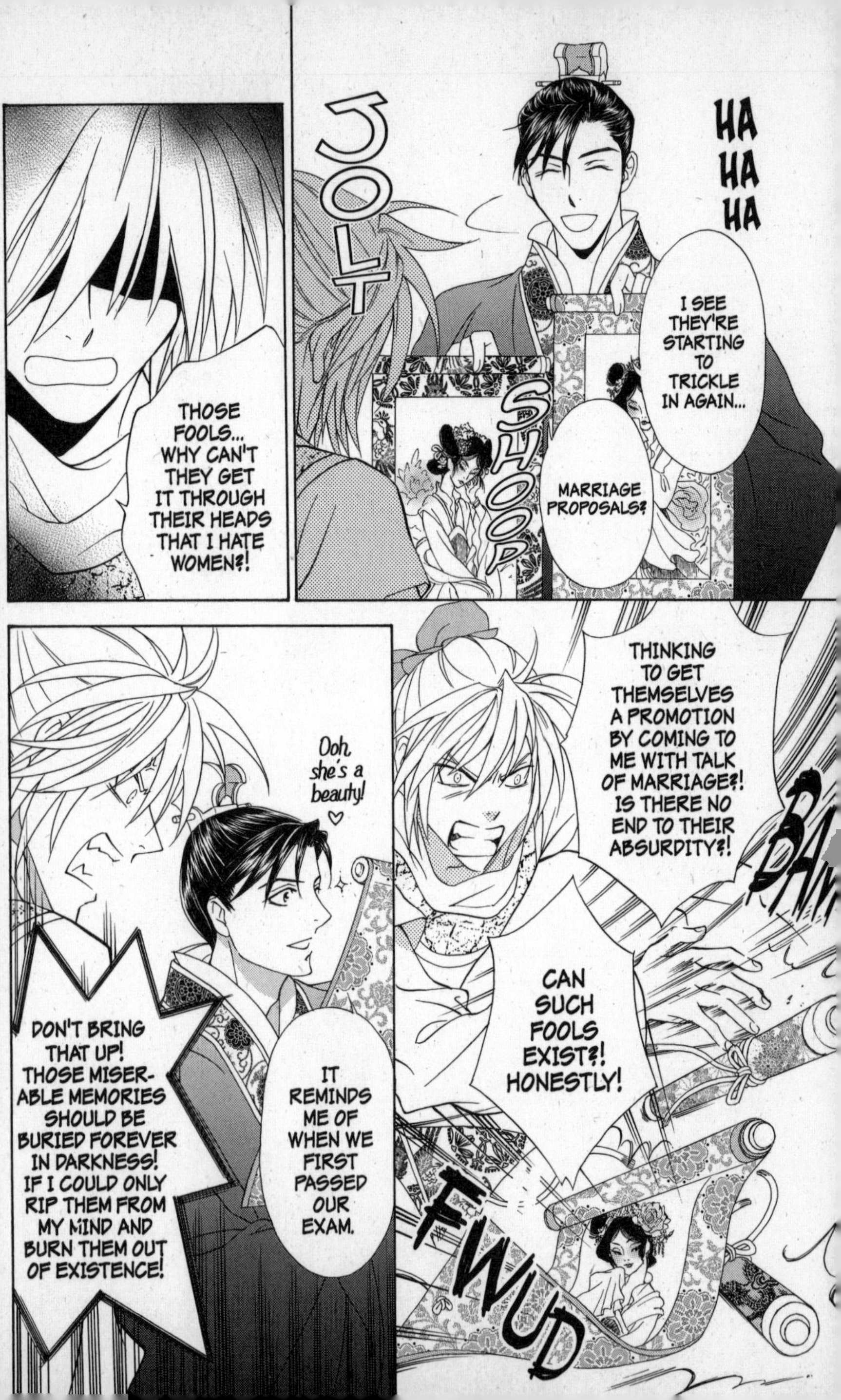
HA HA HA
I SEE THEY'RE STARTING TO TRICKLE IN AGAIN...
JOLT
SHOOP
MARRIAGE PROPOSALS?
THOSE FOOLS... WHY CAN'T THEY GET IT THROUGH THEIR HEADS THAT I HATE WOMEN?!
THINKING TO GET THEMSELVES A PROMOTION BY COMING TO ME WITH TALK OF MARRIAGE?! IS THERE NO END TO THEIR ABSURDITY?!
BAM
CAN SUCH FOOLS EXIST?! HONESTLY!
FWUD
Ooh, she's a beauty! ♡
IT REMINDS ME OF WHEN WE FIRST PASSED OUR EXAM.
DON'T BRING THAT UP! THOSE MISER-ABLE MEMORIES SHOULD BE BURIED FOREVER IN DARKNESS! IF I COULD ONLY RIP THEM FROM MY MIND AND BURN THEM OUT OF EXISTENCE!

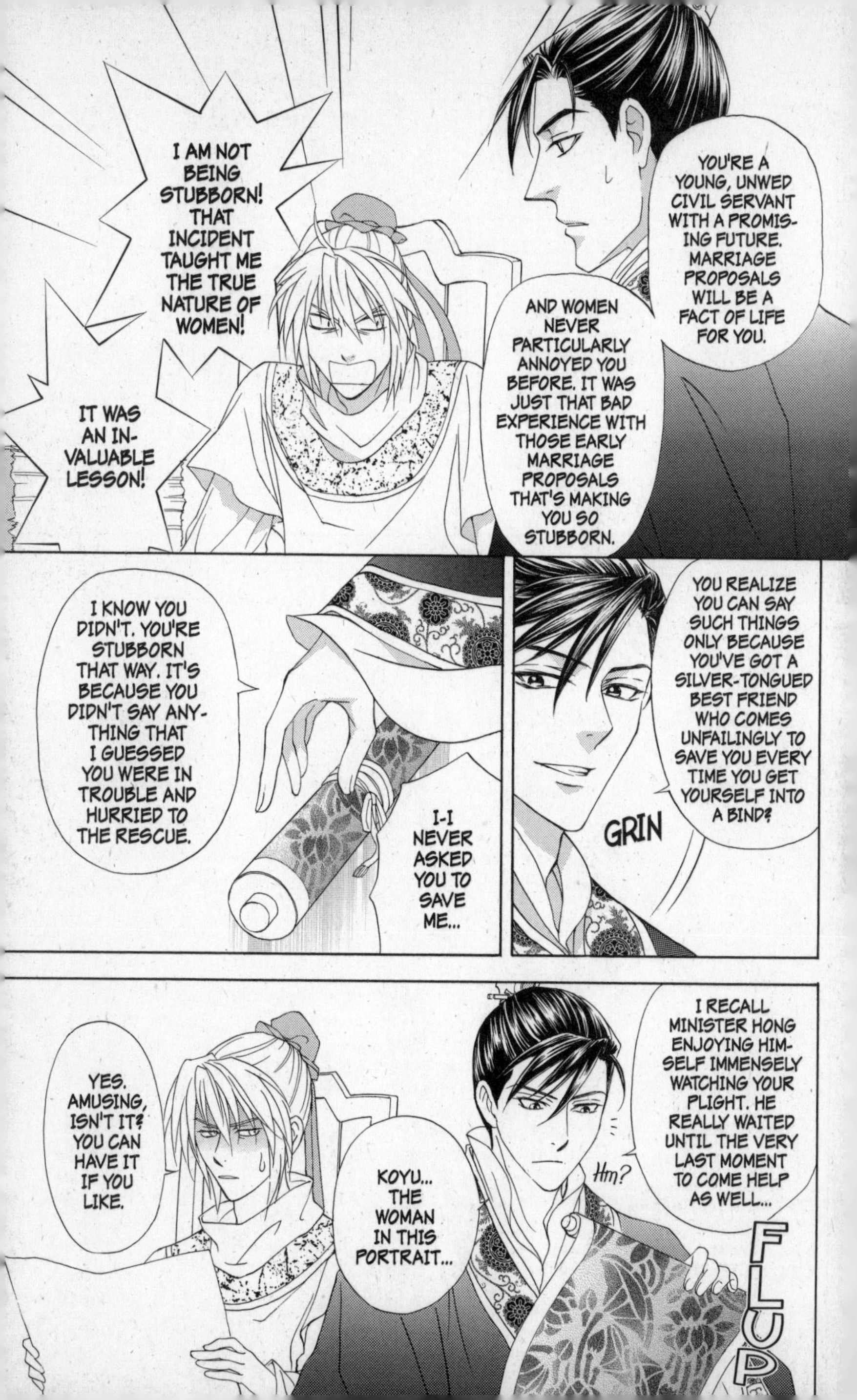
YOU'RE A YOUNG, UNWED CIVIL SERVANT WITH A PROMIS-ING FUTURE. MARRIAGE PROPOSALS WILL BE A FACT OF LIFE FOR YOU.
AND WOMEN NEVER PARTICULARLY ANNOYED YOU BEFORE. IT WAS JUST THAT BAD EXPERIENCE WITH THOSE EARLY MARRIAGE PROPOSALS THAT'S MAKING YOU SO STUBBORN.
I AM NOT BEING STUBBORN! THAT INCIDENT TAUGHT ME THE TRUE NATURE OF WOMEN!
IT WAS AN IN-VALUABLE LESSON!
YOU REALIZE YOU CAN SAY SUCH THINGS ONLY BECAUSE YOU'VE GOT A SILVER-TONGUED BEST FRIEND WHO COMES UNFAILINGLY TO SAVE YOU EVERY TIME YOU GET YOURSELF INTO A BIND?
GRIN
I-I NEVER ASKED YOU TO SAVE ME...
I KNOW YOU DIDN'T. YOU'RE STUBBORN THAT WAY. IT'S BECAUSE YOU DIDN'T SAY ANY-THING THAT I GUESSED YOU WERE IN TROUBLE AND HURRIED TO THE RESCUE.
I RECALL MINISTER HONG ENJOYING HIM-SELF IMMENSELY WATCHING YOUR PLIGHT. HE REALLY WAITED UNTIL THE VERY LAST MOMENT TO COME HELP AS WELL...
FLUP
Hm?
KOYU... THE WOMAN IN THIS PORTRAIT...
YES. AMUSING, ISN'T IT? YOU CAN HAVE IT IF YOU LIKE.

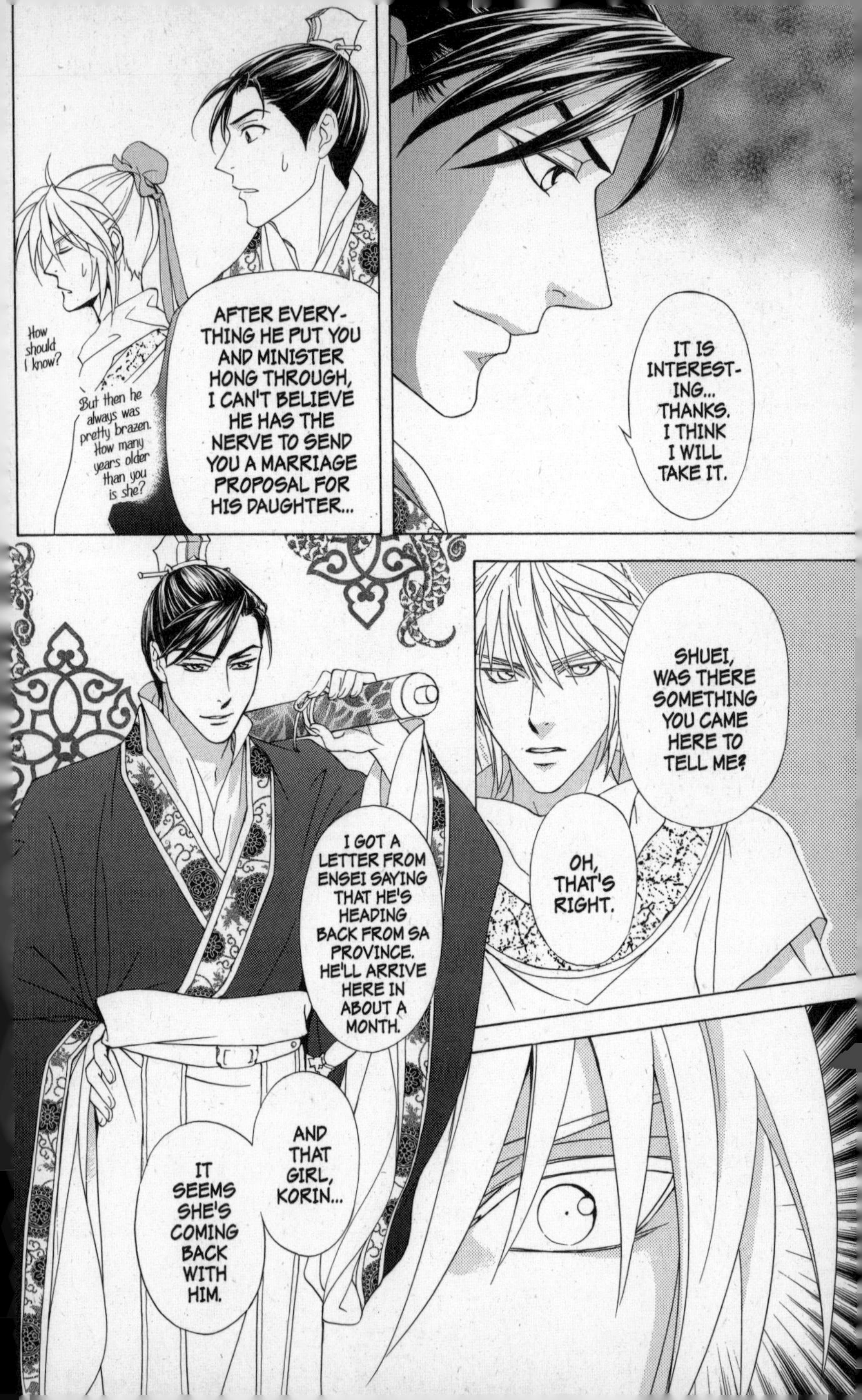
IT IS INTERESTING... THANKS. I THINK I WILL TAKE IT.
AFTER EVERYTHING HE PUT YOU AND MINISTER HONG THROUGH, I CAN'T BELIEVE HE HAS THE NERVE TO SEND YOU A MARRIAGE PROPOSAL FOR HIS DAUGHTER...
How should I know?
But then he always was pretty brazen. How many years older than you is she?
SHUEI, WAS THERE SOMETHING YOU CAME HERE TO TELL ME?
OH, THAT'S RIGHT.
I GOT A LETTER FROM ENSEI SAYING THAT HE'S HEADING BACK FROM SA PROVINCE. HE'LL ARRIVE HERE IN ABOUT A MONTH.
AND THAT GIRL, KORIN...
IT SEEMS SHE'S COMING BACK WITH HIM.

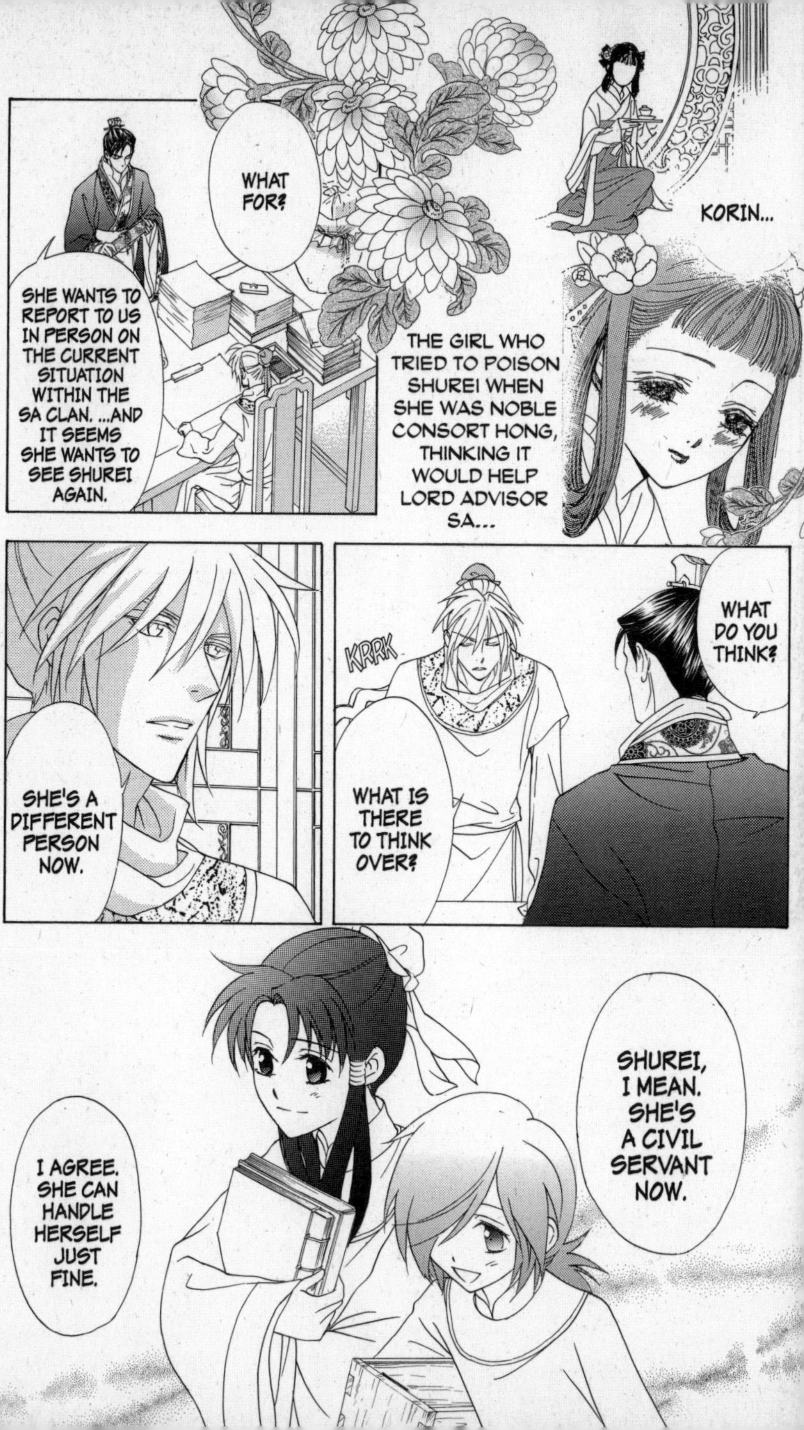
KORIN...
THE GIRL WHO TRIED TO POISON SHUREI WHEN SHE WAS NOBLE CONSORT HONG, THINKING IT WOULD HELP LORD ADVISOR SA...
WHAT FOR?
SHE WANTS TO REPORT TO US IN PERSON ON THE CURRENT SITUATION WITHIN THE SA CLAN. ...AND IT SEEMS SHE WANTS TO SEE SHUREI AGAIN.
WHAT DO YOU THINK?
KRRK
WHAT IS THERE TO THINK OVER?
SHE'S A DIFFERENT PERSON NOW.
SHUREI, I MEAN. SHE'S A CIVIL SERVANT NOW.
I AGREE. SHE CAN HANDLE HERSELF JUST FINE.

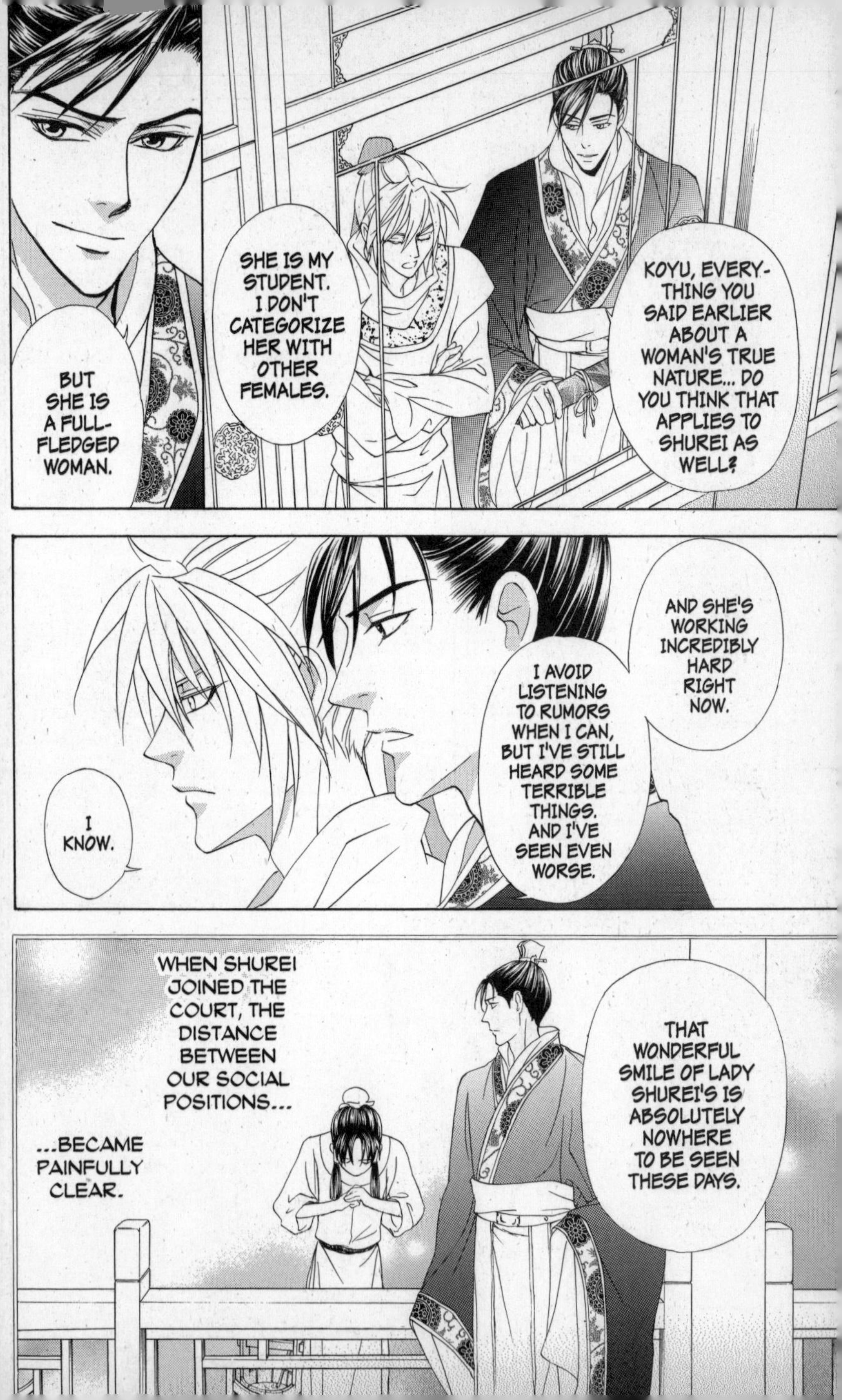
KOYU, EVERY-THING YOU SAID EARLIER ABOUT A WOMAN'S TRUE NATURE... DO YOU THINK THAT APPLIES TO SHUREI AS WELL?
SHE IS MY STUDENT. I DON'T CATEGORIZE HER WITH OTHER FEMALES.
BUT SHE IS A FULL-FLEDGED WOMAN.
AND SHE'S WORKING INCREDIBLY HARD RIGHT NOW.
I AVOID LISTENING TO RUMORS WHEN I CAN, BUT I'VE STILL HEARD SOME TERRIBLE THINGS. AND I'VE SEEN EVEN WORSE.
I KNOW.
THAT WONDERFUL SMILE OF LADY SHUREI'S IS ABSOLUTELY NOWHERE TO BE SEEN THESE DAYS.
WHEN SHUREI JOINED THE COURT, THE DISTANCE BETWEEN OUR SOCIAL POSITIONS...
...BECAME PAINFULLY CLEAR.

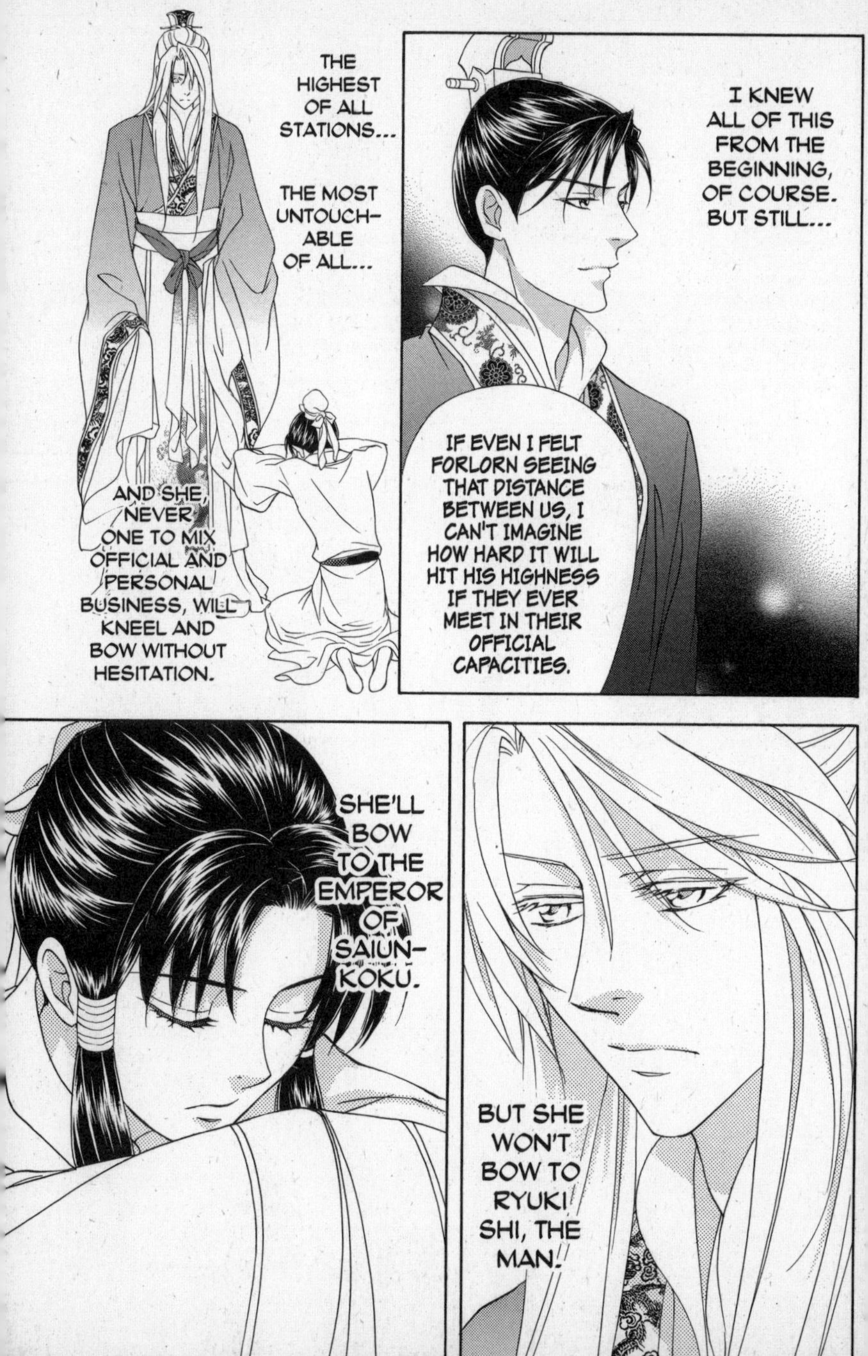
I KNEW ALL OF THIS FROM THE BEGINNING, OF COURSE. BUT STILL...
IF EVEN I FELT FORLORN SEEING THAT DISTANCE BETWEEN US, I CAN'T IMAGINE HOW HARD IT WILL HIT HIS HIGHNESS IF THEY EVER MEET IN THEIR OFFICIAL CAPACITIES.
THE HIGHEST OF ALL STATIONS...
THE MOST UNTOUCH-ABLE OF ALL...
AND SHE, NEVER ONE TO MIX OFFICIAL AND PERSONAL BUSINESS, WILL KNEEL AND BOW WITHOUT HESITATION.
BUT SHE WON'T BOW TO RYUKI SHI, THE MAN.
SHE'LL BOW TO THE EMPEROR OF SAIUN-KOKU.

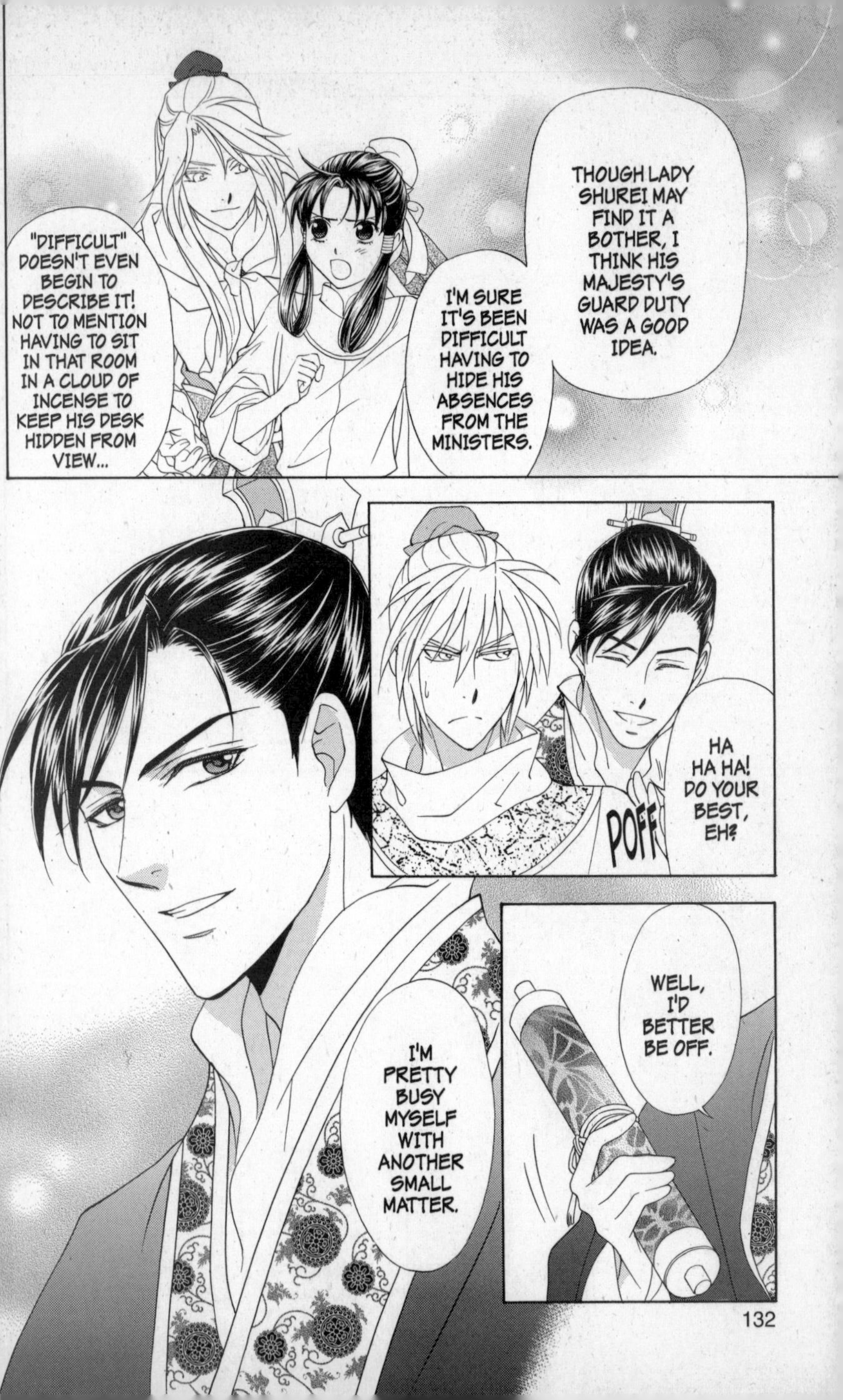
THOUGH LADY SHUREI MAY FIND IT A BOTHER, I THINK HIS MAJESTY'S GUARD DUTY WAS A GOOD IDEA.
I'M SURE IT'S BEEN DIFFICULT HAVING TO HIDE HIS ABSENCES FROM THE MINISTERS.
"DIFFICULT" DOESN'T EVEN BEGIN TO DESCRIBE IT! NOT TO MENTION HAVING TO SIT IN THAT ROOM IN A CLOUD OF INCENSE TO KEEP HIS DESK HIDDEN FROM VIEW...
HA HA HA! DO YOUR BEST, EH?
POFF
WELL, I'D BETTER BE OFF.
I'M PRETTY BUSY MYSELF WITH ANOTHER SMALL MATTER.

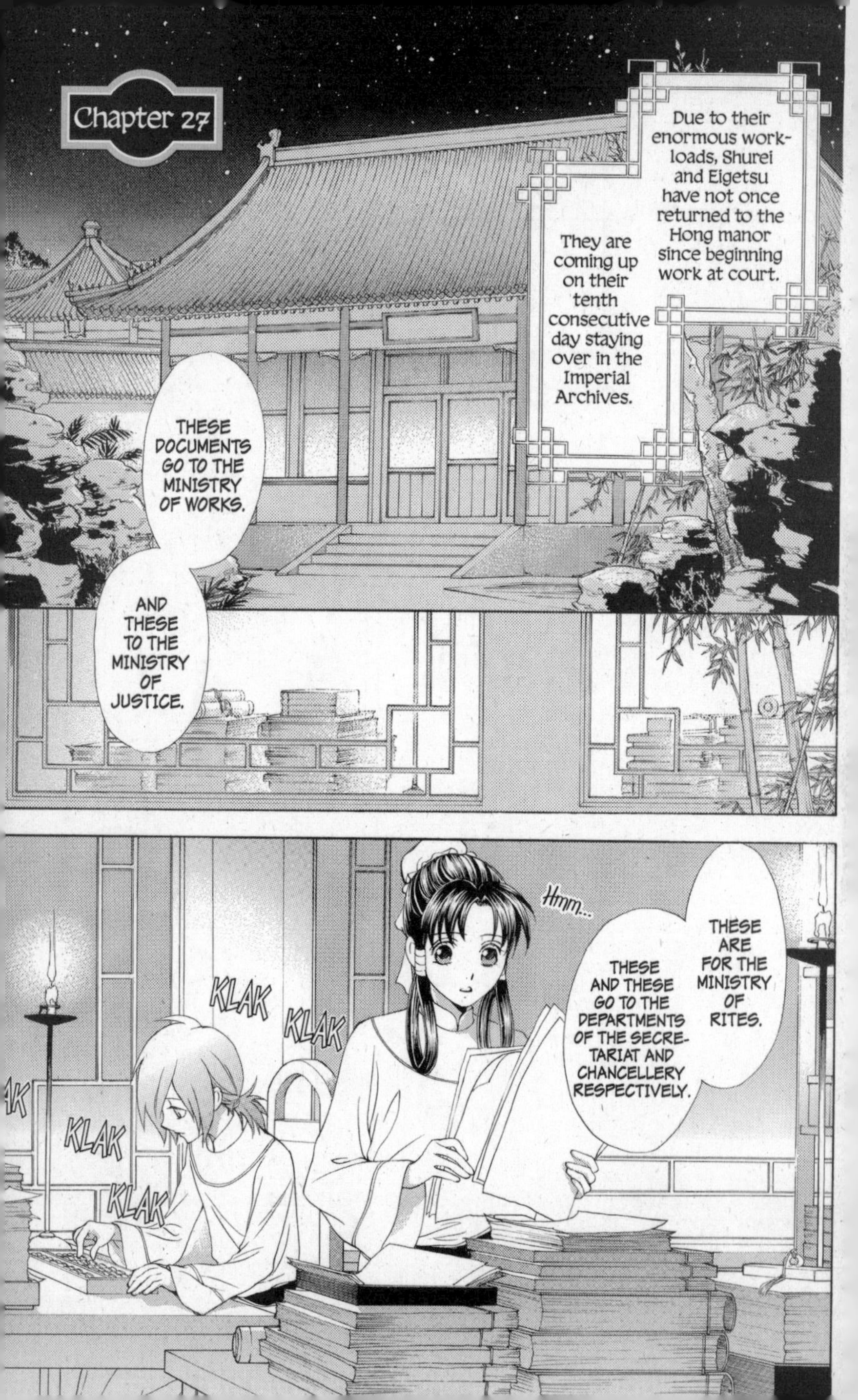
Chapter 27
Due to their enormous work-loads, Shurei and Eigetsu have not once returned to the Hong manor since beginning work at court.
They are coming up on their tenth consecutive day staying over in the Imperial Archives.
THESE DOCUMENTS GO TO THE MINISTRY OF WORKS.
AND THESE TO THE MINISTRY OF JUSTICE.
Hmm...
THESE ARE FOR THE MINISTRY OF RITES.
THESE AND THESE GO TO THE DEPARTMENTS OF THE SECRE-TARIAT AND CHANCELLERY RESPECTIVELY.
KLAK
KLAK
KLAK
KLAK

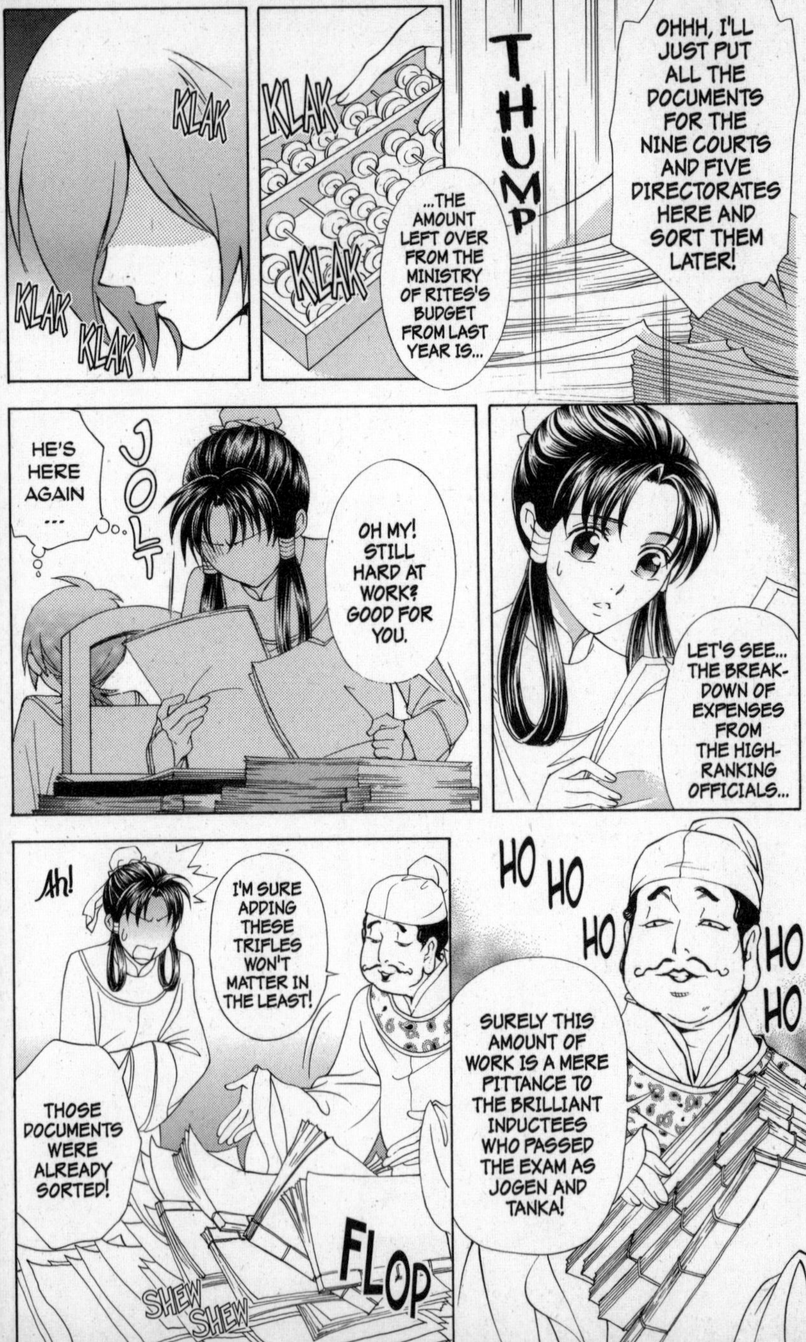
OHHH, I'LL JUST PUT ALL THE DOCUMENTS FOR THE NINE COURTS AND FIVE DIRECTORATES HERE AND SORT THEM LATER!
THUMP
...THE AMOUNT LEFT OVER FROM THE MINISTRY OF RITES'S BUDGET FROM LAST YEAR IS...
KLAK
KLAK
KLAK
KLAK
KLAK
LET'S SEE... THE BREAKDOWN OF EXPENSES FROM THE HIGH-RANKING OFFICIALS...
OH MY! STILL HARD AT WORK? GOOD FOR YOU.
JOLT
HE'S HERE AGAIN ...
HO HO HO HO HO
SURELY THIS AMOUNT OF WORK IS A MERE PITTANCE TO THE BRILLIANT INDUCTEES WHO PASSED THE EXAM AS JOGEN AND TANKA!
I'M SURE ADDING THESE TRIFLES WON'T MATTER IN THE LEAST!
Ah!
THOSE DOCUMENTS WERE ALREADY SORTED!
FLOP
SHEW SHEW

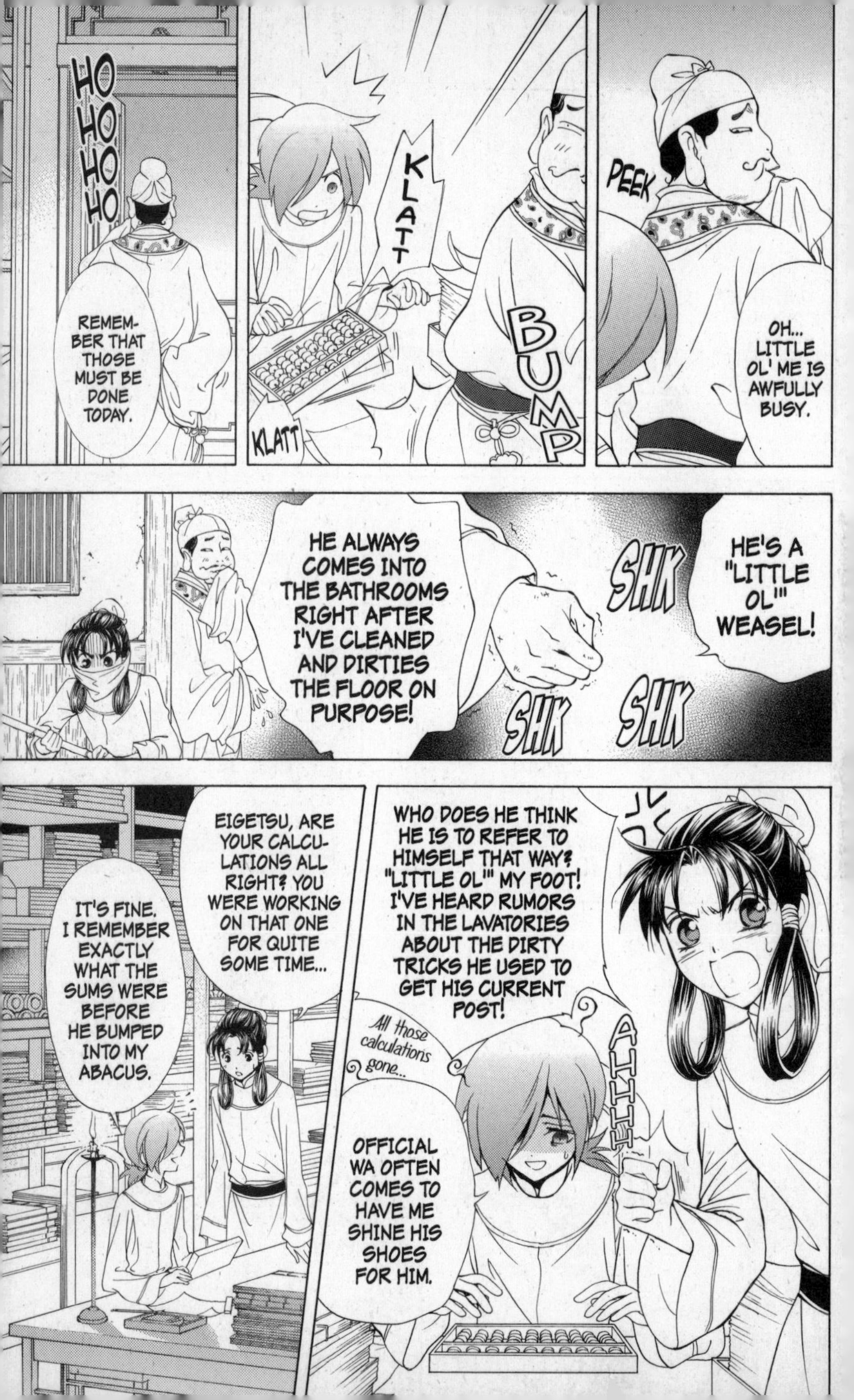
PEEK
OH... LITTLE OL' ME IS AWFULLY BUSY.
KLATT
BUMP
KLATT
HO HO HO HO
REMEMBER THAT THOSE MUST BE DONE TODAY.
HE'S A "LITTLE OL'" WEASEL!
SHK
SHK
SHK
HE ALWAYS COMES INTO THE BATHROOMS RIGHT AFTER I'VE CLEANED AND DIRTIES THE FLOOR ON PURPOSE!
WHO DOES HE THINK HE IS TO REFER TO HIMSELF THAT WAY? "LITTLE OL'" MY FOOT! I'VE HEARD RUMORS IN THE LAVATORIES ABOUT THE DIRTY TRICKS HE USED TO GET HIS CURRENT POST!
AHHHH
All those calculations gone...
OFFICIAL WA OFTEN COMES TO HAVE ME SHINE HIS SHOES FOR HIM.
EIGETSU, ARE YOUR CALCULATIONS ALL RIGHT? YOU WERE WORKING ON THAT ONE FOR QUITE SOME TIME...
IT'S FINE. I REMEMBER EXACTLY WHAT THE SUMS WERE BEFORE HE BUMPED INTO MY ABACUS.

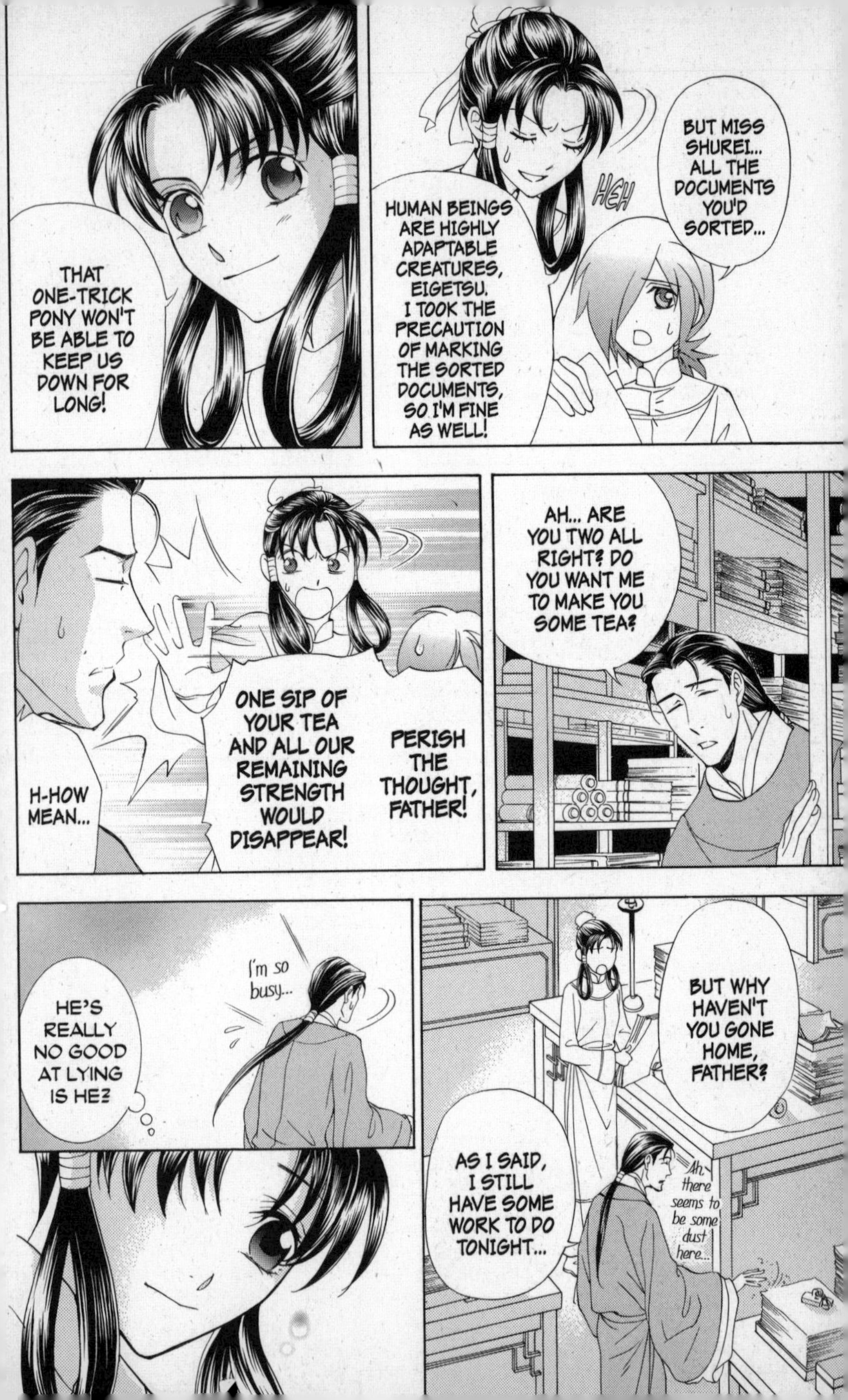
BUT MISS SHUREI... ALL THE DOCUMENTS YOU'D SORTED...
HEH
HUMAN BEINGS ARE HIGHLY ADAPTABLE CREATURES, EIGETSU. I TOOK THE PRECAUTION OF MARKING THE SORTED DOCUMENTS, SO I'M FINE AS WELL!
THAT ONE-TRICK PONY WON'T BE ABLE TO KEEP US DOWN FOR LONG!
AH... ARE YOU TWO ALL RIGHT? DO YOU WANT ME TO MAKE YOU SOME TEA?
PERISH THE THOUGHT, FATHER!
ONE SIP OF YOUR TEA AND ALL OUR REMAINING STRENGTH WOULD DISAPPEAR!
H-HOW MEAN...
BUT WHY HAVEN'T YOU GONE HOME, FATHER?
AS I SAID, I STILL HAVE SOME WORK TO DO TONIGHT...
Ah, there seems to be some dust here...
I'm so busy...
HE'S REALLY NO GOOD AT LYING IS HE?

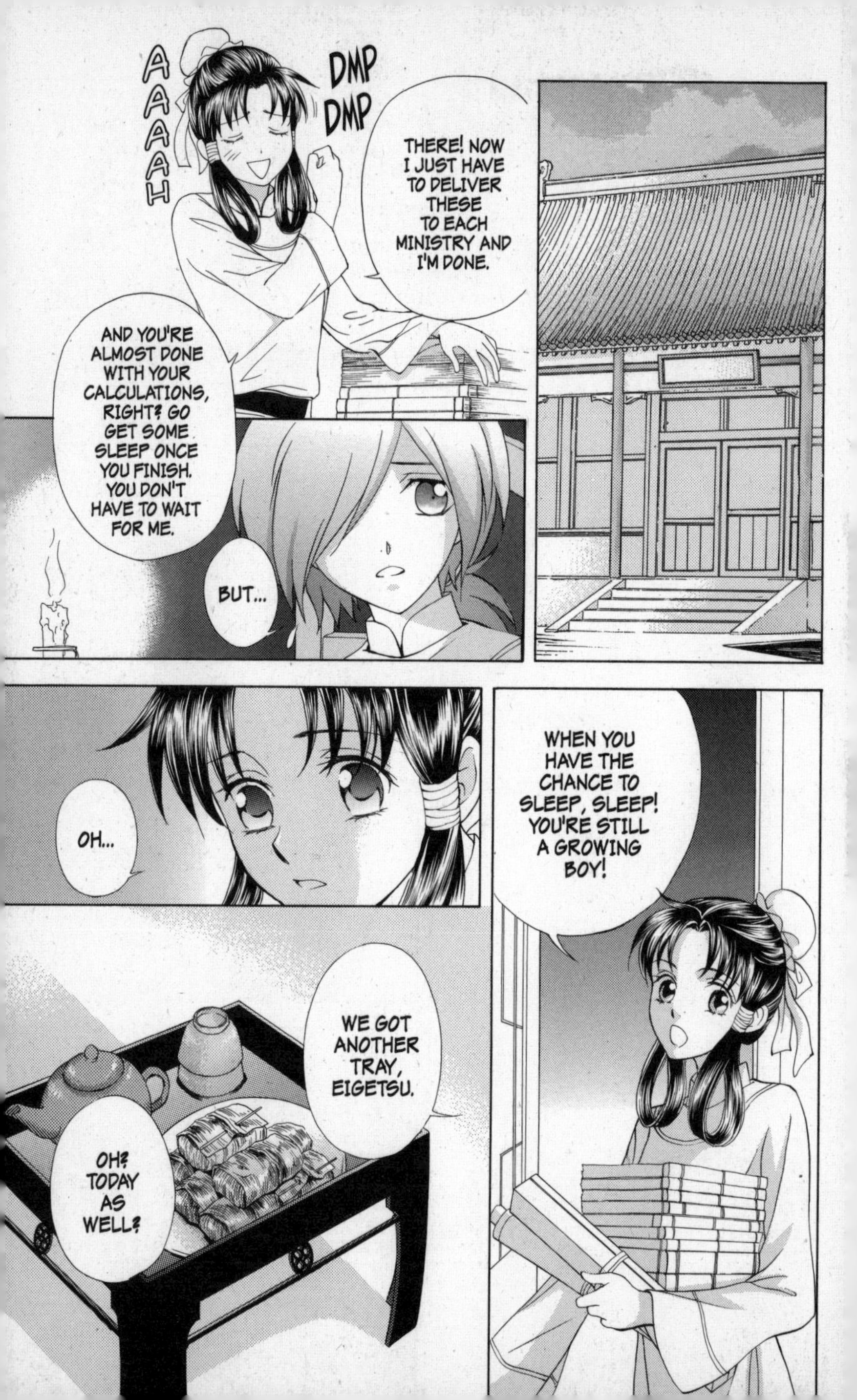
DMP DMP
THERE! NOW I JUST HAVE TO DELIVER THESE TO EACH MINISTRY AND I'M DONE.
AAAAAH
AND YOU'RE ALMOST DONE WITH YOUR CALCULATIONS, RIGHT? GO GET SOME SLEEP ONCE YOU FINISH. YOU DON'T HAVE TO WAIT FOR ME.
BUT...
WHEN YOU HAVE THE CHANCE TO SLEEP, SLEEP! YOU'RE STILL A GROWING BOY!
OH...
WE GOT ANOTHER TRAY, EIGETSU.
OH? TODAY AS WELL?

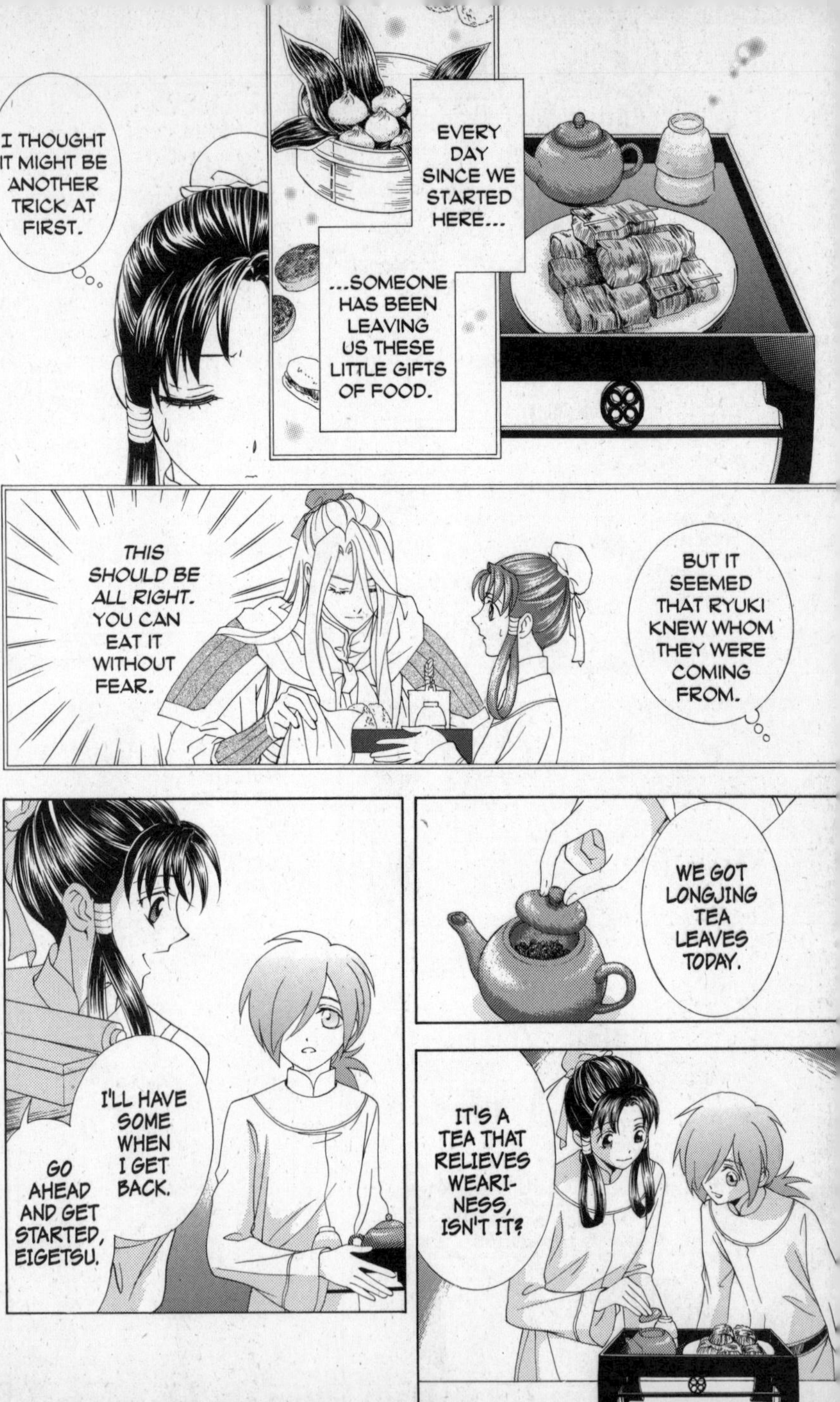
EVERY DAY SINCE WE STARTED HERE...
...SOMEONE HAS BEEN LEAVING US THESE LITTLE GIFTS OF FOOD.
I THOUGHT IT MIGHT BE ANOTHER TRICK AT FIRST.
BUT IT SEEMED THAT RYUKI KNEW WHOM THEY WERE COMING FROM.
THIS SHOULD BE ALL RIGHT. YOU CAN EAT IT WITHOUT FEAR.
WE GOT LONGJING TEA LEAVES TODAY.
IT'S A TEA THAT RELIEVES WEARI-NESS, ISN'T IT?
I'LL HAVE SOME WHEN I GET BACK.
GO AHEAD AND GET STARTED, EIGETSU.

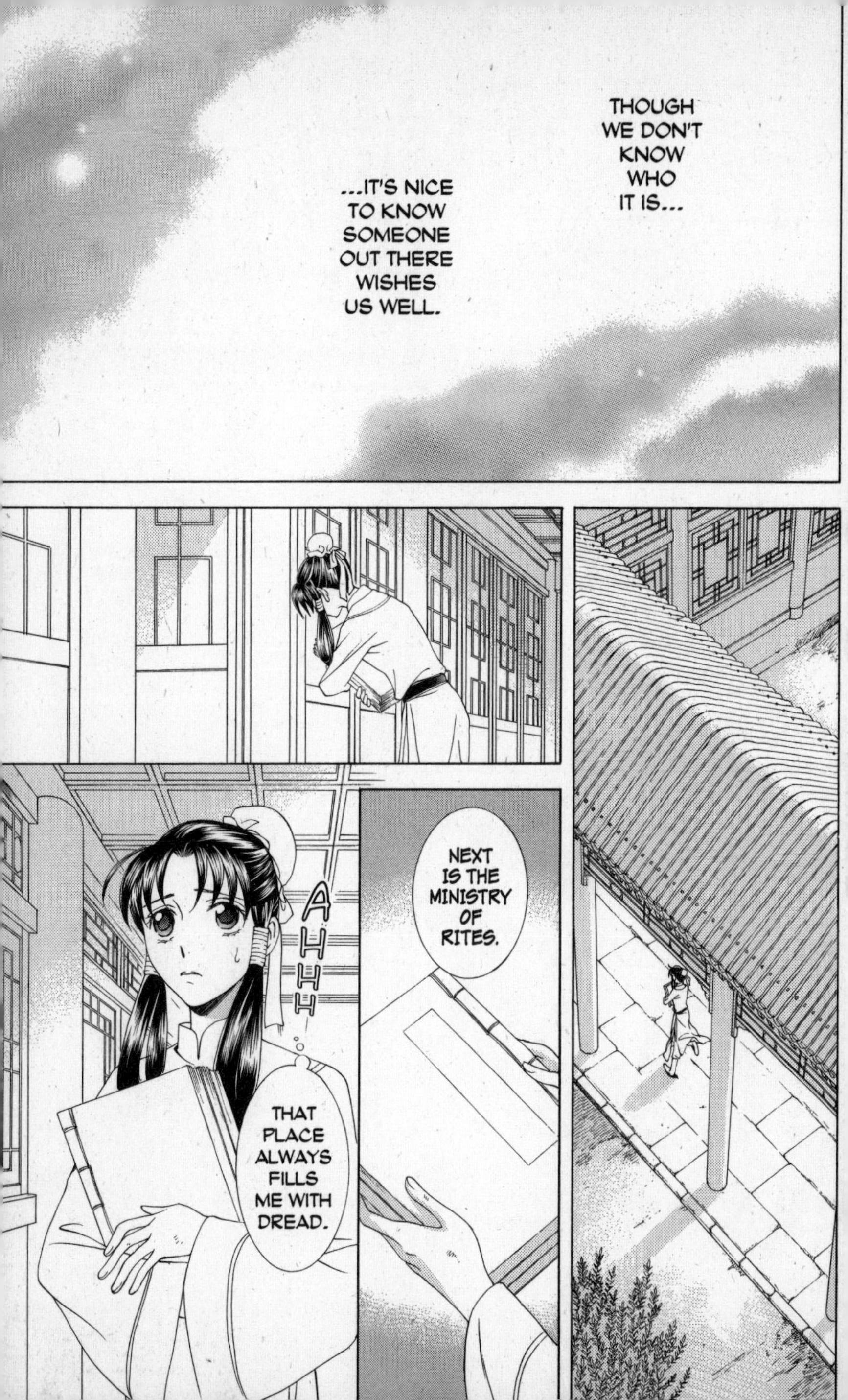
THOUGH WE DON'T KNOW WHO IT IS...
...IT'S NICE TO KNOW SOMEONE OUT THERE WISHES US WELL.
NEXT IS THE MINISTRY OF RITES.
AHHH!
THAT PLACE ALWAYS FILLS ME WITH DREAD.

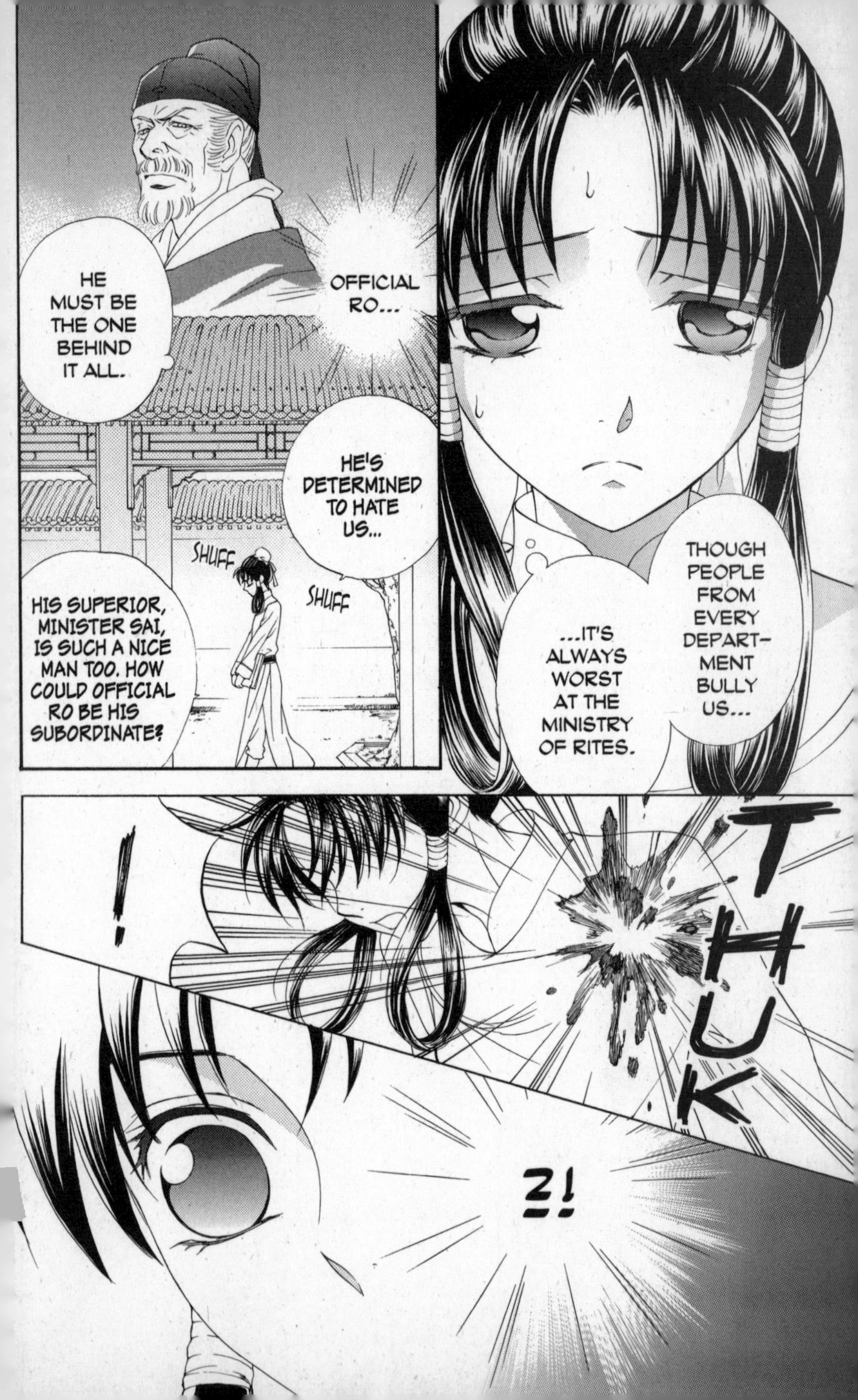
THOUGH PEOPLE FROM EVERY DEPARTMENT BULLY US...
...IT'S ALWAYS WORST AT THE MINISTRY OF RITES.
OFFICIAL RO...
HE MUST BE THE ONE BEHIND IT ALL.
HE'S DETERMINED TO HATE US...
SHUFF
SHUFF
HIS SUPERIOR, MINISTER SAI, IS SUCH A NICE MAN TOO. HOW COULD OFFICIAL RO BE HIS SUBORDINATE?
THUK
!
?!

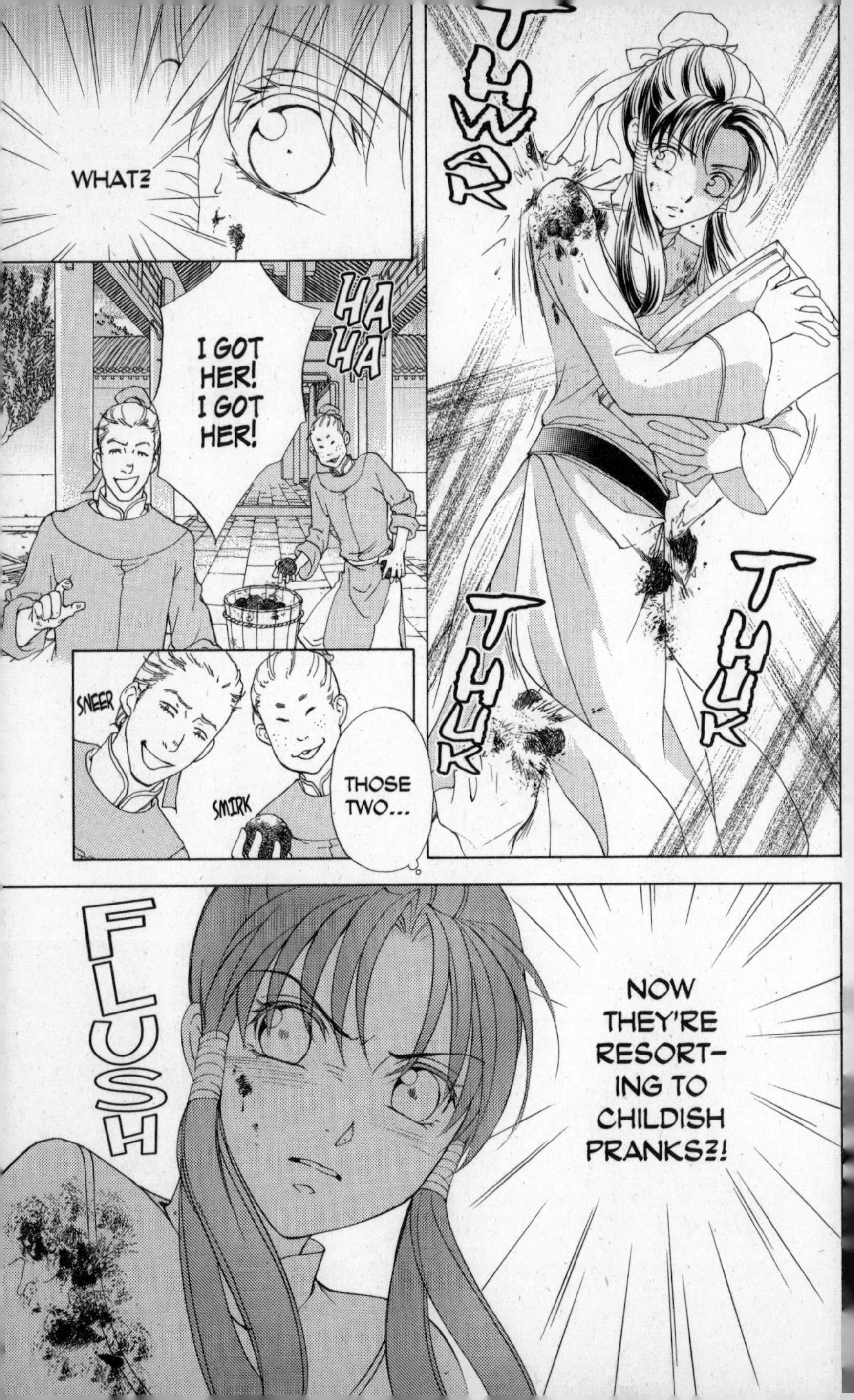
THWAR
THUK
THUK
WHAT?
HA HA
I GOT HER! I GOT HER!
SNEER
SMIRK
THOSE TWO...
NOW THEY'RE RESORT-ING TO CHILDISH PRANKS?!
FLUSH

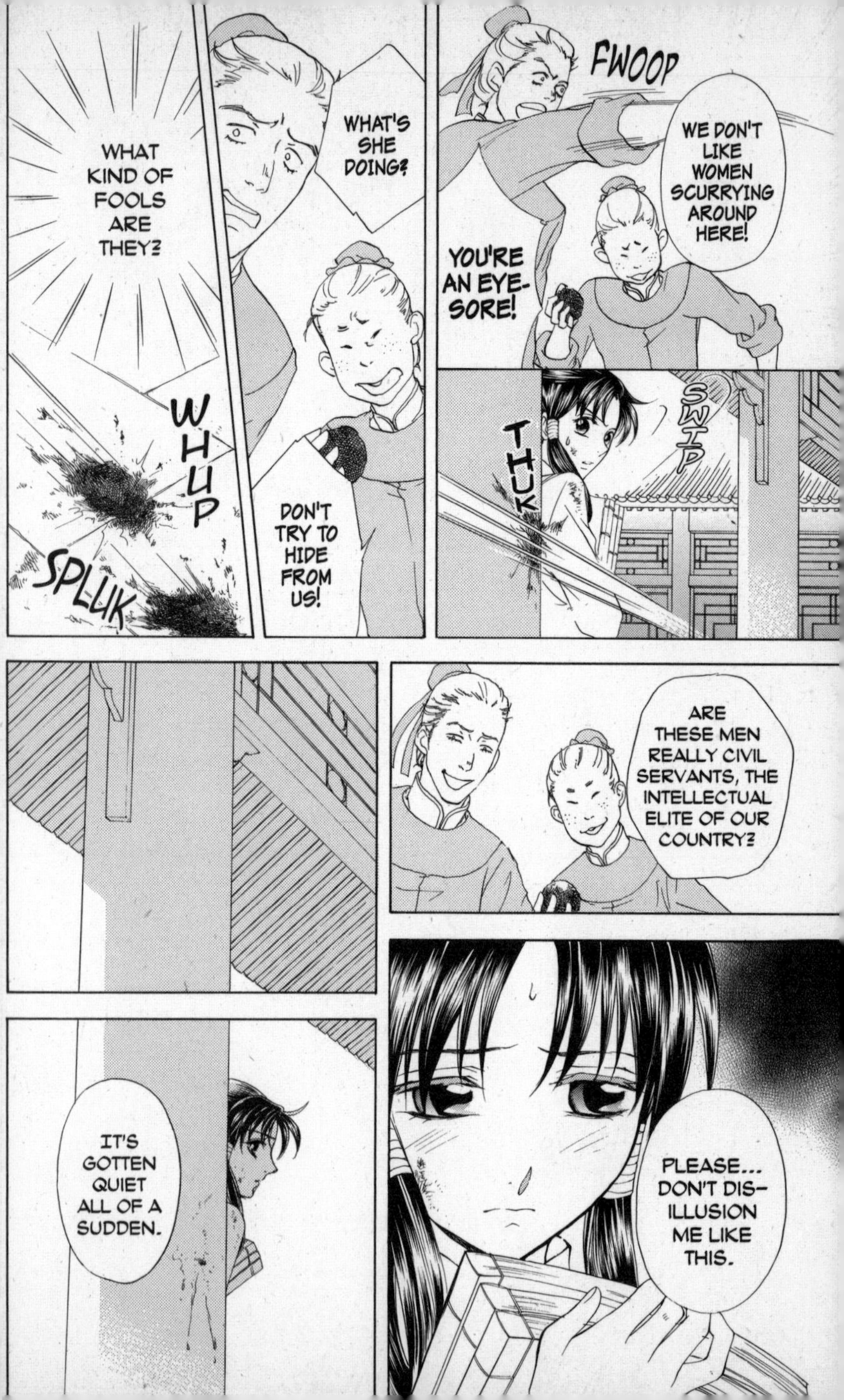
FWOOP
WE DON'T LIKE WOMEN SCURRYING AROUND HERE!
YOU'RE AN EYE-SORE!
SWIP
THUK
WHAT'S SHE DOING?
DON'T TRY TO HIDE FROM US!
WHAT KIND OF FOOLS ARE THEY?
WHUP
SPLUK
ARE THESE MEN REALLY CIVIL SERVANTS, THE INTELLECTUAL ELITE OF OUR COUNTRY?
PLEASE... DON'T DIS-ILLUSION ME LIKE THIS.
IT'S GOTTEN QUIET ALL OF A SUDDEN.

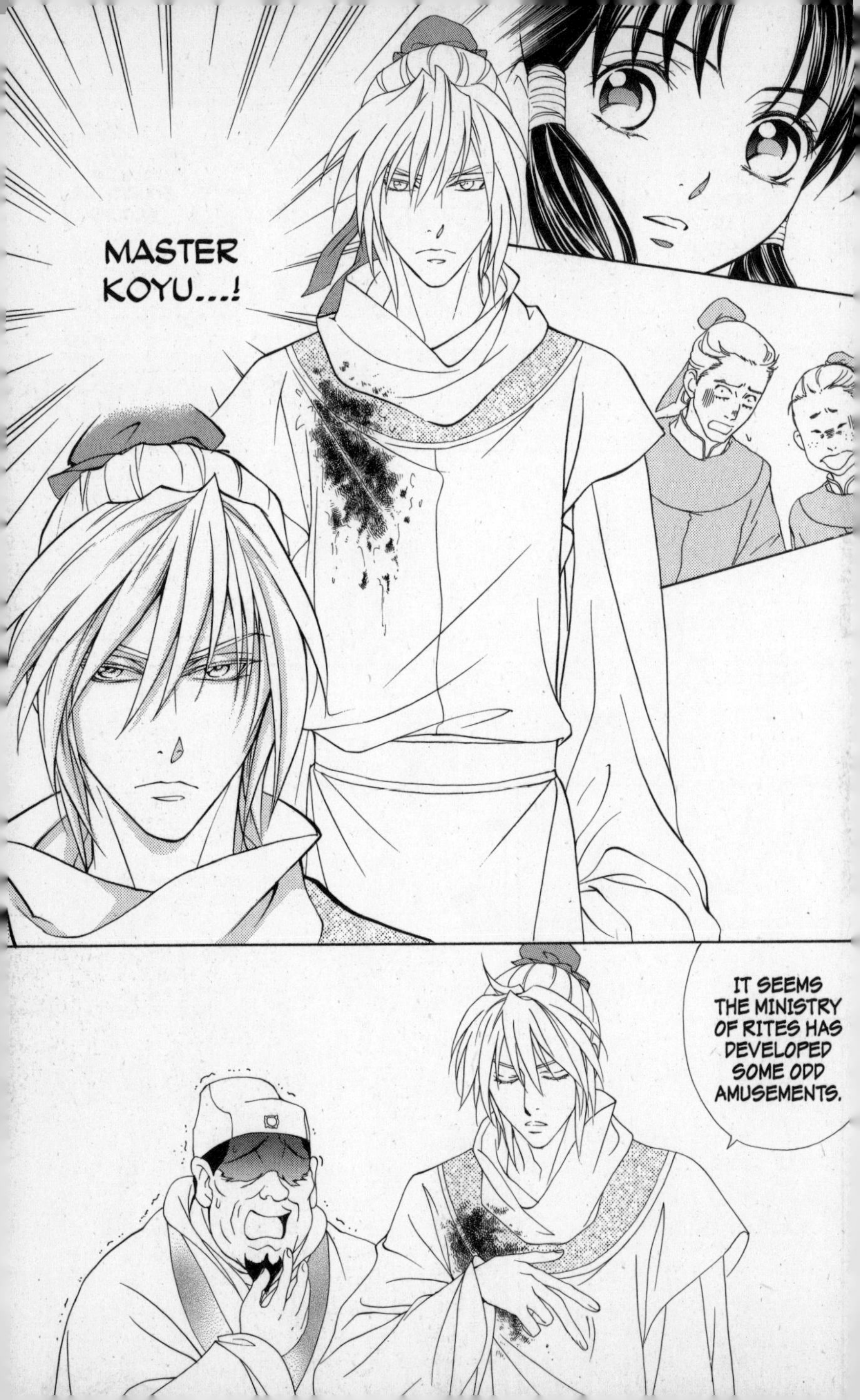
MASTER KOYU...!
IT SEEMS THE MINISTRY OF RITES HAS DEVELOPED SOME ODD AMUSEMENTS.

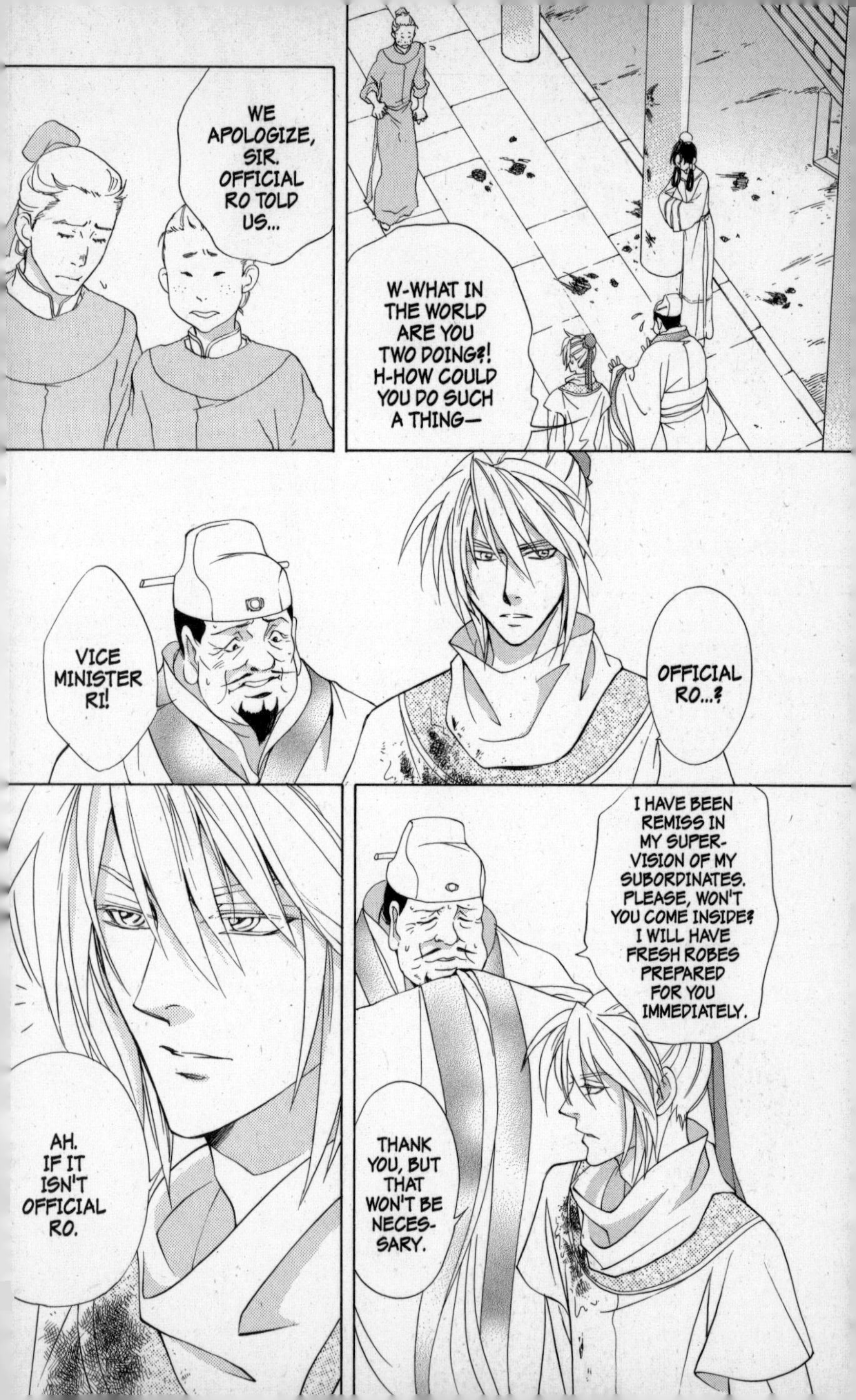
W-WHAT IN THE WORLD ARE YOU TWO DOING?! H-HOW COULD YOU DO SUCH A THING—
WE APOLOGIZE, SIR. OFFICIAL RO TOLD US...
OFFICIAL RO...?
VICE MINISTER RI!
I HAVE BEEN REMISS IN MY SUPER-VISION OF MY SUBORDINATES. PLEASE, WON'T YOU COME INSIDE? I WILL HAVE FRESH ROBES PREPARED FOR YOU IMMEDIATELY.
THANK YOU, BUT THAT WON'T BE NECES-SARY.
AH. IF IT ISN'T OFFICIAL RO.

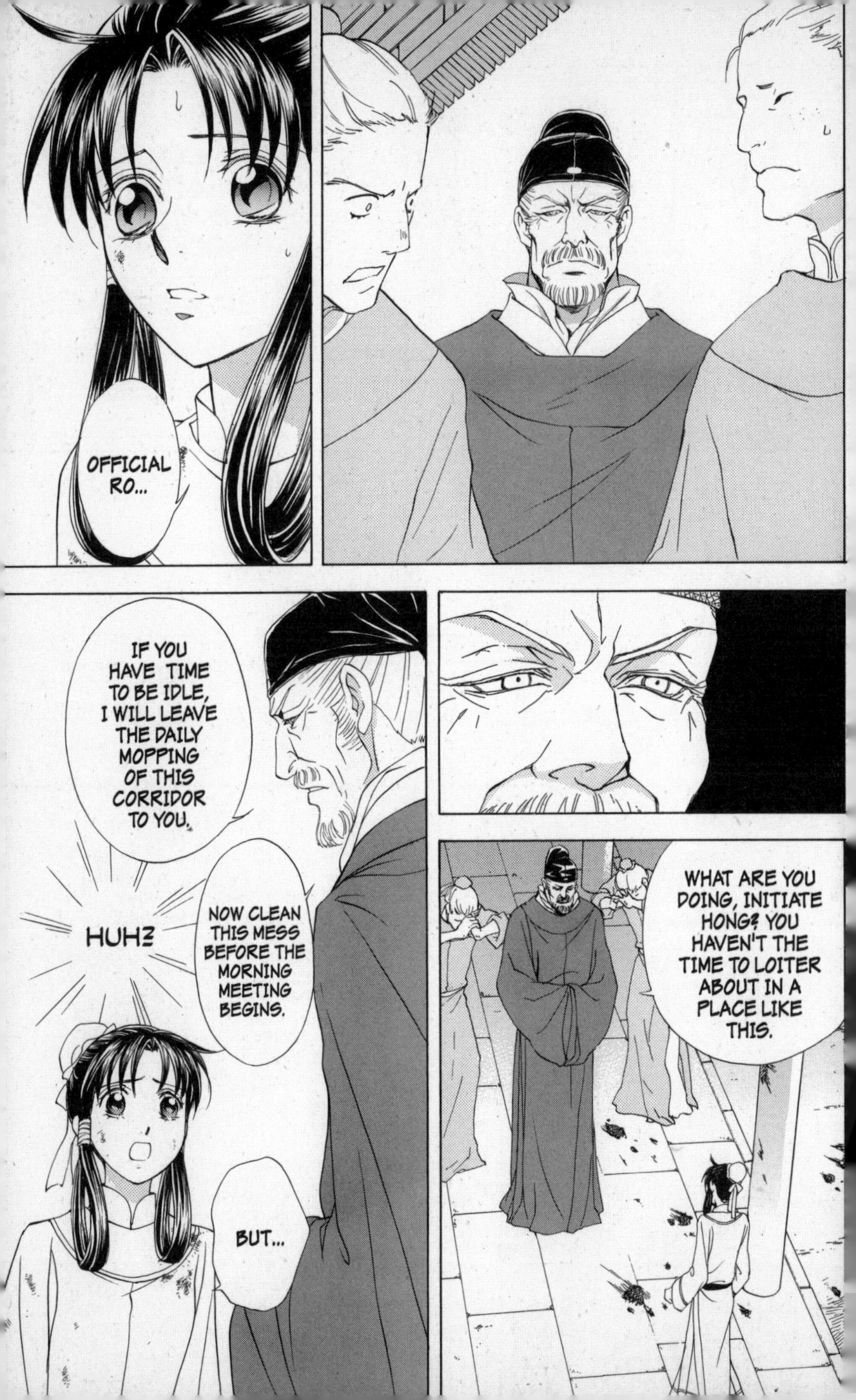
OFFICIAL RO...
WHAT ARE YOU DOING, INITIATE HONG? YOU HAVEN'T THE TIME TO LOITER ABOUT IN A PLACE LIKE THIS.
IF YOU HAVE TIME TO BE IDLE, I WILL LEAVE THE DAILY MOPPING OF THIS CORRIDOR TO YOU.
HUH?
NOW CLEAN THIS MESS BEFORE THE MORNING MEETING BEGINS.
BUT...

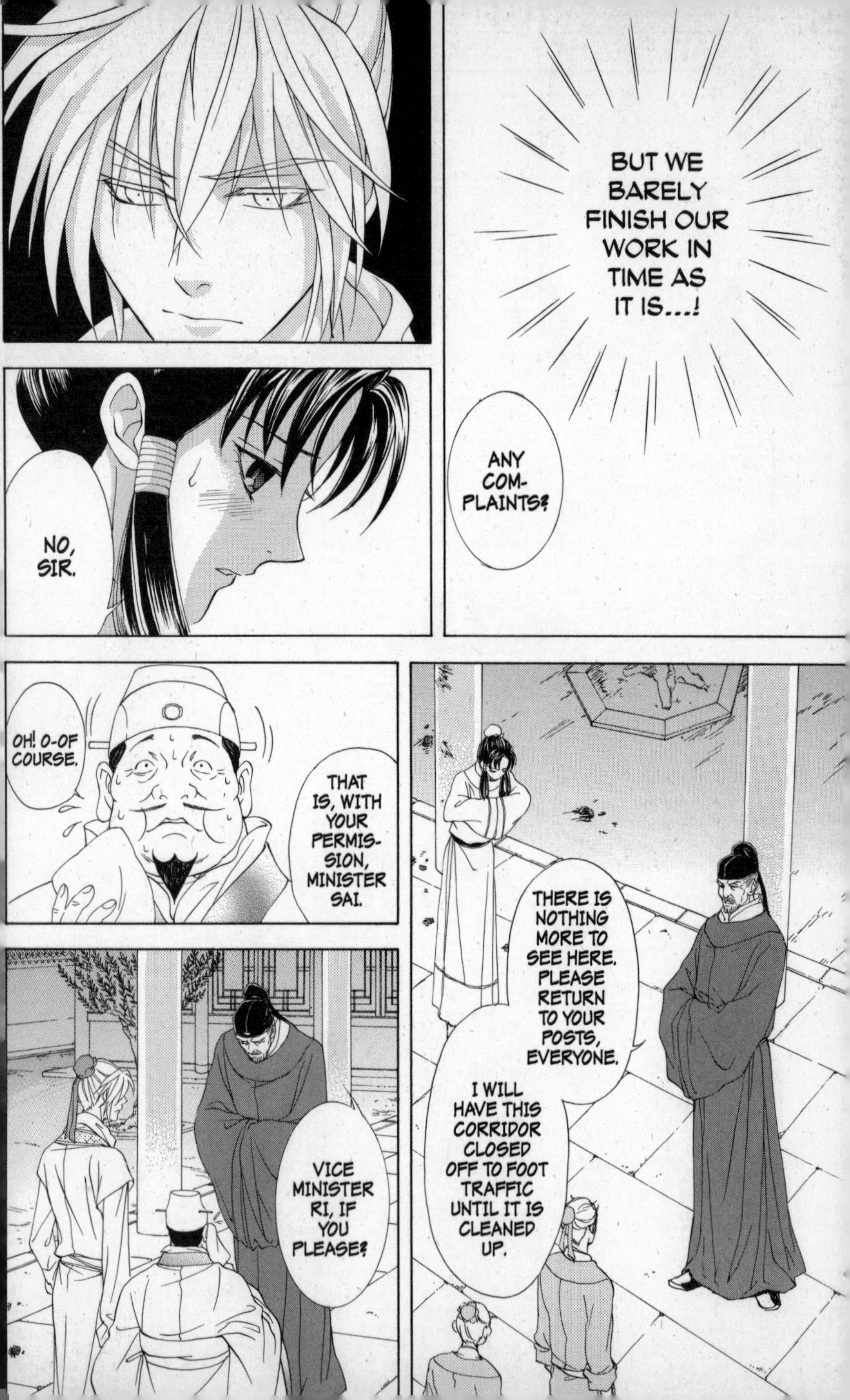
BUT WE BARELY FINISH OUR WORK IN TIME AS IT IS...!
ANY COM-PLAINTS?
NO, SIR.
THERE IS NOTHING MORE TO SEE HERE. PLEASE RETURN TO YOUR POSTS, EVERYONE.
I WILL HAVE THIS CORRIDOR CLOSED OFF TO FOOT TRAFFIC UNTIL IT IS CLEANED UP.
OH! O-OF COURSE.
THAT IS, WITH YOUR PERMIS-SION, MINISTER SAI.
VICE MINISTER RI, IF YOU PLEASE?

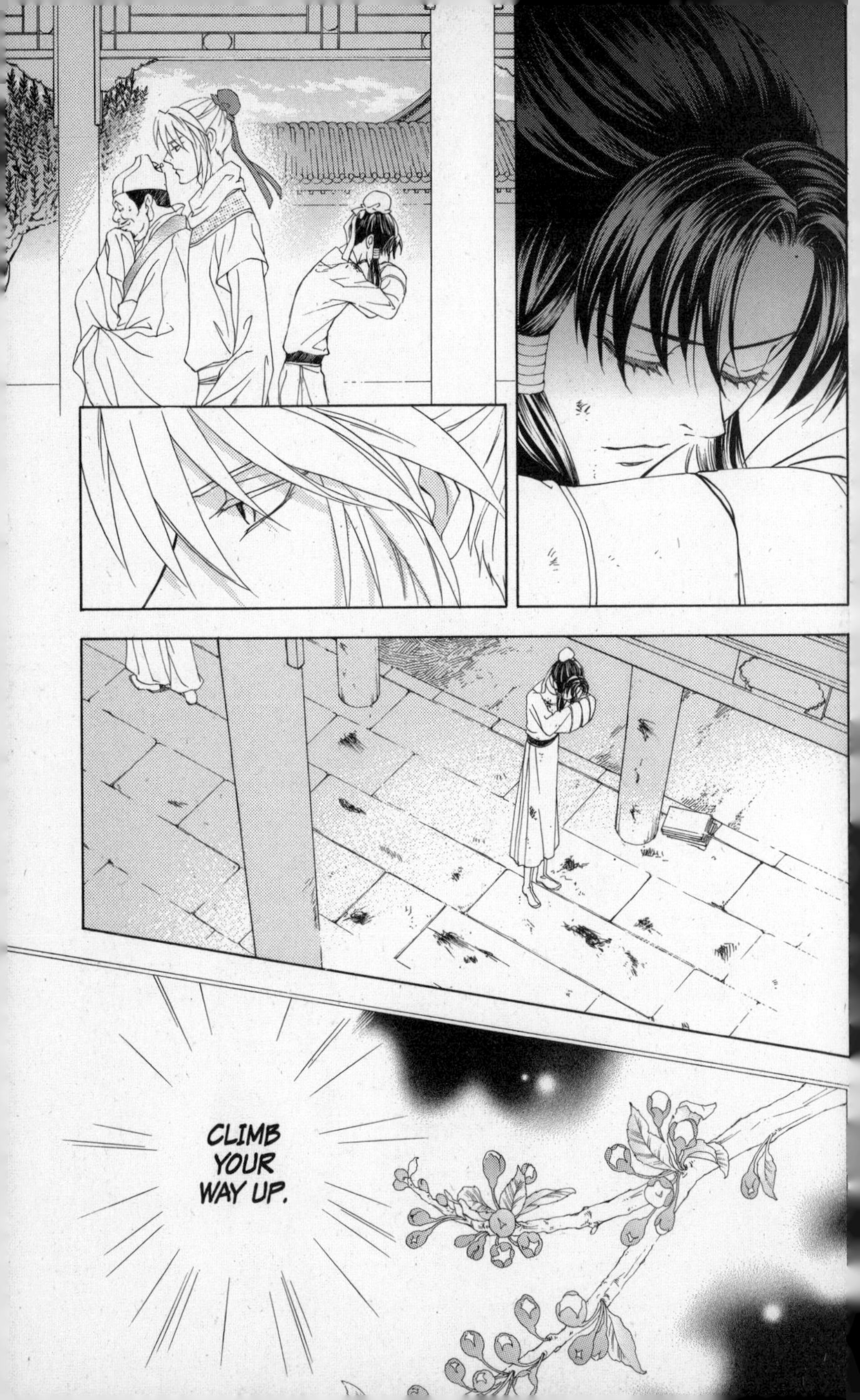
CLIMB YOUR WAY UP.

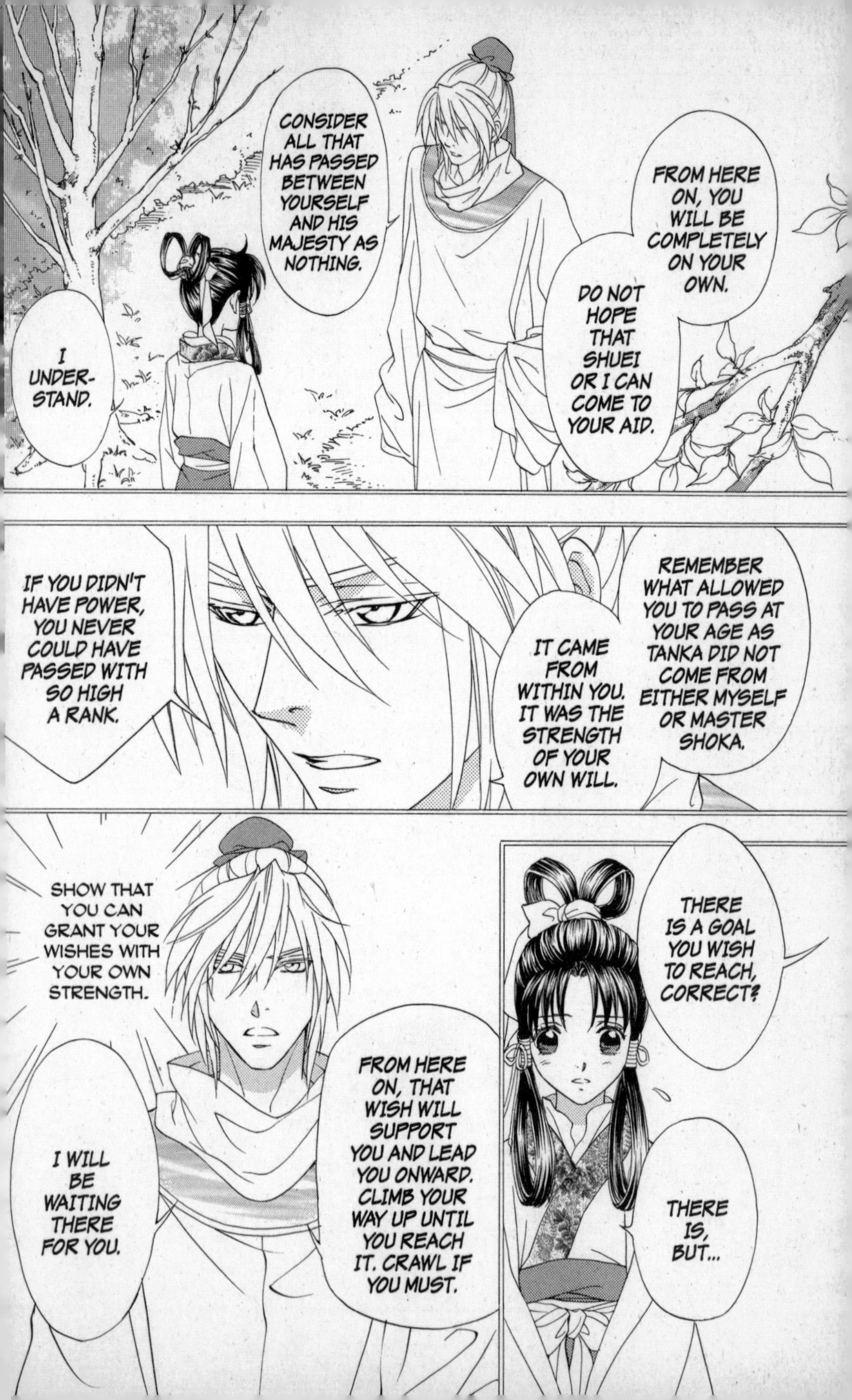
FROM HERE ON, YOU WILL BE COMPLETELY ON YOUR OWN.
DO NOT HOPE THAT SHUEI OR I CAN COME TO YOUR AID.
CONSIDER ALL THAT HAS PASSED BETWEEN YOURSELF AND HIS MAJESTY AS NOTHING.
I UNDER-STAND.
REMEMBER WHAT ALLOWED YOU TO PASS AT YOUR AGE AS TANKA DID NOT COME FROM EITHER MYSELF OR MASTER SHOKA.
IT CAME FROM WITHIN YOU. IT WAS THE STRENGTH OF YOUR OWN WILL.
IF YOU DIDN'T HAVE POWER, YOU NEVER COULD HAVE PASSED WITH SO HIGH A RANK.
THERE IS A GOAL YOU WISH TO REACH, CORRECT?
THERE IS, BUT...
SHOW THAT YOU CAN GRANT YOUR WISHES WITH YOUR OWN STRENGTH.
FROM HERE ON, THAT WISH WILL SUPPORT YOU AND LEAD YOU ONWARD. CLIMB YOUR WAY UP UNTIL YOU REACH IT. CRAWL IF YOU MUST.
I WILL BE WAITING THERE FOR YOU.

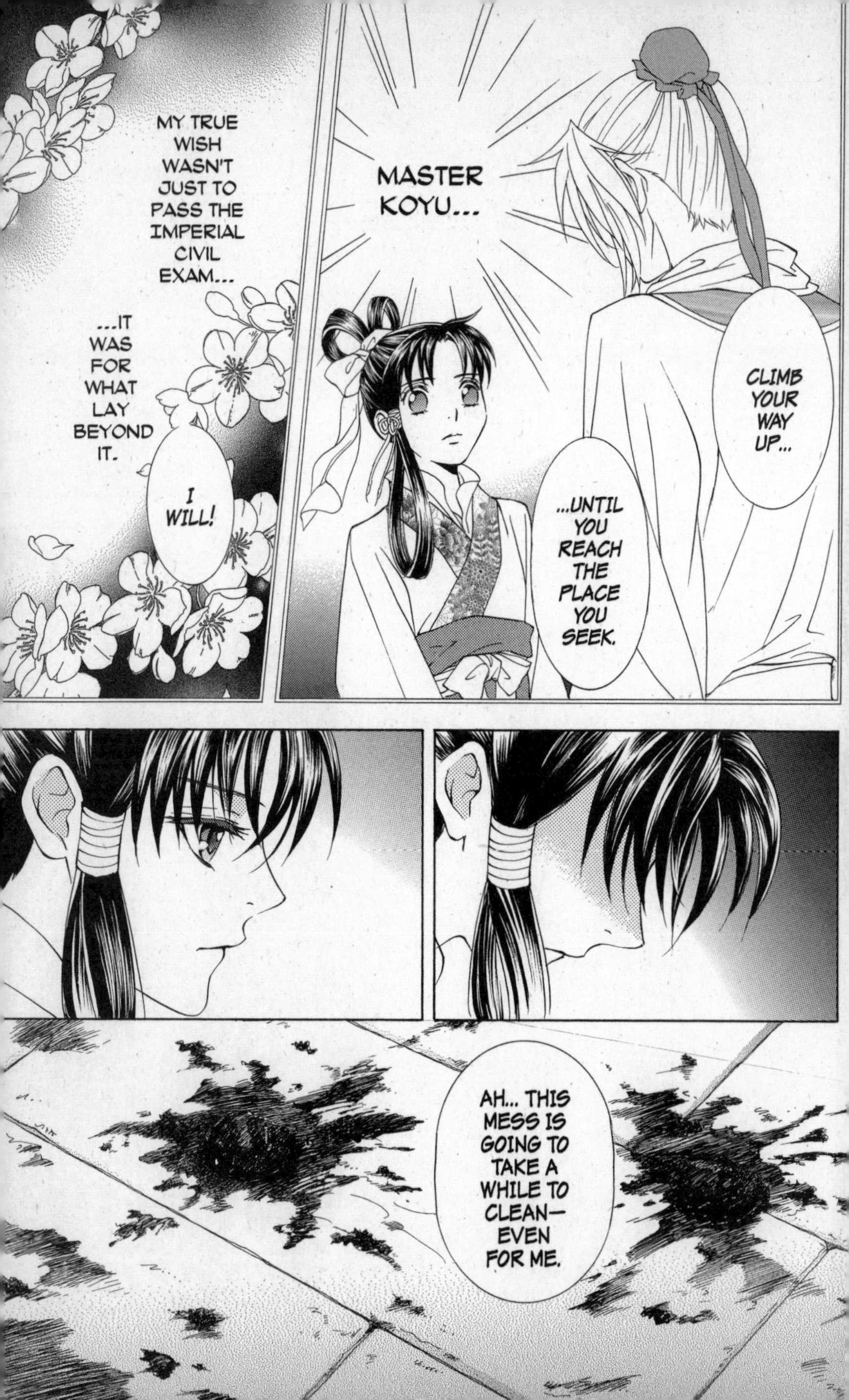
MASTER KOYU...
CLIMB YOUR WAY UP...
...UNTIL YOU REACH THE PLACE YOU SEEK.
MY TRUE WISH WASN'T JUST TO PASS THE IMPERIAL CIVIL EXAM...
...IT WAS FOR WHAT LAY BEYOND IT.
I WILL!
AH... THIS MESS IS GOING TO TAKE A WHILE TO CLEAN— EVEN FOR ME.

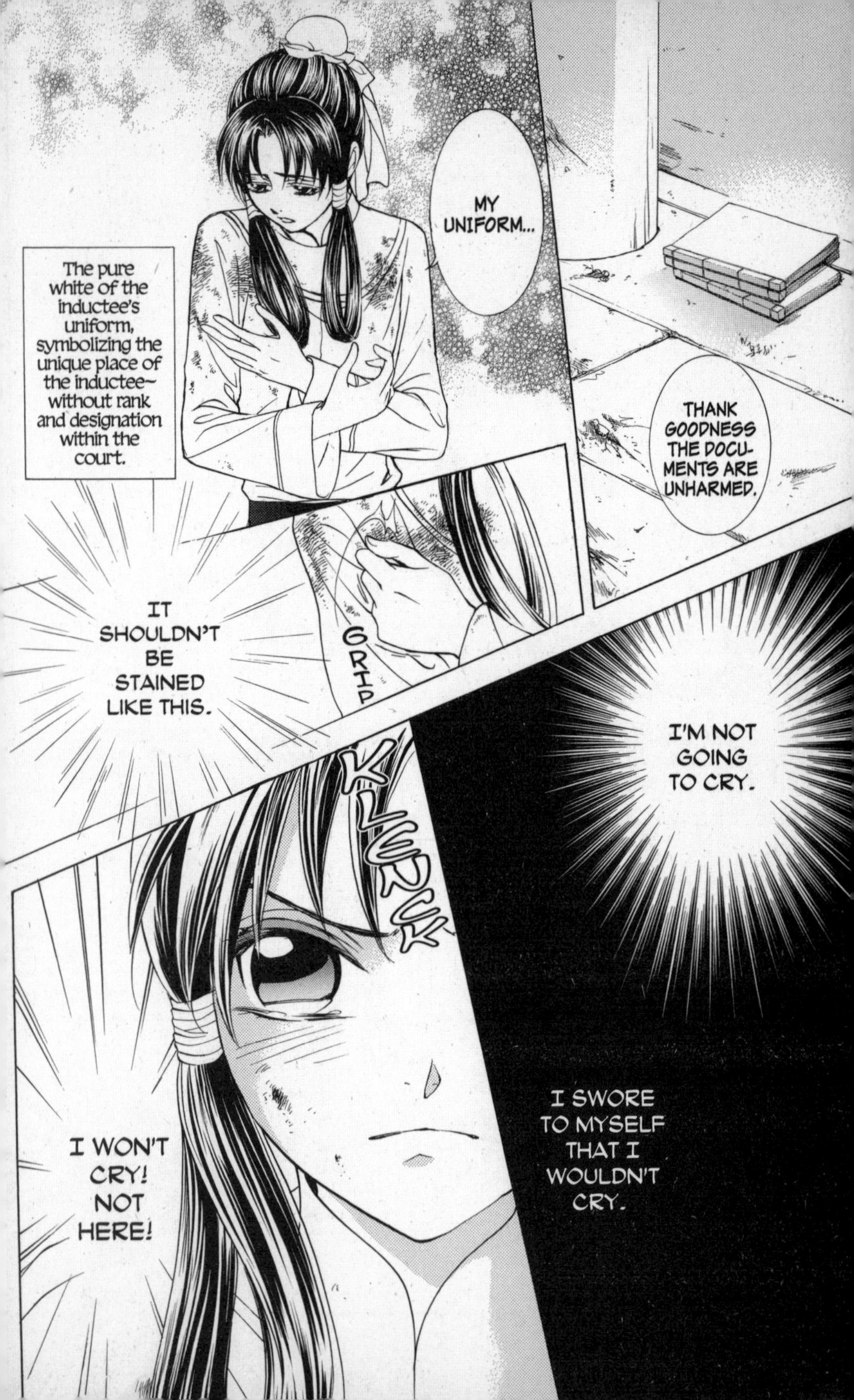
THANK GOODNESS THE DOCUMENTS ARE UNHARMED.
MY UNIFORM...
The pure white of the inductee's uniform, symbolizing the unique place of the inductee—without rank and designation within the court.
GRIP
IT SHOULDN'T BE STAINED LIKE THIS.
I'M NOT GOING TO CRY.
KLENCH
I SWORE TO MYSELF THAT I WOULDN'T CRY.
I WON'T CRY! NOT HERE!

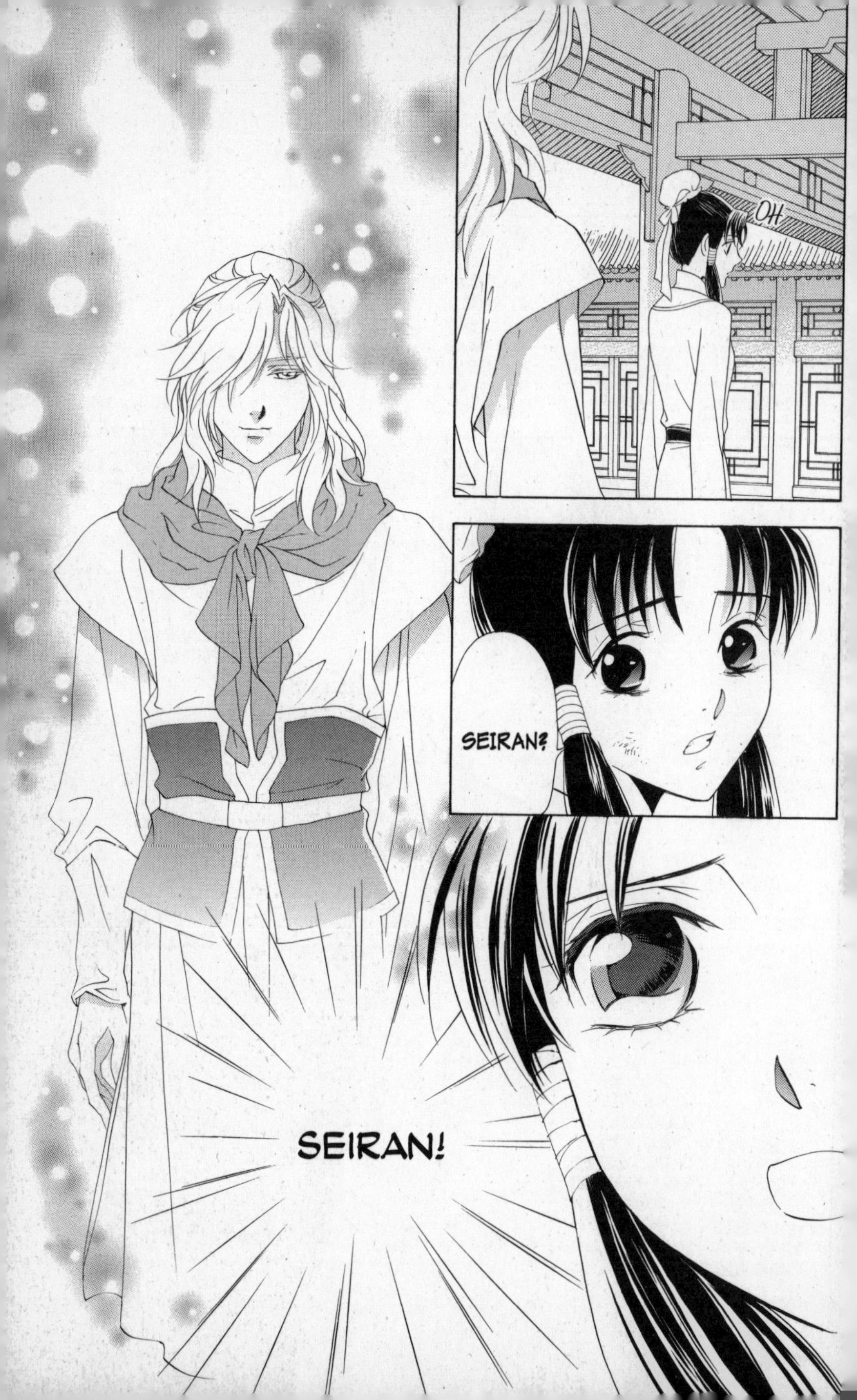
OH
SEIRAN?
SEIRAN!

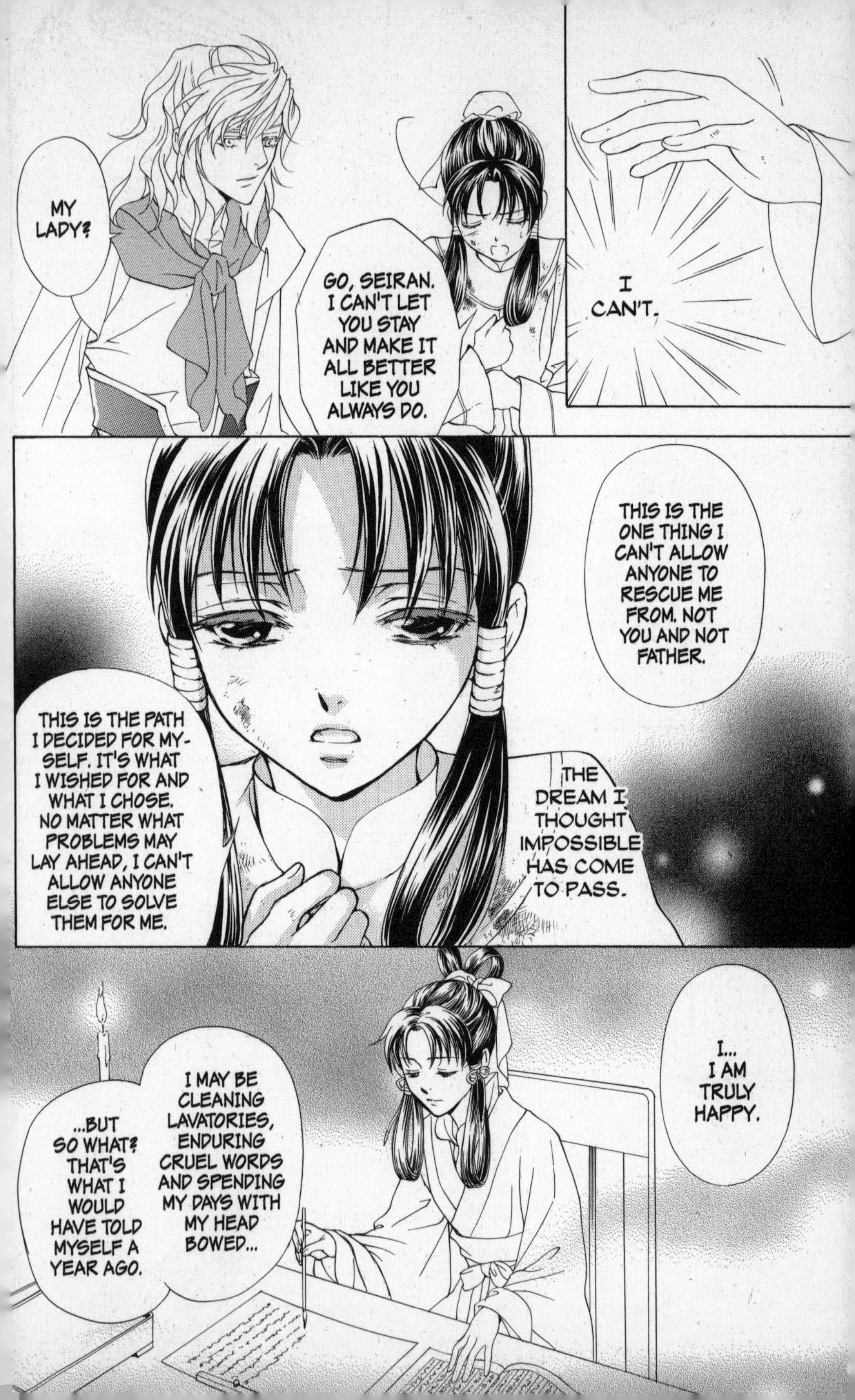
I CAN'T.
GO, SEIRAN. I CAN'T LET YOU STAY AND MAKE IT ALL BETTER LIKE YOU ALWAYS DO.
MY LADY?
THIS IS THE ONE THING I CAN'T ALLOW ANYONE TO RESCUE ME FROM. NOT YOU AND NOT FATHER.
THE DREAM I THOUGHT IMPOSSIBLE HAS COME TO PASS.
THIS IS THE PATH I DECIDED FOR MY-SELF. IT'S WHAT I WISHED FOR AND WHAT I CHOSE. NO MATTER WHAT PROBLEMS MAY LAY AHEAD, I CAN'T ALLOW ANYONE ELSE TO SOLVE THEM FOR ME.
I... I AM TRULY HAPPY.
I MAY BE CLEANING LAVATORIES, ENDURING CRUEL WORDS AND SPENDING MY DAYS WITH MY HEAD BOWED...
...BUT SO WHAT? THAT'S WHAT I WOULD HAVE TOLD MYSELF A YEAR AGO.

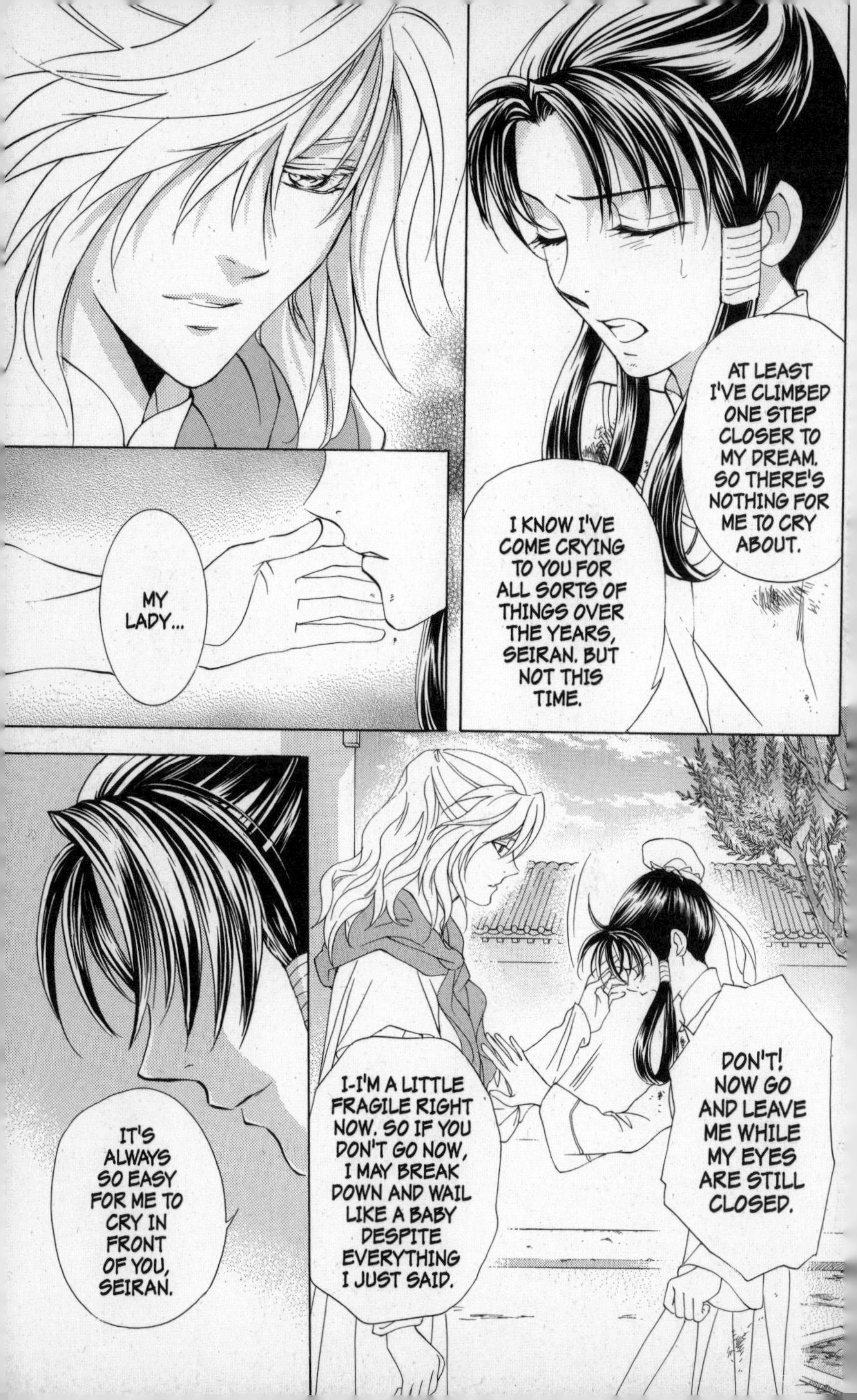
AT LEAST I'VE CLIMBED ONE STEP CLOSER TO MY DREAM. SO THERE'S NOTHING FOR ME TO CRY ABOUT.
I KNOW I'VE COME CRYING TO YOU FOR ALL SORTS OF THINGS OVER THE YEARS, SEIRAN. BUT NOT THIS TIME.
MY LADY...
DON'T! NOW GO AND LEAVE ME WHILE MY EYES ARE STILL CLOSED.
I-I'M A LITTLE FRAGILE RIGHT NOW. SO IF YOU DON'T GO NOW, I MAY BREAK DOWN AND WAIL LIKE A BABY DESPITE EVERYTHING I JUST SAID.
IT'S ALWAYS SO EASY FOR ME TO CRY IN FRONT OF YOU, SEIRAN.

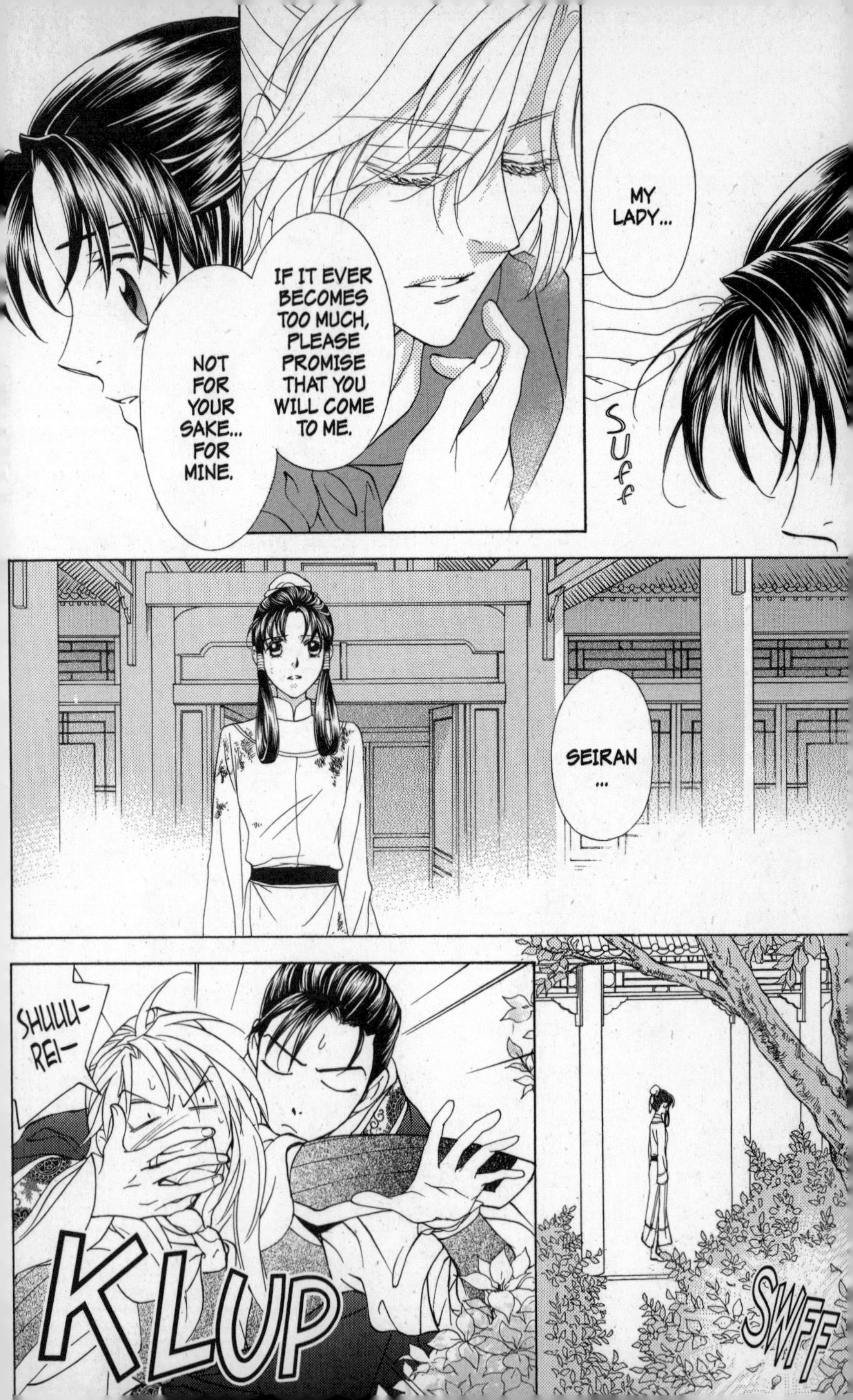
MY LADY...
SUFF
IF IT EVER BECOMES TOO MUCH, PLEASE PROMISE THAT YOU WILL COME TO ME.
NOT FOR YOUR SAKE... FOR MINE.
SEIRAN ...
SWFF
SHUUU-REI-
KLUP

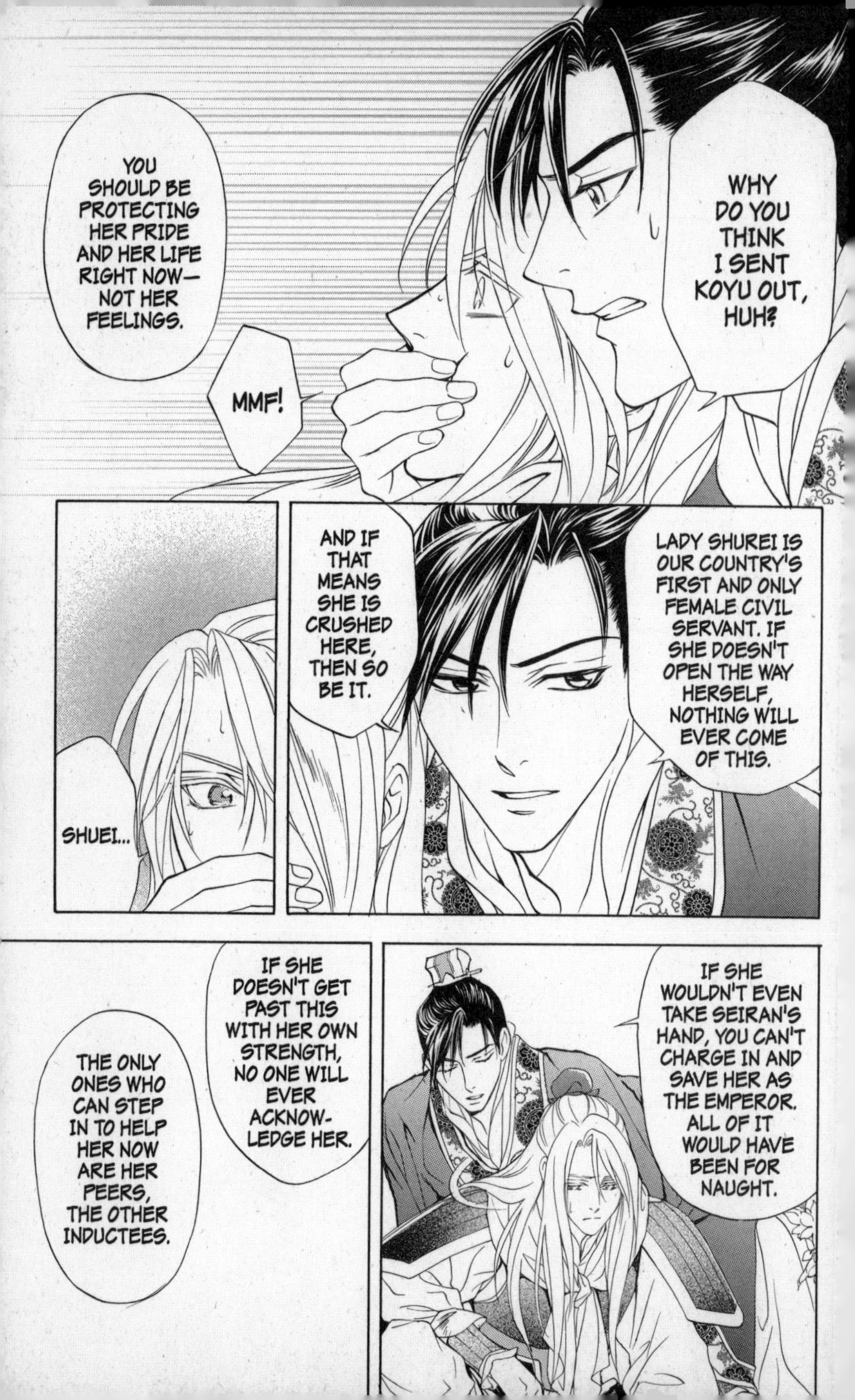
WHY DO YOU THINK I SENT KOYU OUT, HUH?
MMF!
YOU SHOULD BE PROTECTING HER PRIDE AND HER LIFE RIGHT NOW—NOT HER FEELINGS.
LADY SHUREI IS OUR COUNTRY'S FIRST AND ONLY FEMALE CIVIL SERVANT. IF SHE DOESN'T OPEN THE WAY HERSELF, NOTHING WILL EVER COME OF THIS.
AND IF THAT MEANS SHE IS CRUSHED HERE, THEN SO BE IT.
SHUEI...
IF SHE WOULDN'T EVEN TAKE SEIRAN'S HAND, YOU CAN'T CHARGE IN AND SAVE HER AS THE EMPEROR. ALL OF IT WOULD HAVE BEEN FOR NAUGHT.
IF SHE DOESN'T GET PAST THIS WITH HER OWN STRENGTH, NO ONE WILL EVER ACKNOW-LEDGE HER.
THE ONLY ONES WHO CAN STEP IN TO HELP HER NOW ARE HER PEERS, THE OTHER INDUCTEES.

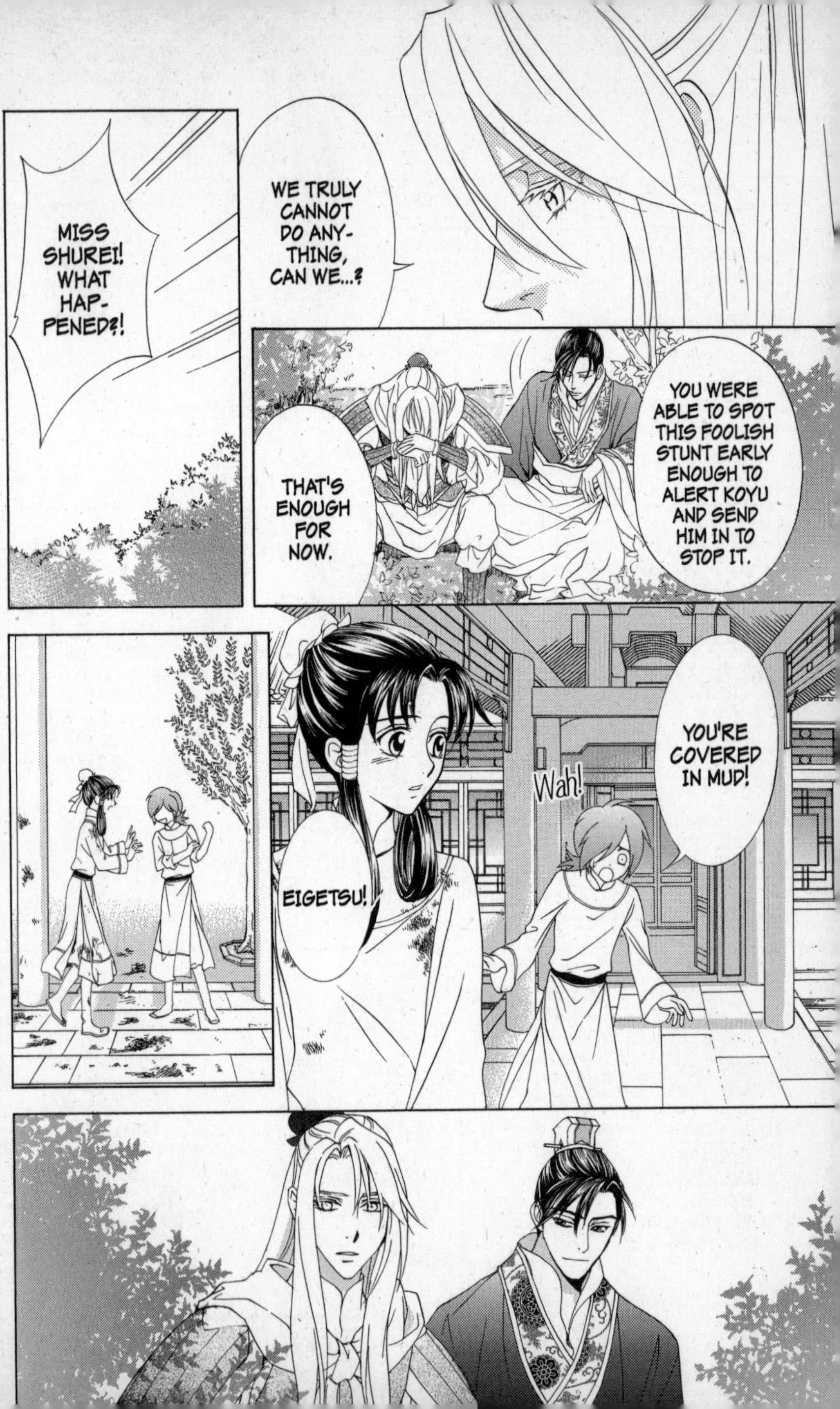
WE TRULY CANNOT DO ANYTHING, CAN WE...?
YOU WERE ABLE TO SPOT THIS FOOLISH STUNT EARLY ENOUGH TO ALERT KOYU AND SEND HIM IN TO STOP IT.
THAT'S ENOUGH FOR NOW.
MISS SHUREI! WHAT HAPPENED?!
YOU'RE COVERED IN MUD!
Wah!
EIGETSU!

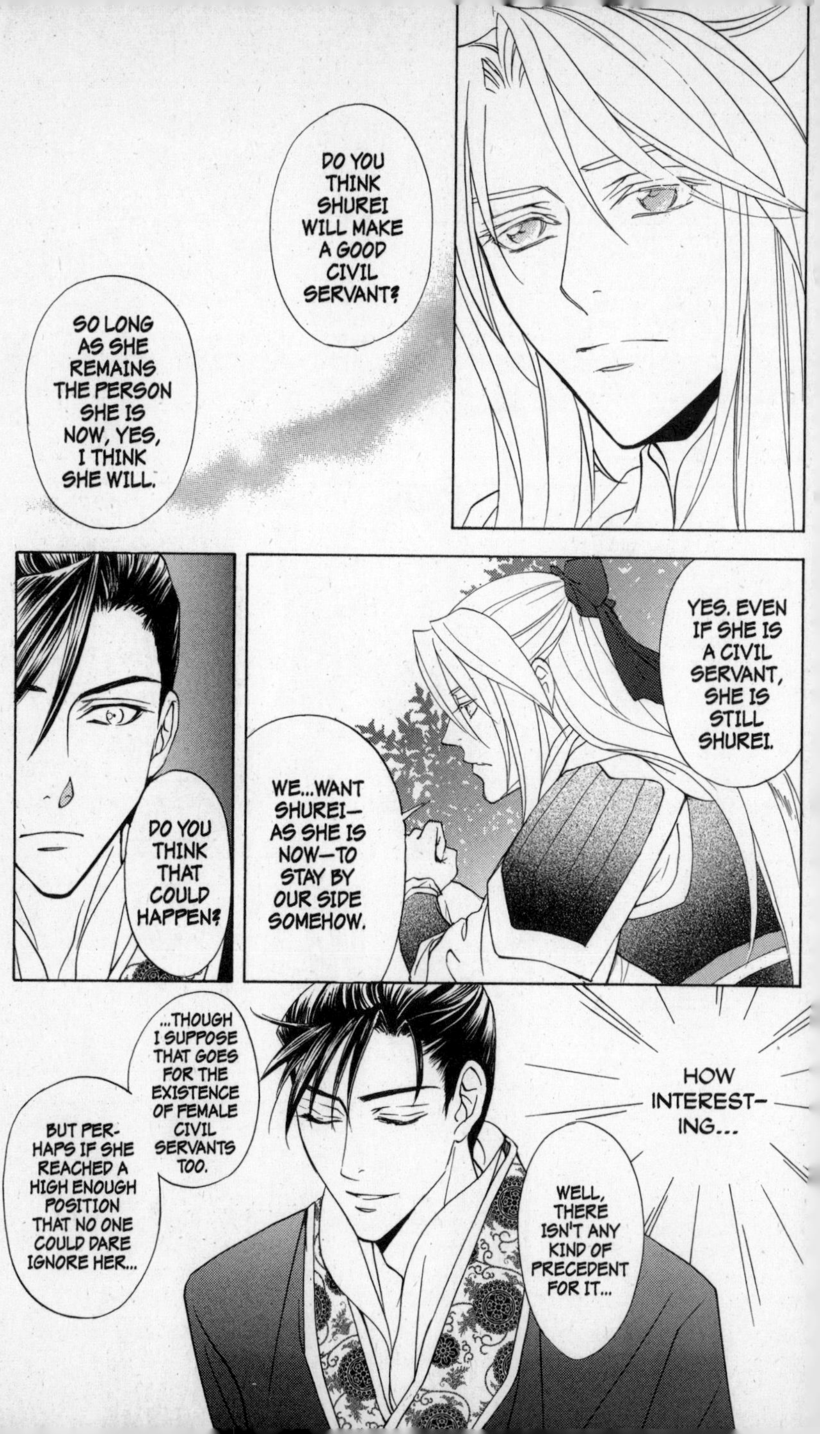
DO YOU THINK SHUREI WILL MAKE A GOOD CIVIL SERVANT?
SO LONG AS SHE REMAINS THE PERSON SHE IS NOW, YES, I THINK SHE WILL.
YES. EVEN IF SHE IS A CIVIL SERVANT, SHE IS STILL SHUREI.
WE...WANT SHUREI—AS SHE IS NOW—TO STAY BY OUR SIDE SOMEHOW.
DO YOU THINK THAT COULD HAPPEN?
HOW INTEREST-ING...
WELL, THERE ISN'T ANY KIND OF PRECEDENT FOR IT...
...THOUGH I SUPPOSE THAT GOES FOR THE EXISTENCE OF FEMALE CIVIL SERVANTS TOO.
BUT PER-HAPS IF SHE REACHED A HIGH ENOUGH POSITION THAT NO ONE COULD DARE IGNORE HER...

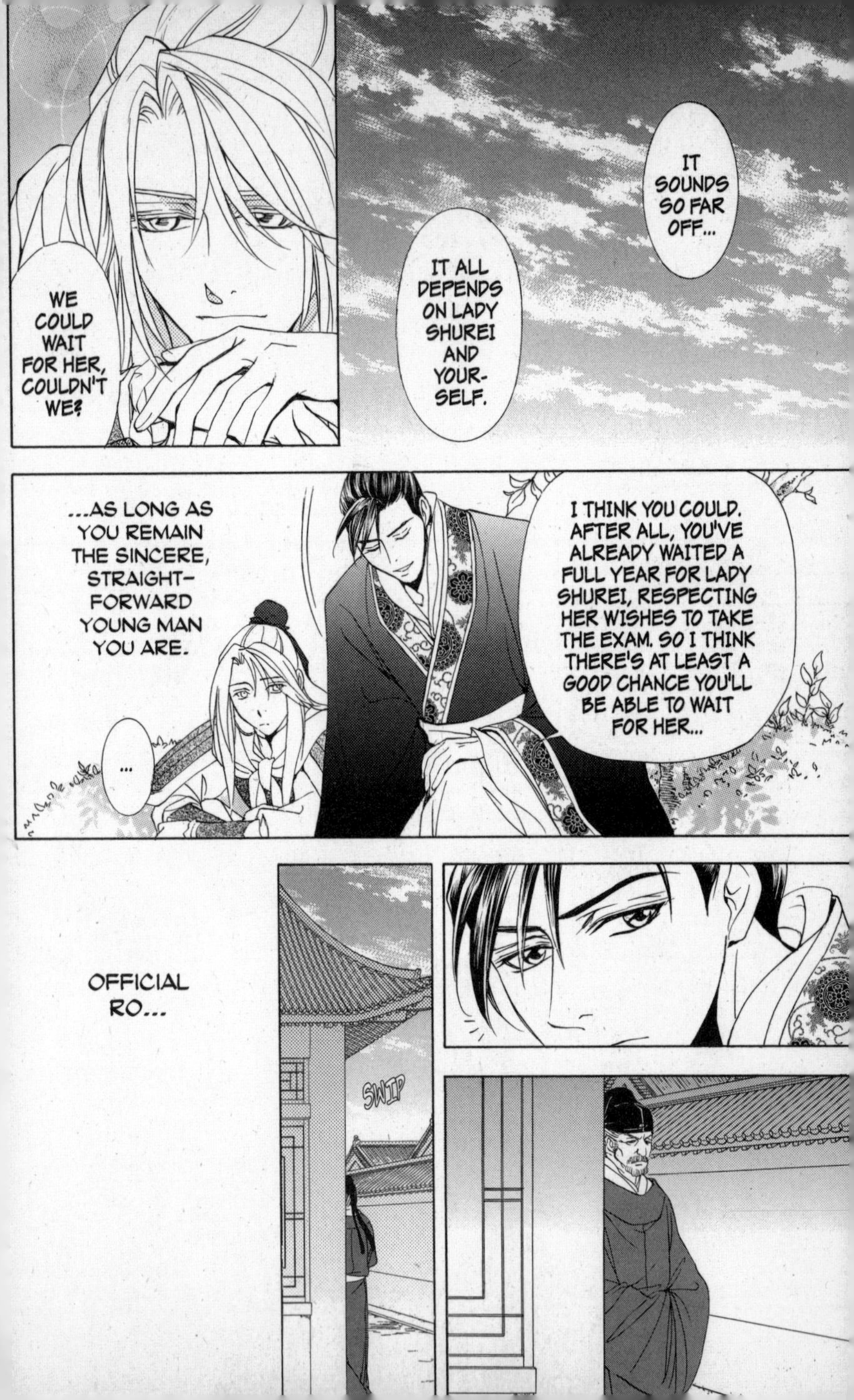
IT SOUNDS SO FAR OFF...
IT ALL DEPENDS ON LADY SHUREI AND YOURSELF.
WE COULD WAIT FOR HER, COULDN'T WE?
I THINK YOU COULD. AFTER ALL, YOU'VE ALREADY WAITED A FULL YEAR FOR LADY SHUREI, RESPECTING HER WISHES TO TAKE THE EXAM. SO I THINK THERE'S AT LEAST A GOOD CHANCE YOU'LL BE ABLE TO WAIT FOR HER...
...AS LONG AS YOU REMAIN THE SINCERE, STRAIGHT-FORWARD YOUNG MAN YOU ARE.
...
SWIP
OFFICIAL RO...

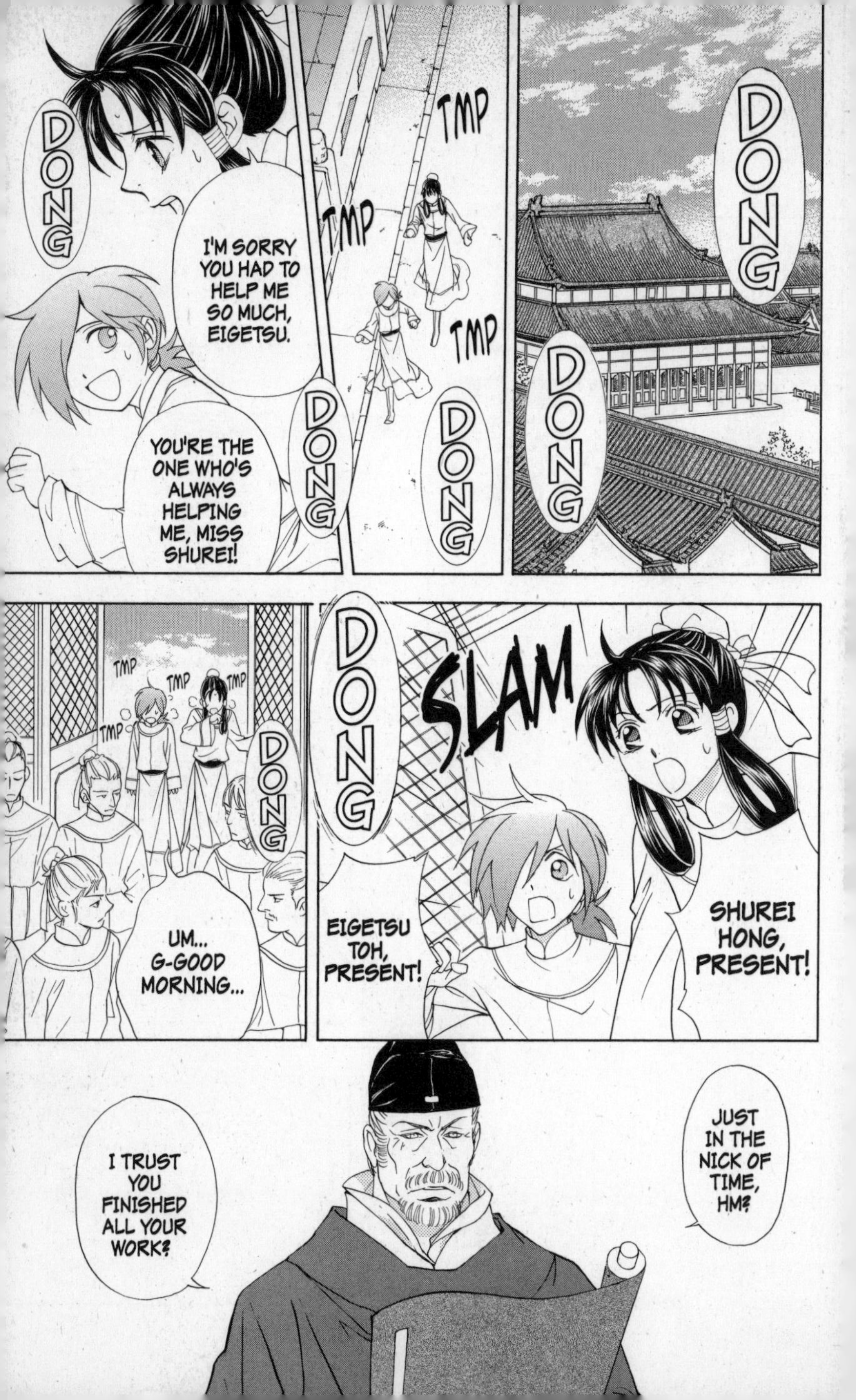
DONG
DONG
TMP
TMP
TMP
DONG
DONG
DONG
I'M SORRY YOU HAD TO HELP ME SO MUCH, EIGETSU.
YOU'RE THE ONE WHO'S ALWAYS HELPING ME, MISS SHUREI!
DONG
SLAM
SHUREI HONG, PRESENT!
EIGETSU TOH, PRESENT!
TMP
TMP
TMP
TMP
DONG
UM... G-GOOD MORNING...
JUST IN THE NICK OF TIME, HM?
I TRUST YOU FINISHED ALL YOUR WORK?

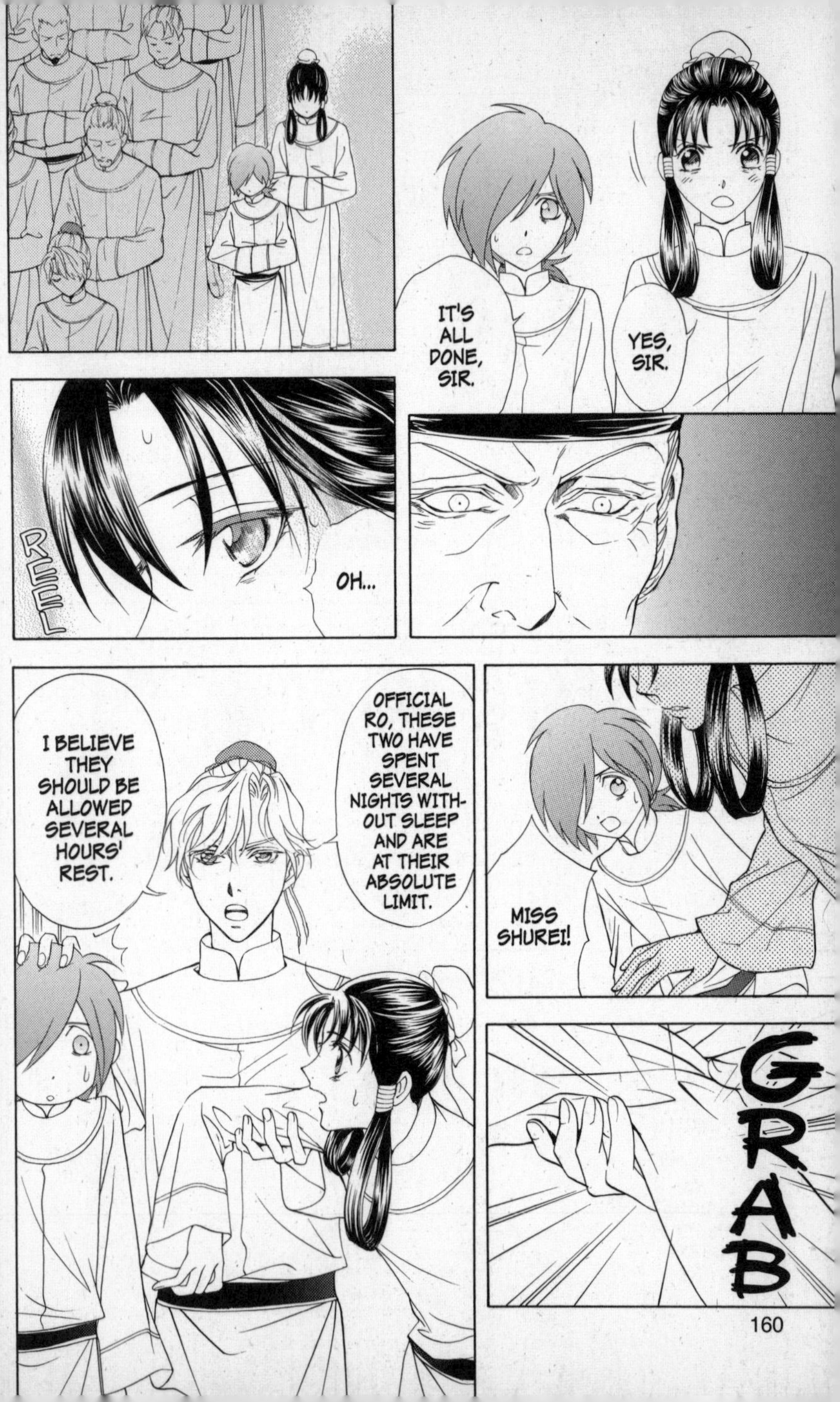
YES, SIR.
IT'S ALL DONE, SIR.
OH...
REEL
MISS SHUREI!
GRAB
OFFICIAL RO, THESE TWO HAVE SPENT SEVERAL NIGHTS WITHOUT SLEEP AND ARE AT THEIR ABSOLUTE LIMIT.
I BELIEVE THEY SHOULD BE ALLOWED SEVERAL HOURS' REST.

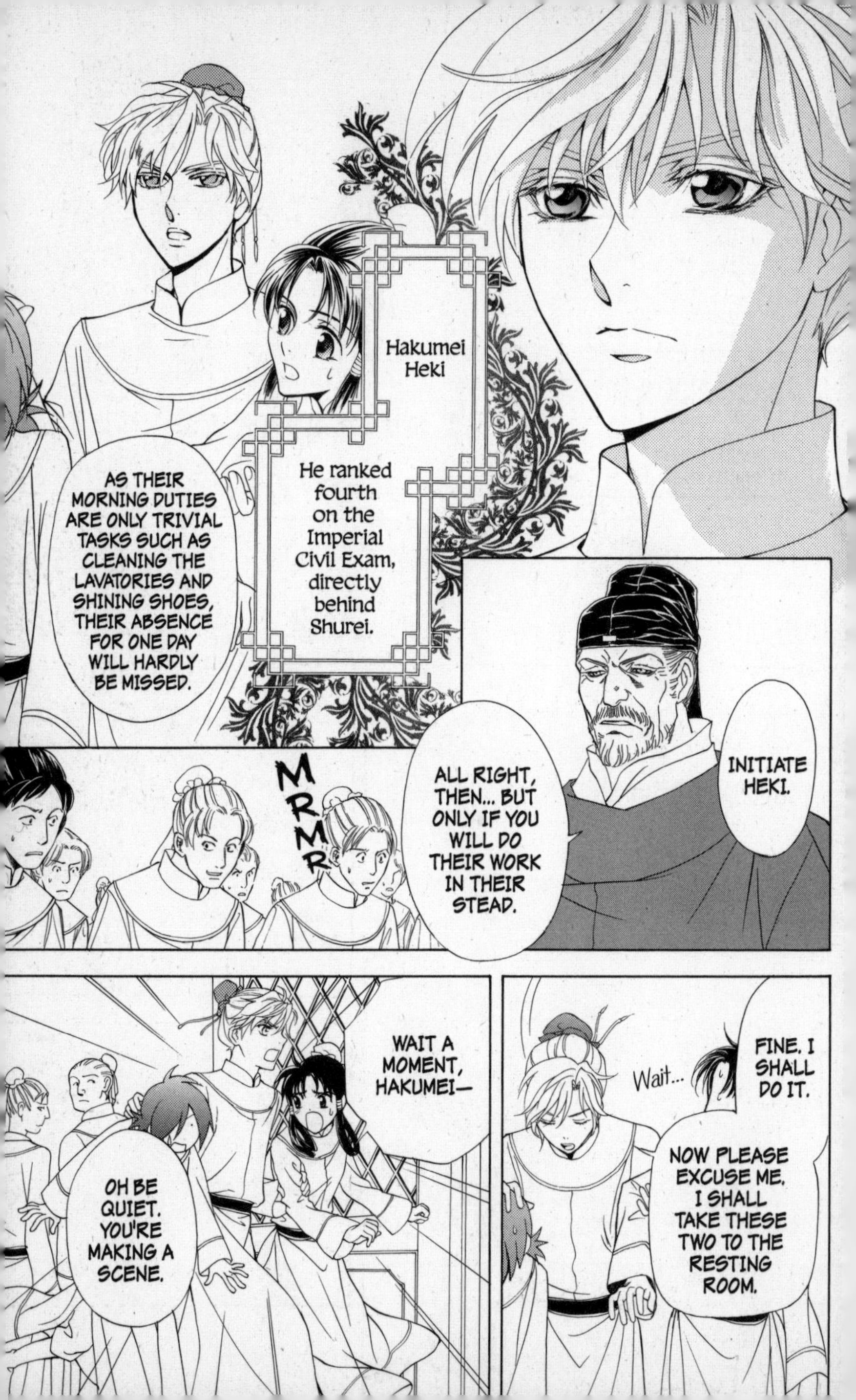
Hakumei Heki
He ranked fourth on the Imperial Civil Exam, directly behind Shurei.
AS THEIR MORNING DUTIES ARE ONLY TRIVIAL TASKS SUCH AS CLEANING THE LAVATORIES AND SHINING SHOES, THEIR ABSENCE FOR ONE DAY WILL HARDLY BE MISSED.
INITIATE HEKI.
ALL RIGHT, THEN... BUT ONLY IF YOU WILL DO THEIR WORK IN THEIR STEAD.
MRMR
FINE. I SHALL DO IT.
Wait...
NOW PLEASE EXCUSE ME. I SHALL TAKE THESE TWO TO THE RESTING ROOM.
WAIT A MOMENT, HAKUMEI—
OH BE QUIET. YOU'RE MAKING A SCENE.

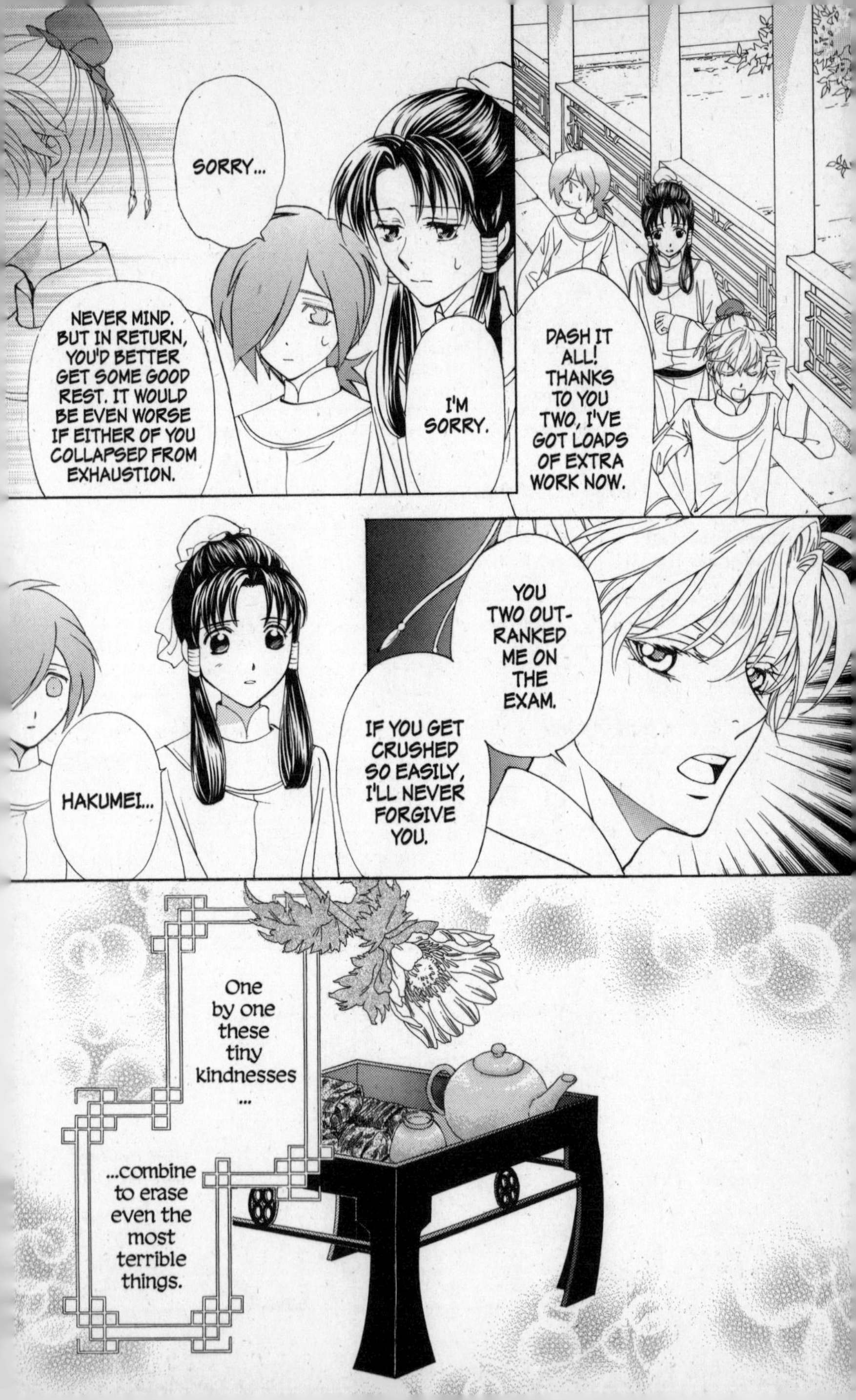
DASH IT ALL! THANKS TO YOU TWO, I'VE GOT LOADS OF EXTRA WORK NOW.
SORRY...
I'M SORRY.
NEVER MIND. BUT IN RETURN, YOU'D BETTER GET SOME GOOD REST. IT WOULD BE EVEN WORSE IF EITHER OF YOU COLLAPSED FROM EXHAUSTION.
YOU TWO OUT-RANKED ME ON THE EXAM.
IF YOU GET CRUSHED SO EASILY, I'LL NEVER FORGIVE YOU.
HAKUMEI...
One by one these tiny kindnesses ...
...combine to erase even the most terrible things.

Kairi Yura was born on January 16. She is the illustrator of both the manga and the YA novels for *The Story of Saiunkoku*. She is also the creator of the *Angelique* series. Yura's hobby is going to the theater.

Sai Yukino was born on January 26. She is author of both the manga and the YA novels for *The Story of Saiunkoku*. She received an honorable mention and the Readers' Award for Kadokawa's Beans Novel Taisho Awards. When she's not busy writing, Yukino enjoys massages.

THE STORY OF SAIUNKOKU
Volume 6

Shojo Beat Edition

ART
KAIRI YURA
STORY
SAI YUKINO

Translation & English Adaptation/Su Mon Han
Touch-up Art & Lettering/Freeman Wong
Design/Yukiko Whitley
Editor/Nancy Thistlethwaite

Saiunkoku Monogatari Volume 6
© Kairi YURA 2010
© Sai YUKINO 2010
First published in Japan in 2010 by KADOKAWA SHOTEN Co., Ltd., Tokyo.
English translation rights arranged with KADOKAWA SHOTEN Co., Ltd., Tokyo.

The stories, characters and incidents mentioned in this publication are
entirely fictional.

No portion of this book may be reproduced or transmitted in any form or by any
means without written permission from the copyright holders.

Printed in the U.S.A.

Published by VIZ Media, LLC
P.O. Box 77010
San Francisco, CA 94107

10 9 8 7 6 5 4 3 2 1
First printing, February 2012

PARENTAL ADVISORY
THE STORY OF SAIUNKOKU is rated T for
Teen and is recommended for ages 13 and
up. This volume contains suggestive themes.
ratings.viz.com

www.viz.com

www.shojobeat.com

Haruka
—Beyond the Stream of Time—
By Tohko Mizuno

Akane is a typical teenage girl...until she swallows a Dragon Jewel and finds herself transported to ancient Japan! What will happen when she learns she's been foreordained to lead the people of Kyou as the Priestess of the Dragon God?

Find out in the *Haruka: Beyond the Stream of Time* manga series!

On Sale Now

On sale at:
www.shojobeat.com

Also avaialble at your local bookstore and comic store.

Harukanaru Toki no Nakade © Tohko Mizuno,
KOEI Co., Ltd. 1999/HAKUSENSHA, Inc.

Natsume's
BOOK of FRIENDS
STORY and ART by
Yuki Midorikawa

Make Some Unusual New Friends

The power to see hidden spirits has always felt like a curse to troubled high schooler Takashi Natsume. But he's about to discover he inherited a lot more than just the Sight from his mysterious grandmother!

$9.99 USA / $12.99 CAN *
ISBN: 978-1-4215-3243-1

On sale at store.viz.com
Also available at your local bookstore or comic store

www.shojobeat.com

Natsume Yujincho © Yuki Midorikawa 2005/HAKUSENSHA, Inc.
* Price subject to change

RATED
T
FOR TEEN
ratings.viz.com

VIZ
MEDIA
www.viz.com

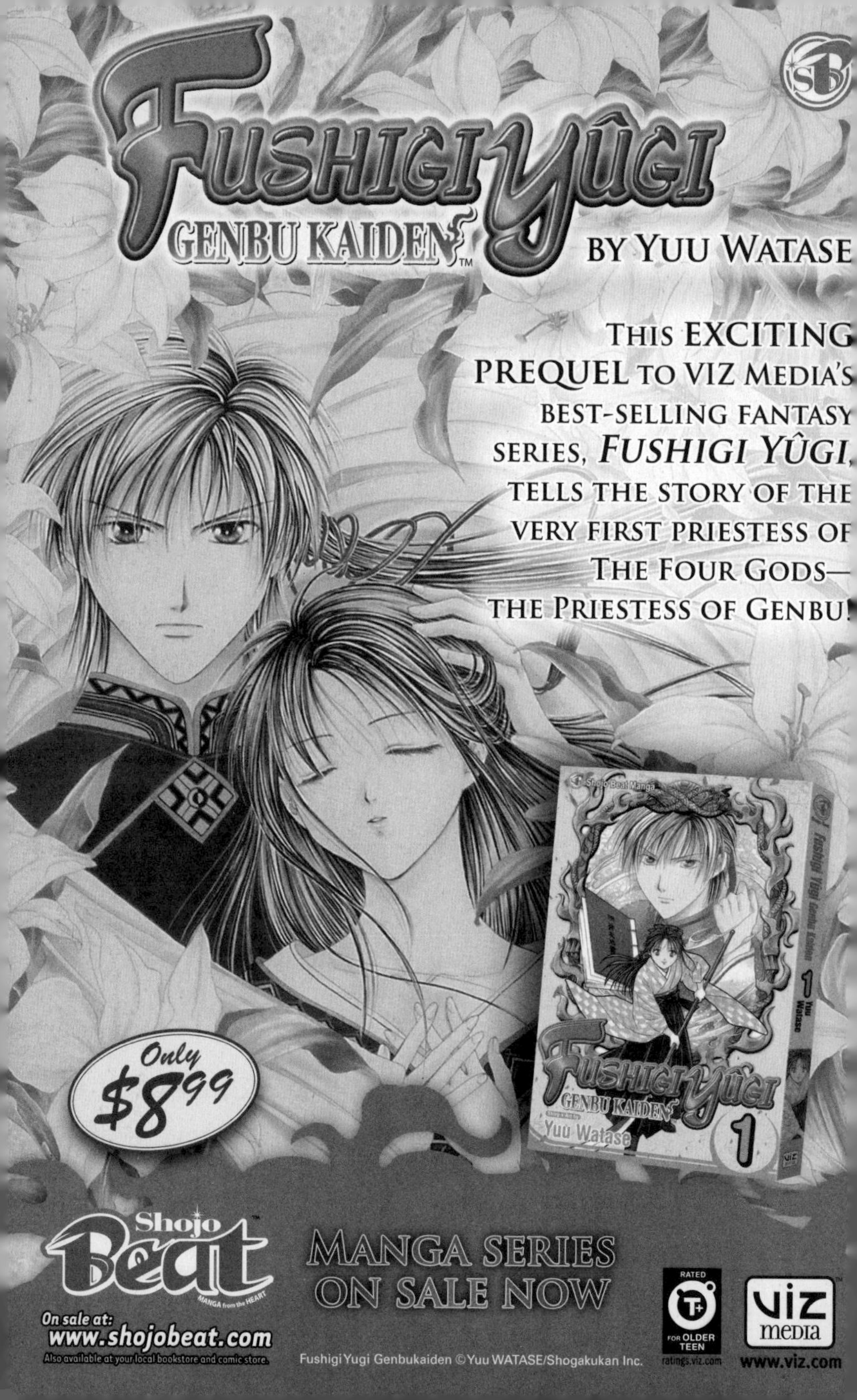
Fushigi Yûgi
Genbu Kaiden™
By Yuu Watase
This exciting prequel to VIZ Media's best-selling fantasy series, *Fushigi Yûgi*, tells the story of the very first priestess of the Four Gods— the Priestess of Genbu!
Only $8.99
Shojo Beat Manga
Fushigi Yûgi Genbu Kaiden 1 Yuu Watase
Shojo Beat™ MANGA from the HEART
On sale at: www.shojobeat.com
Also available at your local bookstore and comic store.
Manga Series On Sale Now
Fushigi Yugi Genbukaiden © Yuu WATASE/Shogakukan Inc.
RATED T+ FOR OLDER TEEN
ratings.viz.com
VIZ media
www.viz.com

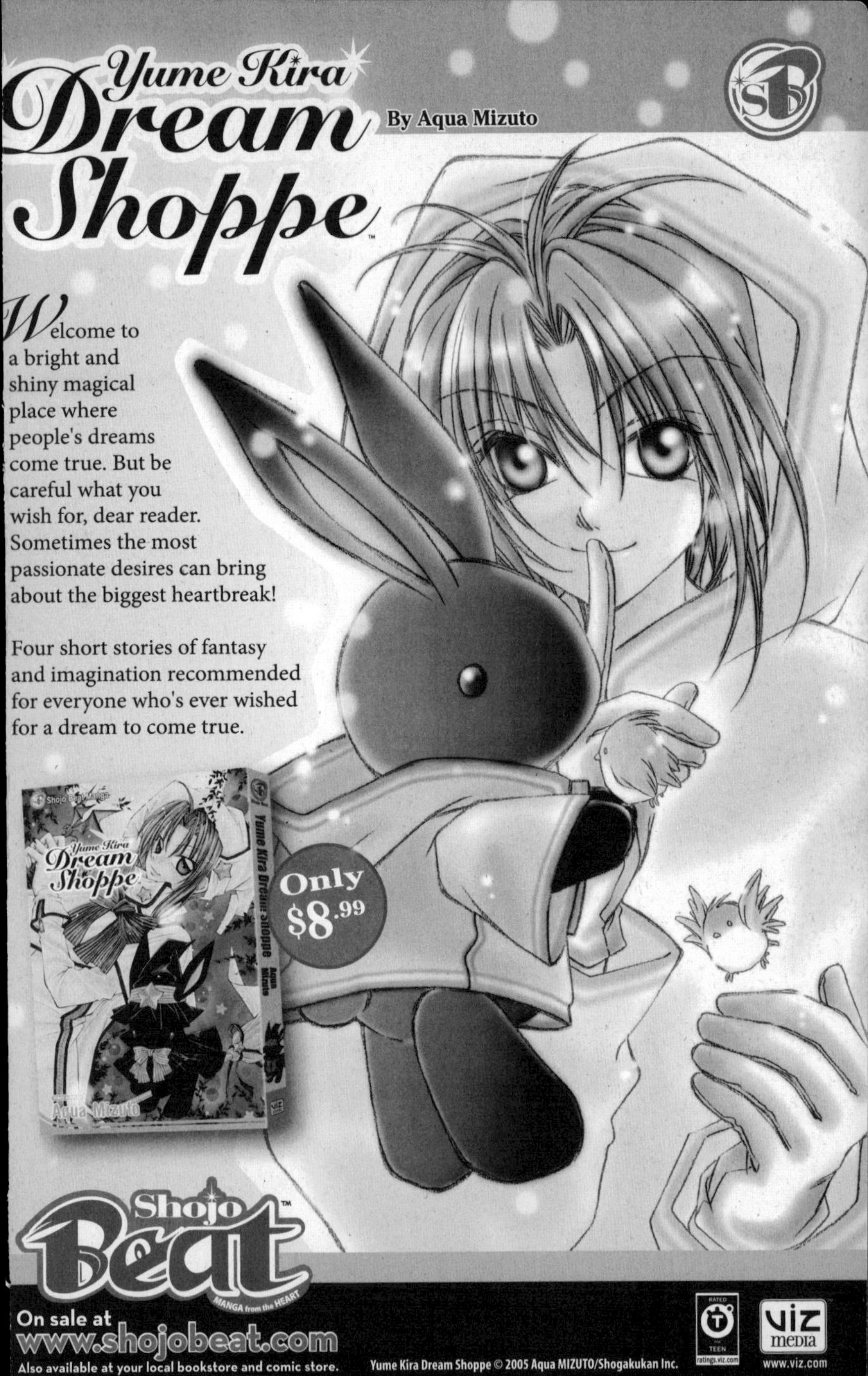
Yume Kira Dream Shoppe™
By Aqua Mizuto
Welcome to a bright and shiny magical place where people's dreams come true. But be careful what you wish for, dear reader. Sometimes the most passionate desires can bring about the biggest heartbreak!
Four short stories of fantasy and imagination recommended for everyone who's ever wished for a dream to come true.
Shojo Beat Manga
Yume Kira Dream Shoppe
Aqua Mizuto
Only $8.99
Shojo Beat™
MANGA from the HEART
On sale at
www.shojobeat.com
Also available at your local bookstore and comic store.
Yume Kira Dream Shoppe © 2005 Aqua MIZUTO/Shogakukan Inc.
RATED T TEEN
ratings.viz.com
VIZ media
www.viz.com

Don't look for the
FULL MOON
lest demons find you.

SAKURA HIME
The Legend of Princess Sakura

Story and Art by
Arina Tanemura
Creator of *Full Moon*
and *Gentlemen's Alliance* †

Available Now
at your local bookstore and comic store

ISBN: 978-1-4215-3882-2
$9.99 USA | $12.99 CAN

SAKURA-HIME KADEN © 2008 by Arina Tanemura/SHUEISHA Inc.

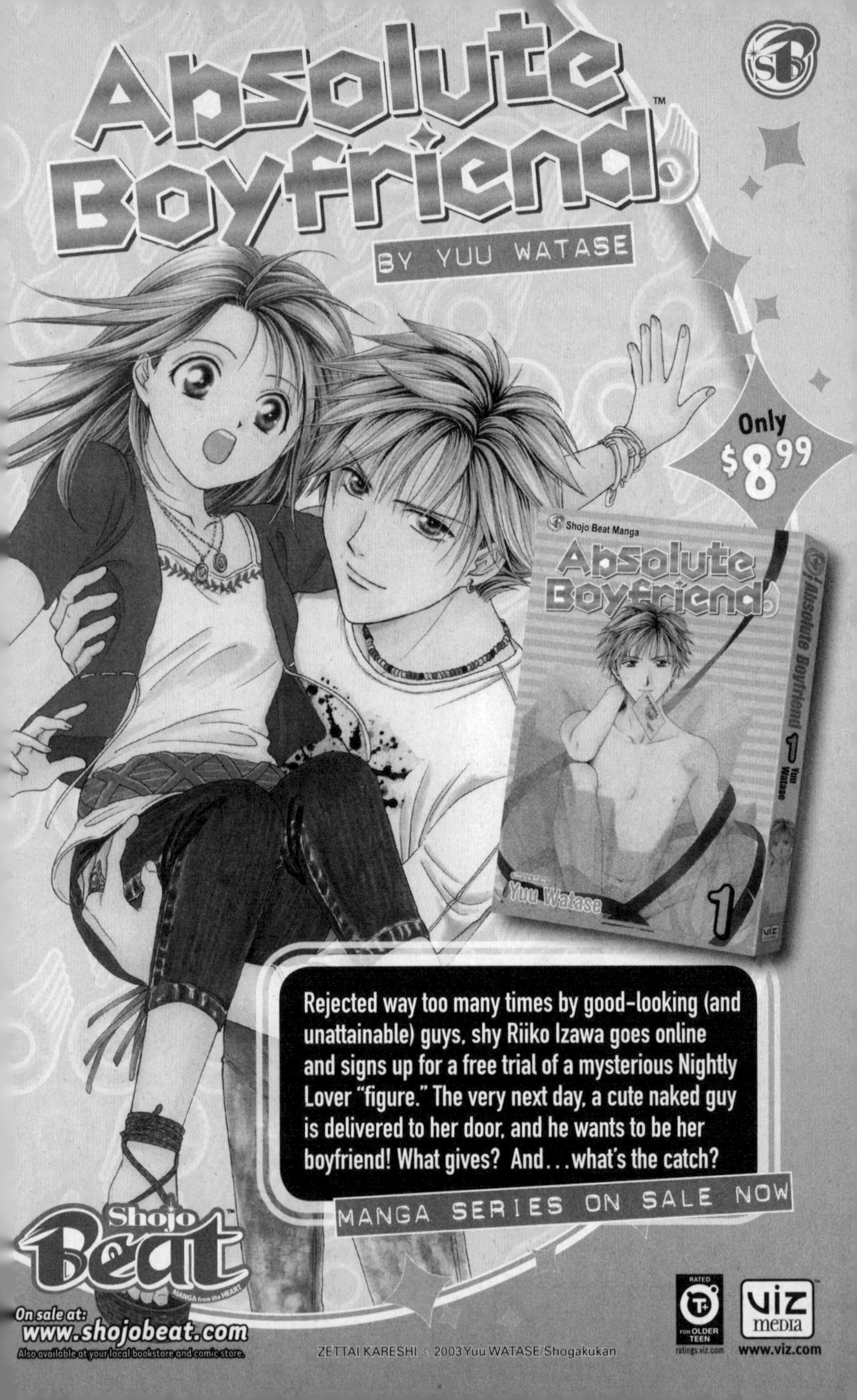
Absolute Boyfriend™
BY YUU WATASE
Only $8.99
Shojo Beat Manga
Absolute Boyfriend
Absolute Boyfriend 1 Yuu Watase
Yuu Watase
1
Rejected way too many times by good-looking (and unattainable) guys, shy Riiko Izawa goes online and signs up for a free trial of a mysterious Nightly Lover "figure." The very next day, a cute naked guy is delivered to her door, and he wants to be her boyfriend! What gives? And…what's the catch?
MANGA SERIES ON SALE NOW
Shojo Beat™
MANGA from the HEART
On sale at:
www.shojobeat.com
Also available at your local bookstore and comic store.
ZETTAI KARESHI © 2003 Yuu WATASE/Shogakukan
RATED T+ FOR OLDER TEEN
ratings.viz.com
VIZ media
www.viz.com

curtain call

Honey Hunt

BY **Miki Aihara**! THE CREATOR OF HOT GIMMICK AND TOKYO BOYS & GIRLS!

Growing up in the shadow of her famous parents, Yura's used to the pressure of being in a celebrity family. But when the spotlight starts to shine directly on her, will Yura have the courage—and talent—to stand on her own?

Find out in the *Honey Hunt* manga— **on sale now!**

On sale at **www.shojobeat.com**
Also available at your local bookstore and comic store.

HONEY HUNT © Miki AIHARA/Shogakukan Inc.

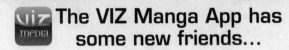

The VIZ Manga App has some new friends...

The world's best manga is now on the iPad,™ iPhone™ and iPod touch™

To learn more, visit viz.com/25years

From legendary manga like *Death Note* to *Absolute Boyfriend*, the best manga in the world is now available on multiple devices through the official VIZ Manga app.

- **Hundreds of volumes available**
- **Free App**
- **New content weekly**
- **Free chapter 1 previews**

TAI KARESHI © 2003 Yuu WATASE/Shogakukan, KEKKAISHI © 2004 Yellow TANABE/Shogakukan, Vampire Knight © Matsuri Hino 2004/HAKUSENSHA, Inc.,
BLACK BIRD © 2007 Kanoko SAKURAKOUJI/Shogakukan, BAKUMAN。© 2008 by Tsugumi Ohba, Takeshi Obata/SHUEISHA Inc.
ONE PIECE © 1997 by Eiichiro Oda/SHUEISHA Inc., BLEACH © 2001 by Tite Kubo/SHUEISHA Inc. NARUTO © 1999 by Masashi Kishimoto/SHUEISHA Inc.
DEATH NOTE © 2003 by Tsugumi Ohba, Takeshi Obata/SHUEISHA Inc.

HEROES OF MANGA
viz.com/25years